The Diary of Alexander the Great

A Chronological Retrospect Centred On Arrian's Anabasis Alexandri

Hutan Ashrafian

DEDICATION

To my wonderful wife Leanne and delightful son Persie.

CONTENTS

ACKNOWLEDGMENTS

The calculated chronology of the diary here-in has been scaffolded onto the original English translation of Arrian's Anabasis of Alexander by E. J. Chinnock (1884).

META-CHRONOLOGY SERIES PREFACE

There seems to be a grand disparity in the world of historians. Whilst the concept of history is relatively robust in society, there is a rift between *Modern* and *Ancient* Historians. Such a dichotomy seems to be artificial, for both study events in the past and both are aim to apply as much objectivity as possible to clarify the causal determinants of past effects; and as a result, to educate and inform contemporaneous society of these facts; ideally to minimize future societal mistakes and to guide beneficial future decisions. Nevertheless, the dichotomy between Ancient and Modern historians seems a pervading distinction that seems largely driven by the very nature of the sources each group has to study.

For example, a very modern historian may have access to *real-time* notes, emails, newspaper articles, television interviews, social media yield and a whole trench of other online media that are contextualized by major world timelines or a *macro-chronology* (such as leadership eras and major calendar events) in addition to a micro-chronology (specific day-to-day, hour-by-hour, minute-by-minute or even second-by-second events). Conversely, an ancient historian may have a few 2nd or 3rd hand sources written in an archaic language, sometimes many centuries after the occurrence of ancient events that predominantly only offer macro-chronological information. Such differences not only seem to affect the analysis of the past but also our interpretation. This seems to limit the interpretation of ancient sources that are treated as having a miasma of 2nd hand source bias, which is not considered to equate with the presumed clarity of modern sources due to their lack of an accepted micro-chronology of events.

My goal therefore has been to offer a micro-chronology of ancient events or an acuity of day-to-day real-time actuality to some ancient individuals and subjects. The integration between both macro- and micro-chronological views can therefore act as a method to cut through the presumed miasma of ancient sources. Sometimes it seems that studying ancient sources offers an encylopaedic appreciation of past events, but this may be tinted with a tone and timing that has a rather ethereal flavor rather than the likely reality of day-to-day events; which were just as real thousands of years ago as they are today. Studying the ancients without the cloak of romanticism, but rather one of scientific daily chronology may offer the reader of ancient sources the context of real-time impetus in decisions and actions. By doing so, it will allow the conceptual bridging of how ancient subjects were actually subjects living in another time, but nonetheless human subjects with comparative sentience and intelligence to their ancient contemporaries in the context of their day-to-day events.

The *real politic* of yester-year was just as real 20,000 years ago as it is today. Sometimes assessing ancient events devoid of time or place can lead to exaggeration and bias, particularly through each iteration of news dissemination. This is one source from which legends can come to exist; for example, there may have been a skirmish between several Mediterranean states and their leaders, which in today's world would be viewed as simply that. The same story devoid of time and place could lead to embellishment to scale in the time of events and size of actions. One could see the origins of Homer's Trojan Wars with demi-gods such as Achilles and magical depictions of Olympian Gods participating in human events. It is interesting to note that Homer by himself may have been aware of loss of time information, for there is a symmetrical chronology of events in the Iliad with times taking from one night to nine nights then to twelve nights then to one night then twelve nights and so on. Additionally the journey of the Odyssey is identical to that of the Trojan War in the Iliad, both ten years; though Odysseus' journey should only take the order of weeks. This likely synthetic approximation of time detracts form the reality of activity that in turn can spawn disinformation. Other examples include those of the Sumerian King List; here we know that some of the kings in this list existed, but clearly their reign length, some at 36,000 years is clearly unfeasible and has obscured analysis of Sumerian regnal time and events.

One classical example at an attempt to quantify the chronology of the past is that of Archbishop James Ussher (1581 – 1656). As a cleric, he expressed his deep devotion to the Bible by considering it as an incontrovertibly factual document. He applied scientific arithmetic to calculate his eponymous Chronology identifing the age of the world according to that text. Others such as Lightfoot, Ben Halafta, Bede and Newton also tried to create their own chronology. Independent to the consideration of the text in question, these attempts offered a quantifiable list of events by which to compare other models of chronology for ancient occurrences and offered a yardstick for which to allow a deeper timeline scrutiny for past events.

It is with this notion, that I have studied the ancient sources for prevailing characters from the ancient world and added a diary-like chronology to them for this 'Meta-Chronology' series (integrating both macro- and micro-chronology) on the most studied events of the most prominent ancient leaders (including the life and leadership of Alexander the Great and Xenophon's Anabasis who of interest where students of amongst the greatest philosophers of all time, Alexander-Aristotle and Xenophon-Socrates). By doing so I aim to discard the shackles of '*Ancient vs. Modern*' or

'*Legendary vs. Contemporary*', but rather to offer anyone interested a common chronological yardstick by which to cover both modern and ancient world events. Here, metaphorically, I have aimed to clarify the nature of each individual's timeline in the same vein that the *Alexander Mosaic* has been reconstructed to give the viewer a sense of its completeness of the original piece of art. Whilst I am aware there may be some inaccuracies in this method, I feel that the bigger picture may offer a stronger sense of existence in the characters discussed, particularly to give a feel of the urgency in decisions and actions as well as times of inaction. A method therefore to directly compare their ancient world with the modern one.

For these works, I have utilised accounts from established ancient sources on day-to-day activities of individuals and have super-imposed a *real-time* date on to those known events. To do this, I calculated specific days using set-dates from accepted or validated known-time points existing in the history of each individual and imputing of extrapolating the remaining dates in an individuals life based on the ancient sources in the texts listed. On occasion I have also imputed some figures based on the description of times, places and travel times (for example if it took 10 days to march from A to B and the distance form C to D resembles that of A to B and the journey speed or impetus was similar then I deduced the journey time would also follow). I have also added to the translation of ancient-to-modern chronology by converting ancient seasons into their modern ones through conversion of the ancient dates into their Julian calendar counterpart. For consistency, I have applied the Julian Calendar in year-month-day (YMD) format. For clarification of my personal comments in the text, I have utilized curly braces {}. These have been used to include relevant travel distances, travel information and the coupling of ancient locations to their current or hypothesized modern-day counterparts. Furthermore, where necessary, other sources have been utlised to clarify dates and events. Specifically for lunar, solar, or astronomical data, sources from NASA (National Aeronautics and Space Administration) or accepted modern astronomical tables/software (including Alcyone) have been applied.

In this series, I have also categorized the listed ancient dates according to modern day designations (Sunday to Saturday utilizing the Computer Support Group [CSGNetwork.com] Calendar Converter and Translator). Whilst these days are based on a cyclical mathematical progression that is arbitrary (these day names did not exist in ancient times) and do not take into account the many calendars (of differing lengths, months and days) applied in the ancient world, the robustness of a continuous mathematically calculated sequential seven day system allows the reader to discern any seven day trends that may have occurred in the chronology of the book. For example, if person A went to war on Monday August 5th in one year and had a celebratory feast on a Monday in August the next year, this may offer an insight regarding the timing and association between these two events. Possibly the 'Monday' or that day in a rolling calendar represented something of note. Additionally it offers the reader an additional sense of tangibility and context within the modern-world calendar timeframe regarding events that occurred thousands of years ago. Significantly however, this *virtual diary* format does carry some limitations. The dates listed are not fact but calculations aiming to offer the most likely factual times. As a result, they cannot be taken as verbatim, but rather they represent the best educated guess as to when the specified ancient events actually took place.

My ultimate aim is therefore to offer a deeper perception of *'real-time'* for ancient events that to-date have suffered from being morphed to exist in an abstract space-time of their own devoid of scale and measure. It is with this I wish the reader a tangibly timely appreciation of ancient historical events.

Hutan Ashrafian
Primrose Hill, London
2017

PREFACE

Alexander the Great remains widely accepted as amongst the most successful military leaders and empire builders of all time. Even though a handful of subsequent leaders (such as Julius Caesar, Genghis Khan and Napoléon Bonaparte) would also succeed in accruing vast geographic areas of dominion, Alexander remains the 'gold-standard' trailblazer against which many of these leaders would compare themselves. This hegemony exists because of several factors including (i) Alexander's unmitigated successes, (ii) the existence of his success in the classical period 330s-320s BC predating many of the other 'Great' title-holders (iii) Alexander's precocious youth rendering him a world emperor in his 20s and (iv) the documentation of his life events by an ancient Greek culture that would go on to have profound impact on subsequent world empires including Rome; which in turn would dominate the academic zeitgeist for modern education and history.

The history of Alexander's rise to power and his epic journey of empire building however remains much more influential than one of a simple list of consistently successful battles. So many factors have subsequently led to his life becoming unquestionably legendary. The powerful influences of ancient Greek religion and the heady days of his youth reflecting a self–reflection of godliness and immortally, a paternal relationship with his army where he would lead from the front and participate in in super-human heroic actions and also an inquisitiveness of new places and cultures. At the same time we see occasional but significant examples of severe rebuke of his close companions if they crossed him. Similalry he also acted as a brutal destroyer of whole populations if they did not accept subjugation. We therefore have a highly complex image of a powerfully driven individual who predominantly demonstrates consistent characteristics of leadership success ranging from physical and military ability, empathy with his 'flock' and also adversaries, a wider vision of empire and an image and charisma that galvanized his countrymen and army. On the other hand, we can nonetheless pick out elements of megalomaniacy and an impish intolerance to questioning his actions that can equate to his clear youth fuelled with almost uncontrollable power.

The activities of this young leader are also laced with many tiers of relationships including several male lovers, royal wives and mistresses who undoubtedly would have had an influence of his decisions. Over the period of his reign, friendships changed, relationships evolved, customs were adopted and eventually we see evidence of Alexander becoming *Persici plus quam Persae* or 'more Persian than the Persians' after having conquered their world empire.

His epic journey through some of the harshest and most fought-over lands of the modern-era remains tantalizing to a wider audience. These include areas corresponding to modern day Bulgaria, Romania, Turkey, Suria, the Levant, Egypt, Palestine, Iraq, Iran, the boarder Arabian Peninsula, Afghanistan, Uzbekistan, Tajikistan, Pakistan and India. In his youth he had gained familiarity with his native Macedonia and ancient Greece as well as his mothers homeland in a region corresponding to modern day Albania. His presence in these nations remains to have a tangible effect on their modern awareness of themselves as nation sates, the presence of Alexander almost validating their existence or used as a yardstick of impact on the prevailing era. Many of the locations in Alexander's journey can be recognized today and therefore offer us a powerful connection with the world-changing events at the time of his conquests and empire.

Alexander can arguably be considered as the greatest leader of all time. This single fact becomes even more significant when one considers that his personal tutor in youth, Aristotle, is correspondingly considered the greatest philosopher-academic of all-time. The coincidence of the crossing of paths of these two individuals is therefore another unique schism in this equaly unique story and most likely had a profound influence of the events in Alexander's lives. The events of his life clearly demonstrate that he was not only an empire builder but that he sought to maintain and expand this realm; not in the accepted method of lead-conquer-subjugate, but rather more attuned with the philosopher-kings. These were supported by Aristotle and exampled by only a few predecessors (such as Cyrus the Great of Persia), who had ruled with an acceptance of local and regional cultures and religions. Alexander himself seems to have gone a step further, and ultimately attempted to create a *hybrid* empire, by formally marrying Persian women and encouraging many of his army to follow suite so that eventually their *hybrid progeny* would live and manage a new world order of a new united race.

To-date Alexander's exploits are widely recognized from stories or classical history books. Whilst many of these offer some ideas of Alexander's actions based on ancient sources, and can give an idea of timing of local events, there has been no comprehensive day-to-day survey of the whole campaign from the crowing of Alexander to his death. As a consequence, whilst some of the macro-chronology of his life is known through the major life events of birth, battles and death dates, much of the micro-chronology in terms of a specific breakdown of day-to-day events remains unknown and largely unappreciated. This is problematic as reading parts of Alexander's massive journey (as many specialists necessarily do) and embellishing the timeframe of events devoid of upstream and downstream markers of time can lead to a warped sense of actions, decisions, activities and travel times. This in turn can lead to serious biases in interpretation of Alexander's life and our appreciation of real events.

We are fortunate in that people, both at the time of Alexander, and also those who followed subsequently realized his massive global impact such that there were multiple sources on his life (of varying accuracy). Although many of those primary sources are now extinct, we have several secondary sources taken from these that remain with us today. These include the five main sources of Arrian, Plutarch, Diodorus, Curtius and Justin. Additionally there are those of Strabo (who gives a summary of Callisthenes), Athenaeus, Polyaenus, Aelian and the Metz Epitome. Furthermore, there are re-created virtual works of Cleitarchus and the more story-based Romance of Alexander by 'pseudo-Callisthenes'. We have additional data from Ancient Egyptian calendars and also those from objective Babylonian Royal Astronomical records. Alexander is also considered by multiple later texts such as the Qoran and the Persian Epic of Kings where he is known as Iskandar; not the conqueror of Persia but rather adopted into their royal line as a native Persian king in his own right!

Whilst no one source is considered perfect, the most reliable source of Alexander's battles and life events is widely considered to be that of Arrian of Nicomedia also known as Lucius Flavius Arrianus. I have therefore utilised Arrian's account (specifically the 1884 English translation of his Anabasis of Alexander by E. J. Chinnock) as a scaffold on which to place diary dates so as to offer and combine both a macro- and micro-chronology of his life.

This has been done to overcome the biases of over-focusing on single events in Alexander's life devoid of the wider context and timing of his actions. I have attempted to calculate the day-to-day micro-chronology of as many individual times and dates in Alexander's epic journey (scaffolded onto the events discussed in Arrian) by utilsing the timeline given in Arrian's own account (for example how long it took for Alexander to Travel from A to B), but have supported this with several additional sources of information to calculate the whole story of Alexander's rise to power and death. These sources include:

(i) Identification of times based on Stellar/lunar events mentioned in Arrian
(ii) Identification of times based on Stellar/lunar events mentioned in other

sources (e.g. Strabo)

(iii) The cross-referencing of ancient Egyptian calendar times where information was available

(iv) The cross-referencing of Babylonian Astronomical tables where information was available

(v) The imputation of army march times based on distances between locations

(vi) Cross-referencing of multiple sources together where times are not known, or if there is a conflict

During the completion of the manuscript, I have identified ten levels of hierarchical evidence that helped complete the timeline in this book. These are in sequential order of reliability:

I – Multiple verifiable sources of objective astronomical data e.g. Eclipse before the Battle of Gaugamela/ Arbela

II – One verifiable source of objective astronomical data (e.g. Setting of the Pleiades)

III – Calculable date based on astronomical data (e.g. 20 Boedromion leaving Patala, sacrifice to Apis which occurred on a winter solstice, 25th Tybi as the founding of Alexandria)

IV – Calculable dates based on described factors (e.g. 3 days march from x to y)

V – Interpolation of multiple aligning sources (e.g. Siege at Tyre)

VI – Interpolation of single source (e.g. Accession date based on Cleitarchus)

VII – Approximation of times, e.g. army march times based on distance and army status

VIII – authors guess based on scant evidence e.g. sacrifice to Ammon/ Amun on the celebration day of Ra-Horakhty

IX – no indication of time in the text

X – totally conflicting source data

The vast majority of evidence falls within the middle and lowest categories of this hierarchy, nonetheless, the author hopes that intermixed with the highest levels of evidence, the reader will now appreciate a completely new and wholistic appreciation of Alexander's campaign; which typically is so large that the concept of time on individual segments of Alexander's campaign can be forgotten, exaggerated or under-expressed. Additionally, this text has offered several new dates on which to identify Alexander's journey; these will be clear in the manuscript. The reader can now select a date and then subsequently look ahead or back by several months and have a deeper perception of what Alexander was doing at a particular time and place. How long did he rest the army?, How fast were the marches? And exactly what proportion of his time was he in battle? These facts have always been assumed, but never addressed in their totality. Hopefully this is something that this book will help answer. To assist the reader in the global contextualization of time within Alexander's journey, the conversion of all dates into the Julian Calendar has been applied (the predominant method of assessing ancient sources with consistency), as this will allow the easiest assessment of time comparisons within the modern world.

The current teaching of Alexander in many institutions suggests that Alexander went to war for many years, almost suggesting that his campaign was literally many years of daily hand-to-hand combat. Whilst undeniably there was much warfare, this manuscript identifies that Alexander's journey consisted of much more than just warfare. The work reveals patterns in times of rest, religious and non-religious celebrations, the adherence to lunar and solar events and his reliance on the ancient Gods. The work also reveals some previously unknown but commonly mistaken times in Alexander's life which render his decisions more apt or more controversial due to their speed or time of year at which they take place. In short, the book offers a new contextualization of how to view Alexander's life and actions.

This new timeline has allowed the identification of some likely misappropriations of locations and times ascribed to Alexander and his army. As a consequence it has uncovered several new findings. These have been highlighted within the text, but a few examples include:

1.   Uxians are Hujians or Bakhtiari's
2.   Alexander met Bistanes, this was likely Ostanes Gandfather to Darius III and son of Darius II
3.   He repeatedly celebrated the winter solstice; likely to Dionysus
4.   Areia (quite possibly Esfarayen in modern day Khorasan Province Iran, considered a focal point for Aryan tribes in Iran)
5.   Journey time and locations of many places in Iran and Iraq have been clarified
6.   Journey time and locations of many places in central Asia have been clarified (raging from unknown places in Afghanistan to hitherto unappreciated travel to Uzbekistan and Tajikistan)
7.   A strong candidate for the Rock of Aornus identified
8.   Journey time and locations of many places in Pakistan and India have been clarified

9.   Flowers in bloom before the journey in the Gadrosian desert are identified as Avicennia marina or Grey Mangrove, so that journey in Gadrosia is better timed.

10.   Ormara is likely the town of Ora that was visited just before the Gadrosian march

11.   The Banquet at Opis was one celebrated by both Greek prophets and Persian Magians, this has been dated to the ancient Zoroastrian feast of friendship also recognized by the Greeks as the autumn equinox

12.   The Nisaean Plain in Media likely corresponds to the Silakhor Plain

13.   The 'Haffar' canal linking the Karun river to the Tigris was likely in prototypical existence in the time of Alexander, who describes it so clearly that the dating of this man-made structure likely goes to the Achaemenids, thirteen centuries before the current approximation of the construction date in the late 10th century AD under Panah Khusraw (also known as Adud ad-Dawlah)

14.   The port of Pallacopas possibly corresponds to Al Chabaish in Iraq

15.   The Ancient Macedonian 'Olympic Games' were likely celebrated more regularly than the 'main' Olympiad as it seems this was also celebrated at the time of the assassination of Philip II in 336 BC and Alexander celebrated this in 335 BC

Within the text, I have also highlighted the date of the ancient Macedonian New Year (first new moon after the autumnal equinox) where pertinent, as this may have had some significance for the Macedonian army and Alexander. Furthermore, Alexander's crowning had occurred on the day of the Autumnal equinox and some ancient sources (e.g. Cleitarchus for his first six books) used this as a date on which to start their books, this may have some resonance. Of note, in contrast, the Athenian new year began on the first new moon after the summer solstice. My calculations for the Macedonian New Year and Athenian New Year are shown in **Table 1**:

Year (BC)	Summer Solstice	Athenian New Year (first new moon after SS)	Autumn Equinox (AE)	Macedonian New Year (first new moon after AE)
336	June 22	July 04	September 22	September 30
335	June 22	June 23	September 22	October 19
334	June 22	July 12	September 22	October 09
333	June 21	July 01	September 22	September 27
332	June 22	July 19	September 22	October 16
331	June 22	July 08	September 22	October 5
330	June 22	June 28	September 22	September 24
329	June 21	July 15	September 22	October 12
328	June 22	July 05	September 22	October 01
327	June 22	June 25	September 22	October 20
326	June 22	July 14	September 22	October 10
325	June 21	July 02	September 22	September 29
324	June 22	July 21	September 22	October 18
323	June 22	July 10	September 22	October 07

Table 1 – Calculated ancient Athenian and Macedonian New Year dates

For both calendars, the first day of spring corresponded to the same date (**Table 2**):

Athenian New Year (first new moon after SS)	First Athenian Calendar day of Spring, 1st Mounichion (Μουνιχιών) or the 10th month	Macedonian New Year (first new moon after AE)	First Macedonian Calendar day of Spring, 1st Artemisios (Ἀρτεμίσιος) or the 7th month
July 04 336 BC	March 27 335 BC	September 30 336 BC	March 27 335 BC
June 23 335 BC	March 16 334 BC	October 19 335 BC	March 16 334 BC
July 12 334 BC	April 03 333 BC	October 09 334 BC	April 03 333 BC
July 01 333 BC	March 23 332 BC	September 27 333 BC	March 23 332 BC
July 19 332 BC	April 11 331 BC	October 16 332 BC	April 11 331 BC
July 08 331 BC	April 01 330 BC	October 5 331 BC	April 01 330 BC
June 28 330 BC	March 20 329 BC	September 24 330 BC	March 20 329 BC
July 15 329 BC	April 08 328 BC	October 12 329 BC	April 08 328 BC
July 05 328 BC	March 29 327 BC	October 01 328 BC	March 29 327 BC
June 25 327 BC	March 18 327 BC	October 20 327 BC	March 18 327 BC
July 14 326 BC	April 04 325 BC	October 10 326 BC	April 04 325 BC
July 02 325 BC	March 24 324 BC	September 29 325 BC	March 24 324 BC
July 21 324 BC	April 12 323 BC	October 18 324 BC	April 12 323 BC
July 10 323 BC	April 02 322 BC	October 07 323 BC	April 02 322 BC

Table 2 – Calculated ancient Athenian and Macedonian Spring start dates

Combining all these elements may offer a useful addition to understanding Alexander's life and journey. As a result, the author hopes that this new approach in offering a day-to-day chronology of Alexander's life; as accurate as possible, will offer the reader a new insight into the scale, efforts and realistic proceedings in the life and times of this world emperor. The calculated weekdays with each calendar entry is hoped to provide an additional level of appreciation for chronology and chronicity in events. It is hoped that such a diary format will generate a new realistic empathy and a common frame of reference by which to analyze Alexander, his life and his actions.

Hutan Ashrafian
Primrose Hill, London
2017

PRELUDE TO ALEXANDER THE GREAT'S REIGN

356 BC

Summer

20 July, Saturday

Alexander the Great is born. Information regarding this date include: (i) Plutarch gives us the date of Hekatombaeon 6 in the Attic Calendar. This would correspond to six days after the summer solstice, which in this year would be six days after June 22, or June 27. (ii) Arrian suggests this was 32 years and 8 months before his death on the June 11 323 BC. (iii) In conflict with this, Arrian also states (based on Aristobulus) that Alexander was around twenty years old when he was crowned with a reign of 12 years and eight months. (iv) Plutarch and (v) Justin both offer the fact that Philip II (Alexander's father) informs his troops of a chariot victory at the Olympic Games and Alexander's birth at the same time as the Olympic Games. These likely occurred on the 2nd full moon after the summer solstice, so that this date would correspond to July 30 that year, and would incorporate Alexander's birthday within that time period. Regarding all this information the 20th July seems the best fit, and regarding Plutarch, he may have miscalculated by approximately one month as the 7th day of the month Metageitnion (just after Hekatombaeon) corresponds to 20th July.

He was the son of Philip II of Macedon (382–336 BC, 3rd son of King

Amyntas III of the Argead Dynasty) and Olympias (daughter of king Neoptolemus I of Epirus, the fourth wife of Philip II). Alexander was born at Pella in Macedonia. Plutarch specifies the date of Alexander's birth as the 6th of Hekatombaion (Ἑκατομβαιών), month corresponding to current July/August or a month known to the Macedonians as 'Lous'. This was also the day that the temple of Diana at Ephesus was burnt.

Hegesias of Magnesia (Ἡγησίας ὁ Μάγνης) suggests that the mistress of the temple was assisting the birth of Alexander and so the temple burnt as she was absent. Additionally, the Eastern soothsayers who happened to be then at Ephesus at that time foresaw this as a portent of a catastrophe that would lead to the destruction of Asia.

343 BC – 340 BC

Tutelage under Aristotle in the Macedonian village of Mieza 'nymph shrine': At some time between the ages of 13-16 years old, Alexander and other notable Macedonian aristocratic children such as Ptolemy (ca. 367 BC - 282 BC) who became king of Egypt and Cassander (ca. 350BC - 297 BC) who became king of Macedonia all studied under the tutelage of the famed philosopher and teacher Aristotle who remains in Macedonia until 335 BC.

339 BC

Autumn

Alexander was 17 years old at this time. His father Philip II placed him in charge of the Macedonian government whilst he waged war and besieging Byzantion (for up to 3 months) as part of his campaign to gain control of Greece.

338 BC

Summer

02 August, Saturday – Battle of Chaeronea

Alexander played a critical role supporting his father in this battle concluding Philip's campaign in Greece (339–338 BC) by achieving a decisive victory for the Macedonians. Alexander was 18 years old at this time and was supported by a group of his father's experienced generals and defeated the Greek right wing comprising mainly of Thebans whilst his father dealt with the left wing of predominantly Athenians. This was a clear indication of Alexander's military ability and his appetite for leadership was also clear following the naming of a nearby city in his own name.

Winter

Philip marries his 7th wife, Cleopatra later named "Eurydice" who is the niece of one of his closest nobles Attalus (ca.390-336). According to Plutarch, he is noted to have made a toast during the wedding celebration that his niece Cleopatra Eurydice may yield a legitimate heir for Philip (presumably as Attalus and Cleopatra Eurydice are both Macedonian whereas Alexander id Macedonian through is father but not his mother's side). This clearly and publicly threatened Alexander's position as crown prince who therefore rebuked the toast to the great anger of his father Philip. According to legend, Alexander threw his drinking cup at Attalus, insulting him for essentially being called a 'bastard child. His father Philip tried to get up and draw his sword and charge his son, but lost his balance and fell due to his inebriation. Alexander is subsequently noted as shouting out load: "Here is the man who was making ready to cross from Europe to Asia, and who cannot even cross from one table to another without losing his balance." Following this both Alexander and his mother Olympias went into exile (temporary) in his mother's homeland of Epirus where her brother Alexander of Molossis was king.

337 BC

Spring

Alexander returns (is recalled) to Macedon but is not accompanied by his mother Olympias as she feels that her position remains risky at the Macedonian court. (Alexander's return may have been partially to ensure that he is upto date on court activity and political shifts).

{The Pixodarus affair (prelude to the assassination of Philip II) – Pixodarus was the regional governor (Satrap) of Caria in south western Asia Minor under the rule of the Persian Empire. He offered his daughter's hand in marriage to Philip's son Arrhidaeus who was Alexander's elder half-brother (Philinna of Larissa was his mother) for likely strategic reasons.

Alexander's mother Olympias and his friends warned that this could act as a overture to the succession of the Macedonian throne going to Arrhidaeus and bypassing Alexander. As a result Alexander sent Thessalus (the tragic actor) as his representative to Pixodarus informing him that Arrhidaeus was an illegitimate child of Philip and suffered from learning difficulties so would not be a fit husband, rather Alexander suggested that he should marry Pixodarus' daughter himself.

Although Pixodarus favoured this idea, Philip heard of the news and disapproved admonishing Alexander for considering marriage to 'a slave of a barbarian king'. Consequently Philip ordered Thessalus to be brought back to Macedon as a prisoner in chains whilst exiling some of Alexander's friends: Erygius, Harpalus, Nearchus, and Ptolemy.

Summer

Diodorus (Diod. Sic. 16.93-5) describes the events of Pausanias as a Macedonian of noble heritage from Orestis who was part of Philip II's bodyguards (somatophylakes) and amongst his lovers. Another individual with the same name became part of the kings entourage so that the King favoured the new Pausanias as a lover. Out of jealousy Pausanias of Orestis called his namesake a slutty hermaphrodite and insinuated his weakness as a man. This led the king's new lover to want to prove himself; and did so by exposing himself and protecting Philip's life during his battle with Pleurias (Pleuratus I), king of the Illyrians (Philip also fought the Illyrians in 344BC but likely again in 337BC). These events resulted in the death of the newer Pausanias as a result of his injuries. In revenge for this death, Attalus, one of the kings closest allies at court invited the Pausanias from Orestis to supper, got him heavily drunk and unconscious and then had multiple individuals rape him as reprisal for the death of his namesake.

Philip's new wife Cleopatra Eurydice attempts to have justice achieved for Pausanias even through her uncle had instigated the event (suggesting an unknown rift in the family of Attalus if the sources suggest it's the same Cleopatra). Pausanias had also asked Alexander for reprisals against his rapists and Alexander is noted as quoting Euripides' Medea, by suggesting the vengeful line of 'The father, bride and bridegroom all at once'.

At this point, Alexander's status as crown prince has thus far been threatened twice:
(1) Indirectly by his older brother Arrhidaeus in the Pixodarus affair
(2) By Cleopatra Eurydice (his fathers newest wife) and her uncle Attalus, suggesting that her offspring would be legitimate

336 BC

Spring

Attalus continues to gain prominence in Philip's court. He appoints Attalus as a senior general under overall command by Parmenion (a relative of Attalus) as commanders of Philip's first military brigades to mobilise against the Persian Empire in Asia Minor.

Autumn

September 18, Sunday
Aegae (modern Vergina)

Philip II's seventh wife, Cleopatra Eurydice gives birth to a baby daughter.

Chapter 1 (Start of Book 1): Death of Philip and Accession of Alexander – His wars with the Thracians

September 21, Wednesday

Assassination of Alexander's father, Philip II. Aegae (modern Vergina). Eve of the Autumnal equinox. The first new moon after this would be the Macedonian New Year. This date was calculated from the day below.

It is said that Philip died[4] when Pythodemus was archon at Athens,[5] {We know from Plutarch that this occurred in Attic Summer, together with the beginning of the archonship of Pythodemus, confirming an early October date. Diodorus of Sicily also suggests that Philip's most recent wife Cleopatra bore him a daughter Europa a few days before his assassination} and that his son Alexander,[6] being then about twenty years of age, marched into Peloponnesus[7] as soon as he had secured the regal power.

{Alexander is 20 years old at this time. Although the assassination was performed by Pausanias; by one of the king's bodyguards for Philip's failure to retaliate against his rapist Attalus who was Philip's new father-in-law from his most recent (7th) wife Cleopatra Eurydice. Both Alexander and his mother Olympias were suspected in the murder. Pausanias was himself killed by some of Alexander's entourage before any evidence could be established.

The assassination occurred at a festival celebrating the marriage of Philip's daughter Cleopatra with Alexander, king of Epirus, and had also coincided with Philip's plans to commence an expedition against Persia; the dominant global empire at the time and largest military threat to Macedonian and Greece. The Persians under the Achaemenid Empire had already attempted an invasion of Greece, though this failed, the Persians had constantly been working toward destabilising Greece and her allies using financial, political and military (mercenary) means. They were the largest threat to Philip's plan of expansion and supremacy in the Greek states. Of note Philip's festivities were jointly celebrated with the Macedonians version of the official Olympic games.

One of the Macedonian aristocracy, Alexander of Lynkestis (son of Aeropus of Lynkestis) declares him as king straightaway and pronounces his loyalty (some authors such as Justin occasionally mislabel him as a brother of Alexander).}

September 22, Thursday

Crowned King on Autumnal Equinox (Chugg suggests this based on his analysis of Cleitarchus. He suggests this occurs 5 years before the day after the Battle of Guagamela, known due its relation to a lunar eclipse. As result, he suggests Boedromion 27, or September 22 In the Julian Calendar used in this book)

{Alexander proclaimed king of Macedon after presenting himself to the army who support his leadership. Recall of his exiled friends back to Macedon.

{NOTE Alexander's reign according to Arrian and Diodorus, lasted 12 years with 7 or 8 months So from September 22 336 BC, this would account to a date of death as: April 22 or May 22 323 BC. Please see 323 BC}

September 23, Friday

{Philip II's dead body was laid out for viewing and likely inhumed (and not cremated [Bartsiokas et al. Proc Natl Acad Sci U S A. 2015 Aug 11;112(32):9844-8. doi: 10.1073/pnas.1510906112]) before dawn the next day. Philip II's killed assassin Pausanias of Orestis was crucified.}

September 24, Saturday

{Alexander's mother Olympias returns to Aegae. Claim that she crowns Philip's killer Pausanias with a garland. Pausanias' 'so-called' conspirators Heromenes and Arrhabaeus of Lynkestis (brothers of Alexander of Lynkestis) are both put under trial and executed.}

September 25, Sunday

{Execution of four or five key individuals threatening his kingship. Two likely ordered by Alexander himself - his cousin Amyntas IV - the legal legitimate heir to the Macedonian throne, a similarly named noble Amyntas of Lynkestis. His mother Olympias ordered the death of Philip II's newest wife Cleopatra Eurydice and her baby Europa, there are additional claims of murder of a rumoured son of Cleopatra and Philip named Caranus, though this remains questionable. Some sources suggest that witnessing the death of her daughter led Cleopatra Eurydice to commit suicide; so much so that it is noted by Plutarch that Alexander was 'angered' by his mother's treachery. Other sources suggest that the method of death for Cleopatra Eurydice and her daughter was being burned alive on the orders of Olympias, which were the source of Alexander's anger toward her. The sources agree that Cleoptra Eurydice gave birth to a daughter just before Philip's assassination, and this is corroborated by the likely remains of Philip II, Cleoptra Eurydice and their newborn child in Tomb I in Vergina, modern-day Greece [Bartsiokas et al. Proc Natl Acad Sci U S A. 2015 Aug 11;112(32):9844-8. doi: 10.1073/pnas.1510906112].

So far at least six (possibly seven) notable individuals have been killed after the death of Philip and his assassin Pausanias. Alexander also sends assassins to kill Attalus, who had been leading some of the army in Troad in northwestern Anatolia, modern Turkey (Biga Yarımadası).}

October 07, Friday

{The Thessalians who occupy a close area to Macedon revolt against Alexander's new rule hoping to take advantage of a presumed leadership vacuum in Macedonia. They start to occupy the Vale of Tempe (Τέμπη) gorge that was a strategic pass linking the capital and central area of Thessaly (modern Larissa) to the coast.

The Amphictyonic League 'of neighbours' which had fought against Philip II of Macedon (primarily by the alliance of Athens and Thebes) and had lost at the Battle of Chaeronea (338 BC) also consider rebellion and arrange to unite near Thermopylae.

Alexander hears of this and arranges to quash this but organising his local army (some are already abroad) to get ready to attack the Thessalians.}

October 10, Monday

{Assassins have covered the 607km between Aegae (modern Vergina) and Troad (on horseback and foot). On arrival at Troad Attalus is killed.}

October 11, Tuesday

{Alexander's army leave for Thessaly}

October 13, Thursday

{Alexander's army cover the approximate 90km from Aegae (Vergina) to arrive in the region of the Vale of Tempe. They however bypass the Thessalian forces by going via Mount Ossa (Όσσα and also known as Kissavos - Κίσσαβος) to surprise the Thessalian force. (Interestingly by Alexander I of Macedon, Alexander the Great's Great Great Great Grandfather had warned that the Vale of Temp could be bypassed in 480BC when Xerxes had tried to invade Greece).}

October 14, Friday
Thessalian capitulation

{The Thessalian's capitulate to Alexander, accepting his kingship and his hegemony over them. As part of this he emphasises his legendary ancestry of descending from the famed hero Achilles.}

October 17, Monday

{Parmenion the overall army chief who is south in Aeolis (near modern-day Smyrna) is informed of the death of Attalus (one of his relatives) and the succession of kings in Macedonia and arrives on this day having travelled 240km to Troad to take over the army.

This is a critical step as Parmenion is the head of the army and could have sided with his dead relative to question Alexander's rule, his capitulation to Alexander's hegemony renders a smooth transition between kings in Macedonia. Some sources actually suggest that Alexander first sent messengers to Parmenion regarding the new leadership in Macedonia ad that Parmenio travelled to Troad an he himself put Attalus to death based on Alexander's orders.}

October 19, Wednesday

{On hearing the news of the Thessalians, The Amphictyonic League now camped at Thermopylae also surrender. Alexander calls for a meeting of this League at Delphi for balloting and appointing him as their head and calls a wider meeting of the League of Corinth.}

October 23, Sunday

{Amphictyonic League meeting at Delphi (50 miles from Thermopylae) and capitulate to Alexander's leadership (Hegemony). Both Athens and Thebes participate in this decision and the former makes Alexander an honorary citizen of Athens and sends him offerings. These members then travel the approximate 100-120 miles from Delphi to attend the pan-Hellenic League of Corinth meeting where Alexander will preside.}

November 01, Tuesday
League of Corinth meeting

There he assembled all the Greeks who were within the limits of Peloponnesus,[8] and asked from them the supreme command of the expedition against the Persians, an, office which they had already conferred upon Philip. He received the honour which he asked from all except the Lacedaemonians,[9] who replied that it was an hereditary custom of theirs, not to follow others but to lead them. The Athenians also attempted to bring about some political change; but they were so alarmed at the very approach of Alexander, that they conceded to him even more ample public honours than those which had been bestowed upon Philip.[10]

November 03, Thursday

{Likely fictional meeting with the philosopher Diogenes (412/404–323BC) in Corinth. The philosopher would have been aged either 68 or 76 at the time. On meeting the king who asked if there was anything the king could offer him, Diogenes is said to have remarked by saying, "Yes, stand out of my sunlight". Alternatively another legend stipulates Alexander finding the philosopher looking at some bones, and asking him why, Diogenes explains that he was looking for the bones of Alexander's father but could not distinguish them from that of a slave.}

November 04, Friday
Leaves Corinth

{Leaves Corinth to travel back to the north of Greece.}

November 10, Thursday
Possible visit to Delphi

{According to another fictional narrative, on his way back to Macedon, Alexander makes a stop at Delphi (approximately 100-125 miles travel from Corinth) to address the oracle of Apollo for prophecies of his future. The temple did not offer prophecies between November and February (hypothesized to be because of ethylene intoxication from mountainous vents – Spiller H, de Boer J, Hale JR, Chanton J. Gaseous emissions at the site of the Delphic Oracle: assessing the ancient evidence. Clin Toxicol (Phila). 2008 Jun;46(5):487-8. doi: 10.1080/15563650701477803. PubMed PMID: 18568810, possibly having less venting during the months between November and February}.

Alexander asked for the high priestess Timocleia to make him a prophecy, however the temple staff asked responded that she did not prophesize on inauspicious days such as the that time, or alternatively to leave and return in a better time such as February. At this Alexander sought out and found the residence of the oracle and grabbed her and dragged her by the hair to the alter insisting on a prophecy.

Her response was transliterated as "you are invincible, my son", possibly as a pejorative outcry. Nevertheless Alexander used this episode to communicate to his soldiers that he was officially confirmed as being indestructible and unconquerable and so returned to Aegae.}

November 12, Saturday

{Leaves Delphi to travel back to Aegae}

November 23, Wednesday
Return to Aegae for the winter

He then returned into Macedonia and busied himself in preparing for the expedition into Asia.

335 BC

Spring

March 24, Friday
Leaves Amphipolis (Ἀμφίπολις) toward Thrace (the vernal equinox that year was on March 20th and caldendar Spring began on March 27th, please see the preface)

However, at the approach of spring (B.C. 335), he marched towards Thrace, into the lands of the Triballians and llyrians,[11] because he ascertained that these nations were meditating a change of policy; and at the same time, as they were lying on his frontier, he thought it inexpedient, when he was about to start on a campaign so far away from his own land, to leave them behind him without being entirely subjugated.

Setting out then from Amphipolis, he invaded the land of the people who were called independent Thracians,[12] keeping the city of Philippi and mount Orbelus on the left.

{Amphipolis corresponds to an area near modern day Sérres in northern Greece. The city of Philippi (originally name was Crenides) and Mt. Orbelos (now called Mt. Lekani or Slavyanka/ Kitka Planina in Bulgarian and Alibotush in Turkish) to its left. The distance between Amphipolis and Mt. Lekani is approximately 85km}

March 30, Thursday
Crosses the river Nessus

Crossing the river Nessus,[13]

{The river Nessus, today known as Nestos (Greek: Νέστος, Bulgarian: Mesta/ Места or Turkish: Mesta Karasu).

April 02, Sunday
Arrival at Mount Haemus, 10 days after the start of his journey

they say he arrived at mount Haemus[14] on the tenth day.

{10 days into his campaign he arrived at Mt. Haemus or modern-day Haemus Mons. The distance between Amphipolis (Sérres) and the Balkan mountain range (Haemus) is approximately 235km}

April 03, Monday
Battle on Mount Haemus (modern day Haemus Mons)

Here, along the defiles up the ascent to the mountain, he was met by many of the traders equipped with arms, as well as by the independent Thracians, who had made preparations to check the further advance of his expedition by seizing the summit of the Haemus, along which was the route for the passage of his army. They had collected their waggons, and placed them in front of them, not only using them as a rampart from which they might defend themselves, in case they should be forced back, but also intending to let them loose upon the phalanx of the Macedonians, where the mountain was most precipitous, if they tried to ascend. They had come to the conclusion[15] that the denser the phalanx was with which the waggons rushing down came into collision, the more easily would they scatter it by the violence of their fall upon it.

But Alexander formed a plan by which he might cross the mountain with the least danger possible; and since he was resolved to run all risks, knowing that there were no means of passing elsewhere, he ordered the heavy-armed soldiers, as soon as the waggons began to rush down the declivity, to open their ranks, and directed that those whom the road was sufficiently wide to permit to do so should stand apart, so that the waggons might roll through the gap; but that those who were hemmed in on all sides should either stoop down together or even fall flat on the ground, and lock their shields compactly together, so that the waggons rushing down upon them, and in all probability by their very impetus leaping over them, might pass on without injuring them. And it turned out just as Alexander had conjectured and exhorted. For some of the men made gaps in the phalanx, and others locked their shields together. The waggons rolled over the shields without doing much injury, not a single man being killed under them. Then the Macedonians regained their courage, inasmuch as the waggons, which they had excessively dreaded, had inflicted no damage upon them. With a loud cry they assaulted the Thracians. Alexander ordered his archers to march from the right wing in front of the rest of the phalanx, because there the passage was easier, and to shoot at the Thracians where they advanced. He himself took his own guard, the shield-bearing infantry and the Agrianians,[16] and led them to the left. Then the archers shot at the Thracians who sallied forward, and repulsed them; and the phalanx, coming to close fighting, easily drove away from their position men who were light-armed and badly equipped barbarians. The consequence was, they no longer waited to receive Alexander marching against them from the left, but casting away their arms they fled down the mountain as each man best could. About 1,500 of them were killed; but only a few were taken prisoners on account of their swiftness of foot and acquaintance with the country. However, all the women who were accompanying them were captured, as were also their children and all their booty.

April 04, Tuesday
Crosses Mount Haemus

Chapter 2: Battle with the Triballians

Alexander sent the booty away southward to the cities on the seashore,[17] entrusting to Lysanias and Philotas[18] the duty of setting it up for sale. But he himself crossed the summit, and advancing through the Haemus into the land of the Triballians,

April 06, Thursday
Arrives at the Lyginus river (modern-day Rositsa river near Resen)

he arrived at the river Lyginus.[19] This river is distant from the Ister[20] three days' march to one intending to go to the Haemus.

{The distance from Haemus to Resen near the Rositsa river is approximately 45km}

April 07, Friday
Travel toward the Island of Peuce at the Daube Delta

Syrmus, king of the Triballians, hearing of Alexander's expedition long before, had sent the women and children of the nation on in advance to the Ister, ordering them to pass over into one of the islands in that river, the name of which was Peuce.[21] To this island also the Thraoians, whose territories were conterminous with those of the Triballians, had fled together for refuge at the approach of Alexander. Syrmns himself likewise, accompanied by his train, had fled for refuge to the same place. But the main body of the Triballians fled back to the river, from which Alexander had started the day before.

{The distance from Resen near the Rositsa river to the Danube Delta (Peuce) is approximately 400km}

April 09, Sunday
Battle against the Triballians

When he heard of their starting, he wheeled round again, and, marching against them, surprised them just as they were encamping. And those who were surprised drew themselves up in battle array in a woody glen along the bank of the river. Alexander drew out his phalanx into a deep column, and led it on in person. He also ordered the archers and slingers to run forward and discharge arrows and stones at the barbarians, hoping to provoke them by this to come out of the woody glen into the ground unencumbered with trees. When they were within reach of the missiles, and were struck by them, they rushed out against the archers, who were undefended by shields, with the purpose of fighting them hand-tohand. But when Alexander had drawn them thus out of the woody glen, he ordered Philotas to take the cavalry which came from upper Macedonia, and to charge their right wing, where they had advanced furthest in their sally. He also commanded Heraclides and Sopolis[22] to lead on the cavalry which came from

Bottiaea[23] and Amphipolis against the left wing; while he himself extended the phalanx of infantry and the rest of the horse in front of the phalanx and led them against the enemy's centre. And indeed as long as there was only skirmishing on both sides, the Triballians did not get the worst of it; but as soon as the phalanx in dense array attacked them with vigour, and the cavalry fell upon them in various quarters, no longer merely striking them with the javelin, but pushing them with their very horses, then at length they turned and fled through the woody glen to the river. Three thousand were slain in the flight; few of them were taken prisoners, both because there was a dense wood in front of the river, and the approach of night deprived the Macedonians of certainty in their pursuit. Ptolemy says, that of the Macedonians themselves eleven horsemen and about forty foot soldiers were killed.

April 12, Wednesday
Arrives at the Ister river (modern-day Danube, possibly near Svishtov)

Chapter 3: Alexander at the Danube and in the Country of the Getae

On the third **day** after the battle, Alexander reached the river Ister, which is the largest of all the rivers in Europe, traverses a very great tract of country, and separates very warlike nations. Most of these belong to the Celtic race,[24] in whose territory the sources of the river take their rise. Of these nations the remotest are the Quadi[25] and Marcomanni[26]; then the Iazygianns,[27] a branch of the Sauromatians[28]; then the Getae,[29] who hold the doctrine of immortality; then the main body of the Sauromatians; and, lastly, the Scythians,[30] whose land stretches as far as the outlets of the river, where through five mouths it discharges its water into the Euxine Sea.[31] Here Alexander found some ships of war which had come to him from Byzantium, through the Euxine Sea and up the river. Filling these with archers and heavy-armed troops, he sailed to the island to which the Triballians and Thracians had fled for refuge. He tried to force a landing; but the barbarians came to meet him at the brink of the river, where the ships were making the assault. But these were only few in number, and the army in them small. The shores of the island, also, were in most places too steep and precipitous for landing, and the current of the river alongside it, being, as it were, shut up into a narrow channel by the nearness of the banks, was rapid and exceedingly difficult to stem.

Alexander therefore led back his ships, and determined to cross the Ister and march against the Getae, who dwelt on the other side of that river; for he observed that many of them had collected on the bank of the river for the purpose of barring his way, if he should cross. There were of them about 4,000 cavalry and more than 10,000 infantry. At the same time a strong desire seized him to advance beyond the Ister. He therefore went on board the fleet himself. He also filled with hay the hides which served them as tent-coverings, and collected from the country around all the boats made from single trunks of trees. Of these there was a great abundance, because the people who dwell near the Ister use them for fishing in the river, sometimes also for journeying to each other for traffic up the river; and most of them carry on piracy with them. Having collected as many of these as he could, upon them he conveyed across as many of his soldiers as was possible in such a fashion. Those who crossed with Alexander amounted in number to 1,500 cavalry and 4,000 infantry.

{The distance from Resen near the Rositsa river to the Danube (near Svishtov) is approximately 50km}

April 16, Sunday
Crosses the Danube (into modern-day Romania, possibly near Zimnicea, south of modern-day Alexandria was named after after a different Alexander, Alexandru II Ghica, prince of Wallachia)

Chapter 4: Alexander Destroys the City of the Getae—the Ambassadors of the Celts

They crossed over by night to a spot where the corn stood high; and in this way they reached the bank more secretly.

April 17, Monday
Defeats the Getae

At the approach of dawn Alexander led his men through the field of standing corn, ordering the infantry to lean upon the corn with their pikes[32] held transversely, and thus to advance into the untilled ground. As long as the phalanx was advancing through the standing corn, the cavalry followed; but when they marched out of the tilled land, Alexander himself led the horse round to the right wing, and commanded Nicanor[33] to lead the phalanx in a square. The Getae did not even sustain the first charge of the cavalry; for Alexander's audacity seemed incredible to them, in having thus easily crossed the Ister, the largest of rivers, in a single night, without throwing a bridge over the stream. Terrible to them also was the closely-looked order of the phalanx, and violent the charge of the cavalry. At first they fled for refuge into their city, which was distant about a parasang[34] from the Ister; but when they saw that Alexander was leading his phalanx carefully along the river, to prevent his infantry being anywhere surrounded by the Getae lying in ambush; whereas he was leading his cavalry straight on, they again abandoned the city, because it was badly fortified. They carried off as many of their women and children as their horses could carry, and betook themselves into the steppes, in a direction which led as far as possible from the river. Alexander took the city and all the booty which the Getae left behind. This he gave to Meleager[35] and Philip[36] to carry off. After razing the city to the ground, he offered sacrifice upon the bank of the river, to Zeus the preserver, to Heracles,[37] and to Ister himself, because he had allowed him to cross; and while it was still day he brought all his men back safe to the camp.

April 21, Friday
Visit by regional ambassadors

There ambassadors came to him from Syrmus, king of the Triballians, and from the other independent nations dwelling near the Ister. Some even arrived from the Celts who dwelt near the Ionian gulf.[38] These people are of great stature, and of a haughty disposition. All the envoys said that they had come to seek Alexander's friendship. To all of them he gave pledges of amity, and received pledges from them in return. He then asked the Celts what thing in the world caused them special alarm, expecting that his own great fame had reached the Celts and had penetrated still further, and that they would say that they feared him most of all things. But the answer of the Celts turned out quite contrary to his expectation; for, as they dwelt so far away from Alexander, inhabiting districts difficult of access, and as they saw he was about to set out in another direction, they said they were afraid that the sky would some time or other fall down upon them. These men also he sent back, calling them friends, and ranking them as allies, making the remark that the Celts were braggarts.[39]

April 26, Wednesday

Chapter 5: Revolt of Clitus and Glaucias

He then advanced into the land of the Agrianians and Paeonians,[40] where messengers reached him, who reported that Clitus, son of Bardylis,[41] had revolted, and that Glaucias,[42] king of the Taulantians,[43] had gone over to him. They also reported that the Autariatians[44] intended to attack him on his way.

{The Agrianians occupied an area west of modern-day Sofia in the region of the Strymon river and the Paeonins were just south of this in an area corresponding to the modern-day Bulgarian Macedonian border, possibly in the region of the town of Makedonska Kamenitsa. Both these areas are approximately 200km from where Alexander had a camp on the southern Danube (near Svishtov).}

April 28, Friday

He accordingly resolved to commence his march without delay. But Langarus, king of the Agrianians, who, in the lifetime of Philip, had been an open and avowed friend of Alexander, and had gone on an embassy to him in his private capacity, at that time also came to him with the finest and best armed of the shield-bearing troops, which he kept as a body-guard. When this man heard that Alexander was inquiring who the Autariatians were, and what was the number of their men, he said that he need take no account of them, since they were the least warlike of the tribes of that district; and that he would himself make an inroad into their land, so that they might have too much occupation about their own affairs to attack others. Accordingly, at Alexander's order, he made an attack upon them; and not only did he attack them, but he swept their land clean of captives and booty. Thus the Autariatians were indeed occupied with their own affairs. Langarus was rewarded by Alexander with the greatest honours, and received from him the gifts which were considered most valuable in the eyes of the king of the Macedonians. Alexander also promised to give him his sister Cyna[45] in marriage when he arrived at Pella.[46] But Langarus fell ill and died on his return home.

May 03, Wednesday
Marches along the Erigon river

After this, Alexander marched along the river Erigon,[47] and proceeded to the city of Pelium;[48] for Clitus had seized this city, as it was the strongest in the country.

{The river Erigon, corresponds to the Crna Reka in the modern-day Republic of Macedonia. Alexander possibly went there from the region of Makedonska Kamenitsa to Kavadarci, neaer which he woud find the Crna river. The distance between these two towns is approximately 80km. Then down the curve of the river to the region of Bitola is a further 100km}

May 9, Tuesday
Arrives at the Eordaicus river (modern-day Devoll river in Albania), possibly south of the town of Cërrik

When Alexander arrived at this place, and had encamped near the river Eordaicus,[49] he resolved to make an assault upon the wall the next day. But Clitus held the mountains which encircled the city, and commanded it from their height; moreover, they were covered with dense thickets. His intention was to fall upon the Macedonians from all sides, if they assaulted the city. But Glaucias, king of the Taulantians, had not yet joined him.

{The distance from Bitola in the modern-day Republic of Macedonia to Cërrik, in Albania is approximately 160km, and therefore the whole journey from the Crna river to the Eordaicus cossresponds to a journey of 240km}

May 10, Wednesday

Alexander, however, led his forces towards the city; and the enemy, after sacrificing three boys, an equal number of girls, and three black rams, sallied forth the purpose of receiving the Macedonians in a hand-to-hand conflict. But as soon as they came to close quarters, they left the positions which they had occupied, strong as they were,[50] in such haste that even their sacrificial victims were captured still lying on the ground.

On this day he shut them up in the city, and encamping near the wall, he resolved to intercept them by a circumvallation; but on the next day

Glaucias, king of the Taulantians, arrived with a great force.

May 11, Thursday

Then, indeed, Alexander gave up the hope of capturing the city with his present force, since many warlike troops had fled for refuge into it, and Glaucias with his large army would be likely to follow him up closely if he assailed the wall.

May 12, Friday

But he sent Philotas on a foraging expedition, with the beasts of burden from the camp and a sufficient body of cavalry to serve as a guard.

May 13, Saturday

When Glaucias heard of the expedition of Philotas he marched out to meet him, and seized the mountains which surrounded the plain, from which Philotas intended to procure forage. As soon as Alexander was informed that his cavalry and beasts of burden would be in danger if night overtook them, taking the shield-bearing troops,[51] the archers, the Agrianians, and about four hundred cavalry, he went with all speed to their aid. The rest of the army he left behind near the city, to prevent the citizens from hastening forth to form a junction with Glaucias (as they would have done), if all the Macedonian army had withdrawn. Directly Glaucias perceived that Alexander was advancing, he evacuated the mountains,

May 14, Sunday

and Philotas and his forces returned to the camp in safety. But Clitus and Glaucias still imagined that they had caught Alexander in a disadvantageous position; for they were occupying the mountains, which commanded the plain by their height, with a large body of cavalry, javelin-throwers, and slingers, besides a considerable number of heavy armed infantry. Moreover, the men who had been beleaguered in the city were expected to pursue the

Macedonians closely if they made a retreat. The ground also through which Alexander had to march was evidently narrow and covered with wood; on one side it was hemmed in by a river, and on the other there was a very lofty and craggy mountain, so that there would not be room for the army to pass, even if only four shieldbearers marched abreast.

May 16, Tuesday

Chapter 6: Defeat of Clitus and Glaucias

Then Alexander drew up his army in such a way that the depth of the phalanx was 120 men; and stationing 200 cavalry on each wing, he ordered them to preserve silence, in order to receive the word of command quickly. Accordingly he gave the signal to the heavy-armed infantry in the first place to hold their spears erect, and then to couch them at the concerted sign; at one time to incline their spears to the right, closely locked together, and at another time towards the left. He then set the phalanx itself into quick motion forward, and marched it towards the wings, now to the right, and then to the left. After thus arranging and re-arranging his army many times very rapidly, he at last formed his phalanx into a sort of wedge, and led it towards the left against the enemy, who had long been in a state of amazement at seeing both the order and the rapidity of his evolutions. Consequently they did not sustain Alexander's attack, but quitted the first ridges of the mountain. Upon this, Alexander ordered the Macedonians to raise the battle cry and make a clatter with their spears upon their shields; and the Taulantians, being still more alarmed at the noise, led their army back to the city with all speed.

Alexander saw only a few of the enemy still occupying a ridge, along which lay his route, he ordered his body-guards and personal companions to take their shields, mount their horses, and ride to the hill; and when they reached it, if those who had occupied the position awaited them, he said that half of them were to leap from their horses, and to fight as foot- soldiers, being mingled with the cavalry. But when the enemy saw Alexander's advance, they quitted the hill and retreated to the mountains in both directions. Then Alexander, with his companions,[52] seized the hill, and sent for the Agrianians and archers, who numbered 2,000. He also ordered the shield-bearing guards to cross the river, and after them the regiments of Macedonian infantry, with instructions that, as soon as they had succeeded in crossing, they should draw out in rank towards the left, so that the phalanx of men crossing might appear compact at once. He himself, in the vanguard, was all the time observing from the ridge the enemy's advance. They, seeing the force crossing the river, marched down the mountains to meet them, with the purpose of attacking Alexander's rear in its retreat. But, as they were just drawing near, Alexander rushed forth with his own division, and the phalanx raised the battle-cry, as if about to advance through the river. When the enemy saw all the Macedonians marching against them, they turned and fled. Upon this, Alexander led the Agrianians and archers at full speed towards the river, and succeeded in being himself the first man to cross it. But when he saw the enemy pressing upon the men in the rear, he stationed his engines of war upon the bank, and ordered the engineers to shoot from them as far forward as possible all sorts of projectiles which are usually shot from military engines.[53] He directed the archers, who had also entered the water, to shoot their arrows from the middle of the river. But Glaucias durst not advance within range of the missiles; so that the Macedonians passed over in such safety, that not one of them lost his life 'in the retreat.

May 19, Friday

Three days after this, Alexander discovered that Clitus and Glaucias lay carelessly encamped; that neither were ' their sentinels on guard in military order, nor had they protected themselves with a rampart or ditch, as if they imagined he had withdrawn through fear; and that they had extended their line to a disadvantageous length. He therefore crossed the river again secretly, at the approach of night, leading with him the shield-bearing guards, the Agrianians, the archers, and the brigades of Perdiccas[54] and Coenus,[55] after having given orders for the rest of the army to follow.

May 20, Saturday

As soon as he saw a favourable opportunity for the attack, without waiting for all to be present, he despatched the archers and Agrianians against the foe. These, being arranged in phalanx, fell unawares with the most furious charge upon their flank, where they were likely to come into conflict with their weakest point, and slew some of them still in their beds, others being easily caught in their flight. Accordingly, many were there captured and killed, as were many also in the disorderly and panic-stricken retreat which ensued. Not a few, moreover, were taken prisoners. Alexander kept up the pursuit as far as the Taulantian mountains; and as many of them as escaped, preserved their lives by throwing away their arms. Clitus first fled for refuge into the city, which, however, he set on fire, and withdrew to Glaucias, in the land of the Taulantians.

May 22, Monday

Chapter 7: Revolt of Thebes (September, B.C. 335)

While these events were occurring, some of the exiles who had been banished from Thebes, coming to the city by night, and being brought in by some of the citizens, in order to effect a change in the government, apprehended and slew outside the Cadmea,[56] Amyntas and Timolaus,[57] two of the men who held that fortress, having no suspicion that any hostile attempt was about to be made.

May 24, Wednesday

Then entering the public assembly, they incited the Thebans to revolt from Alexander, holding out to them as pretexts the ancient and glorious words, liberty and freedom of speech, and urging them now at last to rid themselves of the heavy yoke of the Macedonians. By stoutly maintaining that Alexander had been killed in Illyria they gained more power in persuading the multitude;[58] for this report was prevalent, and for many reasons it gained credit, both because he had been absent a long time, and because no news had arrived from him. Accordingly, as is usual in such cases, not knowing the facts, each man conjectured what was most pleasing to himself.

June 03, Saturday

When Alexander heard what was being done at Thebes, he thought it was a movement not at all to be slighted, inasmuch as he had for a long time suspected the city of Athens and deemed the audacious action of the Thebans no trivial matter, if the Lacedaemonians, who had long been disaffected in their feelings to him, and the Aetolians and certain other States in the Peloponnese, who were not firm in their allegiance to him, should take part with the Thebans in their revolutionary effort.

June 04, Sunday

He therefore led his army through Eordaea and Elimiotis[59] and along the peaks of Stymphaea and Paravaea,[60]

{Eordaea and Elimiotis are respectively north west and south west of ancient Orestis or modern-day Kastoria in Greece both within the Upper Macedonian region of Ancient Greece. The peaks of Stymphaea and Paravaea may respectively correspond to Emporio and Vlasti}

June 11, Sunday

and on the seventh day arrived at Pelina[61] in Thessaly.

{Pelina is in the region of modern-day Pontokomi. The distance between Cërrik, in Albania and Pontokomi in Greece is approximately 165km}

June 17, Saturday

Starting thence, he entered Boeotia on the sixth day; so that the Thebans did not learn that he had passed south of Thermopylae, until he was at Onchestus[62] with the whole of his army. Even then the authors of the revolt asserted that Antipater's army had arrived out of Macedonia, stoutly affirming that Alexander himself was dead, and being very angry with those who announced that it was Alexander himself who was advancing.[63] For they said it must be another Alexander, the son of Aëropus, who was coming.[64]

{Onchestus is approximately 9.25km north-west of Thebes and was on Lake Copais, modern-day Kopais. This is approximately 360km from Pelina (Pontokomi) in Thessaly}

June 18, Sunday

On the following day Alexander set out from Onchestus,

June 20, Tuesday
Sets camp near Thebes

and advanced towards the city along the territory consecrated to Iolaus;[65] where indeed he encamped, in order to give the Thebans further time to repent of their evil resolutions and to send an embassy to him.

{Thebes is approximately 35km from Lake Copais. Sources derived from Cleitarchus suggest it took Alexander three days to prepare his forces for the siege}

June 24, Saturday

But so far were they from showing any sign of wishing to come to an accommodation, that their cavalry and a large body of light-armed infantry sallied forth from the city as far as the camp, and, skirmishing with the Macedonian outposts, slew a few of their men. Alexander hereupon sent forth a party of his light-armed infantry and archers to repel their sortie; and these men repelled them with ease, just as they were approaching the very camp.

June 25, Sunday

The next day he took the whole of his army and marched round towards the gate which led to Eleutherae and Attica. But not even then did he assault the wall itself, but encamped not far away from the Cadmea, in order that succour might be at hand to the Macedonians who were occupying that citadel. For the Thebans had blockaded the Cadmea with a double stockade and were guarding it, so that no one from without might be able to give succour to those who were beleagured, and that the garrison might not be able, by making a sally, to do them any injury, when they were attacking the enemy outside. But Alexander remained encamped near the Cadmea, for he still wished rather to come to friendly terms with the Thebans than to come to a contest with them.[66]

June 26, Monday
Formally commences siege of Thebes

Then those of the Thebans who knew what was for the best interest of the commonwealth were eager to go out to Alexander and obtain pardon for the commonalty of Thebes for their revolt; but the exiles and those who had summoned them home kept on inciting the populace to war by every means in their power, since they despaired of obtaining for themselves any indulgence from Alexander, especially as some of them were also Boeotarchs.[67] However not even for this did Alexander assault the city.

June 28, Wednesday
3 days into the Siege

Chapter 8: Fall of Thebes

But Ptolemy, son of Lagus, tells us that Perdiccas, who had been posted in the advanced guard of the camp with his own brigade, and was not far from the enemy's stockade, did not wait for the signal from Alexander to commence the battle; but of his own accord was the first to assault the stockade, and, having made a breach in it, fell upon the advanced guard of the Thebans.[68] Amyntas,[69] son of Andromenes, followed Perdiccas, because he had been stationed with him. This general also of his own accord led on his brigade when he saw that Perdiccas had advanced within the stockade. When Alexander saw this, he led on the rest of his army, fearing that unsupported they might be intercepted by the Thebans and be in danger of destruction. He gave instructions to the archers and Agrianians to rush within the stockade, but he still retained the guards and shield-bearing troops outside. Then indeed Perdiccas, after forcing his way within the second stockade, fell there wounded with a dart, and was carried back grievously injured to the camp, where he was with difficulty cured of his wound. However the men of Perdiccas, in company with the archers sent by Alexander, fell upon the Thebans and shut them up in the hollow way leading to the temple of Heracles, and followed them in their retreat as far as the temple itself. The Thebans, having wheeled round, again advanced from that position with a shout, and put the Macedonians to flight. Eurybotas the Cretan, the captain of the archers, fell with about seventy of his men; but the rest fled to the Macedonian guard and the royal shield-bearing troops. Now, when Alexander saw that his own men were in flight, and that the Thebans had broken their ranks in pursuit, he attacked them with his phalanx drawn up in proper order, and drove them back within the gates. The Thebans fled in such a panic that being driven into the city through the gates they had not time to shut them; for the Macedonians, who were close behind the fugitives, rushed with them within the fortifications, inasmuch as the walla were destitute of defenders on account of the numerous pickets in front of them. When the Macedonians had entered the Cadmea, some of them marched out of it, in company with those who held the fortress, into the other part of the city opposite the temple of Amphion,[70] but others crossing along the walls, which were now in the possession of those who had rushed in together with the fugitives, advanced with a run into the market-place. Those of the Thebans who had been drawn up opposite the temple of Amphion stood their ground for a short time; but when the Macedonians under the command of Alexander were seen to be pressing hard upon them in various directions, their cavalry rushed through the city and sallied forth into the plain, and their infantry fled for safety as each man found it possible. Then indeed the Thebans, no longer defending themselves, were slain, not so much by the Macedonians as by the Phocians, Plataeans and other Boeotians,[71] who by indiscriminate slaughter vented their rage against them. Some were even attacked in the houses, having there turned to defend themselves from the enemy, and others were slain as they were supplicating the protection of the gods in the temples; not even the women and children being spared.[72]

Chapter 9: Destruction of Thebes

This was felt by the Greeks to be a general calamity for it struck the rest of the Greeks with no less consternation than it did those who had themselves taken part in the struggle, both on account of the magnitude of the captured city and the celerity of the action, the result of which was in the highest degree contrary to the expectation both of the sufferers and the perpetrators. For the disasters which befell the Athenians in relation to Sicily,[73] though in regard to the number of those who perished they brought no less misfortune to the city, yet, because their army was destroyed far away from their own land, being composed for the most part rather of auxiliary troops than of native Athenians, and because their city itself was left to them intact, so that afterwards they held their own in war even for a long time, though fighting against the Lacedaemonians and their allies, as well as the Great King; these disasters, I say, neither produced in the persons who were themselves involved in the calamity an equal sensation of the misfortune, nor did they cause the other Greeks a similar consternation at the catastrophe. Again, the defeat sustained by the Athenians at Aegospotami[74] was a naval one, and the city received no other humiliation than the demolition of the Long Walls, the surrender of most of her ships, and the loss of supremacy. However, they still retained their hereditary form of government, and not long after recovered their former power to such a degree as not only to build up the Long Walls but to recover the rule of the sea[75] and in their turn to preserve from extreme danger those very Lacedaemonians then so formidable to them, who had come and almost obliterated their city. Moreover, the defeat of the Lacedaemonians at Leuctra and Mantinea filled them with consternation rather by the unexpectedness of the disaster than because of the number of those who perished.[76] And the attack made by the Boeotians and Arcadians under Epaminondas upon the city of Sparta, even this terrified both the Lacedaemonians themselves and those who participated with them in the transactions at that time,[77] rather by the novelty of the sight than by the reality of the danger. The capture of the city of the Plataeans was not a great calamity, by reason of the small number of those who were taken in it; most of the citizens having long before escaped to Athens.[78] Again, the capture of Melus and Scione simply related to insular States, and rather brought disgrace to those who perpetrated the outrages than produced great surprise among the Grecian community as[79] a whole.

But the Thebans having effected their revolt suddenly and without any previous consideration, the capture of the city being brought about in so short a time and without difficulty on the part of the captors, the slaughter, being great, as was natural, from its being made by men of the same race who were glutting their revenge on them for ancient injuries, the complete enslavement of a city which excelled among those in Greece at that time both in power and warlike reputation, all this was attributed not without probability to the avenging wrath of the deity. It seemed as if the Thebans had after a long time suffered this punishment for their betrayal of the Greeks in the Median war,[80] for their seizure of the city of Plataeae during the truce, and for their complete enslavement of it, as well as for the un-Hellenic slaughter of the men who had surrendered to the Lacedaemonians, which had been committed at the instigation of the Thebans; and for the devastation of the territory in which the Greeks had stood in battle-array against the Medes and had repelled danger from Greece; lastly, because by their vote they had tried to ruin the Athenians when a motion was brought forward among the allies of the Lacedaemonians for the "enslavement of Athens.[81] Moreover it was reported that before the disaster many portents were sent from the deity, which indeed at the time were treated with neglect, but afterwards when men called them to remembrance they were compelled to consider that the events which occurred had been long before prognosticated.[82]

July 04, Tuesday

The settlement of Theban affairs was entrusted by Alexander to the allies who had taken part in the action. They resolved to occupy the Cadmea with a garrison; to raze the city to the ground; to distribute among themselves all the territory, except what was dedicated to the gods; and to sell into slavery the women and children, and as many of the males as survived, except those who were priests or priestesses, and those who were bound to Philip or Alexander by the ties of hospitality or had been public agents of the Macedonians. It is said that Alexander preserved the house and the descendants of Pindar the poet, out of respect for his memory.[83] In addition to these things, the allies decreed that Orchomenus[84] and Plataeae should be rebuilt and fortified.

July and August

Chapter 10: Alexander's Dealings with Athens

As soon as news of the calamity which had befallen the Thebans reached the other Greeks, the Arcadians, who had set out from their own land for the purpose of giving aid to the Thebans, passed sentence of death on those who had instigated them to render aid. The Eleans also received back their exiles from banishment, because they were Alexander's adherents; and the Aetolians, each tribe for itself, sent embassies to him, begging to receive pardon, because they also had attempted to effect a revolution, on the receipt of the report which had been spread by the Thebans. The Athenians also, who, at the time when some of the Thebans, escaping from the carnage, arrived at Athens, were engaged in celebrating the Great Mysteries,[85] abandoned the sacred rites in great consternation, and carried their goods and chattels from the rural districts into the city. The people came together in public assembly, and, on the motion of Demades, elected from all the citizens ten ambassadors, men whom they knew to be Alexander's special adherents, and sent them to signify to him, though somewhat unseasonably, that the Athenian people rejoiced at his safe return from the land of the Illyrians and Triballians, and at the punishment which he had inflicted upon the Thebans for their rebellion. In regard to other matters he gave the embassy a courteous reply, but wrote a letter to the people demanding the surrender of Demosthenes and Lycurgus, as well as that of Hyperides, Polyeuctus, Chares, Charidemus, Ephialtes, Diotimus, and Moerocles;[86] alleging that these men were the cause of the disaster which befell the city at Chaeronea, and the authors of the subsequent offensive proceedings after Philip's death, both against himself and his father.[87] He also declared that they had instigated the Thebans to revolt no less than had those of the Thebans themselves who favoured a revolution.

September 07, Thursday

The Athenians, however, did not surrender the men, but sent another embassy to Alexander,[88] entreating him to remit his wrath against the persons whom he had demanded.

September 08, Friday

The king did remit his wrath against them, either out of respect for the city of Athens, or from an earnest desire to start on the expedition into Asia, not wishing to leave behind him among the Greeks any cause for distrust. However, he ordered Charidemus alone of the men whom he had demanded as prisoners and who had not been given up, to go into banishment. Charidemus therefore went as an exile to King Darius in Asia.[89]

Chapter 11: Alexander Crosses the Hellespont and Visits Troy

Having settled these affairs, he returned into Macedonia.

September 21, Thursday
Celebration of the Macedonian Olympic Games at Aegae (whilst the 'Official Olympics' took place on the second full moon [August 06] after the summer solstice [June 22], the Macedonian one may have occurred on the eve of the autumn solstice [September 22] as Philip II was suggested to have been assassinated on a Macedonian Olympic celebration day on the eve of the autumnal solstice, please see above. It also suggests that the Macedonian Olympic games were not necessarily every four years but may have been an annual event, opposing the larger, more prominent formal Olympic Games which took place every four years)

He then offered to the Olympian Zeus the sacrifice which had been instituted by Archelaus,[90] and had been customary up to that time; and he celebrated the public contest of the Olympic games at Aegae.[91] It is said that he also held a public contest in honour of the Muses. At this time it was reported that the statue of Orpheus, son of Oeagrus the Thracian, which was in Pieris,[92] sweated incessantly.[93] Various were the explanations of this prodigy given by the soothsayers; but Aristander,[94] a man of Telmissus, a soothsayer, bade Alexander take courage; for he said it was evident from this that there would be much labour for the epic and lyric poets, and for the writers of odes, to compose and sing about Alexander and his achievements.

334 BC

Spring

March 16, Friday
Marches toward the Hellespont, (the vernal equinox that year was on March 20th and caldendar Spring began on March 16th, please see the preface)

(B.C. 334.) At the beginning of the spring he marched towards the Hellespont, entrusting the affairs of Macedonia and Greece to Antipater. He led not much above 30,000 infantry together with light-armed troops and archers, and more than 5,000 cavalry. [95] His march was past the lake Cercinitis,[96] towards Amphipolis and the mouths of the river Strymon. Having crossed this river he passed by the Pangaean mountain,[97] along the road leading to Abdera and Maronea, Grecian cities built on the coast. Thence he arrived at the river Hebrus,[98] and easily crossed it. Thence he proceeded through Paetica to the river Melas, having crossed

April 04, Wednesday
Gallipoli peninsula (Bigalı in modern-day Turkey)

which he arrived at Sestus, in twenty days altogether from the time of his starting from home.

April 05, Thursday
Gallipoli peninsula (Sedd el Bahr in Turkey)

{Military congregation with army and navy}

When he came to Elaēus he offered sacrifice to Protesilaus upon the tomb of that hero, both for other reasons and because Protesilaus seemed to have been the first of the Greeks who took part with Agamemnon in the expedition to Ilium to disembark in Asia. The design of this sacrifice was, that his disembarking in Asia might be more fortunate than that of Protesilaus had been.[99]

{Sedd el Bahr is 40km from Bigalı}

April 10, Tuesday
Crosses the Dardanelles and arrival at the Port of the Achaeans. Likely Kumkale port in Çanakkale Province, Turkey

He then committed to Parmenio the duty of conveying the cavalry and the greater part of the infantry from Sestus to Abydus; and they were transported in 160 triremes, besides many trading vessels.[100]

The prevailing account is, that Alexander started from Elaeus and put into the Port of Achaeans,[101] that with his own hand he steered the general's ship across, and that when he was about the middle of the channel of the Hellespont he sacrificed a bull to Poseidon and the Nereids, and poured forth a libation to them into the sea from a golden goblet.

They say also that he was the first man to step out of the ship in full armour on the land of Asia,[102] and that he erected altars to Zeus, the protector of people landing, to Athena, and to Heracles, at the place in Europe whence he started, and at the place in Asia where he disembarked.

{Kumkale port in Çanakkale Province, 8km from Sedd el Bahr}

April 12, Thursday
Hisarlik and Tevfikiye in Çanakkale Province, Turkey

It is also said that he went up to Ilium and offered sacrifice to the Trojan Athena; that he setup his own panoply in the temple as a votive offering, and in exchange for it took away some of the consecrated arms which had been preserved from the time of the Trojan war. These arms were said to have been carried in front of him into the battles by the shield-bearing guards. A report also prevails that he offered sacrifice to Priam upon the altar of Zeus the household god, deprecating the wrath of Priam against the progeny of Neoptolemus, from whom Alexander himself derived his origin.

Chapter 12: Alexander at the Tomb of Achilles — Memnon's Advice Rejected by the Persian Generals

When he went up to Ilium, Menoetius the pilot crowned him with a golden crown; after him Chares the Athenian,[103] coming from Sigeum, as well as certain others, both Greeks and natives, did the same. Alexander then encircled the tomb of Achilles with a garland; and it is said that Hephaestion[104] decorated that of Patroclus in the same way. There is indeed a report that Alexander pronounced Achilles fortunate in getting Homer as the herald of his fame to posterity.[105] And in truth it was meet that Alexander should deem Achilles fortunate for this reason especially; for to Alexander himself this privilege was wanting, a thing which was not in accordance with the rest of his good fortune. His achievements have, therefore, not been related to mankind in a manner worthy of the hero. Neither in prose nor in verse has any one suitably honoured him; nor has he ever been sung of in a lyric poem, in which style of poetry Hiero, Gelo, Thero, and many others not at all comparable with Alexander, have been praised.[106] Consequently Alexander's deeds are far less known than the meanest achievements of antiquity. For instance, the march of the ten thousand with Cyrus up to Persia against King Artaxerxes, the tragic fate of Clearchus and those who were captured along with him,[107] and the march of the same men down to the sea, in which they were led by Xenophon, are events much better known to men through Xenophon's narrative than are Alexander and his achievements. And yet Alexander neither accompanied another man's expedition, nor did he in flight from the Great King overcome those who obstructed his march down to the sea. And, indeed, there is no other single individual among Greeks or barbarians who achieved exploits so great or important either in regard to number or magnitude as he did. This was the reason which induced me to undertake this history, not thinking myself incompetent to make Alexander's deeds known to men. For whoever I may be, this I know about myself, that there is no need for me to assert my name, for it is not unknown to men; nor is it needful for me to say what my native land and family are, or if I have held any public office in my own country. But this I do assert, that this historical work is and has been from my youth up, in place of native land, family, and public offices to me; and for this reason I do not deem myself unworthy to rank among the first authors in the Greek language, if Alexander indeed is among the first in arms.

{Hisarlik and Tevfikiye in Çanakkale are 8km from Kumkale}

April 13, Friday
Northeast of Troy on the Hellespont Coast

From Ilium Alexander came to Arisbe, where his entire force had encamped after crossing the Hellespont;

April 14, Saturday
Northeast of Troy on the Hellespont Coast

and on the following day he came to Percote.

April 15, Sunday
Near modern Lapseki in Çanakkale Province, Turkey

On the next, passing by Lampsacus, he encamped near the river Practius, which flows from the Idaean mountains and discharges itself into the sea between the Hellespont and the Euxine Sea.

{Practius is possibly a now non-existent river between the Hellespont and the Black sea (Euxine Sea). The Idean mountains likely represent modern Mount Ida}

April 16, Monday
On the Southern Coast of the Sea of Marmara, Turkey

Thence passing by the city of Colonae,

{Colonae is unlikely to be Ancient Kolonai (αἱ Κολωναί), close to modern-day Alemşah in the Ezine district of Çanakkale Province, Turkey, but rather a city on the souther coast of the Sea of Marmara}

April 17, Tuesday
Arrival at Hermotus. On the Southern Coast of the Sea of Marmara, Turkey (possible classification by some sources that Alexander was formally in Asia Minor)

he arrived at Hermotus.

He now sent scouts before the army under the command of Arayntas, son of Arrhabaeus, who had the squadron of the Companion cavalry which came from Apollonia,[108] under the captain Socrates, son of Sathon, and four squadrons of what were called Prodromi (runners forward). In the march he despatched Panegorus, son of Lycagoras, one of the Companions, to take possession of the city of Priapus, which was surrendered by the inhabitants.

{The scouts identified the plain of Adrasteia that Alexander subsequently used as a vantage point for battle. The ancient city of Priapus corresponds to the town of Karabiga (also known as Karabuga) in the Biga District of Çanakkale Province, in the Marmara area of modern Turkey}

The Persian generals were Arsames, Rheomithres, Petines, Niphates, and with them Spithridates, viceroy of Lydia and Ionia, and Arsites, governor of the Phrygia near the Hellespont. These had encamped near the city of Zeleia with the Persian cavalry and the Grecian mercenaries.

{Zeleia was an ancient city allied with Troy, it existed at the foot of Mount Ida, approximately 32km southeast of Troy; along the northeastern side of the Edremit Gulf}

When they were holding a council about the state of affairs, it was reported to them that Alexander had crossed (the Hellespont). Memnon, the Rhodian,[109] advised them not to risk a conflict with the Macedonians, since they were far superior to them in infantry, and Alexander was there in person; whereas Darius was not with them. He advised them to advance and destroy the fodder, by trampling it down under their horses' hoofs, to burn the crops of the country, and not even to spare the very cities. "For then Alexander," said he, "will not be able to stay in the land from lack of provisions."[110] It is said that in the Persian conference Arsites asserted that he would not allow a single house belonging to the people placed under his rule to be burned, and that the other Persians agreed with Arsites, because they had a suspicion that Memnon was deliberately contriving to protract the war for the purpose of obtaining honour from the king.

April 20, Friday
Three days after arriving in Hermotus in the afternoon (circa 4pm), Biga Çayı River, modern Turkey. The sources for the date of this battle come from: (i) Plutarch who suggests the battle took place in Thargelion of the Attic calendar and (ii) Plutarch also suggests this took place in Daisios of the ancient Macedonian calendar. Both commeneced on the same day of the new moon as did the month before (beginning of Spring, please see the book preface). Lastly (iii), Aelian suggests the battle took place on the 6th of Thargelion. Spring in 334 BC was on March 16 (please see the book preface), so that Thargelion and Daisios began on the new moon of April 15 and therefore the 6th Thargelion would be April 20 334 BC.

Chapter 13: Battle of the Granicus (B.C. 334)

Meantime Alexander was advancing to the river Granicus,[111] with his army arranged for battle, having drawn up his heavy-armed troops in a double phalanx, leading the cavalry on the wings, and having ordered that the baggage should follow in the rear. And Hegelochus at the head of the cavalry, who were armed with the long pike,[112] and about 500 of the light-armed troops, was sent by him to reconnoitre the proceedings of the enemy. When Alexander was not far from the river Granicus, some of his scouts rode up to him at full speed and announced that the Persians had taken up their position on the other side of the Granicus, drawn up ready for battle. Thereupon Alexander arranged all his army with the intention of fighting. Then Parmenio approached him and spoke as follows: "I think, O king, that it is advisable for the present to pitch our camp on the bank of the river as we are. For I think that the enemy, being, as they are, much inferior to us in infantry, will not dare to pass the night near us, and therefore they will permit the army to cross the ford with ease at **day**break.

For we shall then pass over before they can put-themselves in order of battle;[113] whereas, I do not think that we can now attempt the operation without evident risk, because it is not possible to lead the army through the river with its front extended. Besides, it is clear that many parts of the stream are deep, 'and you see that these banks are steep and in some places abrupt. Therefore the enemy's cavalry, being formed into a dense square, will attack us as we emerge from the water in broken ranks and in column, in the place where we are weakest. At the present juncture the first repulse would be difficult to retrieve, as well as perilous for the issue of the whole war."

But to this Alexander replied: "I recognise the force of these arguments, O Parmenio; but I should feel it a disgrace, if, after crossing the Hellespont so easily, this brook (for with such an appellation he made light of the Granicus) should bar our passage for a moment. I consider that this would be in accordance neither with the fame of the Macedonians nor with my own eagerness for encountering danger. Moreover, I think that the Persians will regain courage, as being a match in war for Macedonians, since up to the present time they have suffered no defeat from me to warrant the fear they entertain."

Chapter 14: Arrangement of the Hostile Armies

Having spoken thus, he sent Parmenio to command upon the left wing, while he led in person on the right. And at the head of the right wing he placed the following officers:—Philotas, son of Parmenio, with the cavalry Companions, the archers, and the Agrianian javelin-men; and Amyntas, son of Arrhabaeus, with the cavalry carrying the long pike, the Paeonians, and the squadron of Socrates, was posted near Philotas. Close to these were posted the Companions who were shield-bearing infantry under the command of Nicanor, son of Parmenio. Next to these the brigade of Perdiccas, son of Orontes, then that of Coenus, son of Polemocrates; then that of Craterus,[114] son of Alexander, and that of Amyntas, son of Andromenes; finally, the men commanded by Philip, son of Amyntas. The first on the left wing were the Thessalian cavalry, commanded by Calas, son of Harpalus;[115] next to these, the cavalry of the Grecian allies, commanded by Philip, son of Menelaus;[116] next to these the Thracians, commanded by Agatho.[117] Close to these were the infantry, the brigades of Craterus, Meleager, and Philip, reaching as far as the centre of the entire line.

The Persian cavalry were about 20,000 in number, and their infantry, consisting of Grecian mercenaries, fell a little short of the same number.[118] They had extended their horse along the bank of the river in a long phalanx, and had posted the infantry behind the cavalry, for the ground above the bank was steep and commanding. They also marshalled dense squadrons of cavalry upon that part of the bank where they observed Alexander himself advancing against their left wing; for he was conspicuous both by the brightness of his arms and by the respectful service of his attendants. Both armies stood a long time at the margin of the river, keeping quiet from dread of the result; and profound silence was observed on both sides. For the Persians were waiting till the Macedonians should step into the water, with the intention of attacking them as they emerged. Alexander leaped upon his steed, ordering those about him to follow, and exhorting them to show themselves valiant men. He then commanded Amyntas, son of Arrhabaeus, to make the first rush into the river at the head of the skirmishing cavalry, the Paeonians, and one regiment of infantry; and in front of these he had placed Ptolemy, son of Philip, in command of the squadron of Socrates, which body of men indeed on that day happened to have the lead of all the cavalry force. He himself led the right wing with sounding of trumpets, and the men raising the war-cry to Enyalius.[119] He entered the ford, keeping his line always extended obliquely in the direction in which the stream flowed, in order that the Persians might not fall upon him on the flank as he was emerging from the water, but that he might, as far as practicable,[120] encounter them with his phalanx.

Chapter 15: Description of the Battle of the Granicus

The Persians began the contest by hurling missiles from above in the direction where the men of Amyntas and Socrates were the first to reach the bank; some of them casting javelins into the river from their commanding position on the bank, and others stepping down along the flatter parts of it to the very edge of the water. Then ensued a violent struggle on the part of the cavalry, on the one side to emerge from the river, and on the other to prevent the landing. Prom the Persians there was a terrible discharge of darts; but the Macedonians fought with spears. The Macedonians, being far inferior in number, suffered severely at the first onset, because they were obliged to defend themselves in the river, where their footing was unsteady, and where they were below the level of their assailants; whereas the Persians were fighting from the top of the bank, which gave them an advantage, especially as the best of the Persian horse had been posted there. Memnon himself, as well as his sons, were running every risk with these; and the Macedonians who first came into conflict with the Persians, though they showed great valour, were cut down, except those who retreated to Alexander, who was now approaching. For the king was already near, leading with him the right wing. He made his first assault upon the Persians at the place where the whole mass of their horse and the leaders themselves were posted; and around him a desperate conflict raged,[121] during which one rank of the Macedonians after another easily kept on crossing the river. Though they fought on horseback, it seemed more like an infantry than a cavalry battle; for they struggled for the mastery, horses being jammed with horses and men with men, the Macedonians striving to drive the Persians entirely away from the bank and to force them into the plain, and the Persians striving to obstruct their landing and to push them back again into the river. At last Alexander's men began, to gain the advantage, both through their superior strength and military discipline, and because they fought with spearshafts made of cornel-wood, whereas the Persians used only darts.

Then indeed, Alexander's spear being broken to shivers in the conflict, he asked Aretis, one of the royal guards, whose duty it was to assist the king to mount his horse, for another spear. But this man's spear had also been shivered whilst he was in the thickest of the struggle, and he was conspicuous fighting with the half of his broken spear. Showing this to Alexander, he bade him ask some one else for one. Then Demaratus, a man of Corinth, one of his personal Companions, gave him his own spear; which he had no sooner taken than seeing Mithridates, the son-in-law of Darius, riding far in front of the others, and leading with him a body of cavalry arranged like a wedge, he rode on in front of the others, and hitting at the face of Mithridates with his spear, struck him to the ground. But hereupon, Rhoesaces rode up to Alexander and hit him on the head with his scimitar, breaking off a piece of his helmet. But the helmet broke the force of the blow. This man also Alexander struck to the ground, hitting him in the chest through the breastplate with his lance. And now Spithridates from behind had already raised aloft his scimitar against the king, when Clitus, son of Dropidas, anticipated his blow, and hitting him on the arm, cut it off, scimitar and all.[122] Meantime the horsemen, as many as were able, kept on securing a landing all down the river, and were joining Alexander's forces.

Chapter 16: Defeat of the Persians. — Loss on Both Sides

The Persians themselves, as well as their horses, were now being struck on their faces with the lances from all sides, and were being repulsed by the cavalry. They also received much damage from the light-armed troops who were mingled with the cavalry. They first began to give way where Alexander himself was braving danger in the front. When their centre had given way, the horse on both wings were also naturally broken through, and took to speedy flight. Of the Persian cavalry only about 1,000 were killed; for Alexander did not pursue them far, but turned aside to attack the Greek mercenaries, the main body of whom was still remaining where it was posted at first. This they did rather from amazement at the unexpected result of the struggle than from any steady resolution. Leading the phalanx against these, and ordering the cavalry to fall upon them from all sides in the midst, he soon cut them up, so that none of them escaped except such as might have concealed themselves among the dead bodies. About 2,000 were taken prisoners.[123] The following leaders of the Persians also fell, in the battle: Niphates, Petines, Spithridates, viceroy of Lydia, Mithrobuzanes, governor of Cappadocia, Mithridates, the son-in-law of Darius, Arbupales, son of Darius the son of Artaxerxes, Pharnaces, brother of the wife of Darius,[124] and Omares, commander of the auxiliaries. Arsites fled from the battle into Phrygia, where he is reported to have committed suicide, because he was deemed by the Persians the cause of their defeat on that occasion.

April 21, Saturday
The day after battle

Of the Macedonians, about twenty-five of the Companions were killed at the first onset; brazen statues of whom were erected at Dium,[125] executed by Lysippus,[126] at Alexander's order. The same statuary also executed a statue of Alexander himself, being chosen by him for the work in preference to all other artists. Of the other cavalry over sixty were slain, and of the infantry, about thirty.[127] These were buried by Alexander the next day, together with their arms and other decorations. To their parents and children he granted exemption from imposts on agricultural produce, and he relieved them from all personal services and taxes upon property. He also exhibited great solicitude in regard to the wounded, for he himself visited each man, looked at their wounds, and inquired how and in the performance of what duty they had received them, allowing them both to speak and brag of their own deeds. He also buried the Persian commanders and the Greek mercenaries who were killed fighting on the side of the enemy. But as many of them as he took prisoners he bound in fetters and sent them away to Macedonia to till the soil, because, though they were Greeks, they were fighting against Greece on behalf of the foreigners in opposition to the decrees which the Greeks had made in their federal council.[128] To Athens also he sent 300 suits of Persian armour to be hung up in the Acropolis[129] as a votive offering to Athena, and ordered this inscription to be fixed over them: "Alexander, son of Philip, and all the Greeks except the Lacedaemonians, present this offering from the spoils taken from the foreigners, inhabiting Asia."

April 26, Thursday

Chapter 17: Alexander in Sardis and Ephesus

Having appointed Calas to the post of viceroy of the territory which had been under the rule of Arsites, and having commanded the inhabitants to pay to him the same tribute which they had paid to Darius, he ordered as many of the natives as came down from the mountains and surrendered to him to depart to their several abodes. He also acquitted the people of Zeleia[130] of blame, because he knew they had been compelled to assist the Persians in the war.

April 30, Monday

He then despatched Parmenio to occupy Dascylium,[131] which he easily performed; for the garrison evacuated it.

{Dascylium is near Ergili in modern-day Turkey}

May 02, Wednesday

He himself advanced towards Sardis;

{modern-day Sart in Turkey, approximately 666km from Granicus}

May 23, Wednesday

and when he was about 70 stades[132] distant from that city,

{1 stade is approximate to an eighth of a mile or 0.2km, so that Sardis was approximately 14km away}

he was met by Mithrines, the commandant of the garrison in the Acropolis, accompanied by the most influential of the citizens of Sardis. The latter surrendered the city into his hands, and Mithrines the fortress and the money laid up in it.

May 24, Thursday

Alexander encamped near the river Hermus,[133] which is about twenty stades[134] distant from Sardis; but he sent Amyntas, son of Andromenes, to occupy the citadel of Sardis.[135]

May 25, Friday

He took Mithrines with him, treating him with honour; and granted the Sardians and other Lydians the privilege of enjoying the ancient laws of Lydia, and permitted them to be free. He then ascended into the citadel, which was garrisoned by the Persians. And the position seemed to him a strong one; for it was very lofty, precipitous on every side, and fenced round by a triple wall. He therefore resolved to build a temple to the Olympian Zeus on the hill, and to erect an altar in it; but while he was considering which part of the hill was the most suitable site, suddenly a winter storm arose, though it was the summer season, loud claps of thunder were heard, and rain fell on the spot where the palace of the kings of Lydia had stood. From this Alexander thought that the deity had revealed to him where the temple to Zeus ought to be built; and he gave orders accordingly.

May 28, Monday

He left Pausanias, one of the Companions, to be superintendent of the citadel of Sardis, Nicias to supervise the collection of the tribute and taxes, and Asander, son of Philotas, to be superintendent of Lydia and the rest of the dominion of Spithridates, giving him as large a number of cavalry and light-armed infantry as seemed sufficient for present emergencies. He also sent Galas and Alexander, son of Aëropus, into the country of

Memnon,[136] in command of the Peloponnesians and most of the other Grecian allies,, except the Argives, who had been left behind to guard the citadel of Sardis.

Meantime, when the news of the cavalry battle was spread abroad, the Grecian mercenaries who formed the garrison of Ephesus, seized two of the Ephesian. triremes and set off in flight. They were accompanied by Amyntas,[137] son of Antiochus, who had fled from Alexander out of Macedonia, not because he had received any injury from the king, but from ill-will to him, and thinking it not unlikely that he should suffer some ill treatment from him (on account of his disloyalty).

June 01, Friday
Ephesus, just southwest of modern-day Selçuk in İzmir Province, Turkey

On the fourth day Alexander arrived at Ephesus, where he recalled from exile all the men who had been banished from the city on account of their adherence to him; and having broken up the oligarchy, he established a democratical form of government there. He also ordered the Ephesians to contribute to Artemis[138] all the tribute which they were in the habit of paying to the Persians. When the people of Ephesus were relieved of their dread of the oligarchs, they rushed headlong to kill the men who had brought Memnon into the city, as also those who had pillaged the temple of Artemis, and those who had thrown down the statue of Philip which was in the temple, and those who had dug up and carried off from the tomb in. the market place the bones of Heropythus, the liberator of their city. They also led Syrphax and his son Pelagon, and the sons of Syrphax's brothers out of the temple and stoned them to death. But Alexander prevented them making any further quest of the rest of the oligarchs for the purpose of wreaking their vengeance upon them; for he knew that if the people were not checked, they would kill the innocent along with the guilty, some from hatred, and others for the sake of seizing their property. At this time Alexander gained great popularity both by his general course of action and especially by what he did at Ephesus.

June 06, Wednesday

Chapter 18: Alexander Marches to Miletus and Occupies the Island of Lade

Men now came to him both from Magnesia[139] and Tralles, offering to surrender those cities; and to them he sent Parmenio, giving him 2,500 infantry from the Grecian auxiliaries, an equal number of Macedonians, and about 200 of the Cavalry Companions. He also sent Lysimachus, son of Agathocles,[140] with an equal force to the Aeolic cities,[141] and to as many of the Ionic cities[142] as were still under the Persians. He was ordered to break up the oligarchies everywhere, to set up the democratical form of government, to restore their own laws to each of the cities, and to remit the tribute which they were accustomed to pay to the foreigners. But Alexander himself remained behind at Ephesus, where he offered a sacrifice to Artemis and conducted a procession in her honour with the whole of his army fully armed and marshalled for battle.[143]

June 07, Thursday

On the following day he took the rest of his infantry, the archers, the Agrianians, the Thracian cavalry, the royal squadron of the Companions, and three other squadrons in addition, and set out for Miletus.

{Miletus is near the modern-day village of Balat in Aydın Province, Turkey, approximately 84km away from Ephesus or 2 days march}

June 13, Wednesday
Begins Assault of Miletus

At his first assault he captured that which was called the outer city; for the garrison had evacuated it.

June 14, Thursday

There he encamped and resolved to blockade the inner city; for Hegesistratus, to whom the king Darius had entrusted the command of the garrison in Miletus, kept on sending letters before this to Alexander, offering to surrender Miletus to him. But then, having regained his courage from the fact that the Persian fleet was not far off, he made up his mind to preserve the city for Darius.

June 22, Friday

But Nicanor, the commander of the Grecian fleet, anticipated the Persians by sailing into the port of Miletus three days before they approached; and with 160 ships he anchored at the island of Lade, which lies near Miletus.[144] The Persian ships arriving too late, and the admirals discovering that Nicanor had occupied the anchorage at Lade before them, they took moorings near Mount Mycale.[145] Alexander had forestalled them in seizing the island, not only by mooring his ships near it, but also by transporting into it the Thracians and about 4,000 of the other auxiliary troops. The ships of the foreigners were about 400 in number.

Notwithstanding the superiority of the Persian fleet, Parmenio advised Alexander to fight a sea-battle, expecting that the Greeks would be victorious with their fleet both for other reasons and especially because an omen from the deity made him confident of the result; for an eagle had been seen sitting upon the shore, opposite the sterns of Alexander's ships.[146] He also urged that if they won the battle, they would reap a great advantage from it in regard to their main object in the war; and if they were beaten, their defeat would not be of any great moment; for even as it was, the Persians held the sovereignty of the sea. He added that he was willing to go on board the fleet himself and to share the danger. However, Alexander replied that Parmenio was mistaken in his judgment, and did not explain the sign according to probability. For it would be rash for him with a few ships to fight a battle against a fleet far more numerous than his own, and with his unpractised naval force to contend against the disciplined fleet of the Cyprians and Phoenicians. Besides, he did not wish to deliver over to the foreigners on so unstable an element the advantage which the Macedonians derived from their skill and courage; and if they were beaten in the sea battle, their defeat would be no small hindrance to their final success in the war, both for other reasons, and especially because the Greeks, being animated with courage at the news of his naval defeat, would attempt to effect a revolution. Taking all these things into consideration, he declared that he did not think that it was a suitable time for fighting a sea-battle; and for his part, he expounded the divine omen in a different way. He admitted that the eagle was in his favour; but as it was seen sitting on the land, it seemed to him rather to be a sign that he should get the mastery over the Persian fleet by defeating their army on land.

June 23, Saturday

Chapter 19: Siege and Capture of Miletus

At this time Glaucippus, one of the most notable men in Miletus, was sent out to Alexander by the people and the Grecian mercenaries, to whom rather than to the citizens the town had been entrusted, to tell him that the Milesians were willing to make their walls and harbours[147] free to him and the Persians in common; and on these terms to demand that he should raise the siege. But Alexander ordered Glaucippus to depart without delay into the city, and tell the citizens to prepare for a battle at daybreak.

June 24, Sunday

He then stationed his military engines near the wall, and having in a short time partly broken and partly shaken down a large piece of it, he led his army near, that the men might enter wherever the wall had been thrown down or shaken. The Persians from Mycale were following close[148] upon them and could almost see their friends and allies being besieged. In the meantime, Nicanor, observing from Lade Alexander's commencement of the attack, began to sail into the harbour of Miletus, rowing along the shore; and mooring his triremes as close as possible together, with their prows facing the enemy, across the narrowest part of the mouth of the harbour, he shut off the Persian fleet from the port and made it impossible for the Persians to give succour to the Milesians. Then the Macedonians from all sides pressed close upon the citizens and the Grecian mercenaries, who took to flight; some of them, casting themselves into the sea, floated along upon their shields with the hollow upwards to an unnamed islet which lies near the city; others getting into their skiffs and hastening to get the start of the Macedonian triremes, were captured by them at the mouth of the harbour. But the majority of them were slain in the city itself. As soon as Alexander had got possession of the city, he sailed against those who had fled for refuge into the island; ordering the men to carry ladders upon the prows of the triremes, with the intention of effecting a landing along the cliffs of the island, as one would mount a wall. But when he saw that the men on the island were resolved to run every risk, he was moved with pity for them, because they appeared to him both brave and loyal; wherefore he made a truce with them on the condition that they would serve as his soldiers. These Grecian mercenaries were about 300 in number. He likewise pardoned all the citizens of Miletus who had escaped death in the capture of the city, and he granted them their freedom.

June 25 Monday – July 18, Wednesday

The foreigners used to start from Mycale every day and sail up to the Grecian fleet, hoping to induce them to accept the challenge and come forth to a battle; but during the night they used to moor their vessels near Mycale, which was an inconvenient station, because they were under the necessity of fetching water from the mouth of the river Maeander, a great way off.[149] Alexander guarded the harbour of Miletus with his ships, in order to prevent the foreigners from forcing an entrance; and at the same time he sent Philotas to Mycale in command of the cavalry and three regiments of infantry, with instructions to prevent the men in the ships from landing. Accordingly, they, being through the scarcity of fresh water and of the other necessaries of life as good as besieged in their ships, sailed away to Samos; where furnishing themselves with food, they sailed back again to Miletus. They then drew up most of their ships in front of the harbour on the deep sea, with the hope that they might in some way or other induce the Macedonians to come out into the open sea.

July 19, Thursday

Five of their ships sailed into the roadstead which lay between the island of Lade and the camp, expecting to surprise Alexander's ships while empty of their crews; for they had ascertained that the sailors for the most part were dispersed from the ships, some to gather fuel, others to collect provisions, and others being arranged in foraging parties.[150] And indeed it happened that a number of the sailors were absent; but as soon as Alexander observed the five Persian ships sailing towards him, he manned ten ships with the sailors who happened to be at hand, and sent them with all speed against them with orders to attack prow to prow. No sooner did the men in the five Persian ships see the Macedonians bearing up against them, contrary to their expectation, than they immediately tacked about, though far off, and fled to the rest of their fleet. However, the ship of the Iassians,[151] not being a fast sailer, was captured in the flight, men and all; but the other four succeeded in escaping to their own triremes. After this the Persians sailed away from Miletus without effecting anything.

July 20, Friday – August 14, Tuesday

Chapter 20: Siege of Halicarnassus — Abortive Attack on Myndus

Alexander now resolved to disband his fleet, partly from lack of money at the time, and partly because he saw that his own fleet was not a match in battle for that of the Persians. On this account he was unwilling to run the risk of losing even a part of his armament. Besides, he considered, that now he was occupying Asia with his land force, he would no longer be in need of a fleet; and that he would be able to break up that of the Persians, if he captured the maritime cities; since they would neither have any ports from which they could recruit their crews, nor any harbour in Asia to which they could bring their ships. Thus he explained the omen of the eagle to signify that he should get the mastery over the enemy's ships by his land force. After doing this, he set forth into Caria,[152] because it was reported that a considerable force, both of foreigners and of Grecian auxiliaries, had collected in Halicarnassus.[153] Having taken all the cities between Miletus and Halicarnassus as soon as he approached them, he encamped near the latter city, at a distance from it of about five stades,[154] as if he expected a long siege.

{Halicarnassus is sited at modern-day Bodrum in Turkey approximately 110km from ancient Miletus}

For the natural position of the place made it strong; and wherever there seemed to be any deficiency in security, it had been entirely supplied long before by Memnon, who was there in person, having now been proclaimed by Darius governor of lower Asia and commander of the entire fleet. Many Grecian mercenary soldiers had been left in the city, as well as many Persian troops; the triremes also were moored in the harbour, so that the sailors might reader him valuable aid in the operations.

August 19, Sunday

On the first day of the siege, while Alexander was leading his men up to the wall in the direction of the gate leading towards Mylasa,[155] the men in the city made a sortie, and a skirmish took place; but Alexander's men making a rush upon them repulsed them with ease, and shut them up in the city.

August 23, Thursday

A few days after this, the king took the shield-bearing guards, the Cavalry Companions, the infantry regiments of Amyntas, Perdiccas and Meleager, and in addition to these the archers and Agrianians, and went round to the part of the city which is in the direction of Myndus, both for the purpose of inspecting the wall, to see if it happened to be more easy to be assaulted there than elsewhere; and at the same time to see if he could get hold of Myndus[156] by a sudden and secret attack. For he thought that if Myndus were his own, it would be no small help in the siege of Halicarnassus; moreover an offer to surrender had been made by the Myndians if he would approach the town secretly, under the cover of night.

August 24, Friday

About midnight, therefore, he approached the wall, according to the plan agreed on; but as no sign of surrender was made by the men within, and though he had with him no military engines or ladders, inasmuch as he had not set out to besiege the town, but to receive it on surrender, he nevertheless led the Macedonian phalanx near and ordered them to undermine the wall. They threw down one of the towers, which, however, in its fall did not make a breach in the wall. But the men in the city stoutly defending themselves, and at the same time many from Halicarnassus having already come to their aid by sea, made it impossible for Alexander to capture Myndus by surprise or sudden assault.

August 25, Saturday

Wherefore he returned without accomplishing any of the plans for which he had set out, and devoted himself once more to the siege of Halicarnassus.

August 28, Tuesday – August 30, Thursday

In the first place he filled up with earth the ditch which the enemy had dug in front of the city, about thirty cubits wide and fifteen deep; so that it might be easy to bring forward the towers, from which he intended to discharge missiles against the defenders of the wall; and that he might bring up the other engines with which he was planning to batter the wall down. He easily filled up the ditch, and the towers were then brought forward.

{30 x 15 cubits = 13.7 x 6.85 meters, Alexander then had to build the towers}

August 31, Friday

But the men in Halicarnassus made a sally by night with the design of setting fire both to the towers and the other engines which had been brought up to the wall, or were nearly brought up to it. They were, however, easily repelled and shut up again within the walls by the Macedonians who were guarding the engines, and by others who were aroused by the noise of the struggle and who came to their aid. Neoptolemus, the brother of Arrhabaeus, son of Amyntas, one of those who had deserted to Darius, was killed, with about 170 others of the enemy. Of Alexander's soldiers sixteen were killed and 300 wounded; for the sally being made in the night, they were less able to guard themselves from being wounded.

September 03, Monday

Chapter 21: Siege of Halicarnassus

A few days after this, two Macedonian hoplites of the brigade of Perdiccas, living in the same tent and being messmates, happened in the course of conversation each to be extolling himself and his own exploits. Hence a quarrel arose between them as to which of them was the braver, and, being somewhat inflamed with wine, they agreed to arm themselves, and of their own accord go and assault the wall facing the citadel, which for the most part was turned towards Mylasa. This they did rather to make a display of their own valour than to engage in a dangerous conflict with the enemy. Some of the men in the city, however, perceiving that there were only two of them, and that they were approaching the wall inconsiderately, rushed out upon them; but they slew those who came near, and hurled darts at those who stood at a distance. At last, however, they were overmatched both by the number of their assailants and the disadvantage of their own position; for the enemy made the attack upon them, and threw darts at them from a higher level.[157] Meanwhile some other men from the brigade of Perdiccas, and others from Halicarnassus, rushed out against each other; and a sharp contest ensued near the wall. Those who had made the sally from the city were driven back, and again shut up within the gates by the Macedonians. The city also narrowly escaped capture; for the walls at that time were not under strict guard, and two towers, with the whole intermediate space, having already fallen to the ground, would have offered an easy entrance within the wall to the army, if the whole of it had undertaken the task. The third tower, which had been thoroughly shaken, would likewise have been easily thrown down if it had been undermined; but the enemy easily succeeded in building inside a crescent-shaped brick wall to take the place of the one which had fallen. This they were able to do so quickly because of the multitude of hands at their disposal.

September 04, Tuesday

On the following day Alexander brought his engines up to this wall also; and the men in the city made another sally to set them on fire. A part of the wicker-work shed near the wall and a piece of one of the wooden towers were burnt, but the rest were protected by Philotas and Hellanicus, to whom the charge of them had been committed. But as soon as those who were making the sally saw Alexander, the men who had come out to render aid by holding torches threw them away, and the majority of them cast away their arms and fled within the walls of the city. Then at first they had the advantage from the nature of their position, which was commanding on account of its height; for not only did they cast missiles right in front against the men who were guarding the engines, but also from the towers which alone had been left standing at each end of the battered-down wall, they were able to cast them against the sides, and almost against the backs, of those who were assaulting the wall which had just been built in place of the ruined one.[158]

September 09, Sunday

Chapter 22: Siege of Halicarnassus

A few days after this, when Alexander again brought his military engines up to the inner brick wall, and was himself superintending the work, a sortie in mass was made from the city, some advancing by the breach in the wall, where Alexander himself was posted, others by the triple gate, where the Macedonians did not at all expect them. The first party cast torches and other combustibles at the engines, in order to set them on fire and to defy the engineers excessively. But when the men around Alexander attacked them vigorously, hurling ' great stones with the engines from the towers, and launching darts at them, they were easily put to rout and fled into the city; and as a great number of them had sallied forth and great audacity had been exhibited in the fight, no small slaughter of them took place. For some of them were slain fighting hand-to-hand with the Macedonians, others were killed near the ruins of the wall,[159] because the breach was too narrow for such a multitude to pass through, and the fragments of the wall made it difficult for them to scale it. The second party, which sallied forth by the triple gate, was met by Ptolemy,[160] one of the royal body-guards, who had with him the regiments of Addaeus and Timander and some of the light-armed troops. These soldiers by themselves easily put the men of the city to rout; but as the latter in their retreat were fleeing over a narrow bridge which had been made over the ditch, they had the misfortune to break it down by the weight of their multitude. Many of them fell into the ditch, some of whom were trampled to death by their own comrades, and others were killed by the Macedonian weapons from above. A very great slaughter was also made at the very gates, because they were shut before the proper time in a state of panic. For the enemy, being afraid that the Macedonians, who were close upon the fugitives, would rush in with them, shut many of their friends out, who were slain by the Macedonians near the very walls. The city narrowly escaped capture; indeed it would have been taken, had not Alexander called back his army, to see if some friendly sign of surrender would be made by the Halicarnassians; for he was still desirous of saving their city. Of the men in the city about one thousand were slain; and of Alexander's men about forty, among whom were Ptolemy, one of the king's body-guards, Clearchus, a captain of the archers, Addaeus, who had the command of a thousand infantry, and other Macedonians of no mean position.[161]

Chapter 23: Destruction of Halicarnassus — Ada, Queen of Caria

Then Orontobates and Memnon, the commanders of the Persians, met and decided from the state of affairs that they could not hold out long against the siege, seeing that part of the wall had already fallen down and part had been battered and weakened, and that many of their soldiers had either perished in the sorties or been wounded and disabled. Taking these things into consideration, about the second watch of the night they set fire to the wooden tower which they had themselves built to resist the enemy's military engines, and to the magazines in which their weapons were stored. They also cast fire into the houses near the wall; and others were burned by the flames, which were carried with great fury from the magazines and the tower by the wind bearing in that direction. Some of the enemy then withdrew to the stronghold in the island (called Arconnesus), and others to another fortress called Salmacis.

September 10, Monday

When this was reported to Alexander by some deserters from the incendiaries, and he himself could see the raging fire, though the occurrence took place about midnight, yet he led out the Macedonians and slew those who were still engaged in setting fire to the city. But he issued orders to preserve all the Halicarnassians who should be taken in their houses.

As soon as the daylight appeared he could discern the strongholds which the Persians and the Grecian mercenaries had occupied; but he decided not to besiege them, considering that he would meet with no small delay beleaguering them, from the nature of their position, and moreover thinking that they would be of little importance to him now that he had captured the whole city.

Wherefore, burying the dead in the night, he ordered, the men who had been placed in charge of the military engines to convey them to Tralles.

September 18, Tuesday

He himself marched into Phrygia,

{Phrygia is located in the west central part of Anatolia, in modern Turkey, located on the Sakarya River – about 600km from Halicarnassus}

October 25, Thursday

after razing the city to the ground, and leaving 3,000 Grecian infantry and 200 cavalry as a guard both of this place and of the rest of Caria, under the command of Ptolemy. He appointed Ada to act as his viceroy of the whole of Caria.[162] This queen was daughter of Hecatomnus and wife of Hidrieus, who, though he was her brother, lived with her in wedlock, according to the custom of the Carians. When Hidrieus was dying, he confided the administration of affairs to her, for it had been a custom in

Asia, ever since the time of Semiramis, even for women to rule men. But Pixodarus expelled her from the rule, and seized the administration of affairs himself. On the death of Pixodarus, his son-in-law Orontobates was sent by the king of the Persians to rule over the Carians. Ada retained Alinda alone, the strongest place in Caria; and when Alexander invaded Caria she went to meet him, offering to surrender Alinda to him, and adopting him as her son.[163] Alexander confided Alinda to her, and did not think the title of son unworthy of his acceptance; moreover, when he had captured Halicarnassus and become master of the rest of Caria, he granted her the privilege of ruling over the whole country.

October 27, Saturday

Chapter 24: Alexander in Lycia and Pamphylia

Some of the Macedonians who served in Alexander's army had married just before he undertook the expedition. He thought that he ought not to treat these men with neglect, and therefore sent them back from Caria to spend the winter in Macedonia with their wives. He placed them under the command of Ptolemy, son of Seleucus, one of the royal body-guards, and of the two generals Coenus, son of Polemocrates, and Meleager, son of Neoptolemus, because they were also newly married. He gave these officers instructions to levy as many horse and foot soldiers as they could from the country, when they returned to him and brought back the men who had been sent away with them. By this act more than by any other Alexander acquired popularity among the Macedonians. He also sent Cleander, son of Polemocrates, to levy soldiers in Peloponnesus,[164] and Parmenio to Sardis, giving him the command of a regiment of the Cavalry Companions, the Thessalian cavalry, and the rest of the Grecian allies. He ordered him to take the wagons to Sardis and to advance from that place into Phrygia.

October 30, Tuesday

He himself marched towards Lycia and Pamphylia, in order to gain command of the coast-land, and by that means render the enemy's fleet useless.

{Lycia and Pamphylia broadly correspond to the areas of Mugla and Antalya of modern Turkey}

November 15, Thursday

The first place on his route was Hyparna, a strong position, having a garrison of Grecian mercenaries; but he took it at the first assault, and allowed the Greeks to depart from the citadel under a truce.

December 18, Tuesday
Completed invasion of Lycia

Then he invaded Lycia and brought over the Telmissians by capitulation;

{Lycia is approximately 500km from Phrygia}

December 28, Friday

and crossing the river Xanthus,

{Xanthus or Xanthos corresponds to Kınık, in Antalya Province, modern-day Turkey and is approximately 320km from Lycia}

333 BC (LEAP YEAR)

January 08, Tuesday

the cities of Pinara, Xanthus, Patara, and about thirty other smaller towns were surrendered to him.[165]

January 17, Thursday

Having accomplished this, though it was now the very depth of winter, he invaded the land called Milyas,[166] which is a part of Great Phrygia, but at that time paid tribute to Lycia, according to an arrangement made by the Great King.

{Milyas was in the south of Pisidia in northern Lycia, possibly corresponding to an area of the modern district and village of Korkuteli in Turkey. The distance between Xanthus and Korkuteli is approximately 400km}

January 23, Wednesday

Hither came envoys from the Phaselites,[167] to treat for his friendship, and to crown him with a golden crown;

January 25, Friday

and the majority of the maritime Lycians also sent heralds to him as ambassadors to treat for the same object. He ordered the Phaselites and Lycians to surrender their cities to those who were despatched by him to receive them; and they were all surrendered.

January 31, Thursday

He soon afterwards arrived himself at Phaselis, and helped the men of that city to capture a strong fort which had been constructed by the Pisidians to overawe the country; and sallying forth from which those barbarians used to inflict much damage upon the Phaselites who tilled the land.[168]

{Phaselis corresponds to the north of Tekirova in the Kemer district of Antalya Province in modern Turkey}

February 04, Monday

Chapter 25: Treason of Alexander, Son of Aëropus

While the king was still near Phaselis he received information that Alexander, son of Aëropus, who was not only one of the Companions, but also at that time commander of the Thessalian horse, was conspiring against him. This Alexander was brother of Heromenes and Arrhabaeus, who had taken part in the murder of Philip.[169] At that time King Alexander pardoned him, though he was accused of complicity with them, because after Philip's death he was among the first of his friends to come to him, and, helping him on with his breastplate, accompanied him to the palace. The king afterwards showed him honour at his court, sent him as general into Thrace; and when Calas the commander of the Thessalian horse was sent away to a viceroyalty[170] he was appointed to succeed that general. The details of the conspiracy were reported as follows: When Amyntas deserted to Darius,[171] he conveyed to him certain messages and a letter from this Alexander. Darius then sent Sisines, one of his own faithful Persian courtiers, down to the sea-coast, under pretence of going to Atizyes, viceroy of Phrygia, but really to communicate with this Alexander, and to give him pledges, that if he would kill king Alexander, Darius would appoint him king of Macedonia, and would give him 1,000 talents of

60

gold[172] in addition to the kingdom. But Sisines, being captured by Parmenio, told him the real object of his mission. Parmenio sent him immediately under guard to the king, who obtained the same intelligence from him. The king then, having collected his friends, proposed to them as a subject for deliberation what decision he ought to make in regard to this Alexander. The Companions thought that formerly he had not resolved wisely in confiding the best part of his cavalry to a faithless man, and that now it was advisable to put him out of the way as speedily as possible, before he became even more popular among the Thessalians and should try to effect some revolutionary plan with their aid. Moreover they were terrified by a certain divine portent. For, while Alexander the king was still besieging Halicarnassus, it is said that he was once taking rest at mid-**day**, when a swallow flew about over his head loudly twittering, and perched now on this side of his couch and now on that, chirping more noisily than usual. On account of his fatigue he could not be roused from sleep, but being disquieted by the sound he brushed her away gently with his hand. But though struck she was so far from trying to escape, that she perched upon the very head of the king, and did not desist until he was wide awake. Thinking the affair of the swallow of no trivial import, he communicated it to a soothsayer, Aristander the Telmissian,[173] who told him that it signified a plot formed by one of his friends. He said it also signified that the plot would be discovered, because the swallow was a bird fond of man's society and well disposed to him as well as more loquacious than any other bird. Therefore, comparing this with the depositions of the Persian, the king sent Amphoterus, son of Alexander and brother of Craterus to Parmenio; and with him he sent some Pergaeans to show him the way. Amphoterus, putting on a native dress, so that he should not be recognised on the road, reached Parmenio by stealth. He did not carry a letter from Alexander, because it did not appear to the king advisable to write openly about such a matter; but he reported the message entrusted to him by word of mouth. Consequently this Alexander was arrested and kept under guard.

February 13, Wednesday

Chapter 26: Alexander in Pamphylia — Capture of Aspendus and Side.

Alexander then, moving from Phaselis, sent part of his army to Perga through the mountains, where the Thracians had levelled a road for him by a route which was otherwise difficult and long. But he himself led his own brigade by the beach along the sea, where there is no route, except when the north wind blows. But if the south wind prevails it is impossible to journey along the beach. At that time, after a strong south wind, the north winds blew, and rendered his passage easy and quick, not without the divine intervention, as both he and his men interpreted.[174]

{Perga corresponds to Aksu in Antalya in modern Turkey}

February 15, Friday

As he was advancing from Perga, he was met on the road by envoys from the Aspendians[175] with full powers, who offered to surrender their city, but begged him not lead a garrison into it. Having gained their request in regard to the garrison, they went back; but he ordered them to give him fifty talents[176] as pay for his army, as well as the horses which they were rearing as tribute to Darius. Having agreed with him about the money, and having likewise promised to hand over the horses, they departed.

February 19, Tuesday

Alexander then marched to Sidē,[177] the inhabitants of which were Cymaeans from Cyme, in Aeolis. These people give the following account of themselves, saying that their ancestors starting from Cyme, arrived in that country, and disembarked to found a settlement. They immediately forgot the Grecian language, and forthwith began to utter a foreign speech, not, indeed, that of the neighbouring barbarians, but a speech peculiar to themselves, which had never before existed. From that time the Sidetans used to speak a foreign language unlike that of the neighbouring nations. Having left a garrison in Side,

{Side retains its name in modern Turkey in the province of Antalya, approximately 64km from Perga}

February 24, Sunday

Alexander advanced to Syllium,[178] a strong place, containing a garrison' of Grecian mercenaries as well as of native barbarians themselves. But he was unable to take Syllium offhand by a sudden assault,

February 26, Tuesday

for he was informed on his march that the Aspendians refused to perform any of their agreements, and would neither deliver the horses to those who were sent to receive them, nor pay the money; but that they had collected their property out of the fields into the city, shut their gates against his men, and were repairing their walls where they had become dilapidated. Hearing this, he marched off to Aspendus.

{Aspendus or Aspendos is located 7 kilometres or 4.3 miles northeast of central Serik in modern Turkey. It is approximately 32km from Side and Alexander was turning back on himself to get there}

March 01, Saturday

Chapter 27: Alexander in Phrygia and Pisidia

The greater part of Aspendus had been built upon a strong and precipitous rock, at the very foot of which flows the river Eurymedon[179]; but round the rock, on the low ground, were many of the citizens' houses, surrounded by a small wall. As soon as they ascertained that Alexander was approaching, the inhabitants deserted the wall and the houses situated on the low ground, which they thought they were unable to protect; and they fled in a body to the rock.

March 02, Sunday

When he arrived with his forces, he passed within the deserted wall and took up his quarters in the houses which had been abandoned by the Aspendians. When these saw that Alexander himself had come, contrary to their expectation, and that his camp was encircling them on all sides, they sent envoys to him, entreating him to form an agreement with them on the former terms. Alexander, considering the strength of the place, and how unprepared he was to undertake a long siege, entered into an agreement with them, though not on the same terms as before. For he ordered them to give him their most influential men as hostages, to hand over the horses which they had formerly agreed to give him, to pay 100 talents instead of fifty, to obey the viceroy appointed by him, and to pay an annual tribute to the Macedonians. Moreover he directed an inquiry to be held about the land which they were accused of holding by force, though it belonged of right to their neighbours.

March 06, Thursday

When all these concessions had been made to him, he marched away to Perga,

{Perga is approximately 24km Aspendus, Alexander essentially returned to Perga as he had been here a few weeks before}

March 08, Saturday

and thence set out for Phrygia, his route leading him past the city of Termessus.

{Termessus or Termessos corresponds to modern day Güllük Dağı in the Taurus mountains in Turkey approximately 43km from Perga}

March 13, Thursday

The people of this city are foreigners, of the Pisidian race, inhabiting a very lofty place, precipitous on every side; so that the road to the city is a difficult one. For a mountain stretches from the city as far as the road, where it suddenly stops short; and over against it rises another mountain, no less precipitous. These mountains form gates, as it were, upon the road; and it is possible for those who occupy these eminences even with a small guard to render the passage impracticable. On this occasion the Termissians had come out in a body, and were occupying both the mountains; seeing which, Alexander ordered the Macedonians to encamp there, armed as they were, imagining that the Termissians would not remain in a body when they saw them bivouacking, but that most of them would withdraw into their city, which was near, leaving upon the mountains only sufficient men to form a guard.

March 14, Friday

And it turned out just as he conjectured; for most of them retired, and only a guard remained. He forthwith took the archers, the regiments of javelin-throwers, and the lighter hoplites, and led them against those who were guarding the pass. When these were attacked with missiles, they did not stand their ground, but abandoned the position. Alexander then passed through the defile, and encamped near the city.

March 19, Wednesday

Chapter 28: Operations in Pisidia

While he was there, ambassadors came to him from the Selgians, who are also Pisidian barbarians, inhabiting a large city, and being warlike. Because they happened to be inveterate enemies to the Termessians they had despatched this embassy to Alexander, to treat for his friendship. He made a treaty with them, and from this time found them faithful allies in all his proceedings.

March 21, Friday

Despairing of being able to capture Termessus without a great loss of time, he marched on to Sagalassus.

{Sagalassus also known as Sagalassos Σαγαλασσός is about 100 km north of Antalya (ancient Attaleia). It lies 7km from Ağlasun on Mount Akdağ, in the Western Taurus mountains range in the province of Burdur, with an altitude of 1450–1700 metres. It is located approximately 30 km from Burdur and Isparta.}

March 25, Tuesday

This was also a large city, inhabited likewise by Pisidians; and though all the Pisidians are warlike, the men of this city were deemed the most so. On this occasion they had occupied the hill in front of the city, because it was no less strong than the walls, from which to attack the enemy; and there they were awaiting him. But Alexander drew up the phalanx of Macedonians in the following way: on the right wing, where he had himself taken up his position, he held the shield-bearing guards, and next to these he extended the foot Companions as far as the left wing, in the order that each of the generals had precedence in the array that **day**. On the left wing he stationed Amyntas, son of Arrhabaeus, as commander. In front of the right wing were posted the archers and Agrianians, and in front of the left wing the Thracian javelin-throwers under the command of Sitalces. But the cavalry were no use to him in a place so rough and unfavourable. The Termessians also had come to the aid of the Pisidians, and arrayed themselves with them. Alexander had already made an attack upon the mountain which the Pisidians were occupying, advancing up the most abrupt part of the ascent, when the barbarians from an ambuscade attacked him on both wings, in a place where it was very easy for themselves to advance, but where the route was very difficult for their enemy. The archers, who were the first to approach, were put to rout, inasmuch as they were insufficiently armed; but the Agrianians stood their ground, for the Macedonian phalanx was already drawing near, at the head of which Alexander himself was seen. When the battle became a hand-to-hand one, though the barbarians were destitute of armour, they rushed against the Macedonian hoplites, and fell wounded on all sides. Then, indeed, they gave way, after about 500 of them had been killed. As they were nimble and well-acquainted with the locality, they effected their retreat without difficulty; whereas the Macedonians, on account of the heaviness of their arms and their ignorance of the roads, durst not pursue them vigorously. Alexander therefore held off from the fugitives, and took their city by storm. Of those with him, Cleander, the general of the archers, and about twenty others were slain.

March 30, Sunday – April 11, Friday

Alexander then marched against the rest of the Pisidians, and took some of their strongholds by storm; others he won over to him by granting them terms of capitulation.

April 12, Saturday

Chapter 29: Alexander in Phrygia

Thence he went into Phrygia, passing by the lake called Ascania[180] in which salt is naturally concreted. The natives use this salt, and do not need the sea at all for this article.

{Lake Askania typically corresponds to modern day Lake Iznik in Turkey (İznik Gölü) – approximately 450km from Sagalassus, this may not be the same Lake Askania as it is so far away, approximately 18 days of a full war-time military march}

April 17, Thursday

On the fifth day of his march, he arrived at Celaenae,[181] in which city there was a fortified rock, precipitous on all sides. This citadel was occupied by the viceroy of Phrygia with a garrison of 1,000 Carians and 100 Grecian mercenaries.

{Celaenae or Kelainai Greek: Κελαιναί is located near the source of the Maeander River (Büyük Menderes rising from a spring near Dinar) in west central Turkey (Dinar of Afyonkarahisar Province)}

April 18, Friday

These men despatched ambassadors to Alexander, promising to surrender the place to him, if succour did not reach them by a day which had been agreed upon with them, naming the day.[182]

April 21, Monday

This arrangement seemed to Alexander more advantageous than to besiege the fortified rock, which was inaccessible on all sides to attack.

At Celaenae he left a garrison of 1,500 soldiers. Remaining here ten days, he appointed Antigonus, son of Philip,[183] viceroy of Phrygia, placed Balacrus, son of Amyntas[184] as general over the Grecian allies in place of Antigonus,

May 01, Thursday

and then directed his march to Gordium.[185] He sent an order to Parmenio to meet him there with the forces under his command; an order which that general obeyed.

{Gordium (modern-day Yassıhüyük) is 248km from Celaenae}

May 27, Tuesday

The newly-married men also, who had been despatched to Macedonia, now arrived at Gordium, and with them another army which had been levied, and put under the command of Ptolemy, son of Seleucus,[186] Coenus, son of Polemocrates, and Meleager, son of Neoptolemus. This army consisted of 3,000 Macedonian foot-soldiers and 300 horse-soldiers, 200 Thessalian cavalry, and 150 Eleans under the command of Alcias the Elean.

Gordium is in the Phrygia which lies near the Hellespont, and is situated upon the river Sangarius, which takes its rise in Phrygia, but, flowing through the land of the Bithynian Thracians, falls into the Euxine Sea.

June 01, Sunday

Here an embassy reached Alexander from the Athenians, beseeching him to release to them the Athenian prisoners who had been captured at the river Granicus, fighting for the Persians, and were then in Macedonia serving in chains with the two thousand others captured in that battle. The envoys departed without obtaining their request on behalf of the prisoners for the present. For Alexander did not think it safe, whilst the war against the Persian was still going on, to relax in the slightest degree the terror with which he inspired the Greeks, who did not deem it unbecoming for them to serve as soldiers on behalf of the foreigners against Greece. However, he replied that whenever his present enterprise had been successfully achieved, they might then come as ambassadors to treat on behalf of the same persons.[187]

June 05, Thursday onward (Darius)

Chapter 30 (Start of Book 2): Capture of Mitylene by the Persians — Death of Memnon

Soon after this, Memnon, whom King Darius had appointed commander of the whole fleet and of the entire sea-coast, with the design of moving the seat of war into Macedonia and Greece, acquired possession of Chios, which was surrendered to him by treachery. Thence he sailed to Lesbos and brought over to his side all the cities of the island,[188] except Mitylene, the inhabitants of which did not submit to him. When he had gained these cities over, he turned his attention to Mitylene; and walling off the city from the rest of the island by constructing a double stockade from sea to sea, he easily got the mastery on the land side by building five camps. A part of his fleet guarded their harbour, and, intercepting the ships passing by, he kept the rest of his fleet as a guard off Sigrium,[189] the headland of Lesbos, where is the best landing-place for trading vessels from Chios, Geraestus,[190] and Malea.[191] By this means he deprived the Mitylenaeans of all hope of succour by sea. But time be himself fell ill and died, and his death at that crisis, was exceedingly injurious to the king's interests. Nevertheless Autophradates, and Pharnabazns, son of Artabazus, prosecuted the siege with vigour. To the latter indeed, Memnon, when dying, had entrusted his command, as he was his sister's son, till Darius should come to some decision on the matter. The Mitylenaeans, therefore, being excluded from the land, and being blockaded on the sea by many ships lying at anchor, sent to Pharnabazus and came to the following agreement:—That the auxiliary troops which had come to their aid from Alexander should depart, that the citizens should demolish the pillars on which the treaty made by them with Alexander was inscribed,[192] that they should become allies of Darius on the terms of the peace which was made with King Darius in the time of Antalcidas,[193] and that their exiles should return from banishment on condition of receiving back half the property which they possessed when they were banished. Upon these terms the compact was made between the Mitylenaeans and the Persians. But as soon as Pharnabazus and Autophradates once got within the city, they introduced a garrison with Lycomedes, a Rhodian, as its commandant. They also appointed Diogenes, one of the exiles, to be despot of the city, and exacted money from the Mitylenaeans, taking part of it by violence for themselves from the wealthy citizens, and laying the rest as a tax upon the community.

Chapter 31: The Persians Capture Tenedus — They are Defeated at Sea

After accomplishing this, Pharnabazus sailed to Lycia, taking with him the Grecian mercenaries; but Autophradates sailed to the other islands. Meantime Darius sent Thymondas, son of Mentor,[194] down to the maritime districts, to take over the Grecian auxiliaries from Pharnabazus and to lead them up to him; and to tell Pharnabazus that he was to be the ruler of all that Memnon had ruled. So Pharnabazus handed over to him the Grecian auxiliaries and then sailed to join Autophradates and the fleet. When they met, they despatched Datames, a Persian, with ten ships to the islands called Cyclades,[195] whilst they with 100 sailed to Tenedus.[196] Having sailed into the harbour of Tenedus which is called Borēus, they sent a message to the inhabitants, commanding them to demolish the pillars on which the treaty made by them with Alexander and the Greeks was inscribed, and to observe in regard to Darius the terms of the peace which they had ratified with the king of Persia in the time of Antalcidas. The Tenedians preferred to be on terms of amity with Alexander and the Greeks; but in the present crisis it seemed impossible to save themselves except by yielding to the Persians, since Hegelochus, who had been commissioned by Alexander to collect another naval force, had not yet gathered so large a fleet as to warrant them in expecting any speedy succour from him. Accordingly Pharnabazus made the Tenedians comply with his demands rather from fear than good-will.

Meantime Proteas, son of Andronicus, by command of Antipater,[197] succeeded in collecting ships of war from Euboea and the Peloponnese, so that there might be some protection both for the islands and for Greece itself, if the foreigners attacked them by sea, as it was reported they intended to do. Learning that Datames with ten ships was moored near Siphnus,[198] Proteas set out by night with fifteen from Chalcis on the Euripus,[199] and approaching the island of Cythnus[200] at dawn, he spent the **day** there in order to get more certain information of the movements of the ten ships, resolving at the same time to fall upon the Phoenicians by night, when he would be likely to strike them with greater terror. Having discovered with certainty that Datames was moored with his ships at Siphnus, he sailed thither while it was still dark, and just at the very dawn fell upon them when they least expected it, and captured eight of the ships, men and all. But Datames, with the other two triremes, escaped by stealth at the beginning of the attack made by the ships with Proteas, and reached the rest of the Persian fleet in safety.

June 06, Friday

Chapter 32: Alexander at Gordium

When Alexander arrived at Gordium, he was seized with an ardent desire to go up into the citadel, which contained the palace of Gordius and his son Midas.

June 08, Sunday

He was also desirous of seeing the wagon of Gordius and the cord which bound the yoke to the wagon. There was a great deal of talk about this wagon among the neighbouring population. It was said that Gordius was a poor man among the ancient Phrygians, who had a small piece of land to till, and two yoke of oxen. He used one of these in ploughing and the other to draw the wagon. On one occasion, while he was ploughing, an eagle settled upon the yoke,[201] and remained sitting there until the time came for unyoking the oxen. Being alarmed at the sight, he went to the Telmissian soothsayers to consult them about the sign from the deity; for the Telmissians were skilful in interpreting the meaning of Divine manifestations, and the power of divination has been bestowed not only upon the men, but also upon their wives and children from generation to generation. When Gordius was driving his wagon near a certain village of the Telmissians, he met a maiden fetching water from the spring, and to her he related how the sign of the eagle had appeared to him. As she herself was of the prophetic race, she instructed him to return to the very spot and offer sacrifice to Zeus the king. Gordius requested her to accompany him and direct him how to perform the sacrifice. He offered the sacrifice in the way the girl suggested, and afterwards married her. A son was born to them named Midas, who, when he arrived at the age of maturity, was both handsome and valiant. At this time the Phrygians were harassed by civil discord, and consulting the oracle, they were told that a wagon would bring them a king, who would put an end to their discord.[202] "While they were still deliberating about this very matter, Midas arrived with his father and mother, and stopped near the assembly with the very wagon in question. They, interpreting the oracular response to refer to him, decided that this was the person whom the god told them the wagon would bring. They therefore appointed Midas king; and he, putting an end to their discord, dedicated his father's wagon in the citadel as a thank-offering to Zeus the king for sending the eagle. In addition to this the following report was current concerning the wagon, that whosoever could loosen the cord with which the yoke of the wagon was tied, was destined to be the ruler of Asia. The cord was made of cornel bark, and neither end nor beginning to it could be seen. It is said by some that when Alexander could find out no way to loosen the cord and yet was unwilling to allow it to remain unloosened, lest it should exercise some disturbing influence upon the multitude, he struck the cord with his sword and cut it through, saying that it had been untied by him. But Aristobulus says that he pulled out the pin of the wagon-pole, which was a wooden peg driven right through it, holding the cord together. Having done this, he drew out the yoke from the wagon-pole. How Alexander performed the feat in connection with this cord, I cannot affirm with confidence. At any rate both he and his troops departed from the wagon as if the oracular prediction concerning the untying of the cord had been, fulfilled. Moreover, that very night, the thunder and lightning were signs from heaven of its fulfilment;

June 09, Monday

and for this reason Alexander offered sacrifice on the following **day** to the gods who had revealed the signs and assured him that the cord had been untied in a proper way.[203]

June 10, Tuesday

Chapter 33: Conquest of Cappadocia — Alexander's Illness at Tarsus

The next day he sent out to Ancyra[204] in Galatia,

{Ancyra corresponds to modern Ankara and is approximately 225km away from Gordium}

July 05, Saturday

where he was met by an embassy from the Paphlagonians, offering to surrender their nation to him and to enter into an alliance with him; but they requested him not to invade their land with his forces. He therefore commanded them to submit to the authority of Galas, the viceroy of Phrygia.

August 10, Sunday

Marching thence into Cappadocia, he subjugated all that part of it which lies on this side of the river Halys,[205] and much of that which lies beyond it. Having appointed Sabictas viceroy of Cappadocia,

{Cappadocia, Turkish: Kapadokya, Greek: Καππαδοκία (Kappadokía), Ancient Greek: Καππαδοκία, from Old Persian: Katpatuka corresponds to a region in Central Anatolia in the Nevşehir, Kayseri, Kırşehir, Aksaray, and Niğde Provinces of modern Turkey. This region is approximately 320km away from Ankara}

September 01, Monday

he advanced to the Gates of Cilicia,[206] and when he arrived at the Camp of Cyrus, who (went) with Xenophon,[207] and saw that the Gates were occupied by strong guards, he left Parmenio there with the regiments of infantry which were more heavily armed; and about the first watch, taking the shield-bearing guards, the archers, and the Agrianians, he advanced by night to the Gates, in order to fall upon the guards when they least expected it. However, his advance was not unobserved; but his boldness served him equally well, for the guards, perceiving that Alexander was advancing in person, deserted their post and set off in flight.

{The Gates of Cilicia or Cilician Gates or Gülek Pass is a pass running in the Taurus Mountains. They link the low plains of Cilicia with the Anatolian Plateau via a narrow gorge of the Gökoluk River. At it's highest, it's level is approximately 1000m. This pass is approximately 250km away from Cappadocia. Xenophon had also travelled here with Cyrus the Younger.}

September 02, Tuesday

At dawn next day he passed through the Gates with all his forces and descended into Cilicia.[208]

September 04, Thursday

Here he was informed that Arsames had previously intended to preserve Tarsus for the Persians; but when he heard that Alexander had already passed through the Gates, he resolved to abandon the city; and that the Tarsians were therefore afraid he would turn to plunder their city and afterwards evacuate it.

{Tarsus is approximately 36.5km from the Cilician Gates. Xenophon had also travelled here with Cyrus the Younger. It corresponds to the centre of the Çukurova region of modern Turkey's Mersin Province }

September 06, Saturday
Illness at the Cydnus River

Hearing this, Alexander led his cavalry and the lightest of his light infantry to Tarsus with a forced march; consequently Arsames, hearing of his start, fled with speed from Tarsus to King Darius without inflicting any injury upon the city.

Alexander now fell ill from the toils he had undergone, according to the account of Aristobulus; but other authors say that while he was very hot and in profuse perspiration he leaped into the river Cydnus[209] and swam, being eager to bathe in its water. This river flows through the midst of the city; and as its source is in mount Taurus and it flows through a clean district, it is cold and its water is clear. Alexander therefore was seized with convulsions, accompanied with high fever and continuous sleeplessness. None of the physicians thought he was likely to survive,[210] except Philip, an Acarnanian, a physician in attendance on the king, and very much trusted by him in medical matters, who also enjoyed a great reputation in the army in general affairs. This man wished to administer a purgative draught to Alexander, and the king ordered him to administer it. While Philip was preparing the cup, a letter was given to the king from Parmenio, warning him to beware of Philip; for he heard that the physician had been bribed by Darius to poison Alexander with medicine. But he, having read the letter, and still holding it in his hand, took the cup which contained the medicine and gave Philip the letter to read. While Philip was reading the news from Parmenio, Alexander drank the potion. It was at once evident to the king that the physician was acting honourably in giving the medicine, for he was not alarmed at the letter, but only so much the more exhorted the king to obey all the other prescriptions which he might give, promising that his life would be saved if he obeyed his instructions. Alexander was purged by the draught, and his illness then took a favourable turn. He afterwards proved to Philip that he was a faithful friend to him; and to the rest of those about he proved that he had perfect confidence in his friends by refusing to entertain any suspicion of their fidelity; and at the same time he showed that he could meet death with dauntless courage.[211]

{The river Cydnus is known as the Berdan river in modern Turkey. It is likely that Alexander was already suffering from an infective condition that rendered him feeling hot so that he jumped into the Cydnus. There are many possible infective causes for this. Another possibility is that he may have suffered from near-syncope after jumping into the cold water. Please see: Ashrafian H. The death of Alexander the Great—a spinal twist of fate. J Hist Neurosci. 2004 Jun;13(2):138-42. PubMed PMID: 15370319.}

September 27, Saturday

Chapter 34: Alexander at the Tomb of Sardanapalus — Proceedings in Cilicia

After this he sent Parmenio to the other Gates which separate the land of the Cilicians from that of the Assyrians, in order to capture them before the enemy could do so, and to guard the pass.[212] He gave him the allied infantry, the Grecian mercenaries, the Thracians who were under the command of Sitalces, and the Theassalian cavalry.

September 29, Monday

He afterwards marched from Tarsus,

September 30, Tuesday

and on the first day arrived at the city of Anchialus.[213] According to report, this city was founded by Sardanapalus the Assyrian;[214] and both from the circumference and from the foundations of the walls it is evident that a large city had been founded and that it had reached a great pitch of power. Also near the wall of Anchialus was the monument of Sardanapalus, upon the top of which stood the statue of that king with the hands joined to each other just as they are joined for clapping.[215] An inscription had been placed upon it in Assyrian characters,[216] which the Assyrians asserted to be in metre. The meaning which the words expressed was this:—"Sardanapalus, son of Anacyndaraxas, built Anchialus and Tarsus in one day; but do thou, O stranger, eat, drink, and play, since all other human things are not worth this!" referring, as in a riddle, to the empty sound which the hands make in clapping. It was also said that the word translated play had been expressed by a more lewd one in the Assyrian language.

October 5, Sunday

From Anchialus Alexander went to Soli,[217] into which city he introduced a garrison, and imposed upon the inhabitants a fine of 200 talents of silver,[218] because they were more inclined to favour the Persians than himself.

{Soli, Greek: Σόλοι, Soloi corresponds to an area within the Mezitli municipality of Greater Mersin in modern Turkey. It is approximately 40km from Tarsus}

October 7, Tuesday

Then, having taken three regiments of Macedonian infantry, all the archers, and the Agrianians, he marched away thence against the Cilicians, who were holding the mountains;

October 14, Tuesday

and in seven days in all, having expelled some by force, and having brought the rest over by composition, he marched back to Soli.

Here he ascertained that Ptolemy and Asander[219] had gained the mastery over Orontobates the Persian who was guarding the citadel of Halicarnassus, and was also holding Myndus, Caunus, Thera, and Callipolis.[220] Cos and Triopium[221] also had been brought into subjection. They wrote to inform him that Orontobates had been worsted in a great battle; that about 700 of his infantry and 50 of his cavalry had been killed, and not less than 1,000 taken prisoners. In Soli Alexander offered sacrifice to Asclepius,[222] conducting a procession of the entire army, celebrating a torch race, and superintending a gymnastic and musical contest. He granted the Solians the privilege of a democratical constitution; and then marched away to Tarsus, despatching the cavalry under Philotas to march through the Aleian plain to the river Pyramus.[223]

October 21, Tuesday

But he himself with the infantry and the royal squadron of cavalry came to Magarsus, where he offered sacrifice to the Magarsian Athena.

{Margasus is on a hill opposite to Mallus (please see immediately below), approximately 100km from Soli}

October 23, Thursday

Thence he marched to Mallus, where he rendered to Amphilochus the sacrificial honours due to a hero.[224] He also arrested those who were creating a sedition among the citizens, and thus put a stop to it. He remitted the tribute which they were paying to King Darius, because the Malliotes were a colony of the Argives, and he himself claimed to have sprung from Argos, being a descendant of Heracles.

{Mallus, (Greek: η Μαλλός Mallos; was sited near the mouth of the Pyramus (now the Ceyhan Nehri) river, in Anatolia, modern Turkey}

October 27, Monday

Chapter 35: Alexander Advances to Myriandrus — Darius Marches against him

While he was still at Mallus, he was informed that Darius was encamped with all his forces at Sochi, a place in the land of Assyria, distant about two days' march from the Assyrian Gates.[225] Then indeed he collected the Companions and told them what was reported about Darius and his army.

They urged him to lead them on as they were, without delay. At that time he commended them, and broke up the conference;

{The Assyrian Gates are also known as the Syrian Gates correspond to The Belen Pass in modern Turkey (Belen İlçesi), acting as a narrow pass in the Nur mountains. It is one of two passes the the Amanus mountain range, the other being the Amanian Gate, please refer below}

October 28, Tuesday

but next day he led them forward against Darius and the Persians.

October 29, Wednesday

On the second day he passed through the Gates and encamped near the city of Myriandrus;[226] but in the night a heavy tempest and a violent storm of wind and rain occurred which detained him in his camp.

{This would have been a very fast march covering approximately 100km from Mallus to the Syrian Gates: Myriandrus and Issus both correspond to modern day Iskenderun in Turkey. Much of the infantry would not have made this pace and would have followed and caught up at the rear. Xenophon had also travelled to Myriandrus and Issus with Cyrus the Younger.}

Darius, on the other hand, had been spending a long time with his army, having chosen a plain in the land of Assyria which stretches out in every direction, suitable for the immense size of his army and convenient for the evolutions of cavalry. Amyntas, son of Antiochus, the deserter from Alexander, advised him not to abandon this position, because there was plenty of room for the great multitude of the Persians and for the vast quantity of their baggage. So Darius remained. But as Alexander made a long stay at Tarsus on account of his illness, and not a short one at Soli, where he offered sacrifice and conducted his army in procession, and moreover spent some time in marching against the Cilician mountaineers, Darius was induced to swerve from his resolution. He was also not unwilling to be led to form whatever decision was most agreeable to his own wishes; and being influenced by those who gave him the advice which they thought would be pleasant to him, without consideration of its utility (for kings will always have associates to give them bad advice),[227] he came to the conclusion that Alexander was no longer desirous of advancing further, but was shrinking from an encounter on learning that Darius himself was marching against him. On all sides they were urging him on, asserting that he would trample down the army of the Macedonians with his cavalry.[228] Nevertheless, Amyntas, at any rate, confidently affirmed that Alexander would certainly come to any place where he heard Darius might be; and he exhorted him by all means to stay where he was. But the worse advice, because at the immediate time it was more pleasant to hear, prevailed; moreover he was led by some divine influence into that locality where he derived little advantage from his cavalry and from the sheer number of his men, javelins and bows, and where he could not even exhibit the mere magnificence of his army, but surrendered to Alexander and his troops an easy victory. For it was already decreed by fate that the Persians should be deprived of the rule of Asia by the Macedonians, just as the Medes had been deprived of it by the Persians, and still earlier the Assyrians by the Medes.

October 31, Friday (Darius)

Chapter 36: Darius at Issus — Alexander's Speech to his Army

Darius crossed the mountain range by what are called the Amanic Gates, and advancing towards Issus, came without being noticed to the rear of Alexander.[229]

{The Amanic of Amanian Gates correspond to a mountain pass located on the border between Osmaniye and Gaziantep provinces in modern-day south-central Turkey. Here the Aamanus mountains correspond to the modern-day Nur mountains. The pass is approximately 27km away by land.}

November 3, Monday (Darius)

Having reached Issus, he captured as many of the Macedonians as had been left behind there on account of illness. These he cruelly mutilated and slew.

{ancient Issus is close to the modern-day Iskenderun in Turkey}

November 4, Tuesday (Darius)

Next day he proceeded to the river Pinarus.

{This river likely corresponds to the Payas River in southern Anatolia close to today's Turkey—Syria border, though previously it considered to be the modern Deli Çay}

November 02, Sunday

As soon as Alexander heard that Darius was in his rear, because the news did not seem to him trustworthy, he embarked some of the Companions in a ship with thirty oars, and sent them back to Issus, to observe whether the report was true. The men who sailed in the thirty-oared ship, discovered the Persians encamped there more easily, because the sea in this part takes the form of a bay.

November 04, Tuesday

They therefore brought back word to Alexander that Darius was at hand. Alexander then called together the generals, the commanders of cavalry, and the leaders of the Grecian allies, and exhorted them to take courage from the dangers which they had already surmounted, asserting that the struggle would be between themselves who had been previously victorious and a foe who had already been beaten; and that the deity was acting the part of general on their behalf better than himself, by putting it into the mind of Darius to move his forces from the spacious plain and shut them up in a narrow place, where there was sufficient room for them to deepen their phalanx by marching from front to rear, but where their vast multitude would be useless to their enemy in battle. He added that their foes were similar to them neither in strength nor in courage; for the Macedonians, who had long been practised in warlike toils accompanied with danger, were coming into close conflict with Persians and Medes, men who had become enervated by a long course of luxurious ease; and, to crown all, they, being freemen, were about to engage in battle with men who were slaves. He said, moreover, that the Greeks who were in the two armies would not be fighting for the same objects; for those with Darius were braving danger for pay, and that pay not high; whereas, those on their side were voluntarily defending the interests of Greece. Again, of foreigners, the Thracians,

Paeonians, Illyrians, and Agrianians, who were the most robust and warlike of men in Europe, were about to be arrayed against the most sluggish and effeminate races of Asia. In addition to all this, Alexander was commanding in the field against Darius. These things he enumerated as evidences of their superiority in the struggle; and then he began to point out the great rewards they would win from the danger to be incurred. For he told them that on that occasion they would overcome, not merely the viceroys of Darius, nor the cavalry drawn up at the Granicus, nor the 20,000 Grecian mercenaries, but would overcome all the available forces of the Persians and Medes, as well as all the other races subject to them dwelling in Asia, and the Great King present in person. After this conflict nothing would be left for them to do, except to take possession of all Asia, and to put an end to their many labours. In addition to this, he reminded them of their brilliant achievements in their collective capacity in days gone by; and if any man had individually performed any distinguished feat of valour from love of glory, he mentioned him by name in commendation of the deed.[230] He then recapitulated as modestly as possible his own daring deeds in the various battles. He is also said to have reminded them of Xenophon and the ten thousand men who accompanied him, asserting that the latter were in no way comparable with them either in number or in general excellence. Besides, they had had with them neither Thessalian, Boeotian, Peloponnesian, Macedonian, or Thracian horsemen, nor any of the other cavalry which was in the Macedonian army; nor had they any archers or slingers except a few Cretans and Rhodians, and even these were got ready by Xenophon on the spur of the moment in the very crisis of danger.[231] And yet even these put the king and all his forces to rout close to Babylon[232] itself, and succeeded in reaching the Euxine Sea after defeating all the races which lay in their way as they were marching down thither. He also adduced whatever other arguments were suitable for a great commander to use in order to encourage brave men in such a critical moment before the perils of battle. They urged him to lead them against the foe without delay, coming from all sides to grasp the king's right hand, and encouraging him by their promises.

Chapter 37: Arrangement of the Hostile Armies

Alexander then ordered his soldiers to take their dinner, and having sent a few of his horsemen and archers forward to the Gates to reconnoitre the road in the rear, he took the whole of his army and marched in the night to occupy the pass again.

November 05, Wednesday
Battle of Issus (Date of 5th or 6th November corroborated with Babylonian Astronomical diaries)

When about midnight he had again got possession of it, he caused the army to rest the remainder of the night there upon the rocks, having posted vigilant sentries. At the approach of dawn he began to descend from the pass along the road; and as long as the space was narrow everywhere, he led his army in column, but when the mountains parted so as to leave a plain between them, he kept on opening out the column into the phalanx, marching one line of heavy armed infantry after another up into line towards the mountain on the right and towards the sea on the left. Up to this time his cavalry had been ranged behind the infantry; but when they advanced into the open country, he began to draw up his army in order of battle. First, upon the right wing near the mountain he placed his infantry guard and the shield-bearers, under the command of Nicanor, son of Parmenio; next to these the regiment of Coenus, and close to them that of Perdiccas. These troops were posted as far as the middle of the heavy-armed infantry to one beginning from the right. On the left wing first stood the regiment of Amyntas, then that of Ptolemy, and close to this that of Meleager. The infantry on the left had been placed under the command of Craterus; but Parmenio held the chief direction of the "whole left wing. This general had been ordered not to abandon the sea, so that they might not be surrounded by the foreigners, who were likely to outflank them on all sides by their superior numbers.[233]

But as soon as Darius was certified of Alexander's approach for battle, he conveyed about 30,000 of his cavalry and with them 20,000 of his light-armed infantry across the river Pinarus, in order that he might be able to draw up the rest of his forces with ease. Of the heavy armed infantry, he placed first the 30,000 Greek mercenaries to oppose the phalanx of the Macedonians, and on both sides of these he placed 60,000 of the men called Cardaces,[234] who were also heavy-armed infantry.[235] For the place where they were posted was able to contain only this number in a single phalanx.[236] He also posted 20,000 men near the mountain on their left and facing Alexander's right. Some of these troops were also in the rear of Alexander's army; for the mountain near which they were posted in one part sloped a great way back and formed a sort of bay, like a bay in the sea, and afterwards bending forwards caused the men who had been posted at the foot of it to be behind Alexander's right wing. The remaining multitude of Darius's light-armed and heavy-armed infantry was marshalled by nations to an unserviceable depth and placed behind the Grecian mercenaries and the Persian army arranged in phalanx. The whole of the army with Darius was said to number about 600,000 fighting men.[237]

As Alexander advanced, he found that the ground spread out a little in breadth, and he accordingly brought up his horsemen, both those called Companions, and the Thessalians as well as the Macedonians, and posted them with himself on the right wing. The Peloponnesians and the rest of the allied force of Greeks he sent to Parmenio on the left. When Darius had marshalled his phalanx, by a pre-concerted signal he recalled the cavalry which he had posted in front of the river for the express purpose of rendering the arranging of his army easy. Most of these he placed on the right wing near the sea facing Parmenio; because here the ground was more suitable for the evolutions of cavalry. A certain part of them also he led up to the mountain towards the left. But when they were seen to be useless there on account of the narrowness of the ground, he ordered most of these also to ride round to the right wing and join their comrades there. Darius himself occupied the centre of the whole army, inasmuch as it was the custom for the kings of Persia to take up that position, the reason of which arrangement has been recorded by Xenphon, son of Gryllus.[238]

Chapter 38: Alexander Changes the Disposition of his Forces

Meantime when Alexander perceived that nearly all the Persian cavalry had changed their ground and gone to his left towards the sea, and that on his side only the Peloponnesians and the rest of the Grecian cavalry were posted there, he sent the Thessalian cavalry thither with speed, ordering them not to ride along before the front of the whole array, lest they should be seen by the enemy to be shifting their ground, but to proceed by stealth in the rear of the phalanx.[239] In front of the cavalry on the right, he posted the lancers under the command of Protomachus, and the Paeonians under that of Aristo; and of the infantry, the archers under the direction of Antiochus, and the Agrianians under that of Attalus. Some of the cavalry and archers also he drew up so as to form an angle with the centre[240] towards the mountain which was in the rear; so on the right his phalanx had been drawn up separated into two wings, the one fronting Darius and the main body of Persians beyond the river, and the other facing those who had been posted at the mountain in their rear. On the left wing the infantry consisting of the Cretan archers and the Thracians under command of Sitalces were posted in front; and before these the cavalry towards the left. The Grecian mercenaries were drawn up as a reserve for all of them. When he perceived that the phalanx towards the right was too thin, and it seemed likely that the Persians would outflank him here considerably, he ordered two squadrons of the Companion cavalry, viz. the Anthemusian,[241] of which Peroedas, son of Menestheus, was captain, and that which was called Leugaean, under the command of Pantordanus, son of Cleander, to proceed from the centre to the right without being seen. Having also marched the archers, part of the Agrianians and of the Grecian mercenaries up along his right in the front, he extended his phalanx beyond the wing of the Persians. But when those who had been posted upon the mountain did not descend, a charge was made by a few of the Agrianians and archers at Alexander's order, by which they were easily put to the rout from the foot of the mountain. As they fled to the summit he decided that he could make use of the men who had been drawn up to keep these in check, to fill up the ranks of his phalanx. He thought it quite sufficient to post 300 horsemen to watch the men on the mountain.

Chapter 39: Battle of Issus

Having thus marshalled his men, he caused them to rest for some time, and then led them forward, as he thought the enemy's approach was very slow. For Darius was no longer leading the foreigners against him, as he had arranged them at first, but he remained in his position, upon the bank of the river, which was in many parts steep and precipitous; and in certain places, where it seemed more easy to ascend, he extended a stockade along it. By this it was at once evident to Alexander's men that Darius had become cowed in spirit.[242] But when the armies at length met in conflict, Alexander rode about in every direction to exhort his troops to show their valour; mentioning with befitting epithets the names, not only of the generals, but also those of the captains of cavalry and infantry, and of the Grecian mercenaries as many as were more distinguished either by rank or merit. From all sides arose a shout not to delay but to attack the enemy. At first he still led them on in close array with measured step, although he had the forces of Darius already in full view, lest by a more hasty march any part of the phalanx should fluctuate from the line[243] and get separated from the rest. But when they came within range of darts, Alexander himself and those around him being posted on the right wing, advanced first into the river with a run, in order to alarm the Persians by the rapidity of their onset, and by coming sooner to close conflict to receive little damage from the archers. And it turned out just as Alexander had conjectured; for as soon as the battle became a hand-to-hand one, the part of the Persian army stationed on the left wing was put to rout; and here Alexander and his men won a brilliant victory. But the Grecian mercenaries serving under Darius attacked the Macedonians at the point where they saw their phalanx especially disordered. For the Macedonian phalanx had been broken and disjoined towards the right wing; because Alexander had charged into the river with eagerness, and engaging in a hand-to-hand conflict was already driving back the Persians posted there; but the Macedonians in the centre did not execute their task with equal speed; and finding many parts of the bank steep and precipitous, they were unable to preserve the front of the phalanx in the same line. Here then the struggle was desperate; the aim of the Grecian mercenaries of Darius being to push the Macedonians back into the river, and regain the victory, though their own forces were already flying; the aim of the Macedonians being not to fall short of Alexander's good-fortune, which was already manifest, and not to tarnish the glory of the phalanx, which up to that time had been commonly asserted to be invincible. Moreover the feeling of rivalry which existed between the Grecian and Macedonian races inspired each side in the conflict. Here fell Ptolemy, son of Seleucus, after proving, himself a valiant man, besides about one hundred and twenty other Macedonians of no mean repute.[244]

Chapter 40: Defeat and Flight of Darius

Hereupon the regiments on the right wing, perceiving that the Persians opposed to them had already been put to rout, wheeled round towards the Grecian mercenaries of Darius and their own hard-pressed detachment. Having driven the Greeks away from the river, they extended their phalanx beyond the Persian army on the side which had been broken; and attacking the Greeks on the flank, were already beginning to cut them up. However the Persian cavalry which had been posted opposite the Thessalians did not remain on the other side of the river during the struggle, but came through the water and made a vigorous attack upon the Thessalian squadrons.[245] In this place a fierce cavalry battle ensued; for the Persians did not give way until they perceived that Darius had fled and the Grecian mercenaries had been cut up by the phalanx and severed from them. Then at last the flight of all the Persians was plainly visible. Their horses suffered much injury in the retreat, because the riders[246] were heavily armed; and the horsemen themselves, being so many in number and retreating in panic terror without any regard to order along narrow roads, were trampled on and injured no less by each other than by the pursuing enemy. The Thessalians also followed them up with vigour, so that no fewer of the cavalry than of the infantry[247] were slaughtered in the flight.

But as soon as the left wing of Darius was terrified and routed by Alexander, and the Persian king perceived that this part of his army was severed from the rest, without any further delay he began to flee in his chariot along with the first, just as he was.[248] He was conveyed safely in the chariot as long as he met with level ground in his flight; but when he lighted upon ravines and other rough ground, he left the chariot there, divesting himself of his shield and Median mantle. He even left his bow in the chariot; and mounting a horse continued his flight. The night, which came on soon after, alone rescued him from being captured by Alexander;[249] for as long as there was daylight the latter kept up the pursuit at full speed. But when it began to grow dark and the ground before the feet became invisible, he turned back again to the camp, after capturing the chariot of Darius with the shield, the Median mantle, and the bow in it.[250] For his pursuit had been too slow for him to overtake Darius, because, though he wheeled round at the first breaking asunder of the phalanx, yet he did not turn to pursue him until he observed that the Grecian mercenaries and the Persian cavalry had been driven away from the river.

Of the Persians were killed Arsames, Rheomithres, and Atizyes who had commanded the cavalry at the Granicus. Sabaces, viceroy of Egypt, and Bubaces, one of the Persian dignitaries, were also killed, besides about 100,000 of the private soldiers, among them being more than 10,000 cavalry.[251] So great was the slaughter that Ptolemy, son of Lagus, who then accompanied Alexander, says that the men who were with them pursuing Darius, coming in the pursuit to a ravine, filled it up with the corpses and so passed over it. The camp of Darius was taken forthwith at the first assault, containing his mother, his wife,—who was also his sister,— and his infant son.[252] His two daughters, and a few other women, wives of Persian peers,[253] who were in attendance upon them, were likewise captured. For the other Persians happened to have despatched their women along with the rest of their property to Damascus;[254] because Darius had sent to that city the greater part of his money and all the other things which the Great King was in the habit of taking with him as necessary for his luxurious mode of living, even though he was going on a military expedition. The consequence was, that in the camp no more than 3,000 talents[255] were captured; and soon after, the money in Damascus was, also seized by Parmenio, who was despatched thither for that very purpose. Such was the result of this famous battle (which was fought) in the month Maimaoterion, when Nicostratus was archon of the Athenians.[256]

November 6, Thursday

Chapter 41: Kind Treatment of Darius's Family

The next day, Alexander, though suffering from a wound which he had received in the thigh from a sword, visited the wounded, and having collected the bodies of the slain, he gave them a splendid burial with all his forces most brilliantly marshalled in order of battle. He also spoke with eulogy to those whom he himself had recognised performing any gallant deed in the battle, and also to those whose exploits he had learnt by report fully corroborated. He likewise honoured each of them individually with a gift of money in proportion to his desert.[257] He then appointed Balacrus, son of Nicanor, one of the royal body-guards, viceroy of Cilicia; and in his place among the body-guards he chose Menes, son of Dionysius. In the room of Ptolemy, son of Seleucus, who had been killed in the battle, he appointed Polysperchon, son of Simmias, to the command of a brigade. He remitted to the Solians the fifty talents[258] which were still due of the money imposed on them as a fine, and he gave them back their hostages.

Nor did he treat the mother, wife, and children of Darius with neglect; for some of those who have written Alexander's history say that on the very night in which he returned from the pursuit of Darius, entering the Persian king's tent, which had been selected for his use, he heard the lamentation of women and other noise of a similar kind not far from the tent. Inquiring therefore who the women were, and why they were in a tent so near, he was answered by some one as follows:—"O king, the mother, wife, and children of Darius are lamenting for him as slain, since they have been informed that thou hast his bow and his royal mantle, and that his shield has been brought back." When Alexander heard this, he sent Leonnatus,[259] one of his Companions, to them, with injunctions to tell them:—"Darius is still alive; in his flight he left his arms and mantle in the chariot; and these are the only things of his that Alexander has." Leonnatus entered the tent and told them the news about Darius, saying, moreover, that Alexander would allow them to retain the state and retinue befitting their royal rank, as well as the title of queens; for he had not undertaken the war against Darius from a feeling of hatred, but he had conducted it in a legitimate manner for the empire of Asia. Such are the statements of Ptolemy and Aristobulus.[260] But there is another report, to the effect that on the following day Alexander himself went into the tent, accompanied alone by Hephaestion one of his Companions. The mother of Darius,[261] being in doubt which of them was the king (for they had both arrayed themselves in the same style of dress), went up to Hephaestion, because he appeared to her the taller of the two, and prostrated herself before him. But when he drew back, and one of her attendants pointed out Alexander, saying he was the king, she was ashamed of her mistake, and was going to retire. But the king told her she had made no mistake, for Hephaestion was also an Alexander. This I record neither being sure of its truth nor thinking it altogether unreliable. If it really occurred, I commend Alexander for his compassionate treatment of the women, and the confidence he felt in his companion, and the honour bestowed on him; but if it merely seems probable to historians that Alexander would have acted and spoken thus, even for this reason I think him worthy of commendation.[262]

November 6, Thursday onward (Darius)

Chapter 42: Flight of Macedonian Deserters into Egypt — Proceedings of Agis, King of Sparta — Alexander Occupies Phoenicia.

Darius fled through the night with a few attendants; but in the daytime, picking up as he went along the Persians and Grecian mercenaries who had come safely out of the battle, he had in all 4,000 men under his command. He then made a forced march towards the city of Thapsacus[263] and the river Euphrates,[264] in order to put that river as soon as possible between himself and Alexander. But Amyntas son of Antiochus, Thymondas son of Mentor, Aristomedes the Pheraean, and Bianor the Acarnanian, all being deserters, fled without delay from the posts assigned them in the battle, with about 8,000 soldiers under their command, and passing through the mountains, they arrived at Tripolis in Phoenicia.[265] There they seized the ships which had been hauled up on shore in which they had previously been transported from Lesbos; they launched as many of these vessel as they thought sufficient to convey them, and the rest they burnt there in the docks, in order not to supply their enemy with the means of quickly pursuing them. They fled first to Cyprus,[266] thence to Egypt; where Amyntas shortly after, meddling in political disputes, was killed by the natives.

Meantime Pharnabazus and Autophradates were staying near Chios; then having established a garrison in this island they despatched some of their ships to Cos and Halicarnassus, and with 100 of their best sailing vessels they put to sea themselves and landed at Siphnus. And Agis, king of the Lacedaemonians,[267] came to them with one trireme, both to ask for money to carry on the war, and also to urge them to send with him into the Peloponnese as large a force both naval and military as they could. At that very time news reached them of the battle which had been fought at Issus; and being alarmed at the report, Pharnabazus started off to Chios with twelve triremes and 1,500 Grecian mercenaries, for fear that the Chians might attempt to effect a revolution when they received the news of the Persian defeat. Agis, having received from Autophradates thirty talents of silver[268] and ten triremes, despatched Hippias to lead these ships to his brother Agesilaus at Taenarum,[269] ordering him also to instruct Agesilaus to give full pay to the sailors and then to sail as quickly as possible to Crete,[270] in order to set things in order there. For a time he himself remained there among the islands, but afterwards joined Autophradates at Halicarnassus.[271]

332 BC

January 05, Monday

Alexander appointed Menon, son of Cerdimmas, viceroy of Coele-Syria,[272] giving him the cavalry of the Grecian allies to guard the country.

{Alexander would have rested at Issus for as few weeks then would have made a temperate march through an area corresponding to the modern-day Syrian coast and take it over. Coele-Syria (modern) is approximately 410km away from Issus. Coele-Syria or Coelesyria, Greek: Κοίλη Συρία is also known as Hollow Syria corresponds to the Beqaa Valley between the Lebanon and Anti-Lebanon mountain ranges.}

January 07, Wednesday

He then went in person towards Phoenicia;

January 10, Saturday

and on the march he was met by Strato, son of Gerostratus, king of the Aradians and of the people living near Aradus.[273] But Gerostratus himself was serving in the fleet with Autophradates, as were also the other kings both of the Phoenicians and the Cyprians.

{Aradus, formerly known as Arados (Greek: Ἄραδος), Arvad, Arpad, Arphad, and Antiochia in Pieria, now called Arwad or Ruad Island is located in the Mediterranean Sea and is the only inhabited island in Syria.}

January 13, Tuesday

When Strato fell in with Alexander, he placed a golden crown upon his head, promising to surrender to him both the island of Aradus and the great and prosperous city of Marathus, situated on the mainland right opposite Aradus; also Sigon, the city of Mariamme, and all the other places under his own dominion and that of his father.

{Marathus (Ancient Greek: Μάραθος) or Marathos, also known as Amrit or Amrith in Arabic corresponds to an area near Tartus in modern day Syria.}

January 22, Thursday

Chapter 43: Darius's Letter, and Alexander's Reply

While Alexander was still in Marathus, ambassadors came bringing a letter from Darius, entreating him to give up to their king his mother, wife, and children. They were also instructed to support this petition by word of mouth. The letter pointed out to him that friendship and alliance had subsisted between Philip and Artaxerxes;[274] and that when Arses, son of Artaxerxes, ascended the throne, Philip was the first to practise injustice towards him, though he had suffered no injury from the Persians. Alexander also, from the time when Darius began to reign over the Persians, had not sent any one to him to confirm the friendship and alliance which had so long existed, but had crossed over into Asia with his army and had inflicted much injury upon the Persians. For this reason he had come down in person, to defend his country and to preserve the empire of his fathers. As to the battle, it had been decided as seemed good to some one of the gods. And now he, a king, begged his captured wife, mother, and children from a king; and he wished to form a friendship with him and become his ally. For this purpose he requested Alexander to send men to him with Meniscus and Arsimas, the messengers who came from the Persians, to receive pledges of fidelity from him and to give them on behalf of Alexander.

January 26, Monday

To this Alexander wrote a reply, and sent Thersippus with the men who had come from Darius, with instructions to give the letter to Darius, but not to converse about anything. Alexander's letter ran thus: "Your ancestors came into Macedonia and the rest of Greece and treated us ill, without any previous injury from us. I, having been appointed commander-in-chief of the Greeks, and wishing to take revenge on the Persians, crossed over into Asia, hostilities being begun by you. For you sent aid to the Perinthians,[275] who were dealing unjustly with my father; and Ochus sent forces into Thrace, which was under our rule. My father was killed by conspirators whom you instigated, as you have yourself boasted to all in your letters;[276] and after slaying Arses, as well as Bagoas, and unjustly seizing the throne contrary to the law of the Persians,[277] and ruling your subjects unjustly, you sent unfriendly letters about me to the Greeks, urging them to wage war with me. You have also despatched money to the Lacedaemonians, and certain other Greeks; but none of the States received it, except the Lacedaemonians.[278] As your agents destroyed my friends, and were striving to dissolve the league which I had formed among the Greeks, I took the field against you, because you were the party who commenced the hostility. Since I have vanquished your generals and viceroys in the previous battle, and now yourself and your forces in like manner, I am, by the gift of the gods, in possession of your land. As many of the men who fought in your army as were not killed in the battle, but fled to me for refuge, I am protecting; and they are with me, not against their own will, but they are serving in my army as volunteers. Come to me therefore, since I am lord of all Asia; but if you are afraid you may suffer any harsh treatment from me in case you come to me, send some of your friends to receive pledges of safety from me. Come to me then, and ask for your mother, wife, and children, and anything else you wish. For whatever you ask for you will receive; and nothing shall be denied you. But for the future, whenever you send to me, send to me as the king of Asia, and do not address to me your wishes as to an equal; but if you are in need of anything, speak to me as to the man who is lord of all your territories. If you act otherwise, I shall deliberate concerning you as an evil-doer; and if you dispute my right to the kingdom, stay and fight another battle for it; but do not run away. For wherever you may be, I intend to march against you." This is the letter which he sent to Darius.

January 28, Wednesday

Chapter 44: Alexander's Treatment of the Captured Greek Ambassadors — Submission of Byblus and Sidon

When Alexander ascertained that all the money which Darius had sent off to Damascus with Cophen, son of Artabazus, was captured, and also that the Persians who had been left in charge of it, as well as the rest of the royal property, were taken prisoners, he ordered Parmenio to take the treasure back to Damascus, and there guard it.[279] When he also ascertained that the Grecian ambassadors who had reached Darius before the battle had likewise been captured, he ordered them to be sent to him.[280] They were Euthycles, a Spartan; Thessaliscus, son of Ismenias, and Dionysodorus, a victor in the Olympic games, Thebans; and Iphicrates, son of Iphicrates the general, an Athenian.[281]

{The distance from Marathus and the Syrian coast to Damascus is approximately 106km}

February 10, Tuesday

When these men came to Alexander, he immediately released Thessaliscus and Dionysodorus, though they were Thebans, partly out of compassion for Thebes, and partly because they seemed to have acted in a pardonable manner. For their native city had been reduced to slavery by the Macedonians, and they were trying to find whatever succour they could for themselves and perhaps also for their native city from Darius and the Persians. Thinking thus compassionately about both of them, he released them, saying that he dismissed Thessaliscus individually out of respect for his pedigree, for he belonged to the ranks of the distinguished men of Thebes. Dionysodorus also he released because he had been conqueror at the Olympic games; and he kept Iphicrates in attendance on himself as long as he lived, treating him with special honour both from friendship to the city of Athens and from recollection of his father's glory. When he died soon after from sickness, he sent his bones back to his relations at Athens. But Euthycles at first he kept in custody, though without fetters, both because he was a Lacedaemonian of a city at that time openly and eminently hostile to him, and because in the man as an individual he could find nothing to warrant his pardon. Afterwards, when he met with great success, he released even this man also.

February 15, Sunday

He set out from Marathus

February 23, Monday

and took possession of Byblus[282] on terms of capitulation,

{Byblos is known as Jubayl in Arabic. It is approximately 105km from Marathus}

February 28, Saturday

as he did also of Sidon,[283] the inhabitants of which spontaneously invited him from hatred of the Persians and Darius.[284]

{Sidon or Saïda is approximately 80km from Byblos}

March 02, Monday

Thence he advanced towards Tyre;[285]

March 03, Tuesday

ambassadors from which city, despatched by the commonwealth, met him on the march, announcing that the Tyrians had decided to do whatever he might command.[286]

March 04, Wednesday

He commended both the city and its ambassadors, and ordered them to return and tell the Tyrians that he wished to enter their city and offer sacrifice to Heracles. The son of the king of the Tyrians was one of the ambassadors, and the others were conspicuous men in Tyre; but the king Azemilcus[287] himself was sailing with Autophradates.

{Tyre is approximately 39km from Sidon}

Chapter 45: The Worship of Hercules in Tyre — The Tyrians Refuse to Admit Alexander

The reason of this demand was, that in Tyre there existed a temple of Heracles,[288] the most ancient of all those which are mentioned in history. It was not dedicated to the Argive Heracles, the son of Alcmena; for this Heracles was honoured in Tyre many generations before Cadmus set out from Phoenicia and occupied Thebes, and before Semele, the daughter of Cadmus, was born, from whom Dionysus, the son of Zeus, was born. This Dionysus would be third from Cadmus, being a contemporary of Labdacus, son of Polydorus, the son of Cadmus; and the Argive Heracles lived about the time of Oedipus, son of Laius.[289] The Egyptians also worshipped another Heracles, not the one which either the Tyrians or Greeks worship. But Herodotus says that the Egyptians considered Heracles to be one of the twelve gods,[290] just as the Athenians worshipped a different Dionysus, who was the son of Zeus and Core; and the mystic chant called Iacchus was sung to this Dionysus, not to the Theban. So also I think that the Heracles honoured in Tartessus[291] by the Iberians, where are certain pillars named after Heracles, is the Tyrian Heracles; for Tartessus was a colony of the Phœnicians, and the temple to Heracles there was built and the sacrifices offered after the usage of the Phoenicians. Hecataeus the historian[292] says Geryones, against whom the Argive Heracles was despatched by Eurystheus to drive his oxen away and bring them to Mycenae, had nothing to do with the land of the Iberians;[293] nor was Heracles despatched to any island called Erythia[294] outside the Great Sea; but that Geryones was king of the mainland (Epirus) around Ambracia[295] and the Amphilochians, that Heracles drove the oxen from this Epirus, and that this was deemed no mean task. I know that to the present time this part of the mainland is rich in pasture land and rears a very fine breed of oxen; and I do not think it beyond the bounds of probability that the fame of the oxen from Epirus, and the name of the king of Epirus, Geryones, had reached Eurystheus. But I do not think that Eurystheus would know the name of the king of the Iberians, who were the remotest nation in Europe, or whether a fine breed of oxen grazed in their land, unless some one, by introducing Hera into the account, as herself giving these commands to Heracles through Eurystheus, wished, by means of the fable, to disguise the incredibility of the tale.

To this Tyrian Heracles, Alexander said he wished to offer sacrifice.

March 06, Friday

But when this message was brought to Tyre by the ambassadors, the people passed a decree to obey any other command of Alexander, but not to admit into the city any Persian or Macedonian; thinking that under the existing circumstances, this was the most specious answer, and that it would be the safest course for them to pursue in reference to the issue of the war, which was still uncertain.[296]

March 08, Sunday

When the answer from Tyre was brought to Alexander, he sent the ambassadors back in a rage. He then summoned a council of his Companions and the leaders of his army, together with the captains of infantry and cavalry, and spoke as follows:—

Chapter 46: Speech of Alexander to his Officers

"Friends and allies, I see that an expedition to Egypt will not be safe for us, so long as the Persians retain the sovereignty of the sea; nor is it a safe course, both for other reasons, and especially looking at the state of matters in Greece, for us to pursue Darius, leaving in our rear the city of Tyre itself in doubtful allegiance, and Egypt and Cyprus in the occupation of the Persians. I am apprehensive lest while we advance with our forces towards Babylon and in pursuit of Darius, the Persians should again forsooth conquer the maritime districts, and transfer the war into Greece with a larger army, considering that the Lacedaemonians are now waging war against us without disguise, and the city of Athens is restrained for the present rather by fear than by any good-will towards us. But if Tyre were captured, the whole of Phoenicia would be in our possession, and the fleet of the Phoenicians, which is the most numerous and the best in the Persian navy, would in all probability come over to us. For the Phoenician sailors and marines will not put to sea in order to incur danger on behalf of others, when their own cities are occupied by us. After this, Cyprus will either yield to us without delay, or will be captured with ease at the mere arrival of a naval force; and then navigating the sea with the ships from Macedonia in conjunction with those of the Phoenicians, Cyprus at the same time coming over to us, we shall acquire the absolute sovereignty of the sea, and at the same time an expedition into Egypt will become an easy matter for us. After we have brought Egypt into subjection, no anxiety about Greece and our own land will any longer remain, and we shall be able to undertake the expedition to Babylon with safety in regard to affairs at home, and at the same time with greater reputation, in consequence of having cut off from the Persian empire all the maritime provinces and all the land this side of the Euphrates."

Chapter 47: Siege of Tyre — Construction of a Mole from the Mainland to the Island

By this speech he easily persuaded his officers to make an attempt upon Tyre. Moreover he was encouraged by a divine admonition, for that very night in his sleep[297] he seemed to be approaching the Tyrian walls, and Heracles seemed to take him by the right hand and lead him up into the city. This was interpreted by Aristander[298] to mean that Tyre would be taken with labour, because the deeds of Heracles were accomplished with labour. Certainly, the siege of Tyre appeared to be a great enterprise; for the city was an island[299] and fortified all round with lofty walls. Moreover naval operations seemed at that time more favourable to the Tyrians, both because the Persians still possessed the sovereignty of the sea and many ships were still remaining with the citizens themselves. However, as these arguments of his had prevailed, he resolved to construct a mole from the mainland to the city.[300] The place is a narrow strait full of pools; and the part of it near the mainland is shallow water and muddy, but the part near the city itself, where was the deepest part of the channel, was the depth of about three fathoms.

March 09, Monday onward

But there was an abundant supply of stones and wood, which they put on the top of the stones.[301] Stakes were easily fixed down firmly in the mud, which itself served as a cement to the stones to hold them firm. The zeal of the Macedonians in the work was great, and it was increased by the presence of Alexander himself, who took, the lead[302] in everything, now rousing the men to exertion by speech, and now by presents of money, lightening the labour of those who were toiling more than their fellows from the desire of gaining praise for their exertions. As long as the mole was being constructed near the mainland, the work made easy and rapid progress, as the material was poured into a small depth of water, and there was no one to hinder them; but when they began to approach the deeper water, and at the same time came near the city itself, they suffered severely, being assailed with missiles from the walls, which were lofty, inasmuch as they had been expressly equipped for work rather than for fighting. Moreover, as the Tyrians still retained command of the sea, they kept on sailing with their triremes to various parts of the mole, and made it impossible in many places for the Macedonians to pour in the material. But the latter erected two towers upon the mole, which they had now projected over a long stretch of sea, and upon these towers they placed engines of war. Skins and prepared hides served as coverings in front of them, to prevent them being struck by fire-bearing missiles from the wall, and at the same time to be a screen against arrows to those who were working. It was likewise intended that the Tyrians who might sail near to injure the men engaged in the construction of the mole should not retire easily, being assailed by missiles from the towers.

April 20, Monday onward

Chapter 48: The Siege of Tyre

But to counteract this the Tyrians adopted the following contrivance. They filled a vessel, which had been used for transporting horses, with dry twigs and other combustible wood, fixed two masts on the prow, and fenced it round in the form of a circle as large as possible, so that the enclosure might contain as much chaff and as many torches as possible. Moreover they placed upon this vessel quantities of pitch, brimstone, and whatever else was calculated to foment a great flame.[303] They also stretched out a double yard-arm upon each mast; and from these they hung caldrons into which they had poured or cast materials likely to kindle flame which would extend to a great distance. They then put ballast into the stern, in order to raise the prow aloft, the vessel being weighed down abaft.[304] Then watching for a wind bearing towards the mole, they fastened the vessel to some triremes which towed it before the breeze. As soon as they approached the mole and the towers, they threw fire among the wood, and at the same time ran the vessel, with the triremes,, aground as violently as possible, dashing against the end of the mole. The men in the vessel easily swam away, as soon as it was set on fire. A great flame soon caught the towers; and the yard-arms being twisted round poured out into the fire the materials that had been prepared for kindling the flame. The men also in the triremes tarrying near the mole kept on shooting arrows into the towers, so that it was not safe for men to approach in order to bring materials to quench the fire. Upon this, when the towers had already caught fire, many men hastened from the city, and embarking in light vessels, and striking against various parts of the mole, easily tore down the stockade which had been placed in front of it for protection, and burnt up all the engines of war which the fire from the vessel did not reach.[305]

May 03, Sunday

But Alexander began to construct a wider mole from the mainland, capable of containing more towers; and he ordered the enginemakers to prepare fresh engines. While this was being performed, he took the shield-bearing guards and the Agrianians and set out to Sidon, to collect there all the triremes he could; since it was evident that the successful conclusion of the siege would be much more difficult to attain, so long as the Tyrians retained the superiority at sea.[306]

May 06, Wednesday

Chapter 49: Tyre Besieged by Sea as well as Land

About this time Gerostratus, King of Aradus, and Enylus, King of Byblus, ascertaining that their cities were in the possession of Alexander, deserted Autophradates and the fleet under his command, and came to Alexander with their naval force, accompanied by the Sidonian triremes;

May 26, Tuesday

so that about eighty Phoenician ships joined him.

May 28, Thursday

About the same time triremes also came to him from Rhodes, both the one called Peripolus,[307] and with it nine others.

June 02, Tuesday

From Soli and Mallus also came three,

June 11, Thursday

and from Lycia ten;

June 14, Sunday

from Macedonia also a ship with fifty oars, in which sailed Proteas, son of Andronicus.[308]

June 21, Sunday

Not long after, too, the kings of Cyprus put into Sidon with about one hundred and twenty ships, when they heard of the defeat of Darius at Issus, and were terrified, because the whole of Phoenicia was already in the possession of Alexander. To all of these Alexander granted indemnity for their previous conduct, because they seemed to have joined the Persian fleet rather by necessity than by their own choice.

June 23, Tuesday

While the engines of war were being constructed for him, and the ships were being fitted up for a naval attack on the city and for the trial of a sea-battle, he took some squadrons of cavalry, the Agrianians and archers, and made an expedition into the range of mountains called Anti-Libanus.[309] Having subdued some of the mountaineers by force, and drawn others over to him by terms of capitulation,

{The Anti-Libanus mountain range or the Anti-Lebanon Mountains correspond to the The Mounts of Lebanon or Jibāl Lubnan ash-Sharqiyah in Arabic meaning the Eastern Lebanon Mountains. They form a large proportion of the border between modern-day Syria and Lebanon where they exist predominantly on the Syrian side of the border.}

July 03, Friday

he returned to Sidon in ten days.[310] Here he found Cleander, son of Polemocrates, just arrived from Peloponnesus, having 4,000 Grecian mercenaries with him.[311]

July 14, Tuesday

When his fleet had been arranged in due order, he embarked upon the decks as many of his shield-bearing guards as seemed sufficient for his enterprise, unless a sea-battle were to be fought rather by breaking the enemy's line[312] than by a close conflict. He then started from Sidon and sailed towards Tyre with his ships arranged in proper order, himself being on the right wing which stretched out seaward; and with him were the kings of the Cyprians, and all those of the Phoenicians except Pnytagoras, who with Craterus was commanding the left wing of the whole line. The Tyrians had previously resolved to fight a sea-battle, if Alexander should sail against them by sea. But then with surprise they beheld the vast multitude of his ships; for they had not yet learnt that Alexander had all the ships of the Cyprians and Phoenicians. At the same time they were surprised to see that he was sailing against them with his fleet arranged in due order; for Alexander's fleet a little before it came near the city, tarried for a while out in the open sea, with the view of provoking the Tyrians to come out to a battle; but afterwards, as the enemy did not put out to sea against them, though they were thus arranged in line, they advanced to the attack with a great dashing of oars. Seeing this, the Tyrians decided not to fight a battle at sea, but closely blocked up the passage for ships with as many triremes as the mouths of their harbour would contain, and guarded it, so that the enemy's fleet might not find an anchorage in any of the harbours. As the

Tyrians did not put out to sea against him, Alexander sailed near the city, but resolved not to try to force an entrance into the harbour towards Sidon on account of the narrowness of its mouth; and at the same time because he saw that the entrance had been blocked up with many triremes having their prows turned towards him. But the Phoenicians fell upon the three triremes moored furthest out at the mouth of the harbour, and attacking them prow to prow, succeeded in sinking them. However, the men in the ships easily swam off to the land which was friendly to them. Then, indeed, Alexander moored his ships along the shore not far from the mole which had been made, where there appeared to be shelter from the winds;

{Tyre is approximately 40km from Sidon on the coast}

July 15, Wednesday

and on the following day he ordered the Cyprians with their ships and their admiral Andromachus to moor near the city opposite the harbour which faces towards Sidon, and the Phoenicians opposite the harbour which looks towards Egypt, situated on the other side of the mole, where also was his own tent.

July 18, Saturday onward

Chapter 50: Siege of Tyre

He had now collected many engineers both from Cyprus and the whole of Phoenicia, and many engines of war had been constructed,[313] some upon the mole, others upon vessels used for transporting horses, which he brought with him from Sidon, and others upon the triremes which were not fast sailers. When all the preparations had been completed they brought up the engines of war along the mole that had been made and also began to shoot from ships moored near various parts of the wall and making trial of its strength. The Tyrians erected wooden towers on their battlements opposite the mole, from which they might annoy the enemy; and if the engines of war were brought near any other part, they defended themselves with missiles and shot at the very ships with fire-bearing arrows, so that they deterred the Macedonians from approaching the wall. Their walls opposite the mole were about one hundred and fifty feet high, with a breadth in proportion, and constructed with large stones imbedded in gypsum. It was not easy for the horse-transports and the triremes of the Macedonians, which were conveying the engines of war up to the wall, to approach the city, because a great quantity of stones hurled forward into the sea prevented their near assault. These stones Alexander determined to drag out of the sea; but this was a work accomplished with great difficulty, since it was performed from ships and not from the firm earth; especially as the Tyrians, covering their ships with mail, brought them alongside the anchors of the triremes, and cutting the cables of the anchors underneath, made anchoring impossible for the enemy's ships. But Alexander covered many thirty-oared vessels with mail in the same way, and placed them athwart in front of the anchors, so that the assault of the ships was repelled by them. But, notwithstanding this, divers under the sea secretly cut their cables. The Macedonians then used chains to their anchors instead of cables, and let them down so that the divers could do no more harm. Then, fastening slipknots to the stones, they dragged them out of the sea from the mole; and having raised them aloft with cranes, they discharged them into deep water, where they were no longer likely to do injury by being hurled forward. The ships now easily approached the part of the wall where it had been made clear of the stones which had been hurled forward. The Tyrians being now reduced to great straits on all sides, resolved to make an attack on the Cyprian ships, which were moored opposite the harbour turned towards Sidon. For a long time they spread sails across the mouth of the harbour, in order that the filling of the triremes might not be discernible;

August 09, Sunday

and about the middle of the day, when the sailors were scattered in quest of necessaries, and when Alexander usually retired from the fleet to his tent on the other side of the city, they filled three quinqueremes, an equal number of quadriremes and seven triremes with the most expert complement of rowers possible, and with the best-armed men adapted for fighting from the decks, together with the men most daring in naval contests. At first they rowed out slowly and quietly in single file, moving forward the handles of their oars without any signal from the men who give the time to the rowers[314]; but when they were already tacking against the Cyprians, and were near enough to be seen, then indeed with a loud shout and encouragement to each other, and at the same time with impetuous rowing, they commenced the attack.

Chapter 51: Siege of Tyre — Naval Defeat of the Tyrians

It happened on that day that Alexander went away to his tent, but after a short time returned to his ships, not tarrying according to his usual custom. The Tyrians fell all of a sudden upon the ships lying at their moorings, finding some entirely empty and others being filled with difficulty from the men who happened to be present at the very time of the noise and attack. At the first onset they at once sank the quinquereme of the king Pnytagoras, that of Androcles the Amathusiau[315] and that of Pasicrates the Curian;[316] and they shattered the other ships by pushing them ashore. But when Alexander perceived the sailing out of the Tyrian triremes, he ordered most of the ships under his command to be manned and to take position at the mouth of the harbour, so that the rest of the Tyrian ships might not sail out. He then took the quinqueremes which he had and about five of the triremes, which were manned by him in haste before the rest were ready, and sailed round the city against the Tyrians who had sailed out of the harbour. The men on the wall, perceiving the enemy's attack and observing that Alexander himself was in the fleet, began to shout to those in their own ships, urging them to return; but as their shouts were not audible, on account of the noise of those who were engaged in the action, they exhorted them to retreat by various kinds of signals. At last after a long time, perceiving the impending attack of Alexander's fleet, they tacked about and began to flee into the harbour; and a few of their ships succeeded in escaping, but Alexander's vessels assaulted the greater number, and rendered some of them unfit for sailing; and a quinquereme and a quadrireme were captured at the very mouth of the harbour. But the slaughter of the marines was not great; for when they perceived that their ships were in possession of the enemy, they swam off without difficulty into the harbour. As the Tyrians could no longer derive any aid from their ships, the Macedonians now brought up their military engines to the wall itself. Those which were brought near the city along the mole, did no damage worth mentioning on account of the strength of the wall there. Others brought up some of the ships conveying military engines opposite the part of the city turned towards Sidon. But when even there they met with no success, Alexander passed round to the wall projecting towards the south wind and towards Egypt, and tested the strength of the works everywhere. Here first a large piece of the wall was thoroughly shaken, and a part of it was even broken and thrown down. Then indeed for a short time he tried to make an assault to the extent of throwing a bridge upon the part of the wall where a breach had been made. But the Tyrians without much difficulty beat the Macedonians back.

August 17, Monday
Capture of Tyre
Several sources give us a clue as to this date: (1) Arrian informs us that Tyre fell in Hecatombaeon, starting of the new moon (July 19) after the summer solstice (June 22), please refer to this book's preface. (2) Curtius suggest it fell in the seventh month after the start of the siege and both (3) Plutarch and (4) Diodorus suggest the whole siege took seven months. (5) Plutarch further adds that this occurred on the last day of the month (i.e the day before the beginning of the next month/ new moon on August 18) giving a Julian date of August 17. (6) Plutarch additionally suggests that the last day of the month was Hecatombaeon 30, although Alexander considered it a 'hollow' month and ascribed it as the 29th due to a prophecy by Aristander. Nevertheless setting aside the arbitrary 'hollow' title, it is clear that Hecatombeaeon had 30 days and on this date corresponds to August 17

Chapter 52: Siege of Tyre

The third day after this, having waited for a calm sea, after encouraging the leaders of the regiments for the action, he led the ships containing the military engines up to the city. In the first place he shook down a large piece of the wall; and when the breach appeared to be sufficiently wide, he ordered the vessels conveying the military engines to retire, and brought up two others, which carried his bridges, which he intended to throw upon the breach in the wall. The shield-bearing guards occupied one of these vessels, which he had put under the command of Admetus; and the other was occupied by the regiment of Coenus, called the foot Companions. Alexander himself, with the shield-bearing guards, intended to scale the wall where it might be practicable. He ordered some of his triremes to sail against both of the harbours, to see if by any means they could force an entrance when the Tyrians had turned themselves to oppose him. He also ordered those of his triremes which contained the missiles to be hurled from engines, or which were carrying archers upon deck, to sail right round the wall and to put in where it was practicable, and to take up position within shooting range, until it became impossible to put in, so that the Tyrians, being shot at from all quarters, might become distracted, and not know whither to turn in their distress. When Alexander's ships drew close to the city and the bridges were thrown from them upon the wall, the shield-bearing guards mounted valiantly along these upon the wall; for their captain, Admetus, proved himself brave on that occasion, and Alexander accompanied them, both as a courageous participant in the action itself, and as a witness of brilliant and dangerous feats of valour performed by others.

The first part of the wall that was captured was where Alexander had posted himself; the Tyrians being easily beaten back from it, as soon as the Macedonians found firm footing, and at the same time a way of entrance not abrupt on every side. Admetus was the first to mount the wall; but while cheering on his men to mount, he was struck with a spear and died on the spot.

After him, Alexander with the Companions got possession of the wall[317]; and when some of the towers and the parts of the wall between them were in his hands, he advanced through the battlements to the royal palace, because the descent into the city that way seemed the easiest.

Chapter 53: Capture of Tyre

To return to the fleet, the Phoenicians posted opposite the harbour looking towards Egypt, facing which they happened to be moored, forcing their way and bursting the bars asunder, shattered the ships in the harbour, attacking some of them in deep water and driving others ashore. The Cyprians also sailed into the other harbour looking towards Sidon, which had no bar across it, and made a speedy capture of the city on that side. The main body of the Tyrians deserted the wall when they saw it in the enemy's possession; and rallying opposite what was called the chapel of Agenor,[318] they there turned round to resist the Macedonians. Against these Alexander advanced with his shield-bearing guards, destroyed the men who fought there, and pursued those who fled. Great was the slaughter also made both by those who were now occupying the city from the harbour and by the regiment of Coenus, which had also entered it. For the Macedonians were now for the most part advancing full of rage, being angry both at the length of the siege and also because the Tyrians, having captured some of their men sailing from Sidon, had conveyed them to the top of their wall, so that the deed might be visible from the camp, and after slaughtering them, had cast their bodies into the sea. About 8,000 of the Tyrians were killed; and of the Macedonians, besides Admetus, who had proved himself a valiant man, being the first to scale the wall, twenty of the shield-bearing guards were killed in the assault on that occasion. In the whole siege about 400 Macedonians were slain. Alexander gave an amnesty to all those who fled for refuge into the temple of Heracles; among them being most of the Tyrian magistrates, including the king Azemilcus, as well as certain envoys from the Carthaginians, who had come to their mother-city to attend the sacrifice in honour of Heracles, according to an ancient custom.[319] The rest of the prisoners were reduced to slavery; all the Tyrians and mercenary troops, to the number of about 30,000, who had been captured, being sold.[320] Alexander then offered sacrifice to Heracles, and conducted a procession in honour of that deity with all his soldiers fully armed. The ships also took part in this religious procession in honour of Heracles. He moreover held a gymnastic contest in the temple, and celebrated a torch race. The military engine, also, with which the wall had been battered down, was brought into the temple and dedicated as a thank-offering; and the Tyrian ship sacred to Heracles, which had been captured in the naval attack, was likewise dedicated to the god. An inscription was placed on it, either composed by Alexander himself or by some one else; but as it is not worthy of recollection, I have not deemed it worth while to describe it. Thus then was Tyre captured in the month Hecatombaion, when Anicetus was archon at Athens.[321]

Chapter 54: The Offers of Darius Rejected — Batis, Governor of Gaza, Refuses to Submit.

While Alexander was still occupied by the siege of Tyre, ambassadors came to him from Darius, announcing that he would give him ten thousand talents[322] in exchange for his mother, wife, and children; that all the territory west of the river Euphrates, as far as the Grecian Sea, should be Alexander's; and proposing that he should marry the daughter of Darius, and become his friend and ally.[323] When these proposals were announced in a conference of the Companions, Parmenio is said to have told Alexander, that if he were Alexander he should be delighted to put an end to the war on these terms, and incur no further hazard of success. Alexander is said to have replied, So would he also do, if he were Parmenio, but as he was Alexander he replied to Darius as he did. For he said that he was neither in want of money from Darius, nor would he receive a part of his territory instead of the whole; for that all his money and territory were his; and that if he wished to marry the daughter of Darius, he would marry her, even though Darius refused her to him. He commanded Darius to come to him if he wished to experience any generous treatment from him. When Darius heard this answer, he despaired of coming to terms with Alexander, and began to make fresh preparations for war.

{Based on the work of Jim Ulvog (https://attestationupdate.com/2016/07/15/guess-on-the-value-of-all-loot-taken-by-alexander-the-great/), one ancient Athenian talent is equivalent to approximately $28 million in the modern era, so that Darius' offer could amount to $280 billion}

August 27, Thursday

Alexander now resolved to make an expedition into Egypt. All the other parts of what was called Palestine Syria[324] had already yielded to him; but a certain eunuch, named Batis, who was in possession of the city of Gaza, paid no heed to him; but procuring Arabian mercenaries, and having been long employed in laying up sufficient food for a long siege, he resolved not to admit Alexander into the city, feeling confident that the place could never be taken by storm.

Chapter 55: Siege of Gaza

Gaza is about twenty stades from the sea;[325] the approach to it is sandy and over heavy soil, and the sea near the city everywhere shallow. The city of Gaza[326] was large, and had been built upon a lofty mound, around which a strong wall had been carried. It is the last city the traveller meets with going from Phoenicia to Egypt, being situated on the edge of the desert.

{A stade is one eight of a mile or 185m. Gaza is approximately 680km from Tyre}

October 02, Friday

When Alexander arrived near the city, on the first day he encamped at the spot where the wall seemed to him most easy to assail, and ordered his military engines to be constructed.

October 03, Saturday

But the engineers expressed the opinion that it was not possible to capture the wall by force, on account of the height of the mound. However, the more impracticable it seemed to be, the more resolutely Alexander determined that it must be captured. For he said that the action would strike the enemy with great alarm from its being contrary to their expectation; whereas his failure to capture the place would redound to his disgrace when mentioned either to the Greeks or to Darius. He therefore resolved to construct a mound right round the city, so as to be able to bring his military engines up to the walls from the artificial mound which had been raised to the same level with them. The mound was constructed especially over against the southern wall of the city, where it appeared easiest to make an assault.

October 20, Tuesday

When he thought that the mound had been raised to the proper level with the walls, the Macedonians placed their military engines upon it, and brought them close to the wall of Gaza. At this time while Alexander was offering sacrifice, and, crowned with a garland, was about to commence the first sacred rite according to custom, a certain carnivorous bird, flying over the altar, let a stone which it was carrying with its claws fall upon his head. Alexander asked Aristander, the soothsayer,[327] what this omen meant. He replied: "O king, thou wilt indeed capture the city, but thou must take care of thyself on this day."

October 24, Saturday

Chapter 56: Capture of Gaza

When Alexander heard this, he kept himself for a time near the military engines, out of the reach of missiles. But when a vigorous sortie was made from the city, and the Arabs were carrying torches to set fire to the military engines, and from their commanding position above hurling missiles at the Macedonians, who were defending themselves from lower ground, were driving them down from the mound which they had made, then Alexander either wilfully disobeyed the soothsayer, or forgot the prophecy from excitement in the heat of action. Taking the shield-bearing guards, he hastened to the rescue where the Macedonians were especially hard pressed, and prevented them from being driven down from the mound in disgraceful flight. But he was himself wounded by a bolt from a catapult, right through the shield and breastplate into the shoulder. When he perceived that Aristander had spoken the truth about the wound, he rejoiced, because he thought he should also capture the city by the aid of the soothsayer. And yet indeed he was not easily cured of the wound.

October 29, Thursday

In the meantime the military engines with which he had captured Tyre arrived, having been sent for by sea; and he ordered the mound to be constructed quite round the city on all sides, two stades[328] in breadth and 250 feet in height. When his engines had been prepared, and brought up along the mound, they shook down a large extent of wall; and mines being dug in various places, and the earth being drawn out by stealth, the wall fell down in many parts, subsiding into the emptied space.[329]

November 06, Friday

The Macedonians then commanded a large extent of ground with their missiles, driving back the men who were defending the city, from the towers. Nevertheless, the men of the city sustained three assaults, though many of their number were killed or wounded; but at the fourth attack, Alexander led up the phalanx of the Macedonians from all sides, threw down the part of the wall which was undermined, and shook down another large portion of it by battering it with his engines, so that he rendered the assault an easy matter through the breaches with his scaling ladders. Accordingly the ladders were brought up to the wall; and then there arose a great emulation among those of the Macedonians who laid any claim to valour, to see who should be the first to scale the wall. The first to do so was Neoptolemus, one of the Companions, of the family of the Aeacidae; and after him mounted one rank after another with their officers. When once some of the Macedonians got within the wall, they split open in succession the gates which each party happened to light upon, and thus admitted the whole army into the city. But though their city was now in the hands of the enemy, the Gazaeans nevertheless stood together and fought; so that they were all slain fighting there, as each man had been stationed. Alexander sold their wives and children into slavery; and having peopled the city again from the neighbouring settlers, he made use of it as a fortified post for the war.[330]

November 24, Tuesday

Chapter 57 (Start of Book 3): Conquest of Egypt — Foundation of Alexandria

Alexander now led an expedition into Egypt, whither he had set out at first (from Tyre); and marching from Gaza,

December 01, Tuesday

on the seventh day he arrived at Pelusium[331] in Egypt. His fleet had also set sail from Phoenicia to Egypt; and he found the ships already moored at Pelusium.[332]

{Pelusium is approximately 30km southeast of Port Said}

December 04, Friday

When Mazaces the Persian, whom Darius had appointed viceroy of Egypt,[333] ascertained how the battle at Issus had resulted, that Darius had fled in disgraceful flight, and that Phoenicia, Syria, and most of Arabia were already in Alexander's possession, as he had no Persian force with which he could offer resistance, he admitted Alexander into the cities and the country in a friendly way.[334] Alexander introduced a garrison into Pelusium, and ordering the men in the ships to sail up the river as far as the city of Memphis,[335]

December 05, Saturday

he went in person towards Heliopolis,[336] having the river Nile[337] on his right.

{Heliopolis is near the modern day suburb of Ayn Shams in north eastern Cairo; he would have done this on land. This is approximately 195km from Pelusium)

December 15, Tuesday

He reached that city through the desert, after getting possession of all the places on the march through the voluntary surrender of the inhabitants.

{Heliopolis is near the modern day suburb of Ayn Shams in north eastern Cairo; he would have done this on land)

December 17, Thursday

Thence he crossed the stream and came to Memphis;

{The 'stream' would have been the Nile trending toward its lower levels (lowest levels are late February/March to June) when he crossed over to Memphis (near modern day Mit Rahina, in Egypt approximately 20 km (12 miles) south of Giza)}

December 19, Saturday

where he offered sacrifice to Apis[338]and the other gods, and celebrated a gymnastic and musical contest, the most distinguished artists in these matters coming to him from Greece.

{This coincided with the Winter Solstice that year}

December 25, Friday

From Memphis he sailed down the river towards the sea, embarking the shield-bearing guards, the archers, the Agrianians, and of the cavalry the royal squadron of the Companions.

{other sources suggest Alexander also explored up the Nile with this crew}

331 BC

January 20, Wednesday
Founding of Alexandria

Coming to Canobus,[339] he sailed round the Marian lake,[340] and disembarked where now is situated the city of Alexandria, which takes its name from him. The position seemed to him a very fine one in which to found a city, and he foresaw that it would become a prosperous one.[341] Therefore he was seized by an ardent desire to undertake the enterprise, and himself marked out the boundaries of the city, pointing out the place where the agora was to be constructed, where the temples were to be built, stating how many there were to be, and to what Grecian gods they were to be dedicated, and specially marking a spot for a temple to the Egyptian Isis.[342] He also pointed out where the wall was to be carried round it. In regard to these matters he offered sacrifice, and the victims appeared favourable.

Chapter 58: Foundation of Alexandria — Events in the Aegean

The following story is told, which seems to me not worthy of belief[343]:— that Alexander himself wished to leave behind for the builders the marks for the boundaries of the fortification, but that there was nothing at hand with which to make a furrow in the ground. One of the builders[344] hit upon the plan of collecting in vessels the barley which the soldiers were carrying, and throwing it upon the ground where the king led the way; and thus the circle of the fortification which he was making[345] for the city was completely marked out. The soothsayers, and especially Aristander the Telmissian, who was said already to have given many other true predictions,

113

pondering this, told Alexander that the city would become prosperous in every respect, but especially in regard to the fruits of the earth.

{Traditionally the date of 7th April 331 BC in the Julian Calendar is typically used for the finding of Alexandria. This is based on the 25th Tybi (Ancient Egyptian calendar) date from The Alexander Romance of pseudo-Callisthenes. However some dispute has arisen as this source was written in the Roman period were the 25th Tybi corresponded to the 20th January 331 BC in the Julian Calendar. The January date is kept as it is consistent with the rest of the chronology in this calendar. Specifically (i) Alexander fights the battle of Gaugamela later this year and so a later date would not allow his extensive exploits in the interim, (ii) Alexander enters the dessert to go to Siwa soon after this and a date later than April would render a journey through the dessert too hot for likely travel in this time and (iii) the sources formally state that Alexander leaves Egypt at the beginning of spring (see below) which could not axiomatically take place after an April founding of Alexandria.}

January 23, Saturday

At this time Hegelochus[346] sailed to Egypt and informed Alexander that the Tenedians had revolted from the Persians and attached themselves to him; because they had gone over to the Persians against their own wish. He also said that the democracy of Chios were introducing Alexander's adherents in spite of those who held the city, being established in it by Autophradates and Pharnabazus. The latter commander had been caught there and kept as a prisoner, as was also the despot Aristonicus, a Methymnaean,[347] who sailed into the harbour of Chios with five piratical vessels, fitted with one and a half banks of oars, not knowing that the harbour was in the hands of Alexander's adherents, but being misled by those who kept the bars of the harbour, because forsooth the fleet of Pharnabazus was moored in it. All the pirates were there massacred by the Chians; and Hegelochus brought to Alexander, as prisoners Aristonicus, Apollonides the Chian, Phisinus, Megareus, and all the others who had taken part in the revolt of Chios to the Persians, and who at that time were holding the government of the island by force. He also announced that he had deprived Chares[348] of the possession of Mitylene, that he had brought over the other cities in Lesbos by a voluntary agreement, and that he had sent Amphoterus to Cos with sixty ships, for the Coans themselves invited him to their island. He said that he himself had sailed to Cos and found it already in the hands of Amphoterus. Hegelochus brought all the prisoners with him except Pharnabazus, who had eluded his guards at Cos and got away by stealth. Alexander sent the despots who had been brought from the cities back to their fellow-citizens, to be treated as they pleased; but Apollonides and his Chian partisans he sent under a strict guard to Eldamantinē, an Egyptian city.[349]

January 28, Thursday

Chapter 59: Alexander Visits the Temple of Ammon

After these transactions, Alexander was seized by an ardent desire to visit Ammon[350] in Libya, partly in order to consult the god, because the oracle of Ammon was said to be exact in its information, and Perseus and Heracles were said to have consulted it, the former when he was despatched by Polydectes[351] against the Gorgons, and the latter, when he visited Antaeus[352] in Libya and Busiris[353] in Egypt. Alexander was also partly urged by a desire of emulating Perseus and Heracles, from both of whom he traced his descent.[354] He also deduced his pedigree from Ammon, just as the legends traced that of Heracles and Perseus to Zeus.

January 29, Friday

Accordingly he made the expedition to Ammon with the design of learning his own origin more certainly, or at least that he might be able to say that he had learned it.

February 06, Saturday

According to Aristobulus, he advanced along the sea-shore to Paraetonium through a country which was a desert, but not destitute of water, a distance of about 1,600 stades.[355]

{1,600 stades is approximately 296km. Paraetonium corresponds to modern day Mersa Matruh; a seaport in northern Egypt and capital of the Matrouh Governorate lying 240 km west of Alexandria. From modern Alexandria to Mersa Matruh on the coast is a distance of 295/296km, very close to the measurement in Alexander's times.}

February 07, Sunday

Thence he turned into the interior, where the oracle of Ammon was located. The route is desert, and most of it is sand and destitute of water. But there was a copious supply of rain for Alexander, a thing which was attributed to the influence of the deity; as was also the following occurrence. Whenever a south wind blows in that district, it heaps up the sand upon the route far and wide, rendering the tracks of the road invisible, so that it is impossible to discover where one ought to direct one's course in the sand, just as if one were at sea; for there are no landmarks along the road, neither mountain anywhere, nor tree, nor permanent hill standing erect, by which travellers might be able to form a conjecture of the right course, as sailors do by the stars.[356] Consequently, Alexander's army lost the way, and even the guides were in doubt about the course to take. Ptolemy, son of Lagus, says that two serpents went in front of the army, uttering a voice, and Alexander ordered the guides to follow them, trusting in the divine portent. He says too that they showed the way to the oracle and back again. But Aristobulus, whose account is generally admitted as correct, says that two ravens flew in front of the army, and that these acted as Alexander's guides. I am able to assert with confidence that some divine assistance was afforded him, for probability also coincides with the supposition; but the discrepancies in the details of the various narratives have deprived the story of certainty.[357]

February 17, Wednesday

Chapter 60: The Oasis of Ammon

The place where the temple of Ammon is located is entirely surrounded by a desert of far-stretching sand, which is destitute of water. The fertile spot in the midst of this desert, is not extensive; for where it stretches into its greater expanse, it is only about forty stades broad.[358] It is full of cultivated trees, olives and palms; and it is the only place in those parts which is refreshed with dew. A spring also rises from it, quite unlike all the other springs which issue from the earth.[359] For at mid-**day** the water is cold to the taste, and still more so to the touch, as cold as cold can be. But when the sun has sunk into the west, it gets warmer, and from the evening it keeps on growing warmer until midnight, when it reaches the warmest point. After midnight it goes on getting gradually colder: at day-break it is already cold; but at midday it reaches the coldest point. Every day it undergoes these alternate changes in regular succession. In this place also natural salt is procured by digging, and certain of the priests of Ammon convey quantities of it into Egypt. For whenever they set out for Egypt they put it into little boxes plaited out of palm, and carry it as a present to the king, or some other great man. The grains of this salt are large, some of them being even longer than three fingers' breadth; and it is clear like crystal.[360] The Egyptians and others who are respectful to the deity, use this salt in their sacrifices, as it is clearer than that which is procured from the sea. Alexander then was struck with wonder at the place, and consulted the oracle of the god.

{Siwah is 308km from Paraetonium}

February 18, Thursday

Having heard what was agreeable to his wishes, as he himself said,

February 19, Friday

he set out on the journey back to Egypt by the same route, according to the statement of Aristobulus; but according to that of Ptolemy, son of Lagus, he took another road,

March 07, Sunday

leading straight to Memphis.[361]

March 10, Wednesday

Chapter 61: Settlement of the Affairs of Egypt

At Memphis, many embassies from Greece reached him; and he sent away no one disappointed by the rejection of his suit. From Antipater also arrived an army of 400 Grecian mercenaries under the command of Menidas, son of Hegesander: likewise from Thrace 500 cavalry, under the direction of Asclepiodorus, son of Eunicus. Here he offered sacrifice to

Zeus the King, led his soldiers fully armed in solemn procession, and celebrated a gymnastic and musical contest. He then settled the affairs of Egypt, by appointing two Egyptians, Doloaspis and Petisis, governors of the country, dividing between them the whole land; but as Petisis declined his province, Doloaspis received the whole. He appointed two of the Companions to be commandants of garrisons: Pantaleon the Pydnaean in Memphis, and Polemo, son of Megacles, a Pellaean, in Pelusium. He also gave the command of the Grecian auxiliaries to Lycidas, an Aetolian, and pointed Eugnostus, son of Xenophantes, one of the Companions, to be secretary over the same troops. As their overseers he placed Aeschylus and Ephippus the Chalcidean. The government of the neighbouring country of Libya he granted to Apollonius, son of Charinus; and the part of Arabia near Heroöpolis[362] he put under Cleomenes, a man of Naucratis.[363] This last was ordered to allow the governors to rule their respective districts according to the ancient custom; but to collect from them the tribute due to him. The native governors were also ordered to pay it to Cleomenes. He appointed Peucestas, son of Macartatus, and Balacrus, son of Amyntas, generals of the army which he left behind in Egypt; and he placed Polemo, son of Theramenes, over the fleet as admiral. He made Leonnatus, son of Anteas, one of his body-guards instead of Arrhybas, who had died of disease. Antiochus, the commander of the archers, also died; and in his stead Ombrion the Cretan was appointed. When Balacrus was left behind in Egypt, the allied Grecian infantry, which had been under his command, was put under that of Calanus. Alexander was said to have divided the government of Egypt among so many men, because he was surprised at the natural strength of the country, and he thought it unsafe to entrust the rule of the whole to a single person. The Romans also seem to me to have learned a lesson from him, and therefore keep Egypt under strong guard; for they do not send any of the senators thither as proconsul for the same reason, but only men who have the rank among them of Equites (Knights).[364]

March 22, Monday
At the time of spring that year

Chapter 62: March into Syria–Alexander's Kindness to Harpalus and his other early Adherents

As soon as spring began to appear, he went from Memphis to Phoenicia, bridging the stream of the Nile near Memphis, as well as the canals issuing from it.

{The distance between Memphis (modern day Mit Rahina) and Tyre is approximately 1000km along the coast}

June 10, Thursday

When he arrived at Tyre, he found his fleet already there.[365] In this city he again offered sacrifice to Heracles, and celebrated both a gymnastic and musical contest. While there, the state vessel called the Paralus came to him from Athens, bringing Diophantus and Achilleus as envoys to him; and all the crew of the Paralus were joined with them in the embassy.[366] These men obtained all the requests which they were despatched to make, and the king gave up to the Athenians all their fellow-citizens who had been captured at the Granicus.[367] Being informed that revolutionary plans had been carried out in the Peloponnese, he sent Amphoterus thither to assist those of the Peloponnesians who were firm in their support of his war against Persia, and were not under the control of the Lacedaemonians. He also commanded the Phoenicians and Cyprians to despatch to the Peloponnese 100 other ships in addition to those which he was sending with Amphoterus. He now started up into the interior towards Thapsacus and the river Euphrates, after placing Coeranus, a Beroean[368] over the levy of tribute in Phoenicia, and Philoxenus to collect it in Asia as far as the Taurus. In the place of these men he entrusted the custody of the money which he had with him to Harpalus, son of Machatas, who had just returned from exile. For this man at first had been banished, while Philip was still king, because he was an adherent of Alexander; as also was Ptolemy, son of Lagus, for the same reason; likewise Nearchus, son of Androtimus, Erigyius, son of Larichus, and his brother Laomedon. For Alexander fell under Philip's suspicion when the latter married Eurydice[369] and treated Alexander's mother Olympias with dishonour. But after Philip's death those who had been banished on Alexander's account returned from exile and were received into favour. He made Ptolemy one of his confidential body-guards; he placed Harpalus over the money, because his bodily strength was unequal to the fatigues of war. Erigyius was made commander of the allied Grecian cavalry; and his brother Laomedon, because he could speak both the Greek and Persian languages and could read Persian writings, was put in charge of the foreign prisoners. Nearchus also was appointed viceroy of Lycia and of the land adjacent to it as far as mount Taurus. But shortly before the battle which was fought at Issus, Harpalus fell under the influence of Tauriscus, an evil man, and fled in his company. The latter started off to Alexander the Epirote[370] in Italy, where he soon after died. But Harpalus found a refuge in Megaris, whence however Alexander persuaded him to return, giving him a pledge that he should be none the worse on account of his desertion. When he came back, he not only received no punishment, but was even reinstated in the office of treasurer. Menander, one of the Companions, was sent away into Lydia as viceroy; and Clearchus was put in command of the Grecian auxiliaries who had been under Menander. Asclepiodorus, son of Eunicus, was also appointed viceroy of Syria instead of Arimmas, because the latter seemed to have been remiss in collecting the supplies which he had been ordered to collect for the army which the king was about to lead into the interior.

{The distance between Tyre and Thapsacus is approximately 600km. Thapsacus' location Is not formally identified but may include modern day Carchemish/ Karkemish on the Turkish side of the Turkey Syrian border (somewhere between Kargamış in the district of Gaziantep in Turkey and Jarabulus in Syria) or Seleucia at the Zeugma possibly at Killik, Şanlıurfa Province (reader please note that this is different to the famed Zeugma, in Osrohene)}

July 28, Wednesday

Chapter 63: Passage of the Euphrates and Tigris

Alexander arrived at Thapsacus in the month Hecatombaion,[371] in the archonship of Aristophanes at Athens;

July 29, Thursday

and he found that two bridges of boats had been constructed over the stream. But Mazaeus, to whom Darius had committed the duty of guarding the river, with about 3,000 cavalry, 2,000 of which were Grecian mercenaries, was up to that time keeping guard there at the river. For this reason the Macedonians had not constructed the complete bridge as far as the opposite bank, being afraid that Mazaeus might make an assault upon the bridge where it ended. But when he heard that Alexander was approaching, he went off in flight with all his army.

{The stream corresponds to the Euphrates next to Thapsacus which is relatively thin at this point}

July 31, Saturday

As soon as lie had fled, the bridges were completed as far as the further bank, and

August 09, Monday

Alexander crossed upon them with his army.[372]

August 14, Saturday

Thence he marched up into the interior through the land called Mesopotamia, having the river Euphrates and the mountains of Armenia on his left.

When he started from the Euphrates he did not march to Babylon by the direct road; because by going the other route he found all things easier for the march of his army, and it was also easier to obtain fodder for the horses and provisions for the men from the country. Besides this, the heat was not so scorching on the indirect route. Some of the men from Darius's army, who were dispersed for the purpose of scouting, were taken prisoners; and they reported that Darius was encamped near the river Tigris, having resolved to prevent Alexander from crossing that stream. They also said that he had a much larger army than that with which he had fought in Cilicia.

August 18, Wednesday

Hearing this, Alexander went with all speed towards the Tigris;

{He would have got to the Tigris relatively North, somewhere possibly near Mosul. He would have kept relatively north on this route due to the more moderate climate at this time of year. This would be a route just under 600km.}

September 12, Sunday

but when he reached it he found neither Darius himself nor any guard which he had left.

September 15, Wednesday

However he experienced great difficulty in crossing the stream, on account of the swiftness of the current,[373] though no one tried to stop him.

September 19, Sunday

There he made his army rest,

September 20, Monday
Date of lunar eclipse (confirmed by NASA tables) according to the Julian calendar. (Plutarch suggests this was eleven days before the battle of Arbela/ Gaugamela)

and while so doing, an eclipse of the moon nearly total occurred.[374] Alexander thereupon offered sacrifice to the moon, the sun and the earth, whose deed this was, according to common report. Aristander thought that this eclipse of the moon was a portent favourable to Alexander and the Macedonians; that there would be a battle that very month, and that victory for Alexander was signified by the sacrificial victims.

September 21, Tuesday

Having therefore decamped from the Tigris, he went through the land of Aturia,[375] having the mountains of the Gordyaeans[376] on the left and the Tigris itself on the right;
September 25, Saturday

and on the fourth day after the passage of the river, his scouts brought word to him that the enemy's cavalry were visible there along the plain, but how many of them there were they could not guess. Accordingly he drew his army up in order and advanced prepared for battle. Other scouts again riding forward and taking more accurate observations, told him that the cavalry did not seem to them to be more than 1,000 in number.

September 26, Sunday

Chapter 64: Description of Darius's Army at Arbela

Alexander therefore took the royal squadron of cavalry, and one squadron of the Companions, together with the Paeonian scouts, and marched with all speed; having ordered the rest of his army to follow at leisure. The Persian cavalry, seeing Alexander, advancing quickly, began to flee with all their might. Though he pressed close upon them in pursuit, most of them escaped; but a few, whose horses were fatigued by the flight, were slain, others were taken prisoners, horses and all. From these they ascertained that Darius with a large force was not far off. For the Indians who were conterminous with the Bactrians, as also the Bactrians themselves and the Sogdianians had come to the aid of Darius, all being under the command of Bessus, the viceroy of the land of Bactria. They were accompanied by the Sacians, a Scythian tribe belonging to the Scythians who dwell in Asia.[377] These were not subject to Bessus, but were in alliance with Darius. They were commanded by Mavaces, and were horse-bowmen. Barsaentes, the viceroy of Arachotia, led the Arachotians[378] and the men who were called mountaineer Indians. Satibarzanes, the viceroy of Areia, led the Areians,[379] as did Phrataphernes the Parthians, Hyrcanians, and Tapurians,[380] all of whom were horsemen. Atropates commanded the Medes, with whom were arrayed the Cadusians, Albanians, and Sacesinians.[381] The men who dwelt near the Red Sea[382] were marshalled by Ocondobates, Ariobarzanes, and Otanes. The Uxians and Susianians[383] acknowledged Oxathres son of Aboulites as their leader, and the Babylonians were commanded by Boupares. The Carians who had been deported into central Asia, and the Sitacenians[384] had been placed in the same ranks as the Babylonians. The Armenians were commanded by Orontes and Mithraustes, and the Cappadocians by Ariaoes. The Syrians from the vale between Lebanon and Anti-Lebanon (i.e. Coele-Syria) and the men of Syria which lies between the rivers[385] were led by Mazaeus. The whole army of Darius was said to contain 40,000 cavalry, 1,000,000 infantry, and 200 scythe-bearing chariots.[386] There were only a few elephants, about fifteen in number, belonging to the Indians who live this side of the Indus.[387] With these forces Darius had encamped at

Gaugamela, near the river Bumodus, about 600 stades distant from the city of Arbela, in a district everywhere level;[388] for whatever ground thereabouts was unlevel and unfit for the evolutions of cavalry, had long before been levelled by the Persians, and made fit for the easy rolling of chariots and for the galloping of horses. For there were some who persuaded Darius that he had forsooth got the worst of it in the battle fought at Issus, from the narrowness of the battle-field; and this he was easily induced to believe.

Chapter 65: Alexander's Tactics—His Speech to the Officers

When Alexander had received all this information from the Persian scouts who had been captured, he remained four days in the place where he had received the news; and gave his army rest after the march. He meanwhile fortified his camp with a ditch and stockade, as he intended to leave behind the baggage and all the soldiers who were unfit for fighting, and to go into the contest accompanied by his warriors carrying with them nothing except their weapons.

September 30, Thursday

Accordingly he took his forces by night, and began the march about the second watch, in order to come into collision with the foreigners at break of day.

As soon as Darius was informed of Alexander's approach, he at once drew out his army for battle; and Alexander led on his men drawn up in like manner. Though the armies were only sixty stades[389] from each other, yet they were not in sight of each other, for between the hostile forces some hills intervened. But when Alexander was only thirty stades distant from the enemy, and his army was already marching down from the hills just mentioned, catching sight of the foreigners, he caused his phalanx to halt there. Calling a council of the Companions, generals, cavalry officers, and leaders of the Grecian allies and mercenaries, he deliberated with them, whether he should at once lead on the phalanx without delay, as most of them urged him to do; or, whether, as Parmenio thought preferable, to pitch their tents there for the present, to reconnoitre all the ground, in order to see if there was anything there to excite suspicion or to impede their progress, or if there were ditches or stakes firmly fixed in the earth out of sight, as well as to make a more accurate survey of the enemy's tactical arrangements. Parmenio's opinion prevailed, so they encamped there, drawn up in the order in which they intended to enter the battle. But Alexander took the light infantry and the cavalry Companions and went all round, reconnoitring the whole country where he was about to fight the battle. Having returned, he again called together the same leaders, and said that they did not require to be encouraged by him to enter the contest; for they had been long before encouraged by their own valour, and by the gallant deeds which they had already so often achieved. He thought it expedient that each of them individually should stir up his own men separately; the infantry captain the men of his company, the cavalry captain his own squadron, the brigadiers their various brigades, and each of the leaders of the infantry the phalanx entrusted to him. He assured them that in this battle they were going to fight, not as before, either for Coele-Syria, Phoenicia, or Egypt, but for the whole of Asia. For he said this battle would decide who were to be the rulers of that continent. It was not necessary for him to stir them up to gallant deeds by many words, since they had this valour by nature; but they should see that each man took care, so far as in him lay, to preserve discipline in the critical moment of action, and to keep perfect silence when it was expedient to advance in silence. On the other hand, they should see that each man uttered a sonorous shout, where it would be advantageous to shout, and to raise as terrible a battle-cry as possible, when a suitable opportunity occurred of raising the battle-cry. He told them to take care to obey his orders as quickly as possible, and to transmit the orders they had received to the ranks with all rapidity; each man remembering that both as an individual and in the aggregate he was increasing the general danger if he was remiss in the discharge of his duty, and that he was assisting to gain a victory if he zealously put forth his utmost exertions.

Chapter 66: Rejection of Parmenio's Advice

With these words and others like them he briefly exhorted his officers, and in return was exhorted by them to feel confidence in their valour. He then ordered the soldiers to take dinner and to rest themselves. It is said that Parmenio came to him in his tent, and urged him to make a night attack on the Persians; saying that thus he would fall upon them unprepared and in a state of confusion, and at the same time more liable to a panic in the dark.[390] But the reply which he made, as others were listening to their conversation, was, that it would be mean to steal a victory, and that Alexander ought to conquer in open daylight, and without any artifice. This vaunting did not appear any arrogance on his part, but rather to indicate self-confidence amid dangers. To me at any rate, he seems to have used correct reasoning in such a matter. For in the night many accidents have occurred unexpectedly to those who were sufficiently prepared for battle as well as to those who were deficiently prepared, which have caused the superior party to fail in their plans, and have handed the victory over to the inferior party, contrary to the expectations of both sides. Though Alexander was generally fond of encountering danger in battle, the night appeared to him perilous; and, besides, if Darius were again defeated, a furtive and nocturnal attack on the part of the Macedonians would relieve him of the necessity of confessing that he was an inferior general and commanded inferior troops. Moreover, if any unexpected defeat befell his army, the circumjacent country was friendly to the enemy, and they were acquainted with the locality, whereas the Macedonians[391] were unacquainted with it, and surrounded by nothing but foes, of whom there were a great number prisoners. These would be a great source of anxiety, as they would be likely to assist in attacking them in the night, not only if they should meet with defeat, but even if they did not appear to be gaining a decisive victory. For this way of reasoning I commend Alexander; and I think him no less worthy of admiration for his excessive desire to fight in open daylight.

Chapter 67: Tactics of the Opposing Generals

Darius and his army remained drawn up during the night in the same order as that in which they had first arrayed themselves; because they had not surrounded themselves with a completely entrenched camp, and, moreover, they were afraid that the enemy would attack them in the night. The success of the Persians, on this occasion, was impeded especially by this long standing on watch with their arms, and by the fear which usually springs up before great dangers; which, however, was not then suddenly aroused by a momentary panic, but had been experienced for a long time, and had thoroughly cowed their spirits.[392] The army of Darius was drawn up in the following manner: for, according to the statement of Aristobulus, the written scheme of arrangement drawn up by Darius was afterwards captured. His left wing was held by the Bactrian cavalry, in conjunction with the Daans[393] and Arachotians; near these had been posted the Persians, horse and foot mixed together; next to these the Susians, and then the Cadusians. This was the arrangement of the left wing as far as the middle of the whole phalanx. On the right had been posted the men from Coele-Syria and Mesopotamia. On the right again were the Medes; next to them the Parthians and Sacians; then the Tapurians and Hyrcanians, and last the Albanians and Sacesinians, extending as far as the middle of the whole phalanx. In the centre where King Darius was, had been posted the king's kinsmen,[394] the Persian guards carrying spears with golden apples at the butt end,[395] the Indians, the Carians who had been forcibly removed to Central Asia, and the Mardian archers.[396] The Uxians, the Babylonians, the men who dwell near the Red Sea, and the Sitacenians had also been drawn up in deep column. On the left, opposite Alexander's right, had been posted the Scythian cavalry, about 1,000 Bactrians and 100 scythe-bearing chariots. In front of Darius's royal squadron of cavalry stood the elephants and 50 chariots. In front of the right wing the Armenian and Cappadocian cavalry with 50 scythe-bearing chariots bad been posted. The Greek mercenaries, as alone capable of coping with the Macedonians, were stationed right opposite their phalanx, in two divisions close beside Darius himself and his Persian attendants, one division on each side.[397]

Alexander's army was marshalled as follows: The right wing was held by the cavalry Companions, in front of whom had been posted the royal squadron, commanded by Clitus, son of Dropidas. Near this was the squadron of Glaucias, next to it that of Aristo, then that of Sopolis, son of Hermodorus, then that of Heraclides, son of Antiochus. Near this was that of Demetrius, son of Althaemenes, then that of Meleager, and last one of the royal squadrons commanded by Hegelochus, son of Hippostratus. All the cavalry Companions were under the supreme command of Philotas, son of Parmenio. Of the phalanx of Macedonian infantry, nearest to the cavalry had been posted first the select corps of shield-bearing guards, and then the rest of the shield-bearing-guards, under the command of Nicanor, son of Parmenio. Next to these was the brigade of Coenus, son of Polemocrates; after these that of Perdiceas, son of Orontes, then that of Meleager, son of Neoptolemus, then that of Polysperchon,[398] son of Simmias, and last that of Amyntas, son of Andromenes, under the command of Simmias, because Amyntas had been despatched to Macedonia to levy an army. The brigade of Craterus, son of Alexander, held the left end of the Macedonian phalanx, and this general commanded the left wing of the infantry.[399] Next to him was the allied Grecian cavalry, under the command of Erigyius, son of Larichus. Next to these, towards the left wing of the army, were the Thessalian cavalry, under the command of Philip, son of Menelaüs. But the whole left wing was led by Parmenio, son of Philotas, round whose person were ranged the Pharsalian horsemen, who were both the best and most numerous squadron of the Thessalian cavalry.

Chapter 68: Alexander's Tactics

In this way had Alexander marshalled his army in front; but he also posted a second array, so that his phalanx might be a double one.[400] Directions had been given to the commanders of these men posted in reserve, to wheel round and receive the attack of the foreigners, if they should see their own comrades surrounded by the Persian army. Next to the royal squadron on the right wing, half of the Agrianians, under the command of Attalus, in conjunction with the Macedonian archers under Briso's command, were posted angular-wise (i.e. in such a way that the wings were thrown forward at an angle with the centre, so as to take the enemy in flank) in case they should be seized anyhow by the necessity of folding back the phalanx or of closing it up (i.e. of deepening it by countermarching from front to rear). Next to the archers were the men called the veteran mercenaries, whose commander was Cleander. In front of the Agrianians and archers were posted the light cavalry used for skirmishing, and the Paeonians, under the command of Aretes and Aristo. In front of all had been posted the Grecian mercenary cavalry under the direction of Menidas; and in front of the royal squadron of cavalry and the other Companions had been posted half of the Agrianians and archers, and the javelin-men of Balacrus who had been ranged opposite the scythe-bearing chariots. Instructions had been given to Menidas and the troops under him to wheel round and attack the enemy in flank, if they should ride round their wing. Thus had Alexander arranged matters on the right wing. On the left the Thracians under the command of Sitalces had been posted angular-wise, and near them the cavalry of the Grecian allies, under the direction of Coeranus. Next stood the Odrysian cavalry, under the command of Agatho, son of Tyrimmas. In this part, in front of all, were posted the auxiliary cavalry of the Grecian mercenaries, under the direction of Andromachus, son of Hiero. Near the baggage the infantry from Thrace were posted as a guard. The whole of Alexander's army numbered 7,000 cavalry and about 40,000 infantry.

{The Battle of Arbela is also known as The Battle of Gaugamela – the location corresponds to an area in the vicinity of the modern city of Dohuk in Iraqi Kurdistan}

October 01, Friday
Battle of Gaugamela. Three sources of information to corroborate this date: (1) According to Plutarch this was on Boedromion 26, calculated as 25 days after the 3rd new moon (Sep 8) after the summer solstice (Jul 22), please refer to the preface. (2) Plutarch also says this was 11 days after the lunar eclipse (which according to NASA tables fits also). (3) According to Chugg, based on Cleitarchus this was also Boedromion 26, the end of one of his books. This corresponded to the day before the 5th anniversary of Alexander's crowning as king. Of

note, the date of this battle was traditionally set as October 1ˢᵗ in the Julian calendar. Arrian however suggests that this occurred in the month of Pyanepsion, although this doesn't directly agree with the other sources, the battle occurring of the 26ᵗʰ Boedromion and the beginning of Pyanespsion (Oct 5), are nevertheless very close.

Chapter 69: The Battle of Arbela

When the armies drew near each other, Darius and the men around him were observed; viz. the apple-bearing Persians, the Indians, the Albanians, the Carians who had been forcibly transported into Central Asia, the Mardian archers ranged opposite Alexander himself and his royal squadron of cavalry. Alexander led his own army more towards the right, and the Persians marched along parallel with him, far outflanking him upon their left.[401] Then the Scythian cavalry rode along the line, and came into conflict with the front men of Alexander's array; but he nevertheless still continued to march towards the right, and almost entirely got beyond the ground which had been cleared and levelled by the Persians.[402] Then Darius, fearing that his chariots would become useless, if the Macedonians advanced into uneven ground, ordered the front ranks of his left wing to ride round the right wing of the Macedonians, where Alexander was commanding, to prevent him from marching his wing any further. This being done, Alexander ordered the cavalry of the Grecian mercenaries under the command of Menidas to attack them. But the Scythian cavalry and the Bactrians, who had been drawn up with them sallied forth against them, and being much more numerous they put the small body of Greeks to rout. Alexander then ordered Aristo at the head of the Paeonians and Grecian auxiliaries to attack the Scythians; and the barbarians gave way. But the rest of the Bactrians drawing near to the Paeonians and Grecian auxiliaries, caused their own comrades who were already in flight to turn and renew the battle; and thus they brought about a general cavalry engagement, in which many of Alexander's men fell, not only being overwhelmed by the multitude of the barbarians, but also because the Scythians themselves and their horses were much more completely protected with armour for guarding their bodies.[403] Notwithstanding this, the Macedonians sustained their assaults, and assailing them violently squadron by squadron, they succeeded in pushing them out of rank. Meantime the foreigners launched their scythe-bearing chariots against Alexander himself, for the purpose of throwing his phalanx into confusion; but in this they were grievously deceived. For as soon as some of them approached, the Agrianians and the javelin-men with Balacrus, who had been posted in front of the Companion cavalry, hurled their javelins at them; others they seized by the reins and pulled the drivers off, and standing round the horses killed them. Yet some rolled right through the ranks; for the men stood apart and opened their ranks, as they had been instructed, in the places where the chariots assaulted them. In this way it generally happened that the chariots passed through safely, and the men by whom they were driven were uninjured. But these also were afterwards overpowered by the grooms of Alexander's army and by the royal shield-bearing guards.[404]

Chapter 70: Battle of Arbela — Flight of Darius

As soon as Darius began to set his whole phalanx in motion, Alexander ordered Aretes to attack those who were riding completely round his right wing; and up to that time he was himself leading his men in column. But when the Persians had made a break in the front line of their army, in consequence of the cavalry sallying forth to assist those who were surrounding the right wing, Alexander wheeled round towards the gap, and forming a wedge as it were of the Companion cavalry and of the part of the phalanx which was posted here, he led them with a quick charge and loud battle-cry straight towards Darius himself. For a short time there ensued a hand-to-hand fight; but when the Macedonian cavalry, commanded by Alexander himself, pressed on vigorously, thrusting themselves against the Persians and striking their faces with their spears, and when the Macedonian phalanx in dense array and bristling[405] with long pikes had also made an attack upon them, all things at once appeared full of terror to Darius, who had already long been in a state of fear, so that he was the first to turn and flee.[406] The Persians also who were riding round the wing were seized with alarm when Aretes made a vigorous attack upon them. In this quarter indeed the Persians took to speedy flight; and the Macedonians followed up the fugitives and slaughtered them.[407] Simmias and his brigade were not yet able to start with Alexander in pursuit, but causing the phalanx to halt there, he took part in the struggle, because the left wing of the Macedonians was reported to be hard pressed. In this part of the field, their line being broken, some of the Indians and of the Persian cavalry burst through the gap towards the baggage of the Macedonians; and there the action became desperate. For the Persians fell boldly on the men, who were most of them unarmed, and never expected that any men would cut through the double phalanx and break through upon them.[408] When the Persians made this attack, the foreign prisoners also assisted them by falling upon the Macedonians in the midst of the action. But the commanders of the men who had been posted as a reserve to the first phalanx, learning what was taking place, quickly moved from the position which they had been ordered to take, and coming upon the Persians in the rear, killed many of them there collected round the baggage. But the rest of them gave way and fled. The Persians on the right wing, who had not yet become aware of the flight of Darius, rode round Alexander's left wing and attacked Parmenio in flank.[409]

Chapter 71: Defeat of the Persians and Pursuit of Darius

At this juncture, while the Macedonians were doubtful as to the result of the battle, Parmenio sent a messenger to Alexander in haste, to tell him that their side was in a critical position and that he must send him aid.[410] When this news was brought to Alexander, he immediately turned back again from the pursuit, and wheeling round with the Companion cavalry, led them with great speed against the right wing of the foreigners. In the first place he assaulted the fleeing cavalry of the enemy, the Parthians, some of the Indians, and the most numerous and the bravest division of the Persians. Then ensued the most obstinately contested cavalry fight in the whole engagement. For being drawn up by squadrons as it were, the foreigners wheeled round and falling on Alexander's men face to face, they no longer relied on the hurling of javelins or the dexterous deploying of horses, as is the common practice in cavalry battles, but every one on his own account strove eagerly to break through what stood in his way, as if this were their only means of safety. They struck and were struck without quarter, as if they were no longer struggling to secure the victory for another, but were contending for their own personal safety. Here about sixty of Alexander's Companions fell; and Hephaestion himself, as well as Coenus and Menidas, was wounded. But even these troops were overcome by Alexander; and as many of them as could force their way through his ranks fled with all their might. And now Alexander had nearly come into conflict with the enemy's right wing, but in the meantime the Thessalian cavalry in a splendid struggle, had not fallen short of Alexander's success in the engagement. For the foreigners on the right wing were already beginning to fly when he came on the scene of conflict; so that he wheeled round again and started off in pursuit of Darius once more, keeping up the chase as long as there was daylight. Parmenio's brigade also followed in pursuit of those who were opposed to them. But Alexander crossed the river Lycus[411] and pitched his camp there, to give his men and horses a little rest; while Parmenio seized the Persian camp with their baggage, elephants, and camels. After giving his horsemen rest until midnight,

{The Lycus river would be different to the Lycus river in Phrygia (Çürüksu) which is a tributary of the Maeander (Büyük Menderes Irmağı) in Turkey}

October 02, Saturday
The day after the battle (according to Chugg, based on Cleitarchus this was the fifth anniversary of Alexander's crowing, as it was the start of one of his books, whereupon he would start each book on the anniversary of Alexander's crowning)

Alexander again advanced by a forced march towards Arbela, with the hope of seizing Darius there, together with his money and the rest of his royal property. He reached Arbela the next day, having pursued altogether about 600 stades from the battle-field.[412] But as Darius went on fleeing without taking any rest,[413] he did not find him at Arbela. However the money and all the other property were captured, as was also the chariot of Darius. His spear and bow were likewise taken, as had been the case after the battle of Issus.[414] Of Alexander's men about 100 were killed, and more than 1,000 of his horses were lost either from wounds or from fatigue in the pursuit, nearly half of them belonging to the Companion cavalry. Of the foreigners there were said to have been about 300,000 slain, and far more were taken prisoners than were killed.[415] The elephants and all the chariots which had not been destroyed in the battle were also captured. Such was the result of this battle, which was fought in the archonship of Aristophanes at Athens, in the month Pyanepsion;[416] and thus Aristander's prediction was accomplished, that Alexander would both fight a battle and gain a victory in the same month in which the moon was seen to be eclipsed.[417]

Chapter 72: Escape of Darius into Media — March of Alexander to Babylon and Susa

Immediately after the battle, Darius marched through the mountains of Armenia towards Media, accompanied in his flight by the Bactrian cavalry, as they had then been posted with him in the battle; also by those Persians who were called the king's kinsmen, and by a few of the men called apple-bearers.[418] About 2,000 of his Grecian mercenaries also accompanied him in his flight, under the command of Paron the Phocian, and Glaucus the Aetolian. He fled towards Media for this reason, because he thought Alexander would take the road to Susa and Babylon immediately after the battle, inasmuch as the whole of that country was inhabited and the road was not difficult for the transit of baggage; and besides Babylon and Susa appeared to be the prizes of the war; whereas the road towards Media was by no means easy for the march of a large army. In this conjecture Darius was mistaken;

October 03, Sunday

for when Alexander started from Arbela, he advanced straight towards Babylon;

{Babylon corresponds to modern day Hillah in the Babil Governorate of Iraq, approximately 600km from Arbela/Gaugamela. Alexander would have done this at rapid pace as he was still likely in 'war mode', so that unusually he did not wait long for his troops to recuperate as usual. He would have been travelling at a war travel pace rather than a more relaxed pace that he took at other times.}

October 21, Thursday

and when he was now not far from that city, he drew up his army in order of battle and marched forward.

October 22, Friday
Enters Babylon

The Babylonians came out to meet him in mass, with their priests and rulers, each of whom individually brought gifts, and offered to surrender their city, citadel, and money.[419] Entering the city, he commanded the Babylonians to rebuild all the temples which Xerxes had destroyed, and especially that of Belus, whom the Babylonians venerate more than any other god.[420] He then appointed Mazaeus viceroy of the Babylonians, Apollodorus the Amphipolitan general of the soldiers who were left behind with Mazaeus, and Asclepiodorus, son of Philo, collector of the revenue. He also sent Mithrines, who had surrendered to him the citadel of Sardis, down into Armenia to be viceroy there.[421] Here also he met with the Chaldaeans; and whatever they directed in regard to the religious rites of Babylon he performed, and in particular he offered sacrifice to Belus according to their instructions.[422]

{The Babylonian Tablet archive suggests the 21st or 22nd October arrival here. Curtius and Justin state he was here for 34 days.}

November 24, Wednesday

He then marched away to Susa[423]; and on the way he was met by the son of the viceroy of the Susians,[424] and a man bearing a letter from Philoxenus, whom he had despatched to Susa directly after the battle. In the letter Philoxenus had written that the Susians had surrendered their city to him, and that all the money was safe for Alexander.

{Curtius and Diodorus (based on Cleitarchus) suggest that six days into his march Alexander arrived Sittacene on **November 29, Monday** where he reorganised his army, although Arrian suggests this took place at Susa.

Susa corresponds to modern day Shush in Iran and is approximately 515km from Babylon (Hillah).}

December 14, Tuesday
Arrival at Susa

In twenty days the king arrived at Susa from Babylon; and entering the city he took possession of the money, which amounted to 50,000 talents, as well as the rest of the royal property.[425] Many other things were also captured there, which Xerxes brought with him from Greece, especially the brazen statues of Harmodius and Aristogeiton.[426] These Alexander sent back to the Athenians, and they are now standing at Athens in the Ceramicus, where we go up into the Acropolis,[427] right opposite the temple of Rhea, the mother of the gods, not far from the altar of the Eudanemi. Whoever has been initiated in the mysteries of the two goddesses[428] at Eleusis, knows the altar of Eudanemus which is upon the plain.

{50,000 talents and the total haul from Susa has been estimated by James Ulvog as approximately 20 Billion US dollars (https://attestationupdate.com/2016/05/23/alexanders-haul-from-looting-susa-the-capital-of-persia-revised-estimate-of-value-of-one-athenian-talent/), although some authors have even suggested figures of over 500 billion US dollars}

December 20, Monday

At Susa Alexander offered sacrifice after the custom of his fathers, and celebrated a torch race and a gymnastic contest; and then, leaving Abulites, a Persian, as viceroy of Susiana, Mazarus, one of his Companions, as commander of the garrison in the citadel of Susa, and Archelaüs, son of Theodorus, as general, he advanced towards the land of the Persians. He also sent Menes down to the sea, as governor of Syria, Phœnicia, and Cilicia, giving him 3,000 talents of silver[429] to convey to the sea, with orders to despatch as many of them to Antipater as he might need to carry on the war against the Lacedaemonians.[430] There also Amyntas, son of Andromenes, reached him with the forces which he was leading from Macedonia[431]; of whom Alexander placed the horsemen in the ranks of the Companion cavalry, and the foot he added to the various regiments of infantry, arranging each according to nationalities. He also established two companies in each squadron of cavalry, whereas before this time companies did not exist in the cavalry; and over them he set as captains those of the Companions who were pre-eminent for merit.

{December 20th 331 BC corresponds to the winter solstice for that year. Alexander had also celebrated this the year before.}

December 25, Saturday

Chapter 73: Subjugation of the Uxians

He now set out from Susa,

December 28, Tuesday

and, crossing the river Pasitigris,[432] invaded the country of the Uxians.

{The Pasitigris river corresponds to the Kārun or Karoun in modern day Iran. It is listed as one of the four rivers of Paradise or the Biblical Eden. Alexander traversed the river at Šurkutir (modern Shushtar) and confronted the Uxians in the area of Masjid-e Solaiman, the Macedonian army was divided near modern Haftgel. The distance from Susa to the Pasitigris is approximately 80km.

It is the author's opinion that the term Uxians corresponds to the indigenous people of ancient Elam (the Elamites) corresponding to people in modern day Khuzestan Province, Ostān-e Khūzestān in Iran. The term

Khuzestan corresponds to the 'The Land of the Khuz People' which in the Achaemiend era (Alexander's time) was called
Huza/ Huzia or Hujiyā/ Huja in Achaemenid Old Persian. The similar geography and transliteration of the name between Uxian, Huxian and Huzian renders a likely link. Furthermore these people may also possibly correspond to the prominent Bakhtiari People of this area.}

Some of these people who inhabit the plains were under the rule of the viceroy of the Persians, and on this occasion surrendered to Alexander; but those who are called the mountaineers were not in subjection to the Persians, and at this time sent word to Alexander that they would not permit him to march with his forces into Persis, unless they received from him as much as they were in the habit of receiving from the king of the Persians for the passage through their mountains.[433]

{This should fit with the Elamites having their own laws in the Achaemenid Empire based on their very ancient history as an empire in themselves and likely some powerful local political influence. This 'special status' may have been recognised by the Darius' mother who below demonstrates her sympathy for these people.}

December 29, Wednesday

He sent the messengers back with instructions to come to the defiles, the possession of which made them think that the passage into Persis was in their power, promising them that they should there receive from him the prescribed toll. He then took the royal body-guards, the shield-bearing infantry, and 8,000 men from the rest of his army, and, under the guidance of the Susians, marched by night along a different road from the frequented one. Advancing by a route rough and difficult, on the same day he fell upon the villages of the Uxians, where he captured much booty and killed many of the people while still in their beds; but others escaped into the mountains. He then made a forced march to the defiles, where the Uxians resolved to meet him in mass in order to receive the prescribed toll. But he had already previously despatched Craterus to seize the heights, to which he thought the Uxians would retire if they were repelled by force; and he himself went with great celerity, and got possession of the pass before their arrival. He then drew up his men in battle array, and led them from the higher and more commanding position against the barbarians. They, being alarmed at Alexander's celerity, and finding themselves deprived by stratagem[434] of the position in which they had especially confided, took to flight without ever coming to close combat. Some of them were killed by Alexander's men in their flight, and many lost their lives by falling over the precipices along the road; but most of them fled up into the mountains for refuge, and falling in with Craterus, were destroyed by his men. Having received these gifts of honour[435] from Alexander, they with difficulty, after much entreaty, procured from him the privilege of retaining possession of their own land on condition of paying him an annual tribute. Ptolemy, son of Lagus, says that the mother of Darius,[436] on their behalf, entreated Alexander to grant them the privilege of inhabiting the land. The tribute agreed upon was a hundred horses, five hundred oxen, and 30,000 sheep a year; for the Uxians had no money, nor was their country fit for tillage; but most of them were shepherds and herdsmen.

{Clement Augustus Gregory Peter Louis de Bode (1806 – 1887), or Baron De Bode suggested in a paper in The Journal of the Royal Geographic Society of London (Volume 13, 1843) that the town of the Uxians corresponds to the modern day city of Malamir or Izeh in Iran.}

330 BC

January 12, Wednesday

Chapter 74: Defeat of Ariobarzanes and Capture of Persepolis

After this, Alexander despatched Parmenio with the baggage, the Thessalian cavalry, the Grecian allies, the mercenary auxiliaries, and the rest of the more heavily armed soldiers, to march into Persis along the carriage road leading into that country.

He himself took the Macedonian infantry, the Companion cavalry, the light cavalry used for skirmishing, the Agrianians, and the archers, and made a forced march through the mountains.

{The distance between the Uxian land and the Persian Gates is an approximately 220-270km journey}

January 19, Wednesday

But when he arrived at the Persian Gates, he found that Ariobarzanes, the viceroy of Persis, with 40,000 infantry and 700 cavalry, had built a wall across the pass, and had pitched his camp there near the wall to block Alexander's passage. Then indeed he pitched his camp there;

{The 'Persian Gates' acts as gate (and therefore powerful strategic area) between the Persian Gulf and inland area of Fras that corresponds to the modern day pass of Tang-e Meyran. In the east it links Yasuj with Sedeh and travels south of the Kuh-e-Dinar massif of the Zagros Mountain of Iran.}

January 20, Thursday
Battle of the Persian Gate

but next day he marshalled his army, and led it up to the wall. When it was evident that it would be difficult to capture it on account of the rugged nature of the ground, and as many of his men were being wounded, the enemy assailing them with missiles from engines of war placed upon higher ground, which gave them an advantage over their assailants, he retreated to his camp. He was informed by the prisoners that they could lead him round by another route, so that he might get to the other end of the pass; but when he ascertained that this road was rough and narrow, he left Craterus there at the camp with his own brigade and that of Meleager, as well as a few archers and 500 cavalry, with orders that when he perceived he had got right round and was approaching the camp of the Persians (which he could easily perceive, because the trumpets would give him the signal), he should then assault the wall. Alexander advanced by night, and travelling about 100 stades, he took the shield-bearing guards, the brigade of Perdiccas, the lightest armed of the archers, the Agrianians, the royal squadron of cavalry Companions, and one regiment of cavalry besides these, containing four companies; and wheeling round with these troops, he marched towards the pass in the direction the prisoners led him. He ordered Amyntas, Philotas, and Coenus to lead the rest of the army towards the plain, and to make a bridge over the river[437] which one must cross to go into Persis. He himself went by a route difficult and rough, along which he nevertheless marched for the most part at full speed. Falling upon the first guard of the barbarians before daylight,[438] he destroyed them, and so he did most of the second; but the majority of the third guard escaped, not indeed by fleeing into the camp of Ariobarzanes, but into the mountains as they were, being seized with a sudden panic. Consequently he fell upon the enemy's camp at the approach of dawn without being observed. At the very time he began to assault the trench, the trumpets gave the signal to Craterus, who at once attacked the advanced fortification. The enemy then, being in a state of confusion from being attacked on all sides, fled without coming to close conflict; but they were hemmed in on all hands, Alexander pressing upon them in one direction and the men of Craterus running up in another. Therefore most of them were compelled to wheel round and flee into the fortifications, which were already in the hands of the Macedonians. For Alexander, expecting the very thing which really occurred, had left Ptolemy there with three thousand infantry; so that most of the barbarians were cut to pieces by the Macedonians at close quarters. Others perished in the terrible flight which ensued, hurling themselves over the precipices; but Ariobarzanes himself, with a few horsemen, escaped into the mountains.[439]

{100 stades is approximately 18.5km}

January 21, Friday

Alexander now marched back with all speed to the river, and finding the bridge already constructed over it, he easily crossed with his army.[440] Thence he again continued his march to Persepolis,

{Persepolis is approximately 150km from the Persian Gates}

January 27, Thursday
Arrival at Persepolis

so that he arrived before the guards of the city could pillage the treasury.[441] He also captured the money which was at Pasargadae[442] in the treasury of the first Cyrus, and appointed Phrasaortes, son of Rheomithres, viceroy over the Persians. He burnt down the Persian palace, though Parmenio advised him to preserve it, for many reasons, and especially because it was not well to destroy what was now his own property, and because the men of Asia would not by this course of action be induced to come over to him, thinking that he himself had decided not to retain the rule of Asia, but only to conquer it and depart. But Alexander said that he wished to take vengeance on the Persians, in retaliation for their deeds in the invasion of Greece, when they razed Athens to the ground and burnt down the temples. He also desired to punish the Persians for all the other injuries they had done the Greeks. But Alexander does not seem to me to have acted on this occasion with prudence; nor do I think that this was any retributive penalty at all on the ancient Persians.[443]

{The march to Persepolis would have been at a fast march rate. According to Plutarch, Alexander stayed at Persepolis for 120 days. Diodorus adds that Alexander destroyed Persepolis, cajoled during a drunken celebration by an Athenian woman Thais. This could correspond to a date of **May 23, Monday**

Furthermore, based on the work of Jim Ulvog (https://attestationupdate.com/2016/07/15/guess-on-the-value-of-all-loot-taken-by-alexander-the-great/), one ancient Athenian talent is equivalent to approximately $28 million. Working of the figures from Frank Holt, he applies 6 thousand talents from Pasargadae and 120 thousand talents from Persepolis such that the total from both these treasuries would be approximately $3.5 trillion. For context, he suggests that overall value of the booty from Persia was approximately $7 trillion and Alexander's overall plunder was equivalent to approximately $11 trillion}

May 27, Friday
Leaves Persepolis

Chapter 75: Darius Pursued into Media and Parthia

After bringing these matters to a successful issue, he advanced towards Media; for he ascertained that Darius was there. Now Darius had formed the resolution, if Alexander remained at Susa or Babylon, to stay there among the Medes, in order to see if any change of policy were made by Alexander. But if the latter marched against him, he resolved to proceed into the interior towards Parthia and Hyrcania, as far as Bactria, laying waste all the land and making it impossible for Alexander to advance any further. He therefore sent the women and the rest of the property which he still retained, together with the covered carriages, to what were called the Caspian Gates[444]; but he himself stayed at Ecbatana,[445] with the forces which had been collected from those who were at hand. Hearing this, Alexander advanced towards Media, and invading the land of the Paraetacae,[446] he subdued it, and appointed Oxathres, son of Abulites, the former viceroy of Susa, to rule as viceroy. Being informed on the march that Darius had determined to meet him for battle, and to try the fortune of war again (for the Scythians and Cadusians had come to him as allies), he ordered that the beasts of burden, with their guards and the rest of the baggage, should follow;

{the land of the Paraetacae corresponds to the province of Mazandaran in modern day Iran. It is approximately 800-950km travel from Persepolis.}

June 18, Saturday
Starts the chase for Darius III

and taking the rest of his army, he led it in order of battle,

June 30, Thursday

and on the twelfth day arrived in Media. There he ascertained that the forces of Darius were not fit for battle, and that his allies, the Cadusians and Scythians, had not arrived; but that he had resolved to flee.

July 01, Friday
Meets Prince Bistanes son of Darius II (possible Grandfather of Darius III)

He therefore marched on with still greater speed; and when he was only three days' journey from Ecbatana, he was met by Bistanes, son of Ochus, who reigned over the Persians before Darius. This man announced that Darius had fled five days before, taking with him 7,000 talents of money[447] from the Medes, and an army of 3,000 cavalry and 6,000 infantry.

July 04, Monday
Arrives at Ecbatana

When Alexander reached Ecbatana, he sent the Thessalian cavalry and the other Grecian allies back to the sea, paying them the full hire which had been stipulated, and making them an additional donation from himself of 2,000 talents. He issued an order that if any man of his own accord wished still to continue to serve for hire with him, he should enlist; and those who enlisted in his service were not a few. He then ordered Epocillus, son of Polyeides, to conduct the rest down to the sea, taking other cavalry as a guard for them, since the Thessalians sold their horses there. He also sent word to Menes to take upon himself the duty of seeing that they were conveyed in triremes to Euboea, when they arrived at the sea.[448] He instructed Parmenio to deposit the money which was being conveyed from Persis in the citadel at Ecbatana, and to hand it over to the charge of Harpalus;[449] for he had left this man over the money with a guard of 6,000 Macedonians and a few horsemen and light-armed infantry to take care of it. He told Parmenio himself to take the Grecian mercenaries, the Thracians, and all the other horsemen except the Companion cavalry, and march by the land of the Cadusians into Hyrcania. He also sent word to Clitus, the commander of the royal squadron of cavalry, who had been left behind at Susa ill, that when he arrived at Ecbatana from Susa he should take the Macedonians who had been left there in charge of the money, and go in the direction of Parthia, where also he himself intended soon to arrive.

{Bistanes listed here seems to be of the royal line but not a recognised Achaemenid king in modern times. Based on Transliteration, this individual could correspond to Ostanes who was son of Darius II (originally called Ochus and sometimes Nothos, "Bastard" by the Greeks as his mother was Cosmartidene of Babylon). Through this line he would be the son od Darius II and the Grandfather of Darius III (via his son Arsames of Ostanes) whom Alexander was chasing. His name in Old Iranian comes as (H)uštāna with a meaning of aristocrat or holder of high rank. This would be a different Ostanes (Αὐστάνης of Paraetakene, north-east of Bactria) that subsequently joins Alexander on his expedition to India.

If Bistanes was Darius III's grandfather, this would fit with Arrian's text that Bistanes was son of Ochus (Darius II), he may also have been brother to the Persian Queen Mother Sisygambis who was captured in Alexander's camp on good terms and she may have facilitated this meeting offering a 'trustworthy Alexander'. This may be a mechanism for the ancient sources to imply that Alexander was on 'good terms' with the imperial Persian monarchy and so that he would have been freed from the suspicion of contributing to Darius' subsequent death.

Based on the work of Jim Ulvog (https://attestationupdate.com/2016/07/15/guess-on-the-value-of-all-loot-taken-by-alexander-the-great/), one ancient Athenian talent is equivalent to approximately $28 million. As a result, the extra 'bonus' 2000 talents given by Alexander to the Thessalian cavalry and the other Grecian allies is equivalent to approximately $56 billion.

Mazandaran province is approximately 480km from Ecbatana (modern day Hamadan in Iran).}

July 07, Thursday

Chapter 76: March through the Caspian Gates

Then taking the Companion cavalry, the light cavalry used for skirmishing, he Greek mercenary cavalry, under the command of Erigyius, the Macedonian phalanx, except the men who had been placed in charge of the money, the archers, and the Agrianians, he marched against Darius. In the forced march which he made, many of his soldiers were left behind, worn out with fatigue, and many of the horses died.

July 18, Monday

He nevertheless pressed on, and on the eleventh day arrived at Rhagae.[450] This place is distant from the Caspian Gates one day's journey to one marching as Alexander did. But Darius had already passed through this defile before Alexander came up, though many of those who were his companions in flight deserted him on the way and retired to their own abodes. Many also surrendered to Alexander. The latter now gave up the hope of capturing Darius by close pursuit, and remained there five days to give his troops repose. He appointed Oxodates a Persian, who had the ill fortune to be arrested by Darius and shut up at Susa, to the office of viceroy of Media; for this treatment was an inducement to Alexander to rely on his fidelity.

July 23, Saturday

He then marched towards Parthia; and on the first day encamped near the Caspian Gates,

{The Caspian Gates or Gates of Alexander; likely Pass of Dariel (a gorge on the border between Russia and Georgia) although a less likely possibility is the Pass of Derbent in Dagestan, Russia.}

July 24, Sunday

which he passed through on the second day as far as the country was inhabited.[451] Hearing that the country further on was desert, he resolved to procure a stock of provisions from the place where he was encamped, and accordingly sent Coenus out on a foraging expedition with the cavalry and a small body of infantry.

July 25, Monday

Chapter 77: Darius is Assassinated by Bessus

At this time Bagistanes, one of the Babylonian nobles, came to him from the camp of Darius, accompanied by Antibelus, one of the sons of Mazaeus. These men informed him that Nabarzanes, the commander of the cavalry which accompanied Darius in his flight, Bessus, viceroy of Bactria, and Barsaentes, viceroy of the Arachotians and Drangians,[452] had jointly arrested the king. When Alexander heard this, he marched with still greater speed than ever, taking with him only the Companions and the skirmishing cavalry, as well as some of the foot-soldiers selected as the strongest and lightest men. He did not even wait for Coenus to return from the foraging expedition; but placed Craterus over the men left behind, with instructions to follow in short marches. His own men took with them nothing but their arms and provisions for two days. After marching the whole night

July 26, Tuesday

and till noon of the next day, he gave his army a short rest, then went on again all night,

July 27, Wednesday

and when day began to break reached the camp from which Bagistanes had set out to meet him; but he did not catch the enemy. However, in regard to Darius, he ascertained that he had been arrested and was being conveyed in a covered carriage[453]; that Bessus possessed the command instead of Darius, and had been nominated leader by the Bactrian cavalry and all the other barbarians who were companions of Darius in his flight, except Artabazus and his sons, together with the Grecian mercenaries, who still remained faithful to Darius; but they, not being able to prevent what was being done, had turned aside their march from the public thoroughfare and were marching towards the mountains by themselves, refusing to take part with Bessus and his adherents in their enterprise. He also learnt that those who had arrested Darius had come to the decision to surrender him to Alexander, and to procure some advantage for themselves, if they should find that Alexander was pursuing them; but if they should learn that he had gone back again, they had resolved to collect as large an army as they could and to preserve the rule for the commonwealth. He also ascertained that for the present Bessus held the supreme command, both on account of his relationship to Darius and because the war was being carried on in his viceregal province. Hearing this, Alexander thought it was advisable to pursue with all his might; and though his men and horses were already quite fatigued by the incessant severity of their labours, he nevertheless proceeded, and, travelling a long way all through the night

July 28, Thursday

and the next day till noon, arrived at a certain village, where those who were leading Darius had encamped the day before. Hearing there that the barbarians had decided to continue their march by night, he inquired of the natives if they knew any shorter road to the fugitives. They said they did know one, but that it ran through a country which was desert through lack of water. He nevertheless ordered them to show him this way, and perceiving that the infantry could not keep up with him if he marched at full speed, he caused 500 of the cavalry to dismount from their horses; and selecting the officers of the infantry and the best of the other foot-soldiers, he ordered them to mount the horses armed just as they were. He also directed Nicanor, the commander of the shield-bearing guards, and Attalus, commander of the Agrianians, to lead their men who were left behind, by the same route which Bessus had taken, having equipped them as lightly as possible; and he ordered that the rest of the infantry should follow in regular marching order. He himself began to march in the afternoon, and led the way with great rapidity.[454]

July 29, Friday
The Death of Darius

Having travelled 400 stades in the night, he came upon the barbarians just before daybreak, going along without any order and unarmed; so that few of them rushed to defend themselves, but most of them, as soon as they saw Alexander himself, took to flight without even coming to blows. A few of those who turned to resist being killed, the rest of these also took to flight. Up to this time Bessus and his adherents were still conveying Darius with them in a covered carriage; but when Alexander was already close upon their heels Nabarzanes and Barsaëntes wounded him and left him there, and with 600 horsemen took to flight. Darius died from his wounds

146

soon after, before Alexander had seen him.[455]

{In the month of Hekatombaion when Aristophon was archon in Athens corresponding to the end of July and beginning of August, additionally the Babylonian Chronicle BCHP 1 offers July 330 BC as a date for this. 400 stades is equivalent to approximately 74km. According to Plutarch the Macedonian solider Polystratus found the dying Darius who was asking for water and received this from him. The location of death is reported as being near Skirmish (near Shahrud/ Shahroud in modern day Iran).}

July 31, Sunday

Chapter 78: Reflections on the Fate of Darius

Alexander sent the body of Darius into Persis, with orders that it should be buried in the royal sepulchre, in the same way as the other Persian kings before him had been buried.[456]

August 03, Wednesday

He then proclaimed Amminaspes, a Parthian, viceroy over the Parthians and Hyrcanians. This man was one of those who with Mazaces had surrendered Egypt to Alexander. He also appointed Tlepolemus, son of Pythophanes, one of the Companions, to guard his interests in Parthia and Hyrcania. Such was the end of Darius, in the archonship of Aristophon at Athens, in the month Hecatombaion.[457] This king was a man pre-eminently effeminate and lacking in self-reliance in military enterprises; but as to civil matters he never exhibited any disposition to indulge in arbitrary conduct; nor indeed was it in his power to exhibit it. For it happened that he was involved in a war with the Macedonians and Greeks at the very time he succeeded to the regal power[458]; and consequently it was no longer possible for him to act the tyrant towards his subjects, even if he had been so inclined, standing as he did in greater danger than they. As long as he lived, one misfortune after another was accumulated upon him; nor did he experience any cessation of calamity from the time when he first succeeded to the rule. At the beginning of his reign the cavalry defeat was sustained by his viceroys at the Granicus, and forthwith Ionia Aeolis, both the Phrygias, Lydia, and all Caria[459] except Halicarnassus were occupied by his foe; soon after, Halicarnassus also was captured, as well as all the littoral as far as Cilicia. Then came his own discomfiture at Issus, where he saw his mother, wife, and children taken prisoners. Upon this Phoenicia and the whole of Egypt were lost; and then at Arbela he himself fled disgracefully among the first, and lost a very vast army composed of all the nations of his empire. After this, wandering as an exile from his own dominions, he died after being betrayed by his personal attendants to the worst treatment possible, being at the same time king and a prisoner ignominiously led in chains; and at last he perished through a conspiracy formed of those most intimately acquainted with him. Such were the misfortunes that befell Darius in his life-time; but after his death he received a royal burial; his children received from Alexander a princely rearing and education, just as if their father had still been king; and Alexander himself became his son-in-law.[460] When he died he was about fifty years of age.

August 10, Wednesday
Advance into Hyrcania

Chapter 79: Expedition into Hyrcania

Alexander now took the soldiers who had been left behind in his pursuit and advanced into Hyrcania,[461] which is the country lying on the left of the road leading to Bactra.[462] On one side it is bounded by lofty mountains densely covered with wood, and on the other it is a plain stretching as far as the Great Sea[463] in this part of the world. He led his army by this route, because he ascertained that the Grecian mercenaries serving under Darius had succeeded in escaping by it into the mountains of Tapuria; at the same time he resolved to subdue the Tapurians themselves. Having divided his army into three parts, he himself led the way by the shortest and most difficult route, at the head of the most numerous and at the same time the lightest division of his forces. He despatched Craterus at the head of his own brigade and that of Amyntas, some of the archers, and a few of the cavalry against the Tapurians; and he ordered Erigyius to take the Grecian mercenaries and the rest of the cavalry, and lead the way by the public thoroughfare, though it was longer, conducting the waggons, the baggage, and the crowd of camp-followers.

{Hyrcania corresponds to Varkâna (Old Persian) corresponds to the area between the Caspian sea and Alborz mountains in North Eastern Iran. The description between the sea and mountains likely corresponds to an area near modern-day Gorgan (previously Astrabad), approximately 80km from the location of the death of Darius (possibly Shahroud). Sources based on

Cleitarchus suggest that on the 3rd day of march, **August 12, Friday Alexander arrived at Hecatompylos** (Εκατόμπυλος), supposedly founded by Greeks and corresponding to the ancient city of Šahr-e-Qumis (Saddarvazeh) in Iran, between Semnan and Damqan in Semnan Province of West Khurasan. Possibly leaves **August 16, Tuesday**}

August 18, Thursday

After crossing the first mountains, and encamping there,

August 20, Saturday

he took the shield-bearing guards together with the lightest men in the Macedonian phalanx and some of the archers, and went along a road difficult and hard to travel upon, leaving guards for the roads wherever he thought there was any peril, so that the barbarians who held the mountains might not at those points fall upon the men who were following.

August 22, Monday

Having passed through the defiles with his archers, he encamped in the plain near a small river[464];

August 23, Tuesday
Surrender of Darius' senior generals near the Stiboetis/ Ziobetis river

and while he was here, Nabarzanes, the commander of Darius's cavalry, Phrataphernes, the viceroy of Hyrcania and Parthia, and the other most distinguished of the Persians in attendance on Darius, arrived and surrendered themselves.

{The Stiboetis/ Ziobetis river likely corresponds to the river between Ahvanu and Astane in modern day Iran}

August 27, Saturday

After waiting four days in the camp, he took up those who had been left behind on the march, all of them advancing in safety except the Agrianians, who, while guarding the rear, were attacked by the barbarian mountaineers. But these soon drew off when they got the worst of it in the skirmish. Starting from this place, he advanced into Hyrcania

September 01, Thursday
Arrives at Zadracarta (possibly Gorgan in modern day Iran)

as far as Zadracarta, the capital of the Hyrcanians.

{Zadracarta is possibly Gorgan in modern day Iran and approximately 70km from the area Ahvanu and Astane in modern day Iran }

September 07, Wednesday

In this place[465] he was rejoined by Craterus, who had not succeeded in falling in with the Grecian mercenaries of Darius; but he had thoroughly traversed the whole country, gaining over part of it by force and the other part by the voluntary capitulation of the inhabitants.

September 12, Monday

Erigyius also arrived here with the baggage and waggons;

September 14, Wednesday

and soon after Artabazus[466] came to Alexander with three of his sons, Cophen, Ariobarzanes, and Arsames, accompanied by Autophradates, viceroy of Tapuria, and envoys from the Grecian mercenaries in the service of Darius.

September 17, Saturday

To Autophradates he restored his viceregal office; but Artabazus and his sons he kept near himself in a position of honour, both on account of their fidelity to Darius and because they were among the first nobles of Persia. To the envoys from the Greeks, begging him to make a truce with them on behalf of the whole mercenary force, he replied that he would not make any agreement with them; because they were acting with great guilt in serving as soldiers on the side of the barbarians against Greece, in contravention of the resolution of the Greeks. He commanded them to come in a body and surrender, leaving it to him to treat them as he pleased, or to preserve themselves as best they could. The envoys said that they yielded both themselves and their comrades to Alexander, and urged him to send some one with them to act as their leader, so that they might be conducted to him with safety. They said they were 1,500 in number. Accordingly he sent Andronicus, son of Agerrhus, and Artabazus to them.

September 22, Thursday
Commencement of march Against the Mardians west along the Caspian shoreline

Chapter 80: Expedition against the Mardians

He then marched forward against the Mardians[467] taking with him the shield-bearing guards, the archers, the Agrianians, the brigades of Coenus and Amyntas, half of the Companion cavalry, and the horse-lancers; for he had now a troop of horse-lancers.
Traversing the greater part of the land of the Mardians, he killed many of them in their flight, some indeed having turned to defend themselves; and many were taken prisoners. No one for a long time had invaded their land in a hostile manner, not only on account of its ruggedness, but also because the people were poor, and besides being poor were warlike. Therefore they never feared that Alexander would attack them, especially as he had already advanced, further than their country. For this reason they were caught more easily off their guard. Many of them, however, escaped into the mountains, which in their land are very lofty and craggy, thinking that Alexander would not penetrate to these at any rate.

{The Mardians likely correspond to the Mazandaranians or people of Mazandaran; an area that sources based on Cleitarcus was near the shore line of the Caspian sea and west of Hyrcania. The Babylonian Astronomial

Diaries suggest that in October Alexander was in the eastern land of Uzuianu, which the author hypothesises may be Zanjan)

October 29, Saturday
Pardoning the Mardians

But when he was approaching them even here, they sent envoys to surrender both the people and their land to him. He pardoned them, and appointed Autophradates, whom he had also recently placed over the Tapurians, viceroy over them.

{possibly occured in central Mazandaran, corresponding to the area of Mount Alam in the Alborz mountain range of Mazandaran Province that form a peak of the Takht-e Suleyman Massif}

November 17, Thursday

Returning to the camp, from which he had started to invade the country of the Mardians, he found that the Grecian mercenaries of Darius had arrived, accompanied by the envoys from the Lacedaemonians who were on an embassy to king Darius. The names of these men were, Callicratidas, Pausippus, Monimus, Onomas, and Dropides, a man from Athens. These were arrested and kept under guard; but he released the envoys from the Sinopeans,[468] because these people had no share in the commonwealth of the Greeks; and as they were in subjection to the Persians, they did not seem to be doing anything unreasonable in going on an embassy to their own king. He also released the rest of the Greeks who were serving for pay with the Persians before the peace and alliance which had been made by the Greeks with the Macedonians. He likewise released Heraclides, the ambassador from the Chalcedonians[469] to Darius. The rest he ordered to serve in his army for the same pay as they had received from the Persian king, putting them under the command of Andronicus, who had led them, and had evidently been taking prudent measures to save the lives of the men.

Chapter 81: March to Bactra — Bessus Aided by Satibaezanes

Having settled these affairs, he marched

December 05, Monday
Return to Zadracarta

to Zadracarta, the largest city of Hyrcania, where also was the seat of the Hyrcanian government. Tarrying here fifteen **day**s,

{Zadracarta is possibly Gorgan in modern day Iran. He returned here as he was here before.}

December 20, Tuesday

he offered sacrifice to the gods according to his custom, and celebrated a gymnastic contest,

{Possibly at the winter solstice that is on this date in 330 BC. He repeatedly did this in previous years}

December 22, Thursday
Leaves Zadracarta

after which he began his march towards Parthia;

December 30, Friday
Passes Areia

thence to the confines of Areia[470]

{quite possibly in the area of Esfarayen in modern day Khorasan Province

Iran, considered a focal point for Aryan tribes in Iran. This is approximately 360km from Gorgan}

329 BC (LEAP YEAR)

January 04, Wednesday
Arrives at Susia

and to Susia, a city in that province, where Satibarzanes, the viceroy of the Areians, came to meet him. To this man he restored his viceregal dignity, and with him sent Anaxippus, one of the Companions, to whom he gave forty horse-lancers so that he might be able to station them as guards of the localities, in order that the Areians might not be injured by the army in its march through their land. At this time came to him some Persians, who informed him that Bessus had assumed the erect tiara[471] and was wearing the Persian dress,[472] calling himself Artaxerxes instead of Bessus, and asserting that he was king of Asia. They said he had in attendance upon him the Persians who had escaped into Bactra and many of the Bactrians themselves; and that he was expecting the Scythians also to come to him as allies.

{Susia corresponds to Tus/ Tous in Khorasan Province of modern day Iran. The distance between Zadacarta and Susia is approximately 566km – minimum 14 day march}

January 06, Friday
Leaves Susia

Alexander, having now all his forces together, went towards Bactra, where Philip son of Menelaüs came to him out of Media with the Greek mercenary cavalry which were under his own command, those of the

Thessalians who had volunteered to remain, and the men of Andromachus. Nicanor, the son of Parmenio, the commander of the shield-bearing guards, had already died of disease.

January 07, Saturday

While Alexander was on his way to Bactra, he was informed that Satibarzanes, viceroy of Areia, had killed Anaxippus and the horse-lancers who were with him, had armed the Areians and collected them in the city of Artacoana, which was the capital of that nation. It was also said that he had resolved, as soon as he ascertained that Alexander had advanced, to leave that place and go with his forces to Bessus, with the intention of joining that prince in an attack upon the Macedonians, wherever a chance might occur. When he received this news, he stopped the march towards Bactra, and taking with him the Companion cavalry, the horse-lancers, the archers, the Agrianians and the regiments of Amyntas and Coenus, and leaving the rest of his forces there under the command of Craterus, he made a forced march against Satibarzanes and the Areians;

January 09, Monday

and having travelled 600 stades in two days came near Artacoana. Satibarzanes, however, no sooner perceived that Alexander was near, than being struck with terror at the quickness of his arrival, he took to flight with a few Areian horsemen. For he was deserted by the majority of his soldiers in his flight, when they also learned that Alexander was at hand.

January 10, Tuesday

The latter made rapid marches in pursuit of the enemy, killed some of the men whom he discovered to be guilty of the revolt and who at that time had left their villages, fleeing, some one way, some another; and others of them he sold into slavery. He then proclaimed Arsames, a Persian, viceroy over the Areians. Being now joined by the men who had been left behind with Oraterus,

January 21, Saturday

he marched into the land of the Zarangaeans,[473]

{also known as Zarangiana or Drangiana, an area corresponding to Lake Hāmūn (or Daryācheh-ye Hāmūn) at the Irano-Afghan border, approximately 400miles from modern Tous or ancient Susia}

January 24, Tuesday

and reached the place where their seat of government was. But Barsaentes, who at that time had possession of the land, being one of those who had fallen upon Darius in his flight, learning that Alexander was approaching, fled to the Indians who live this side of the river Indus. But they arrested him and sent him back to Alexander, by whom he was put to death on account of his guilty conduct towards Darius.

{The capital city of Zarangiana likely corresponds to the archaeological site of Dahan-e-Gholaman or Dahaneh-e-Gholaman ("Gateway of the Slaves"), approximately 30 km southeast of Zabol in Iran near the modern day Iran-Afghanistan border }

January 25, Wednesday

Chapter 82: Philotas and Parmenio put to Death

Here also Alexander discovered the conspiracy of Philotas, son of Parmenio. Ptolemy and Aristobiilus say that it had already been reported to him before in Egypt[474]; but that it did not appear to him credible, both on account of the long- existing friendship between them, the honour which he publicly conferred upon his father Parmenio, and the confidence he reposed in Philotas himself. Ptolemy, son of Lagus, says that Philotas was brought before the Macedonians,[475] that Alexander vehemently accused him, and that he defended himself from the charges. He says also that the divulgers[476] of the plot came forward and convicted him and his accomplices both by other clear proofs and especially because Philotas himself confessed that he had heard of a certain conspiracy which was being formed against Alexander. He was convicted of having said nothing to the king about this plot, though he visited the royal tent twice a day.[477]

He and all the others who had taken part with him in the conspiracy were killed by the Macedonians with their javelins;[478] and Polydamas, one of the Companions, was despatched to Parmenio, carrying letters from Alexander to the generals in Media, Oleander, Sitalces, and Menidas, who had been placed over the army commanded by Parmenio. By these men Parmenio was put to death, perhaps because Alexander deemed it incredible that Philotas should conspire against him and Parmenio not participate in his son's plan; or perhaps, he thought that even if he had no share in it, he would now be a dangerous man if he survived, after the king had violently made away with his son. Moreover he was held in very great respect both by Alexander himself and by all the army, having great influence not only among the Macedonian troops but also among the Grecian auxiliaries, whom lie often used to command according to Alexander's order, both in his own turn and out of his turn, with his sovereign's approbation and satisfaction.[479]

January 26, Thursday

Chapter 83: Treatment of Amyntas — The Ariaspians

They also say that about the same time Amyntas, son of Andromenes, was brought to trial, together with his brothers Polemo, Attains, and Simmias, on the charge of being accessory to the conspiracy against Alexander, on account of their trust in Philotas and their intimate friendship with him. The belief in their participation in the plot was strengthened among the mass of men by the fact that when Philotas was arrested, Polemo, one of the brothers of Amyntas, fled to the enemy. But Amyntas with his other two brothers stayed to await the trial, and defended himself so vigorously among the Macedonians that he was declared innocent of the charge. As soon as he was acquitted in the assembly, he demanded that permission should be given him to go to his brother and bring him back to Alexander. To this the Macedonians acceded; so he went away and on the same day brought Polemo back. On this account he now seemed free from guilt much more than ' before. But soon after, as he was besieging a certain village, he was shot with an arrow and died of the wound; so that he derived no other advantage from his acquittal except that of dying with an unsullied reputation.[480]

Alexander appointed two commanders over the Companion cavalry, Hephaestion, son of Amyntor, and Clitus, son of Dropidas, dividing the brigade of the Companions into two parts, because he did not wish any one of his friends to have the sole command of so many horsemen, especially as they were the best of all his cavalry, both in public estimation and in martial discipline.[481]

January 28, Saturday

He now arrived in the land of the people formerly called Ariaspians, but afterwards named Euergetae, because they assisted Cyrus, son of Cambyses, in his invasion of Scythia.[482] Alexander treated these people, whose ancestors had been serviceable to Cyrus, with honour; and when he ascertained that the men not only enjoyed a form of government unlike that of the other barbarians in that part of the world, but laid claim to justice equally with the best of the Greeks, he set them free, and gave them besides as much of the adjacent country as they asked for themselves; but they did not ask for much. Here he offered sacrifice to Apollo, and arrested Demetrius, one of his confidential body-guards, on suspicion of having been implicated with Philotas in the conspiracy. Ptolemy, son of Lagus, was appointed to the post vacated by Demetrius.

{February 02, Thursday Alexander hears that Satibarzanes had defected to Bessus in Aria so that a force was sent against him}

March 28, Wednesday
Leaves Euergetae after 60 days according to Strabo

Chapter 84: Alexander Crosses the Hindu-Koosh

After the transaction of this business, he advanced against Bactra and Bessus,

{Bactra corresponds to the city of Balkh in Afghanistan; also known as Zariaspa in the ancient world associated with the location where Zoroaster first preached his religion.}

March 30, Friday

reducing the Drangians

{Drangiana or Zarangiana (Old Western Iranian: Zranka corresponds to the area of Hamun Lake and the Sistan Basin on the Irano-Afghan-Pakistan border. This is in the region of Zabol, where the legendary Persian Hero Rostam and his line originated according to the Persian Epic of Kings; the Shahnameh}

April 01, Sunday

and Gadrosians[483] to subjection on his march.

{Gadrosia is likely different to the Gedrosia (in Blauchistan on the Iran-Pakistan border) later on in Alexander's journey and is likely much further north in the southern Farah region of Afghanistan, approximately 80 miles north of Zabol}

April 03, Tuesady

He also reduced the Arachosians to subjection and appointed Menon viceroy over them.

April 04, Wednesday

He then reached the Indians, who inhabit the land bordering on that of the Arachosians. All these nations he reached marching through deep snow and his soldiers experiencing scarcity of provisions and severe hardship. Learning that the Areians had again revolted, in consequence of Satibarzanes invading their land with 2,000 cavalry, which he had received from Bessus, he despatched against them Artabazus the Persian with Erigyius and Caranus two of the Companions, also ordering Phrataphernea, viceroy of the Parthians, to assist them in attacking the Areians. An obstinately contested battle then took place between the troops of Erigyius and Caranus and those of Satibarzanes; nor did the barbarians give way until Satibarzanes, encountering Erigyius, was struck in the face with a spear and killed. Then the barbarians gave way and fled with headlong speed.

April 05, Thursday

Meantime Alexander was leading his army towards Mount Caucasus,[484] where he founded a city and named it Alexandreia.[485]

{Mount Caucasus is likely in the area west of Farah (approximately 300 miles west), approaching the far western Hindu Kush in the Bayan Mountain Range leading up to the Kowtal Pass (Kowtal-e Kermu) and just south of the Baba Mountain Range and west of the Foladi peak (Shah Fuladi) or the nearby area of Band-e-Amir national park. This area considered the Afghanistan's 'Grand Canyon' would offer an ideal area for a new city in view of its multiple water supplies and strategic location within the mountain range. Some scholars feel that this may also have been Alexandria in the Caucasus and corresponds to an area near Begram, sited north of Kabul in modern day Afghanistan, though this does not fit here in this chronology.}

April 07, Saturday

Having offered sacrifice here to the gods to whom it was his custom to sacrifice,

April 08, Sunday
(Evening Setting of the Pleiades / last visibility, date suggested by Strabo)

he crossed Mount Caucasus, after appointing Proexes, a Persian, viceroy over the land, and leaving Neiloxenus son of Satyrus, one of the Companions, with an army as superintendent. According to the account of Aristobulus, Mount Caucasus is as lofty as any in Asia, and most of it is bare, at any rate in that part where Alexander crossed it. This range of mountains stretches out so far that they say even that Mount Taurus, which forms the boundary of Cilicia and Pamphylia, springs from it, as do other great ranges which have been distinguished from the Caucasus by various names according to the position of each, Aristobulus says that in this part of the Caucasus nothing grew except terebinth trees and silphium;[486] notwithstanding which, it was inhabited by many people, and many sheep and oxen graze there; because sheep are very fond of silphium. For if a sheep smells it even from a distance, it runs to it and feeds upon the flower. They also dig up the root, which is devoured by the sheep. For this reason in Gyrene,[487] some drive their flocks as far as possible away from the places where their silphium is growing; others even enclose the place with a fence, so that even if the sheep should approach it they would not be able to get within the enclosure. For the silphium is very valuable to the Cyrenaeans.

Bessus, accompanied by the Persians who had taken part with him in the seizure of Darius, and by 7,000 of the Bactrians themselves and the Daans who dwelt on this side the Tanais,[488] was laying waste the country at the foot of Mount Caucasus, in order to prevent Alexander from marching any further, both by the desolation of the land between the enemy and himself and by the lack of provisions. But none the less did Alexander keep up the march, though with difficulty, both on account of the deep snow and from the want of necessaries; but yet he persevered in his journey. When Bessus was informed that Alexander was now not far off, he crossed the river Oxus,[489] and having burnt the boats upon which he had crossed, he withdrew to Nautaca[490] in the land of Sogdiana. He was followed by Spitamenes and Oxyartes, with the cavalry from Sogdiana, as well as by the Daans from the Tanais. But the Bactrian cavalry, perceiving that, Bessus had resolved to take to flight, all dispersed in various directions to their own abodes.

April 21, Saturday
(16 days after The designation of Alexandria on the Caucasus according to sources derived from Cleitarchus)

Chapter 85: Conquest of Bactria, and Pursuit of Bessus across the Oxus

Alexander now arrived at Drapsaca, and having there given his army a rest,

{Drapsaca may correspond with the city of Kunduz in modern day Afghanistan}

May 03, Thursday

he marched

May 09, Wednesday

to Aornus and

{The location of Aornos is not clear but has been associated to an area at Pir Sar at the Upper Indus river or Mount Ilam (Elum Ghar) between Swat and Bunir regions in Pakistan}

May 27, Sunday

Bactra, which are the largest cities in the land of the Bactrians.

These he took at the first assault; and left a garrison in the citadel of Aornus, over which he placed Archelaüs son of Androcles, one of the Companions. He appointed Artabazus the Persian, viceroy over the rest of the Bactrians, who were easily reduced to submission.

{Bactra corresponds to the city of Balkh in Afghanistan; also known as Zariaspa in the ancient world associated with the location where Zoroaster first preached his religion.}

June 06, Wednesday

Then he marched towards the river Oxus, which flows from mount Caucasus, and is the largest of all the rivers in Asia which Alexander and his army reached, except the Indian rivers; but the Indian rivers are the largest in the world. The Oxus discharges its water into the great sea which is near Hyrcania.

June 10, Sunday
On the banks of the Oxus [possibly in Qarqin in modern Afghanistan where the Oxus is narrow]

When he attempted to cross the river it appeared altogether impassable; for its breadth was about six stades, and its depth was much greater than the proportion of its breadth. The bed of the river was sandy, and the stream so rapid, that stakes fixed deep into the bottom were easily rooted up from the earth by the mere force of the current, inasmuch as they could not be securely fixed in the sand. Besides this, there was a scarcity of timber in the locality, and he thought it would take a long time and cause great delay, if they brought from a distance the materials needful for making a bridge over the river.

{Qarqin is approximately 120km from Balkh}

June 11, Monday

Therefore he collected the skins which the soldiers used for tentcoverings, and ordered them to be filled with chaff as dry as possible, and tied and stitched tightly together, so that the water might not penetrate into them.[491]

June 16, Saturday
Crossing the Oxus

When these were filled and stitched together, they were sufficient to convey the army across in five days. But before he crossed the river, he selected the oldest of the Macedonians, who were now unfit for military service, and such of the Thessalians as had volunteered to remain in the army, and sent them back home. He then dispatched Stasanor, one of the Companions, into the land of the Areians, with instructions to arrest Arsames, the viceroy of that people, because he thought him disaffected, and to assume the office of viceroy of Areia himself.

June 21, Thursday

After passing over the river Oxus,

June 24, Sunday

he made a forced march to the place where he heard that Bessus was with his forces; but at this time messengers reached him from Spitamenes and Dataphernes, to announce that they would arrest Bessus and hand him over to Alexander if he would send to them a small army and a commander for it; since even at that very time they were holding him under guard, though they had not bound him with fetters. When Alexander heard this, he gave his army rest, and marched more slowly than before. But he despatched Ptolemy, son of Lagus, at the head of three troops of the Companion cavalry and all the horse-lancers, and of the infantry, the brigade of Philotas, one regiment of 1,000 shield-bearing guards, all the Agrianians, and half the archers, with orders to make a forced march to Spitamenes and Dataphernes.

June 28, Thursday
Ptolemy marches toward Spitamenes and Dataphernes

Ptolemy went according to his instructions,, and completing ten days' march in four days, arrived at the camp where on the preceding day the barbarians under Spitamenes had bivouacked.

Chapter 86: Capture of Bessus — Exploits in Sogdiana

Here Ptolemy learned that Spitamenes and Dataphernes were not firmly resolved about the betrayal of Bessus. He therefore left the infantry behind with orders to follow him in regular order,

July 01, Sunday
Ptolemy reaches Bessus

and advanced with the cavalry till he arrived at a certain village, where Bessus was with a few soldiers for Spitamenes and his party had already retired from thence, being ashamed to betray Bessus themselves. Ptolemy posted his cavalry right round the village, which was enclosed by a wall supplied with gates. He then issued a proclamation to the barbarians in the village, that they would be allowed to depart uninjured if they surrendered Bessus to him. They accordingly admitted Ptolemy and his men into the village. He then seized Bessus

July 02, Monday
Ptolemy transports Bessus to Alexander

and departed; but sent a messenger on before to ask Alexander how he was to conduct Bessus into his presence. Alexander ordered him to bind the prisoner naked in a wooden collar, and thus to lead him and place him on the righthand side of the road along which he was about to march with the army. Thus did Ptolemy.

July 05, Thursday
Bessus presented to Alexander

When Alexander saw Bessus, he caused his chariot to stop, and asked him, for what reason he had in the first place arrested Darius, his own king, who was also his kinsman and benefactor, and then led him as a prisoner in chains, and at last killed him? Bessus said that he was not the only person who had decided to do this, but that it was the joint act of those who were at the time in attendance upon Darius, with the view of procuring safety for themselves from Alexander. For this Alexander ordered that he should be scourged, and that the herald should repeat the very same reproaches which he had himself made to Bessus in his inquiry. After being thus disgracefully tortured, he was sent away to Bactra to be put to death. Such is the account given by Ptolemy in relation to Bessus; but Aristobulus says that Spitamenes and Dataphernes brought Bessus to Ptolemy, and having bound him naked in a wooden collar betrayed him to Alexander.[492]

July 08, Sunday

Alexander supplied his cavalry with horses from that district, for many of his own horses had perished in the passage of the Caucasus and in the march to and from the Oxus.

July 12, Thursday

He then led his army

July 16, Monday
Arrival at Marcanda (Samarkand), a journey of four days according to sources deriving from Cleitarchus

to Maracanda,[493] which is the capital of the land of the Sogdianians.

August 05, Sunday
Arrival at River Tanais (also known as Jaxartes, also known as Syr Darya), a journey of six days according to sources deriving from Cleitarchus

Thence he advanced to the river Tanais. This river, which Aristobulus says the neighbouring barbarians call by a different name, Jaxartes, has its source, like the Oxus, in mount Caucasus, and also discharges itself into the Hyrcanian Sea.[494] It must be a different Tanais from that of which Herodotus the historian speaks, saying that it is the eighth of the Scythian rivers, that it flows out of a great lake in which it originates, and discharges itself into a still larger lake, called the Maeotis.[495] There are some who make this Tanais the boundary of Europe and Asia, saying that the Palus Maeotis, issuing from the furthest recess of the Euxine[496] Sea, and this river Tanais, which discharges itself into the Maeotis, separate Asia and Europe,[497] just in the same way as the sea near Gadeira and the Nomad Libyans opposite Gadeira separates Libya and Europe.[498] Libya also is said by these men to be divided from the rest of Asia by the river Nile.

August 08, Wednesday
Possibly near the Syrdarya are of northern Uzbekistan and close to Atakent in modern Kazakhstan and to Chinaz on the opposite side of the Syr Darya

In this place (viz. at the river Tanais), some of the Macedonians, being engaged in foraging, were cut to pieces by the barbarians. The perpetrators of this deed escaped to a mountain, which was very rugged and precipitous on all sides. In number they were about 30,000.

August 09, Thursday
Alexander injured

Alexander took the lightest men in his army and marched against these. Then the Macedonians made many ineffectual assaults upon the mountain. At first they were beaten back by the missiles of the barbarians, and many of them were wounded, including Alexander himself, who was shot right through the leg with an arrow, and the fibula of his leg was broken. Notwithstanding this, he captured the place, and some of the barbarians were cut to pieces there by the Macedonians, while many also cast themselves down from the rocks and perished; so that out of 30,000 not more than 8,000 were preserved.[499]

August 13, Monday
Arrival of the Abii

Chapter 87 (Start of Book 4): Rebellion of the Sogdianians
A few days after this, envoys reached Alexander from the people called Abian Scythians, whom Homer commended in his poem, calling them the justest of men.[500] This nation dwells in Asia and is independent, chiefly by reason of its poverty and love of justice. Envoys also came from the Scythians of Europe, who are the largest nation dwelling in that continent.[501]

August 16, Thursday

Alexander sent some of the Companions with them, under the pretext indeed that they were to conclude a friendly alliance by the embassy; but the real object of the mission was rather to spy into the natural features of the Scythian land, the number of the inhabitants and their customs, as well as the armaments which they possessed for making military expeditions.[502]

August 18, Saturday

He formed a plan of founding a city near the river Tanais, which was to be named after himself; for the site seemed to him suitable and likely to cause the city to grow to large dimensions. He also thought it would be built in a place which would serve as a favourable basis of operations for an invasion of Scythia, if such an event should ever occur; and not only so, but it would also be a bulwark to secure the land against the incursions of the barbarians dwelling on the further side of the river. Moreover he thought that the city would become great, both by reason of the multitude of those who would join in colonizing it, and on account of the celebrity of the name conferred upon it.[503]

August 20, Monday

Meantime the barbarians dwelling near the river seized upon the Macedonian soldiers who were garrisoning their cities and killed them; after which they began to strengthen the cities for their greater security.

August 25, Saturday

Most of the Sogdianians joined them in this revolt, being urged on to it by the men who had arrested, Bessus. These men were so energetic that they even induced some of the Bactrians to join in the rebellion, either because they were afraid of Alexander, or because their seducers assigned as a reason for their revolt, that he had sent instructions to the rulers of that land to assemble for a conference at Zariaspa, the chief city; which conference, they said, would be for no good purpose.[504].

August 27, Monday

Chapter 88: Capture of Five Cities in Two Days

When Alexander was informed of this, he gave instructions to the infantry, company by company, to prepare the ladders which were assigned to each company.

August 29, Wednesday

He then started from the camp and advanced to the nearest city, the name of which was Gaza; for the barbarians of the land were said to have fled for refuge into seven cities. He sent Craterus to the one called Cyropolis, the largest of them all, into which most of the barbarians had gathered.[505] The orders of Craterus were to encamp near the city, to dig a trench round it, to surround it with a stockade, and to fix together the military engines which were required for use, so that the men in this city, having had their attention drawn to his forces,/ might be unable to render aid to the other cities.

As soon as Alexander arrived at Gaza, without any delay he gave the signal to his men to place the ladders against the wall all round and to take it by assault at once, as it was made merely of earth and was not at all high. Simultaneously with the assault of the infantry, his slingers, archers, and javelin-throwers assailed the defenders on the wall, and missiles were hurled from the military engines, so that the wall was quickly cleared of its defenders by the multitude of the missiles. Then the fixing of the ladders against the wall and the mounting of the Macedonians were matters soon effected. They killed all the men, according to Alexander's injunctions; but the women, the children, and the rest of the booty they carried off as plunder. Thence he immediately marched to the city situated next to that one; and this he took in the same way and on the same day, treating the captives in the same manner. Then he marched against the third city, and

August 30, Thursday

took it on the next day at the first assault. While he was thus occupied by these matters with the infantry, he sent out his cavalry to the two neighbouring cities, with orders to guard the men within them closely, so that when they heard of the capture of the neighbouring cities, and at the same time of his own near approach, they should not betake themselves to flight and render it impossible for him to pursue them. It turned out just as he had conjectured; and his despatch of the cavalry was made just at the nick of time. For when the barbarians who occupied the two cities still uncaptured, saw the smoke rising from the city in front of them which was then on fire, (and some men, escaping even from the midst of the calamity itself, became the reporters of the capture which they had themselves witnessed,) they began to flee in crowds out of the cities as fast as each man could; but falling in with the dense body of cavalry drawn up in array of battle, most of them were cut to pieces.

{Cyropolis likely corresponds to Khujand in modern daynorthern Tajikistan, approximately 65 miles from Alexander's Camp at the Syr Darya}

August 31, Friday

Chapter 89: Storming of Cyropolis — Revolt of the Scythians

Having thus captured the five cities and reduced them to slavery in two days,[506] he went

September 02, Sunday

to Cyropolis, the largest city in the country. It was fortified with a wall higher than those of the others, as it had been founded by Cyrus. The majority of the barbarians of this district, and at the same time the most warlike of them, had fled for refuge thither, and consequently it was not possible for the Macedonians to capture it so easily at the first assault.

September 03, Monday

Wherefore Alexander brought his military engines up to the wall with the determination of battering it down in this way, and of making assaults wherever breaches might be made in it. When he observed that the channel of the river, which flows through the city when it is swollen by the winter rains, was at that time nearly dry and did not reach up to the wall, and would thus afford his soldiers a passage by which to penetrate into the city, he took the body-guards, the shield-bearing guards, the, archers, and Agrianians, and made his way secretly into the city along the channel, at first with a few men, while the barbarians had turned their attention towards the military engines and those who were assailing them in that quarter. Having from within broken open the gates which were opposite this position, he gave an easy admittance to the rest of his soldiers. Then the barbarians, though they perceived that their city was already in the hands of the enemy, nevertheless turned against Alexander and his men and made a desperate assault upon them, in which Alexander himself received a violent blow on the head and neck with a stone, and Craterus was wounded with an arrow, as were also many other officers. Notwithstanding this, however, they drove the barbarians out of the market-place. Meantime, those who had made the assault upon the wall, took it, as it was now void of defenders. In the first capture of the city about 8,000 of the enemy were killed. The rest fled for refuge into the citadel; for 15,000 warriors in all had gathered together in the city.

September 04, Tuesday

Alexander encamped around these and besieged them for one day,[507] and

September 05, Wednesday

then they surrendered through lack of water.

September 10, Monday

The seventh city he took at the first assault. Ptolemy says that the men in it surrendered; but Aristobulus asserts that this city was also taken by storm, and that he slew all who were captured therein. Ptolemy also says that he distributed the men among the army and ordered that they should be kept guarded in chains until he should depart from the country, so that none of those who had effected the revolt should be left behind.

September 13, Thursday

Meantime an army of the Asiatic Scythians arrived at the bank of the river Tanais, because most of them had heard that some of the barbarians on the opposite side of the river had revolted from Alexander. They intended to attack the Macedonians, if any revolutionary movement worthy of consideration were effected.

September 14, Friday

News was also brought that Spitamenes was besieging the men who had been left in the citadel at Maracanda. Against him Alexander then despatched Andromachus, Menedemus, and Caranus with sixty of the Companion cavalry, 800 of the mercenary cavalry under the command of Caranus, and 1,500 mercenary infantry. Over them he placed Pharnuches the interpreter, who, though by birth a Lycian, was skilled in the language of the barbarians of this country, and in other respects appeared clever in dealing with them.

September 15, Saturday
Beginning of building a new City of Alexandria near the Tanais River (Syr Darya) known as Alexandria Eschate or 'the farthest Alexandria' possibly near Chinaz and Olmazor in Uzbekistan

Chapter 90: Defeat of the Scythians beyond the Tanais

October 05, Friday

In twenty days he fortified the city which he was projecting, and settled in it some of the Grecian mercenaries and those of the neighbouring barbarians who volunteered to take part in the settlement, as well as the Macedonians from his army who were now unfit for military service.[508]

October 07, Sunday

He then offered sacrifice to the gods in his customary manner and celebrated an equestrian and gymnastic contest.

October 09, Tuesday

When he saw that the Scythians were not retiring from the river's bank, but were seen to be shooting arrows into the river, which was not wide here, and were uttering audacious words in their barbaric tongue to insult

Alexander, to the effect that he durst not touch Scythians, or if he did, he would learn what was the difference between them and the Asiatic barbarians, he was irritated by these remarks, and having resolved to cross over against them, he began to prepare the skins for the passage of the river.[509] But when he offered sacrifice with a view to crossing, the victims proved to be unfavourable; and though he was vexed at this, he nevertheless controlled himself and remained where he was.

October 10, Wenesday

But as the Scythians did not desist from their insults, he again offered sacrifice with a view to crossing; and Aristander told him that the omens still portended danger to himself. But Alexander said that it was better for him to come into extreme danger than that, after having subdued almost the whole of Asia, he should be a laughing-stock to the Scythians, as Darius, the father of Xerxes, had been in days of yore.[510] Aristander refused to explain the will of the gods contrary to the revelations made by the deity simply because Alexander wished to hear the contrary.

October 14, Sunday

When the skins had been prepared for the passage, and the army, fully equipped, had been posted near the river, the military engines, at the signal preconcerted, began to shoot at the Scythians riding along the river's bank. Some of them were wounded by the missiles, and one was struck right through the wicker-shield and breastplate and fell from his horse. The others, being alarmed at the discharge of missiles from so great a distance, and at the death of their champion, retreated a little from the bank. But Alexander, seeing them thrown into confusion by the effect of his missiles, began to cross the river with trumpets sounding, himself leading the way; and the rest of the army followed him. Having first got the archers and slingers across, he ordered them to sling and shoot at the Scythians, to prevent them approaching the phalanx of infantry stepping out of the water, until all his cavalry had passed over. When they were upon the bank in dense mass, he first of all launched against the Scythians one regiment of the Grecian auxiliary cavalry and four squadrons of pike-men. These the Scythians received, and in great numbers riding round them in circles, wounded them, as they were few in number, themselves escaping with ease. But Alexander mixed the archers, the Agrianians, and other light troops under the command of Balacrus, with the cavalry, and then led them against the enemy. As soon as they came to close quarters, he ordered three regiments of the cavalry Companions and all the horse-lancers to charge them. The rest of the cavalry he himself led, and made a rapid attack with his squadrons in column. Accordingly the enemy were no longer able as before to wheel their cavalry force round in circles, for at one and the same time the cavalry and the light-armed infantry mixed with the horsemen pressed upon them, and did not permit them to wheel about in safety. Then the flight of the Scythians was already apparent. 1,000 of them fell, including Satraces, one of their chiefs; and 150 were captured. But as the pursuit was keen and fatiguing on account of the excessive heat, the entire army was seized with thirst; and Alexander himself while riding drank of such water as was procurable in that country. He was seized with an incessant diarrhoea; for the water was bad; and for this reason he could not pursue all the Scythians. Otherwise I think all of them would have perished in the flight, if Alexander had not fallen ill. He was carried back to the camp, having fallen into extreme danger; and thus Aristander's prophecy was fulfilled.

October 17, Wednesday

Chapter 91: Spitamenes Destroys a Macedonian Detachment

Soon after this, arrived envoys from the king of the Scythians, who were sent to apologize for what had been done, and to state that it was not the act of the Scythian State, but of certain men who set out for plunder after the manner of freebooters. They also assured him that their king was willing to obey the commands laid upon him. Alexander sent to him a courteous reply, because it did not seem honourable for him to abstain from marching against him if he distrusted him, and at that time there was not a convenient opportunity to do so.

October 20, Saturday

The Macedonians who were garrisoning the citadel at Maracanda, when an assault was made upon it by Spitamenes and his adherents, sallied forth, and killing some of the enemy and repulsing all the rest, retreated into the citadel without any loss.

October 31, Wednesday
Some of Alexander's troops race back to Samarkand

But when Spitamenes was informed that the men despatched by Alexander to Maracanda were now drawing near, he raised the siege of the citadel, and retired to the capital of Sogdiana.[511] Pharnuches and the generals with him, being eager to drive him out altogether, followed him up as he was retreating towards the frontiers of Sogdiana, and without due consideration made a joint attack upon the Nomad Scythians.

{Samarkand is approximately 240km or 6 days fast march from Chinaz}

November 02, Friday

Then Spitamenes, having received a reinforcement of 600 Scythian horsemen, was further emboldened by the Scythian alliance to wait and receive the Macedonians who were advancing upon him.

November 03, Saturday
Loss of Alexander's men at Samarkand's Zarafshan River

Posting his men in a level place near the Scythian desert, he was not willing either to wait for the enemy or to attack them himself; but rode round and discharged arrows at the phalanx of infantry. When the forces of Pharnuches made a charge upon them, they easily escaped, since at that time their horses were swifter and more vigorous, while the horse of Andromachus had been damaged by the incessant marching, as well as by lack of fodder; and the Scythians pressed upon them with all their might whether they halted or retreated. Many of them then were wounded by the arrows, and some were killed. They therefore arranged the soldiers into the form of a square and proceeded to the river Polytimetus,[512] because there was a woody glen near it, and it would consequently no longer be easy for the barbarians to shoot arrows at them, and their infantry would be more useful to them. But Caranus, the commander of the cavalry, without communicating with Andromachus, attempted to cross the river in order to put the cavalry in a place of safety on the other side. The infantry followed him without any word of command; their descent into the river being made in a panic and without any discipline down the precipitous banks. When the barbarians perceived the error of the Macedonians, they sprang into the ford here and there, horses and all. Some of them seized and held tight those who had already crossed and were departing; others being posted right in front of those who were crossing, rolled them over into the river; others shot arrows at them from the flanks; while others pressed upon the man who were just entering the water. The Macedonians being thus encompassed with difficulty on all sides, fled for refuge into one of the small islands in the river, where they were entirely surrounded by the Scythians and the cavalry of Spitamenes, and all killed with arrows, except a few of them, whom they reduced to slavery. All of these were afterwards killed.

Chapter 92: Spitamenes Driven into the Desert

But Aristobulus says the greater part of this army was destroyed by an ambuscade, the Scythians having hidden themselves in a park and fallen upon the Macedonians from their place of concealment, when Pharnuches was in the very act of retiring from the command in favour of the Macedonians who had been sent with him, on the ground of his not being skilled in military affairs, and of his having been sent by Alexander rather to win the favour of the barbarians than to take the supreme command in battles. He also alleged that the Macedonian officers present were the king's Companions. But Andromachus, Menedemus, and Caranus declined to accept the chief command, partly because it did not seem right to make any alteration on their own responsibility contrary to Alexander's instructions to them, and partly because in the very crisis of danger, they were unwilling, if they met with any defeat, not only individually to take a share of the blame, but also collectively to exercise the command unsuccessfully. In this confusion and disorder the barbarians fell upon them, and cut them all off, so that not more than forty horsemen and 300 foot preserved their lives.[513]

{The Polytimetus river corresponds to the modern Zarafshan river, previously known as the Sughd}

November 06, Tuesday
Alexander hears of the Zarafshan defeat

When the report of this reached Alexander, he was chagrined at the loss of his soldiers, and resolved to march with all speed against Spitamenes and his barbarian adherents.

November 08, Thursday

He therefore took half of the Companion cavalry, all the shield-bearing guards, the archers, the Agrianians, and the lightest men of the phalanx, and went towards Maracanda, where he ascertained Spitamenes had returned and was again besieging the men in the citadel.

November 10, Saturday

Having travelled 1,500 stades in three days,

{1,500 stades is equivalent to 277.5km, accommodating the complex terrain between the area of Chinaz and Olmazor with Samarkand, this distance fits the journey}

November 11, Sunday

at the approach of dawn on the fourth day he came near the city;[514] but when Spitamenes was informed of Alexander's approach, he did not remain, but abandoned the city and fled.

November 12, Monday

Alexander pursued him closely; and coming to the place where the battle was fought, he buried his soldiers as well as the circumstances permitted,

November 13, Tuesday

and then followed the fugitives

November 15, Thursday

as far as the desert.

November 16, Friday

Returning thence, he laid the land waste, and slew the barbarians who had fled for refuge into the fortified places, because they were reported to have taken part in the attack upon the Macedonians.[515] He traversed the whole country which the river Polytimetus waters in its course; but the country beyond the place where the water of this river disappears is desert; for though it has abundance of water, it disappears into the sand.[516] Other large and perennial rivers in that region disappear in a similar way:—the Epardus, which flows through the land of the Mardians; the Areius, after which the country of the Areians is named; and the Etymander, which flows through the territory of the Euergetae.[517] All of these are rivers of such a size that none of them is smaller than the Thessalian river Peneius, which flows through Tempē and discharges itself into the sea. The Polytimetus is much too large to be compared with the river Peneius.[518]

December 02, Sunday

Chapter 93: Treatment of Bessus.

When he had accomplished this,

December 19, Wednesday
Arrival at Zariaspa (Balkh)

he came to Zariaspa;

{Balkh is approximately 200miles from the Samarakand area. December 19th in 329BC is also the date of the winter solstice on this year}

328 BC

January 09, Wednesday

where he remained until the depth of winter arrived.[519]

January 11, Saturday

At this time came to him Phrataphernes the viceroy of Parthia, and Stasanor, who had been sent into the land of the Areians to arrest Arsames.[520] Him they brought with them in chains, as also Barzanes, whom Bessus had appointed viceroy of the land of the Parthians, and some others of those who at that time had joined Bessus in revolt.

January 14, Monday

At the same time arrived from the sea, Epocillus,[521]Melamnidas and Ptolemy, the general of the Thracians who had convoyed down to the sea the Grecian allies and the money sent with Menes.[522] At this time also arrived Asander and Nearchus at the head of an army of Grecian mercenaries.[523] Asclepiodorus, viceroy of Syria, and Menes the deputy also arrived from the sea, at the head of another army. Then Alexander gathered a conference of those who were then at hand, and led Bessus in before them. Having accused him of the betrayal of Darius, he ordered his nose and ears to be cut off, and that he should be taken to Ecbatana to be put to death there in the council of the Medes and Persians.[524] I do not commend this excessive punishment; on the contrary, I consider that the mutilation of the prominent features of the body is a barbaric[525] custom, and I agree with those who say that Alexander was induced to indulge his desire of emulating the Median and Persian wealth and to treat his subjects as inferior beings according to the custom of the foreign kings. Nor do I by any means commend him for changing the Macedonian style of dress which his fathers had adopted, for the Median one,[526] being as he was a descendant of Heracles.[527] Besides, he was not ashamed to exchange the head-dress which he the conqueror had so long worn, for that of the conquered Persians. None of these things do I commend; but I consider Alexander's great achievements prove, if anything can, that supposing a man to have a vigorous bodily constitution, to be illustrious in descent, and to be even more successful in war than Alexander himself; even supposing he could sail right round Libya as well as Asia, and hold them both in subjection as Alexander indeed designed; even if he could add the possession of Europe to that of Asia and Libya; all these things would be no furtherance to such a man's happiness, unless at the same time he possess the power of self-control, though he has performed the great deeds which have been supposed.

Chapter 94: The Murder of Clitus

Here also I shall give an account of the tragic fate of Clitus, son of Dropidas, and of Alexander's mishap in regard to it. Though it occurred a little while after this, it will not be out place here. The Macedonians kept a day sacred to Dionysus, and on that day Alexander used to offer sacrifice to him every year. But they say that on this occasion he was neglectful of Dionysus,[528]

{Dionysus Day: In ancient Athens this was based at the January/February full moon. In 328BC the first full moon was on the January 24, which may correspond to the Dionysia mentioned here. As a comparison, the ancient Athenian 'Rural Dionysia' (possibly from the early era of farming/ Neolithic times) was around the winter solstice in winter during the month of Posiden between December and January which may correspond to a similar time for Alexander, it should however be noted that there were four Athenian festivals for Dionysis (the Dionysia) including The Anthesteria that was an annual three day festival during the eleventh to thirteenth of the month of Anthesterion which corresponded to the full moon between January and February. The winter solstice was celebrated in Ancient Persia with a tradition that can be witnessed today as the Yalda festival or Shab-e

Yalda/ Shab-e Chelleh. This date may have been a common cultural link between the Macedonians and the Persians. As Alexander had recently celebrated an event around the time of the 329 winter solstice, the events here could correspond to a similar time to that of the Athenian Anthesteria in honour of Dionysis}

February 22, Friday
The Murder of Clitus (A day of a full moon in this year)

and sacrificed to the Dioscūri[529] instead; for he had resolved to offer sacrifice to those deities for some reason or other. When the drinking-party on this occasion had already gone on too long (for Alexander had now made innovations even in regard to drinking, by imitating the custom of foreigners), and in the midst of the carouse a discussion had arisen about the Dioscuri, how their procreation had been taken away from Tyndareus and ascribed to Zeus, some of those present, in order to flatter Alexander, maintained that Polydeaces and Castor were in no way worthy to compare with him who had performed so many exploits. Such men have always corrupted the character of kings and will never cease to ruin the interests of those who happen to be reigning.[530] In their carousal they did not even abstain from (comparing him with) Heracles; saying that envy prevented the living from receiving the honours due to them from their associates. It was well known that Clitus had long been vexed at Alexander for the change in his style of living in imitation of foreign kings, and at those who flattered him with their speech. At that time also, being heated with wine, he would not permit them either to insult the deity or, by depreciating the deeds of the ancient heroes, to confer upon Alexander a gratification which deserved no thanks. He affirmed Alexander's deeds were neither in fact so great or marvellous as they represented in their laudation; nor had he achieved them by himself, but for the most part they were the deeds of the Macedonians. The delivery of this speech annoyed Alexander; and I do not commend it, for I think, in such a drunken bout, it would have been sufficient if, so far as he was personally concerned, he had kept silence, and not committed the error of indulging in the same flattery as the others. But when some even mentioned Philip's actions without exercising a just judgment, declaring that he had performed nothing great or marvellous, they gratified Alexander; but Clitus being then no longer able" to contain himself, began to put Philip's achievements in the first rank, and to depreciate Alexander and his performances.[531] Clitus being now quite intoxicated, made other insolent remarks and even greatly reviled him, because forsooth he had saved his life, when the cavalry battle had been fought with the Persians at the

Granicus. Then indeed, arrogantly stretching out his right hand, he said:—" This hand, Alexander, preserved thee on that occasion." Alexander could now no longer endure the drunken insolence of Clitus; but jumped up against him in a great rage. He was however restrained by his boon-companions. As Clitus did not desist from his insulting remarks, Alexander shouted out a summons for his shieldbearing guards to attend him; but when no one obeyed him, he said that he was reduced to the same position as Darius, when he was led about under arrest by Bessus and his adherents, and that he now possessed the mere name of king. Then his companions were no longer able to restrain him; for according to some he leaped up and snatched a javelin from one of his confidential bodyguards; according to others, a long pike from one of his ordinary guards, with which he struck Clitus and killed him.[532] Aristobulas does not say whence the drunken quarrel originated, but asserts that the fault was entirely on the side of Clitus, who, when Alexander bad got so enraged with him as to jump up against him with the intention of making an end of him, was led away by Ptolemy, son of Lagus, the confidential body-guard, through the gateway, beyond the wall and ditch of the citadel where the quarrel occurred. He adds that Clitus could not control himself, but went back again, and falling in with Alexander who was calling out for Clitus, he exclaimed:— "Alexander, here is Clitus!" Thereupon he was struck with a long pike and killed.

Chapter 95: Alexander's Grief for Clitus

I think Clitus deserving of severe censure for his insolent behaviour to his king, while at the same time I pity Alexander for his mishap, because on that occasion he showed himself the slave of two vices, anger and drunkenness, by neither of which is it seemly for a prudent man to be enslaved. But then on the other hand I think his subsequent behaviour worthy of praise, because directly after he had done the deed he recognised that it was a horrible one. Some of his biographers even say that he propped the pike against the wall with the intention of falling upon it himself, thinking that it was not proper for him to live who had killed his friend when under the influence of wine. Most historians do not mention this, but say that he went off to bed and lay there lamenting, calling Clitus himself by name, and his sister Lanice, daughter of Dropidas, who had been his nurse. He exclaimed that having reached man's estate he had forsooth bestowed on her a noble reward for her care in rearing him, as she lived to see her own sons die fighting on his behalf, and the king slaying her brother with his own hand.[533] He did not cease calling himself the murderer of his friends; and for three days rigidly abstained from food and drink, and paid no attention whatever to his personal appearance. Some of the soothsayers revealed that, the avenging wrath of Dionysus had been the cause of his conduct, because he had omitted the sacrifice to that deity.[534]

February 26, Tuesday

At last with great difficulty he was induced by his companions to touch food and to pay proper attention to his person.[535] He then paid to Dionysus the sacrifice due to him, since he was not at all unwilling to attribute the fatality rather to the avenging wrath of the deity than to his own depravity. I think Alexander deserves great praise for this, that he did not obstinately persevere in evil, or still worse become a defender and advocate of the wrong which had been done, but confessed that he had committed a crime, being a man and not a god. There are some who say that Anaxarchus the Sophist[536] was summoned into Alexander's presence to give him consolation. Finding him lying down and groaning, he laughed at him, and said that he did not know that the wise men of old for this reason made Justice an assessor of Zeus, because whatever was done by him was justly done[537]; and therefore also that which was done by the Great King ought to be deemed just, in the first place by the king himself, and then by the rest of men. They say that Alexander was then greatly consoled by these remarks.[538] But I assert that Anaxarchus did Alexander a great injury and one still greater than that by which he was then oppressed, if he really thought this to be the opinion of a wise man, that forsooth it is proper for a king to come to hasty conclusions and act unjustly, and that whatever is done by a king must be deemed just, no matter how it is done. There is also a current report that Alexander wished men to prostrate themselves before him as to a god, entertaining the notion that Ammon was his father, rather than Philip; and that he now showed his admiration of the customs of the Persians and Medea by changing the style of his dress, and by the alteration he made in the general etiquette of his court. There were not wanting those who in regard to these matters gave way to his wishes with the design of flattering him;" among others being Anaxarchus, one of the philosophers attending his court, and Agia, an Argive who was an epic poet.[539]

March 16, Saturday

Chapter 96: Dispute between Callisthenes and Anaxarchus

But it is said that Callisthenes the Olynthian, who had studied philosophy under Aristotle, and was somewhat brusque in his manner, did not approve of this conduct; and so far as this is concerned I quite agree with him. But the following remark of his, if indeed it has been correctly recorded, I do not think at all proper, when he declared that Alexander and his exploits were dependent upon him and his history, and that he had not come to him to acquire reputation from him, but to make him renowned in the eyes of men;[540] consequently that Alexander's participation in divinity did not depend on the false assertion of Olympias in regard to the author of his birth, but on what he might report to mankind in his history of the king. There are some writers also who have said that on one occasion Philotas forsooth asked him, what man he thought to be held in especial honour by the people of Athens; and that he replied:—"Harmodius and Aristogeiton; because they slew one of the two despots, and put an end to the despotism."[541] Philotas again asked:—"If it happened now that a man should kill a despot, to which of the Grecian States would you wish him to flee for - preservation? " Callisthenes again replied:—" If not among others, at any rate among the Athenians an exile would find preservation; for they waged war on behalf of the sons of Heracles against Burystheus, who at that time was ruling as a despot over Greece."[542] How he resisted Alexander in regard to the ceremony of prostration, the following is the most received account.[543] An arrangement was made between Alexander and the Sophists in conjunction with the most illustrious of the Persians and Medes who were in attendance upon him, that this topic should be mentioned at a wine-party. Anaxarchus commenced the discussion[544] by saying that he considered Alexander much more worthy of being deemed a god than either Dionysus or Heracles, not only on account of the very numerous and mighty exploits which he had performed, but also because Dionysus was only a Theban, in no way related to Macedonians; and Heracles was an Argive, not at all related to them, except that Alexander deduced his descent from him. He added that the Macedonians might with greater justice gratify their king with divine honours, for there was no doubt about this, that when he departed from men they would honour him as a god. How much more just then would it be to worship him while alive, than after his death, when it would be no advantage to him to be honoured.

Chapter 97: Callisthenes Opposes the Proposal to Honour Alexander by Prostration

When Anaxarchus had uttered these remarks and others of a similar kind, those who were privy to the plan applauded his speech, and wished at once to begin the ceremony of prostration. Most of the Macedonians, however, were vexed[545] at the speech and kept silence. But Callisthenes interposed and said:— "O Anaxarchus, I openly declare that there is no honour which Alexander is unworthy to receive, provided that it is consistent with his being human; but men have made distinctions between those honours which are due to men, and those due to gods, in many ifferent ways, as for instance by the building of temples and by the erection of statues. Moreover for the gods sacred enclosures are selected, to them sacrifice is offered, and to them libations are made. Hymns also are composed in honour of the gods, and eulogies for men. But the greatest distinction is made by the custom of prostration. For it is the practice that men should be kissed by those who salute them[546]; but because the deity is located somewhere above, it is not lawful even to touch him, and this is the reason no doubt why he is honoured by prostration. Bands of choral dancers are also appointed for the gods, and paeans are sung in their honour. And this is not at all wonderful, seeing that certain honours are specially assigned to some of the gods and certain others to other gods, and, by Zeus, quite different ones again are assigned to heroes, which are very distinct from those paid to the deities.[547] It is not therefore reasonable to confound all these distinctions without discrimination, exalting men to a rank above their condition by extravagant accumulation of honours, and debasing the gods, as far as lies in human power, to an unseemly level, by paying them honours only equal to those paid to men." He said that Alexander would not endure the affront, if some private individual were to be thrust into his royal honours by an unjust vote, either by show of hand or by ballot. Much more justly then would the gods be indignant at those mortals who usurp divine honours or suffer themselves to be thrust into them by others. "Alexander not only seems to be, but is in reality beyond any competition the bravest of brave men, of kings the most kingly, and of generals the most worthy to command an army. Anaxarchus, it was thy duty, rather than any other man's, to become the special advocate of these arguments now adduced by me, and the opponent of those contrary to them, seeing that thou associatest with him for the purpose of imparting philosophy and instruction. Therefore it was unseemly to begin this discussion, when thou oughtest to have remembered that thou art not associating with and giving advice to Cambyses or Xerxes, but to the son of Philip, who derives his origin from Heracles and Aeacus,[548] whose ancestors came to Macedonia from Argos, and have continued to rule the Macedonians, not by force, but by law. Not even to Heracles himself while still alive were divine honours paid by the Greeks; and even after his death they were withheld until a decree had been published by the oracle of the god at Delphi that men should honour Heracles as a god. But if, because the discussion is held[549] in the land of foreigners, we ought to adopt the sentiments of foreigners, I demand, Alexander, that thou shouldst bethink thyself of Greece, for whose sake the whole of this expedition was undertaken by thee, that thou mightest join Asia to Greece. Therefore make up thy mind whether thou wilt return thither and compel the Greeks, who are men most devoted to freedom, to pay thee the honour of prostration, or whether thou wilt keep aloof from Greece, and inflict this honour on the Macedonians alone, or thirdly whether thou wilt thyself make a difference in every respect as to the honours to be paid thee, so as to be honoured by the Greeks and Macedonians as a human being and after the manner of the Greeks, and by foreigners alone after the foreign fashion of prostration. But if it is said that Cyrus, son of Cambyses, was the first man to whom the honour of prostration was paid, and that afterwards this degrading ceremony continued in vogue among the Persians and Medes, we ought to bear in mind that the Scythians, men poor but independent, chastised that Cyrus;[550] that other Scythians again chastised Darius, as the Athenians and Lacedaemonians did Xerxes, as Clearchus and Xenophon with their 10,000 followers did Artaxerxes; and finally, that Alexander, though not honoured with prostration, has conquered this Darius."

Chapter 98: Callisthenes Refuses to Prostrate Himself

By making these and other remarks of a similar kind, Callisthenes greatly annoyed Alexander, but spoke the exact sentiments of the Macedonians. When the king perceived this, he sent to prevent the Macedonians from making any farther mention of the ceremony of prostration. But after the discussion silence ensued; and then the most honourable of the Persians arose in due order and prostrated their bodies before him. But when one of the Persians seemed to have performed the ceremony in an awkward way, Leonnatus, one of the Companions, laughed at his posture as mean. Alexander at the time was angry with him for this,

March 20, Wednesday
Date of the Vernal Equinox in 328 BC

but was afterwards reconciled to him.[551] The following account has also been given:— Alexander drank from a golden goblet the health of the circle of guests, and handed it first to those with whom he had concerted the ceremony of prostration. The first who drank from the goblet rose up and perforated the act of prostration, and received a kiss from him. This ceremony proceeded from one to another in due order. But when the pledging of health came to the turn of Callisthenes, he rose up and drank from the goblet, and drew near, wishing to kiss the king without performing the act of prostration. Alexander happened then to be conversing with

Hephaestion, and consequently did not observe whether Callisthenes performed the ceremony properly or not. But when Callisthenes was approaching to kiss him, Demetrius, son of Pythouax, one of the Companions, said that he was doing so without having prostrated himself. So the king would not permit him to kiss him; whereupon the philosopher said:—"I am going away only with the loss of a kiss." I by no means approve any of these proceedings, which manifested both the insolence of Alexander on the present occasion and the churlish nature of Callisthenes. But I think that, so far as regards himself, it would have been quite sufficient if he had given his opinion discreetly, magnifying as much as possible the exploits of the king, with whom no one thought it a dishonour to associate. Therefore I consider that not without reason Callisthenes became odious to Alexander on account of the unseasonable freedom of speech in which he indulged,[552] as well as from the egregious fatuity of his conduct. I surmise that this was the reason why such easy credit was given to those who accused him of participating in the conspiracy formed against Alexander by his pages, and to those also who affirmed that they had been incited to engage in the conspiracy by him alone. The facts of this conspiracy were as follows:—

Chapter 99: Conspiracy of the Pages

It was a custom introduced by Philip, that the sons of those Macedonians who had enjoyed high office, should, as soon as they reached the age of puberty, be selected to attend the king's court. These youths were entrusted with the general attendance on the king's person and the protection of his body while he was asleep. Whenever the king rode out, some of them received the horses from the grooms, and brought them to him, and others assisted him to mount in the Persian fashion. They were also companions of the king in the emulation of the chase.[553] Among these youths was Hermolaus, son of Sopolis, who seemed to be applying his mind to the study of philosophy, and to be cultivating the society of Callisthenes for this purpose. There is current a tale about this youth to the effect that in the chase, a boar rushed at Alexander, and that Hermolaus anticipated him by casting a javelin at the beast, by which it was smitten and killed. But Alexander, having lost the opportunity of distinguishing himself by being too late in the assault, was indignant with Hermolaus, and in his wrath ordered him to receive a scourging in sight of the other pages; and also deprived him of his horse.

This Hermolaus, being chagrined at the disgrace he had incurred, told Sostratus son of Amyntas, who was his equal in age and intimate confidential friend, that life would be insupportable to him unless he could take vengeance upon Alexander for the affront. He easily persuaded

Sostratus to join in the enterprise, since he was fondly attached to him.

They gained over to their plans Antipater, son of Asclepiodorus, viceroy of Syria, Epimenes son of Arseas, Anticles son of Theocritus, and Philotas son of Carsis the Thracian. They therefore agreed to kill the king by attacking him in his sleep, on the night when the nocturnal watch came round to Antipater's turn.

Some say that Alexander accidentally happened to be drinking

until day-break; but Aristobulus has given the following account: A Syrian woman, who was under the inspiration of the deity, used to follow Alexander about. At first she was a subject of mirth to Alexander and his courtiers; but when all that she said in her inspiration was seen to be true, he no longer treated her with neglect, but she was allowed to have free access to him both by night and day, and she often took her stand near him even when he was asleep. And indeed on that occasion, when he was withdrawing from the drinking-party she met him, being under the inspiration of the deity at the time, and besought him to return and drink all night. Alexander, thinking that there was something divine in the warning, returned and went on drinking; and thus the enterprise of the pages fell through.[554]

The next day, Epimenes son of Arseas, one of those who took part in the conspiracy, spoke of the undertaking to Charicles son of Menander, who had become his confidential friend; and Charicles told it to Eurylochus, brother of Epimenes. Eurylochus went to Alexander's tent and related the whole affair to Ptolemy son of Lagus, one of the confidential body-guards. He told Alexander, who ordered those whose names had been mentioned by Eurylochus to be arrested. These, being put on the rack, confessed their own conspiracy, and mentioned the names of certain others.

Chapter 100: Execution of Callisthenes and Hermolaus

Aristobulus says that the youths asserted it was Callisthenes who instigated them to make the daring attempt; and Ptolemy says the same.[555] Most writers, however, do not agree with this, but represent that Alexander readily believed the worst about Callisthenes, from the hatred which he already felt towards him and because Hermolaus was known to be exceedingly intimate with him. Some authors have also recorded the following particulars:—

that Hermolaus was brought before the Macedonians, to whom he confessed that he had conspired against the king's life, because it was no longer possible for a free man to bear his insolent tyranny. He then recounted all his acts of despotism, the illegal execution of Philotas, the still more illegal one of his father Parmenio and of the others who were put to death at that time, the murder of Clitus in a fit of drunkenness, his assumption of the Median garb, the introduction of the ceremony of prostration, which had been planned and not yet relinquished, and the drinking-bouts and lethargic sleep arising from them, to which he was addicting himself.[556] He said that, being no longer able to bear these things, he wished to free both himself and the other Macedonians. These same authors say that Hermolaus himself and those who had been arrested with him were stoned to death by those who were present. Aristobulus says that Callisthenes was carried about with the army bound with fetters, and afterwards died a natural death; but Ptolemy, son of Lagus, says that he was stretched upon the rack and then hanged.[557] Thus not even did these authors, whose narratives are very trustworthy, and who at the time were in intimate association with Alexander, give accounts consistent with each other of events so well known, and the circumstances of which could not have escaped their notice. Other writers have given many various details of these same proceedings which are inconsistent with each other; but I think I have written quite sufficient on this subject. Though these events took place shortly after the death of Clitus[558] I have described them among those which happened to Alexander in reference to that General, because, for the purposes of narrative, I consider them very intimately connected with each other.

May 17, Friday

Chapter 101: Alliance with the Scythians and Chorasmians

Another embassy from the European Scythians came to Alexander with the envoys whom he had despatched to those people; for the king who was reigning over them at the time when he sent these envoys, happened to die, and his brother was reigning in his stead. The object of the embassy was to state that the Scythians were willing to do whatsoever Alexander commanded. They were also bringing to him from their king the gifts which among them are deemed most valuable. They said their monarch was willing to give his daughter to Alexander in marriage, in order to confirm the friendship and alliance with him; but if Alexander himself deigned not to marry the princess of the Scythians, then he was willing at any rate to give the daughters of the viceroys of the Scythian territory and of the other mighty men throughout the country of Scythia to the most faithful of Alexander's officers. He also sent word that he would come in person if bidden, in order to hear from Alexander's own mouth what his orders were.

May 23, Thursday

At this time also came Pharasmanes, king of the Chorasmians,[559] to Alexander with 1,500 horsemen, who affirmed that he dwelt on the confines of the nations of the Colchians and the women called Amazons,[560] and promised, if Alexander was willing to march against these nations in order to subjugate the races in this district whose territories extended to the Euxine Sea, to act as his guide through the mountains and to supply his army with provisions. Alexander then gave a courteous reply to the men who had come from the Scythians, and one that was adapted to the exigencies of that particular time; but said that he had no need of a Scythian wedding. He also commended Pharasmanes and concluded a friendship and alliance with him, saying that at present it was not convenient for him to march towards the Euxine Sea. After introducing Pharasmanes as a friend to Artabazus the Persian, to whom he had intrusted the government of the Bactrians,[561] and to all the other viceroys who were his neighbours, he sent him back to his own abode. He said that his mind at that time was engrossed by the desire of conquering the Indians; for when he had subdued them, he should possess the whole of Asia. He added that when Asia was in his power he would return to Greece, and thence make an expedition with all his naval and military forces to the eastern extremity of the Euxine Sea through the Hellespont and Propontis.[562] He desired Pharasmanes to reserve the fulfilment of his present promises until then.

June 02, Sunday

Alexander then returned to the river Oxus, with the intention of advancing into Sogdiana, because news was brought that many of the Sogdianians had fled for refuge into their strongholds and refused to submit to the viceroy whom he had placed over them.

{The Oxus is approximately 100km from Balkh, only a few days march. However according to sources derived from Cleitarchus, Alexander left

Balkh and then first crossed the River Ochus and then crossed the Oxus before going to the city of Margania. The river Ochus is sometimes considered to be the Oxus-tributary the Panj, (modern-day Pyandzh river) crossing from Afghanistan to Tajikistan. A stronger possibility could be that the Ochus was the Kunduz river (an earlier tributary of the Oxus) in Afghanistan, so that Alexander would have gone west from Balkh toward it (Kunduz river) in the northern area of Qala-I-Zal and then only a short journey north to cross the Oxus (now in its Tajikistan territory). This would fit both accounts (Arrian not emphasizing on the much smaller Kunduz crossing) and would render Alexander's journey to the Oxus 100-120 miles or 160-195km}

June 03, Monday

While he was encamping near the river Oxus, a spring of water and near it another of oil rose from the ground not far from Alexander's own tent. When this prodigy was announced to Ptolemy, son of Lagus, the confidential body-guard, he told Alexander, who offered the sacrifices which the prophets directed on account of the phenomenon. Aristander affirmed that the spring of oil was the sign of labours; but it also signified that after the labours there would be victory.

June 05, Wednesday
Alexander Crosses Oxus (again at a time of year when it can be traversed)

Chapter 102: Subjucation of Sogdiana–Revolt of Spitamenes

He therefore crossed the river with a part of his army and entered Sogdiana, leaving Polysperchon, Attalus, Gorgias, and Meleager there among the Bactrians, with instructions to guard the land, to prevent the barbarians of that region from making any revolutionary change, and to reduce those who had already rebelled. He divided the army which he had with him into five parts; the first of which he put under the command of Hephaestion, the second under that of Ptolemy, son of Lagus, the confidential body-guard; over the third he put Perdiccas; Ooenus and Artabazus commanded the fourth brigade for him, while he himself took the fifth division and penetrated into the land towards Maracanda.[563] The others also advanced as each found it practicable, reducing by force some of those who had fled for refuge into the strongholds, and capturing others who surrendered to them on terms of capitulation.

July 12, Friday
Arrival back at Samarkand

When all his forces reached Maracanda, after traversing the greater part of the land of the Sogdianians,

{Samarkand is approximately 200miles away from Kunduz area of Afghanistan (near the Afghanistan/Tajikistan border)}

August 03, Saturday

he sent Hephaestion away to plant colonies in the cities of Sogdiana.

August 15, Thursday

He also sent Coenus and Artabazus into Scythia, because he was informed that Spitamenes had fled for refuge thither;

August 21, Wednesday

but he himself with the rest of his army traversed Sogdiana and easily reduced all the places still held by the rebels. While Alexander was thus engaged,

October 02, Wednesday
Spitamenes arrives in the land of the Massagetians

Spitamenes, accompanied by some of the Sogdianian exiles, fled into the land of the Scythians called Massagetians,[564]

{The land of the Massagetians possibly corresponds to the confluence of the borders of Afghanistan, Turkmenistan and Uzbekistan, in the Jawzjan region of Afghanistan}

October 15, Tuesday
Spitamenes organises his forces

and having collected 600 horsemen from this nation,

October 20, Sunday
Spitamenes attacks a Bactrain fort

he came to one of the forts in Bactriana. Falling upon the commander of this fort, who was not expecting any hostile demonstration, and upon those who were keeping guard with him, he destroyed the soldiers, and capturing the commander, kept him in custody.

October 22, Tuesday
Spitamenes arrives in the land of the Massagetians

Being emboldened by the capture of this fort,

October 28, Monday
Spitamenes arrives outside Zariaspa

a few days after he approached Zariaspa; but resolving not to attack the city,

October 30, Wednesday
Spitamenes leaves Zariaspa with booty

he marched away after collecting a great quantity of booty.

November 02, Saturday
Macedonians and Greek Mercenaries chase after Spitamenes

But at Zariaspa a few of the Companion cavalry had been left behind on the score of illness, and with them Peithon, son of Sosicles,[565] who had been placed over the royal household of attendants at Zariaspa, and Aristonicus the harper. These men, hearing of the incursion of the Scythians, and having now recovered from their illness, took their arms and mounted their horses. Then collecting eighty mercenary Grecian horsemen, who had been left behind to guard Zariaspa, and some of the royal pages, they sallied forth against the Massagetians.

November 04, Monday
Macedonians and Greek Mercenaries chase after Spitamenes

Falling upon the Scythians, who had no suspicion of such an event, they deprived them of all the booty at the first onset, and killed many of those who were driving it off.

November 06, Wednesday
Spitamenes ambushes the Macedonians and the Greek Mercenaries

But as no one was in command, they returned without any regard to order: and being drawn into an ambush by Spitamenes and other Scythians, they lost seven of the Companions and sixty of the mercenary cavalry. Aristonicus the harper was also slain there, having proved himself a brave man, beyond what might have been expected of a harper. Peithon, being wounded, was taken prisoner by the Scythians.[566]

November 10, Sunday
Craterus hears of the ambush

Chapter 103: Defeat and Death of Spitamenes

When this news was brought to Craterus,

November 11, Monday
Craterus chases the Massagetians

he made a forced march against the Massagetians, who, when they heard that he was marching against them, fled as fast as they could towards the desert.

November 15, Friday
Craterus reaches the Massagetians near the desert (possibly near the desert area just beyond the Andkhoy district in the Faryab Province of northern Afghanistan)

Following them up closely, he overtook those very men and more than 1,000 other Massagetian horsemen, not far from the desert.

November 16, Saturday
Craterus battles with the Scythians

A fierce battle ensued, in which the Macedonians were victorious. Of the Scythians, 150 horsemen were slain; but the rest of them easily escaped into the desert, for it was impossible for the Macedonians to pursue them any further.

November 22, Friday

At this time, Alexander relieved Artabazus of the viceroyalty of the Bactrians, at his own request, on the ground of his advanced age; and Amyntas, son of Nicolaus, was appointed viceroy in his stead.[567] Coenus was left with his own brigade and that of Meleager, 400 of the Companion cavalry, and all the horsearchers, besides the Bactrians, Sogdianians and others who were under the command of Amyntas. They were all under strict injunctions to obey Coenus and to winter there in Sogdiana, in order to protect the country and to arrest Spitamenes, if anyhow they might be able to draw him into an ambush, as he was wandering about during the winter.

December 02, Monday

But when Spitamenes saw that every place was occupied by the Macedonians for a garrison, and that there would soon be no way of flight left open to him,

December 04, Wednesday
Spitamenes resolved to confront Coenus

he turned round against Coenus and the army with him, thinking that he would be better able to fight in this way.

December 11, Wednesday
Spitamenes comes to Bagae

Coming to Bagae, a fortified place in Sogdiana, situated on the confines of the countries of the Sogdianians and the Massagetian Scythians,

{Bagae may correspond to Basaga in Turkmenistan as this fits with the description of the Sogdian-Massagetian confines}

December 15, Sunday
Spitamenes assembles his forces

he easily persuaded 3,000 Scythian horsemen to join him in an invasion of Sogdiana. It is an easy matter to induce these Scythians to engage in one war after another, because they are pinched by poverty, and at the same time have no cities or settled abodes, to give them cause for anxiety about what is most dear to them.

December 21, Saturday

When Coenus ascertained that Spitamenes was advancing with his cavalry,

December 23, Monday
Coenus leaves for confronting Spitamenes

he went to meet him with his army.

December 27, Friday
Battle between Coenus and Spitamenes

A sharp contest ensued, in which the Macedonians were victorious, so that of the barbarian cavalry over 800 fell in the battle, while Coenus lost 25 horsemen and twelve foot-soldiers. The consequence was, that the Sogdianians who were still left with Spitamenes, as well as most of the Bactrians, deserted him in the flight, and came to Coenus to surrender. The Massagetian Scythians having met with ill-success in the battle, plundered the baggage of the Bactrians and Sogdianians who were serving in the same army as themselves, and then fled into the desert in company with Spitamenes.

327 BC

January 04, Saturday
Spitamenes Beheaded by the Massagetians

But when they were informed that Alexander was already on the start to march into the desert, they cut off the head of Spitamenes and sent it to him, with the hope by this deed of diverting him from pursuing them.[568]

January 15, Wednesday
Coenus returns to Alexander at Nautaca

Chapter 104: Oxyartes Besieged in the Sogdian Rock

Meantime Coenus returned to Alexander at Nautaca, as also did Craterus, Phrataphernes the viceroy of the Parthians, and Stasanor the viceroy of the Areians, after executing all the orders which Alexander had given them.

{Nautaca could be found between Bactra (possibly modern-day Balkh) and Marcanda (quite likely Samarkand), bisected around the point where the Kashka river (likely modern-day Qashqadaryo River in south Uzbekistan) joins the passage to the Iron-Gate of Derbent toward modern-day Termez. It has been traditionally associated with the city of Shakhrisabz in the Qashqadaryo Region of southern Uzbekistan, although it may fit with the area of the city of Qarshi in Uzbekistan}

January 19, Sunday

The king then caused his army to rest around Nautaca, because it was now mid-winter; but he despatched Phrataphernes into the land of the Mardiaus and Tapurians to fetch Autophradates the viceroy, because, though he had often been sent for, he did not obey the summons. He also sent Stasanor into the land of the Drangians, and Atropates into Media,[569] with the appointment of viceroy over the Medes, because Oxodates seemed disaffected to him. Stamenes also he despatched to Babylon, because news came to him that Mazaeus the Babylonian governor was dead. Sopolis, Epocillus, and Menidas he sent away to Macedonia, to bring him the army up from that country.

March 02, Sunday

At the first appearance of spring,[570] he advanced towards the rock in Sogdiana, to which he was informed many of the Sogdianians had fled for refuge; among whom were said to be the wife and daughters of Oxyartes the Bactrian, who had deposited them for safety in that place, as if forsooth it were impregnable. For lie also had revolted from Alexander. If this rock was captured, it seemed that nothing would be left to those of the Sogdianians who wished to throw off their allegiance.

{The location of the Sogdian Rock or Rock of Ariamazes has never been fully elucidated. It was a fort located in Bactrian Sogdiana and would have likely been in a mountainous region on the southern Uzbekistan/ western Tajikistan border. The author hypothesizes this could have been in Surkhandarya Province in the Gissar Mountains of the Pamir-Alay Range (the highest mountain being the Khazret Sultan) or more likely on the western border of the Pamir-Alay Range located at eastern Kashkadarya(Qashqadaryo) Province. In the latter region there is a historical town named Jayraxona which would offer some possible association for the Sogdian Rock in this area based on the name of Roxanna whom Alexander would meet here, somewhere near Sarnashma in Uzbekistan or the Seven Lakes in Tajikistan. This would have been approximately 160-200km from Nautaca}

March 10, Monday

When Alexander approached it, he found it precipitous on all sides against assault, and that the barbarians had collected provisions for a long siege. The great quantity of snow which had fallen helped to make the approach more difficult to the Macedonians, while at the same time it kept the barbarians supplied with plenty of water.

March 12, Wednesday

But notwithstanding all this, he resolved to assault the place; for a certain overweening and insolent boast uttered by the barbarians had thrown him into a wrathful state of ambitious pertinacity. For when they were invited to come to terms of capitulation, and it was held out to them as an inducement, that if they surrendered the place, they would be allowed to withdraw in safety to their own abodes, they burst out laughing, and in their barbaric tongue bade Alexander seek winged soldiers, to capture the mountain for him, since they had no apprehension of danger from other men.[571]

March 13, Thursday

He then issued a proclamation that the first man who mounted should have a reward of twelve talents,[572] the man who came next to him the second prize, and the third so on in proportion, so that the last reward should be three hundred darics[573] to the last prize-taker who reached the top. This proclamation excited the valour of the Macedonians still more, though they were even before very eager to commence the assault.

Chapter 105: Alexander Captures the Rock and Marries Roxana

All the men who had gained practice in scaling rocks in sieges, banded themselves together to the number of three hundred, and provided themselves with the small iron pegs with which their tents had been fastened to the ground, with the intention of fixing them into the snow, where it might be seen to be frozen hard, or into the ground, if it should anywhere exhibit itself free from snow. Tying strong ropes made of flax to these pegs, they advanced in the night towards the most precipitous part of the rock, which was also most unguarded; and fixing some of these pegs into the earth, where it made itself visible, and others into the snow where it seemed least likely to break up, they hoisted themselves up the rock, some in one place and some in another. Thirty of them perished in the ascent; and as they fell into various parts of the snows, not even could their bodies be found for burial.

March 14, Friday

The rest, however, reached the top of the mountain at the approach of dawn; and taking possession of it, they waved linen flags towards the camp of the Macedonians,[574] as Alexander had directed them to do. He now sent a herald with instructions to shout to the sentries of the barbarians to make no further delay, but surrender at once; since "the winged men" had been found, and the summits of the mountain were in their possession. At the same time the herald pointed at the soldiers upon the crest of the mountain. The barbarians, being alarmed by the unexpectedness of the sight, and suspecting that the men who were occupying the peaks were more numerous than they really were, and that they were completely armed, surrendered, so frightened did they become at the sight of those few Macedonians. The wives and children of many important men were there captured, including those of Oxyartes. This chief had a daughter, a maiden of marriageable age, named Roxana,[575] who was asserted by the men who served in Alexander's army to have been the most beautiful of all Asiatic women, with the single exception of the wife of Darius.[576] They also say that no sooner did Alexander see her than he fell in love with her; but though he was in love with her, he refused to offer violence to her as a captive, and did not think it derogatory to his dignity to marry her. This conduct of Alexander I think worthy rather of praise than blame. Moreover, in regard to the wife of Darius, who was said to be the most beautiful woman in Asia, he either did not entertain a passion for her, or else he exercised control over himself,[577] though he was young, and in the very meridian of success, when men usually act with insolence and violence. On the contrary, he acted with modesty and spared her honour, exercising a great amount of chastity, and at the same time exhibiting a very proper desire to obtain a good reputation.[578]

Chapter 106: Magnanimous Treatment of the Family of Darius

In relation to this subject there is a story current, that soon after the battle which was fought at Issus between Darius and Alexander, the eunuch who was guardian of Darius's wife escaped and came to him. When Darius saw this man, his first inquiry was, whether his children, wife, and mother were alive? Ascertaining that they were not only alive, but were called queens, and enjoyed the same personal service and attention which they had been accustomed to have with Darius, he thereupon made a second inquiry, whether his wife was still chaste? When he ascertained that she remained so, he asked again whether Alexander had not offered any violence to her to gratify his lust? The eunuch took an oath and said: "O king, thy wife is just as thou didst leave her; and Alexander is the best and most chaste of men."

Upon this Darius stretched his hands towards heaven and prayed as follows:— "King Zeus,[579] to whom power has been assigned to regulate the affairs of kings among men, do thou now protect for me especially the empire of the Persians and Medes, as indeed thou didst give it to me. But if I am no longer king of Asia according to thy behest, at any rate do thou hand over my power to no other man but Alexander." Thus not even to enemies, I ween, are chaste actions a matter of unconcern. Oxyartes, hearing that his children were in the power of Alexander, and that he was treating his daughter Roxana with respect, took courage and came to him. He was held in honour at the king's court, as was natural after such a piece of good fortune.[580]

March 18, Tuesday

Chapter 107: Capture of the Rock of Chorienes

When Alexander had finished his operations among the Sogdianians, and was now in possession of the rock,

March 23, Sunday

he advanced into the land of the Paraetacians, because many of the barbarians were said to be holding another rock, a strongly fortified place in that country. This was called the rock of Chorienes; and to it Chorienes himself and many other chiefs had fled for refuge. The height of this rock was about twenty stades, and the circuit about sixty. It was precipitous on all sides, and there was only one ascent to it, which was narrow and not easy to mount, since it had been constructed in spite of the nature of the place. It was therefore difficult to ascend even by men in single file and when no one barred the way. A deep ravine also enclosed[581] the rock all round, so that whoever intended to lead an army up to it, must long before make a causeway of earth over this ravine in order that he might start from level ground, when he led his troops to the assault.

{Rock of Chorienes AKA Rock of Sisimithres may possibly have been deeper in the Pamir-Alay Range, may be corresponding to the similar sounding Khayronbed town in western Tajikistan's Sughd province. This is approximately 100km from the area of the Sogdian Rock}

March 24, Monday

Notwithstanding all this, Alexander undertook the enterprise. To so great a pitch of audacity had he advanced through his career of success, that he thought every place ought to be accessible to him,[582] and to be captured by him. He cut down the pines, which were very abundant and lofty all round the mountain, and made ladders of them, so that by means of them the soldiers might be able to descend into the ravine[583]; for otherwise it was impossible for them to do so. During the **day**-time he himself superintended the work, keeping half of his army engaged in it; and during the night his confidential body-guards, Perdiccas, Leonnatus, and Ptolemy, son of Lagus, in turn with the other half of the army divided into three parts, performed the duty which had been assigned to each for the night. But they could complete no more than twenty cubits in a day, and not quite so much in a night, though the whole army engaged in the labour; so difficult was the place to approach and so hard was the work in it. Descending into the ravine, they fastened pegs into the sharpest and narrowest part of it, distant from each other as far as was consistent with strength to support the weight of what was placed upon them. Upon these they placed hurdles made of willow and osiers, very much in the form of a bridge. Binding these together, they loaded earth above them, so that there might be an approach to the rock for the army on level ground. At first the barbarians derided, as if the attempt was altogether abortive;

April 01, Tuesday

but when the arrows began to reach the rock, and they were unable to drive back the Macedonians, though they themselves were on a higher level, because the former had constructed screens to ward off the missiles, that they might carry on their labour under them without receiving injury,

April 02, Wednesday

Chorienes grew alarmed at what was being done, and sent a herald to Alexander, beseeching him to send Oxyartes up to him.

April 03, Thursday

Alexander accordingly sent Oxyartes, who on his arrival persuaded Chorienes to entrust himself and the place to Alexander; for he told him that there was nothing which Alexander and his army could not take by storm; and as he himself had entered into an alliance of fidelity and friendship with him, he commended the king's honour and justice in high terms, adducing other examples, and above all his own case for the confirmation of his arguments. By these representations Chorienes was persuaded and came himself to Alexander, accompanied by some of his relations and companions. When he arrived, the king gave him a courteous answer to his inquiries, and retained him after pledging his fidelity and friendship. But he bade him send to the rock some of those who came down with him to order his men to surrender the place; and it was surrendered by those who had fled to it for refuge. Alexander therefore took 500 of his shield-bearing guards and went up to get a view of the rock; and was so far from inflicting any harsh treatment upon Chorienes that he entrusted that very place to him again, and made him governor of all that he had ruled before. It happened that the army suffered much hardship from the severity of the winter, a great quantity of snow having fallen during the siege; while at the same time the men were reduced to great straits from lack of provisions. But Chorienes said he would give the army food for two months; and he gave the men in every tent corn, wine, and salted meat out of the stores in the rock. When he had given them this, he said he had not exhausted even the tenth part of what had been laid up for the siege. Hence Alexander held him in still greater honour, inasmuch as he had surrendered the rock, not so much from compulsion as from his own inclination.

April 10, Thursday

Chapter 108: Alexander Reaches the River Cabul, and Receives the Homage of Taxiles

After performing this exploit,

April 27, Sunday

Alexander himself went to Bactra;

{Bactra/Balkh is approximately 200miles from the Rock of Chorienes}

but sent Craterus with 600 of the cavalry Gompanions and his own brigade of infantry as well those of Polysperchon, Attalus, and Alcetas, against Catanes and Austanes, who were the only rebels still remaining in the land of the Paraetacenians.[584]

May 12, Monday
Battle between Craterus and rebel Paraetacenians

A sharp battle was fought with them in which Craterus was victorious; Catanes being killed there while fighting, and Austanes being captured

May 20, Tuesday
Austanes brought to Alexander

and brought to Alexander. Of the barbarians with them 120 horsemen and about 1,500 foot soldiers were killed. When Craterus had done this, he also went to Bactra, where the tragedy in reference to Callisthenes and the pages befell Alexander.

May 27, Tuesday

As the spring was now over, he took the army and advanced from Bactra towards India,[585] leaving Amyntas in the land of the Bactrians with 3,500 horses and 10,000 foot.

June 02, Monday
Returns to the Caucasus Mountain Range

He crossed the Caucasus[586] in ten days and

{His entry to the mountains may have been directly south of Bactra at the entrance to the mountains, possibly the town of Baybul in modern-day Afghanistan, a distance of approximately 70miles}

June 12, Thursday
Returns to Alexandria in the Caucasus

arrived at the city of Alexandria, which had been founded in the land of the Parapamisadae when he made his first expedition to Bactra.

{Alexandria in the Caucasus as discussed earlier may have corresponded approximately to modern-day Band-e-Amir National Park}

June 16, Monday

He dismissed from office the governor whom he had then placed over the city, because he thought he was not ruling well.

July 03, Thursday

He also settled in Alexandria others from the neighbouring tribes and the soldiers who were now unfit for service in addition to the first settlers, and commanded Nicanor, one of the Companions, to regulate the affairs of the city itself. Moreover he appointed Tyriaspes viceroy of the land of the Parapamisadae and of the rest of the country as far as the river Cophen.[587]

{The river Cophen likely corresponds to the modern-day Kabul River that originates in the Sanglakh Range corresponding to ancient Gandara}

July 29, Tuesday
Arrival at the City of Nicaea

Arriving at the city of Nicaea, he offered sacrifice to Athena

{Nicea could correspond to the strategically well sited ancient town of Charikar as gateway to the Panjshir Valley (valley of five lions). This would be approximately 240km from Band-e-Amir (possible Alexandria in the Caucasus)}

August 05, Tuesday
Arrival at the Kabul River

and then advanced towards the Cophen, sending a herald forward to Taxiles[588] and the other chiefs on this side the river Indus, to bid them come and meet him as each might find it convenient.

{The area of the river Cophen (Kabul) that Alexander travelled towards would fit with Kabul's outside district of Surobi that accommodates the river where a town named Surobi exists today}

August 24, Sunday
Arrival of the Taxiles and other Indian Chiefs

Taxiles and the other chiefs accordingly did come to meet him, bringing the gifts which are reckoned of most value among the Indians. They said that they would also present to him the elephants which they had with them, twenty-five in number. There he divided his army, and sent Hephaestion and Perdiccas away into the land of Peucelaotis,[589] towards the river Indus, with the brigades of Gorgias, Clitus,[590] and Meleager, half of the Companion cavalry, and all the cavalry of the Grecian mercenaries. He gave them instructions either to capture the places on their route by force, or to bring them over on terms of capitulation; and when they reached the river Indus, to make the necessary preparations for the passage of the army.

{Taxila from where Taxiles rules is approximately 360km from the outskirts of Kabul so that the process of sending messengers and coming back with elephants would have taken approximately this time}

September 02, Tuesday
Sending Hephaestion and Perdiccas toward the Indus

With them Taxiles and the other chiefs also marched.

September 17, Wednesday
Hephaestion and Perdiccas arrive at the Indus

When they reached the river Indus

{The journey of Hephaestion and Perdiccas has been suggested as following the Khyper Pass, passing the Peshawar area in modern-day Pakistan the heading straight down to the Indus river via a route possibly passing towns such as modern-day Saleh Khana and Cherat, in Pakistan's Khyber Pakhtunkhwa province. Thence straight down to the Indus, a total journey of approximately 300km}

October 03, Friday
Hephaestion and Perdiccas at the Indus

they carried out all Alexander's orders. But Astes, the ruler of the land of Peucelaotis, effected a revolt, which both ruined himself and brought ruin also upon the city into which he had fled for refuge.

{Peucelaotis likely the Sanskrit name of Puskalavati (lotus flower city) likely corresponds to a town in modern-day Charsadda Valley near Peshawar, capital of the ancient Gandara area. This would be approximately 80-100km from the Indus }

November 02, Sunday
Hephaestion successfully sieges Peucelaotis and its leader Astes

For Hephaestion captured it after a siege of thirty days, and Astes himself was killed. Sangaeus, who had some time before fled from Astes and deserted to Taxiles, was appointed to take charge of the city. This desertion was a pledge to Alexander of his fidelity.

September 04, Thursday

Chapter 109: Battles with the Aspasians

Alexander now took command of the shield-bearing guards, the Companion cavalry with the exception of those who had been joined with Hephaestion's division, the regiments of what were called foot-Companions, the archers, the Agrianians and the horse-lancers, and advanced with them into the land of the Aspasians, Gnraeans and Assacenians.[591]

September 16, Tuesday
Crosses the Choes River

Marching by a mountainous and rough road along the river called Choes,[592] which he crossed with difficulty,

{The Choes river is likely the Kunar river. The crossing may have been near Asadabad (ancient Chega Serai or Chughansuraee) near the Afghanistan/Pakistan border approximately 160km from his Kabul river base (possibly at Surobi)}

September 18, Wednesday

he ordered the main body of his infantry to follow at leisure; while he himself took all the cavalry, and 800 of the Macedonian infantry whom he mounted upon horses with their infantry shields,

September 19, Thursday

and made a forced march, because he had received information that the barbarians who inhabited that district had fled for safety into the mountains which extend through the land and into as many of their cities as were strong enough to resist attack.

September 22, Monday

Assaulting the first of these cities which was situated on his route, he routed, at the first attack without any delay, the men whom he found drawn up in front of the city, and shut them up in it. He was himself wounded by a dart which penetrated through the breastplate into his shoulder; but the wound was only a slight one, for the breastplate prevented the dart from penetrating right through his shoulder. Leonnatus and Ptolemy, son of Lagus, were also wounded. Then he encamped near the city at the place where the wall seemed most easy to assault.

September 23, Tuesday

At dawn on the following day the Macedonians easily forced their way through the first wall, as it had not been strongly built. The city had been surrounded with a double wall. At the second wall the barbarians stood their ground for a short time; but when the scaling ladders were now being fixed, and the defenders were being wounded with darts from all sides, they no longer stayed; but rushed through the gates out of the city towards the mountains. Some of them were killed in the flight and the Macedonians, being enraged because they had wounded Alexander, slew all whom they took prisoners. Most of them, however, escaped into the mountains, because they were not far from the city.

September 24, Wednesday

Having levelled this city with the ground,

September 25, Thursday

he marched to another,

September 28, Sunday
Capture of Audaca

named Audaca, which he got possession of by capitulation. He left Craterus there with the other commanders of the infantry to capture all the remaining cities which would not yield of their own accord, and to set the affairs of the whole country in such order as he should find most convenient under the circumstances.

Chapter 110: Operations against the Aspasians

October 02, Thursday

Alexander now took command of the shield-bearing guards, the archers, the Agrianians, the brigade of Coenus and Attains, the royal body-guard of cavalry, about four regiments of the other Companion cavalry, and half of the horse-archers, and advanced towards the river Euaspla,[593] where the chieftain of the Aspasians was.

{The Euaspla could correspond to the tributary links between the Kunar river and the Panjkora river, possibly near/ east of the town of Khaar/Khar in the Bajaur Agency of the Federally Administered Tribal Areas of Pakistan. This is approximately 50km from Asadabad and would fit this journey}

October 04, Saturday

After a long journey he arrived at the city on the second day. When the barbarians ascertained that he was approaching they set fire to the city and fled to the mountains.

{This city would fit with a place near the town of Pashat in northern Pakistan}

October 06, Monday
Ptolemy's battle with an Indian leader

But Alexander followed close upon the fugitives as far as the mountains, and slaughtered many of them before they could manage to get away into the places which were difficult of access. Ptolemy, son of Lagus, observing that the leader himself of the Indians of that district was on a certain hill, and that he had some of his shield-bearing guards round him, though he had with himself far fewer men, yet he still continued to pursue him on horseback. But as the hill was difficult for his horse to run up, lie left it there, handing it over to one of the shield-bearing guards to lead. He then followed the Indian on foot, without any delay. When the latter observed Ptolemy approaching, he turned round, and so did the shield-bearing guards with him. The Indian at close quarters struck Ptolemy on the chest through the breastplate with a long spear, but the breastplate checked the violence of the blow. Then Ptolemy, smiting right through the Indian's thigh, overthrew him, and stripped him of his arms. When his men saw their leader lying dead, they stood their ground no longer; but the men on the mountains, seeing their chieftain's corpse being carried off by the enemy, were seized with indignation, and running down engaged in a desperate conflict over him on the hill. For Alexander himself was now on the hill with the infantry who had dismounted from the horses. These, falling upon the Indians, drove them away to the mountains after a hard struggle, and remained in possession of the corpse.

October 10, Friday
Arrival at Arigaeum

Then crossing the mountains he descended to a city called Arigaeum, and found that this had been set on fire by the inhabitants, who had afterwards fled.

{It has been suggested that Arigaeum and ancient Arjunayana correspond (Based on the Sanskrit Arjunava, please refer to V. S. Agarwala). The author suggests it might be associated with the town of Ajabay/Arjabay in northern Pakistan. This location lies across the mountains from Pashat. Ajabay is in the region of Chamar Talai near a major tributary of the Panjkora river}

October 16, Thursday
Craterus Arrives at Arigaeum

There Craterus with his army reached him, after accomplishing all the king's orders; and because this city seemed to be built in a convenient place, he directed that general to fortify it well, and settle in it as many of the neighbouring people as were willing to live there, together with any of the soldiers who were unfit for service.

October 20, Monday
Leaves Arigaeum

He then advanced

October 22, Wednesday
Arrives at the Barbarian Stronghold

to the place where he heard that most of the barbarians of the district had fled for refuge; and coming to a certain mountain, he encamped at the foot of it. Meantime Ptolemy, son of Lagus, being sent out by Alexander on a foraging expedition, and advancing a considerable distance with a few men to reconnoitre, brought back word to the king that he had observed many more fires in the camp of the barbarians than there were in Alexander's. But the latter did not believe in the multitude of the enemy's fires. Discovering, however, that the barbarians of the district had joined their forces into one body,

{The area of the stronghold may correspond to the Barawal Bandi mountainous area in the Khyber region of northern Pakistan}

October 23, Thursday
Division of army into three parts

he left a part of his army there near the mountain, encamped as they were, and taking as many men as seemed sufficient, according to the reports he had received, as soon as they could descry the fires near at hand, he divided his army into three parts. Over one part he placed Leonnatus, the confidential body-guard, joining the brigades of Attains and Balacrus with his own; the second division he put under the lead of Ptolemy, son of Lagus, including the third part of the royal shield-bearing guards, the brigades of Philip and Philotas, two regiments of horse-archers, the Agrianians, and half of the cavalry. The third division he himself led towards the place where most of the barbarians were visible.

Chapter 111: Defeat of the Aspasians.—The Assacenians and Guraeans Attacked

October 24, Friday
Defeat of the Gandaran Barbarians by the Triumvirate

When the enemy who were occupying the commanding heights perceived the Macedonians approaching, they descended into the plain, being emboldened by their superiority in number and despising the Macedonians, because they were seen to be few. A sharp contest ensued; but Alexander won the victory with ease. Ptolemy's men did not range themselves on the level ground, for the barbarians were occupying a hill. Wherefore Ptolemy, forming his battalions into column, led them to the point where the hill seemed most easily assailable, not surrounding it entirely, but leaving room for the barbarians to flee if they were inclined to do so. A sharp contest also ensued with these men, both from the difficult nature of the ground, and because the Indians are not like the other barbarians of this district, but are far stronger than their neighbours. These men also were driven away from the mountain by the Macedonians. In the same way did Leonnatus with the third division of the army; for his men also defeated those opposed to them. Ptolemy indeed says that all the men were captured, to a number exceeding 40,000, and that 230,000 oxen were also taken, of which Alexander picked out the finest, because they seemed to him to excel both in beauty and size, wishing to send them into Macedonia to till the soil.

{This defeat would have likely taken place in the hills in the north Pakistan/west Afghanistan border, maybe in the Barawal Bandi Hills. The Oxen here could correspond to the Gandaran Oxen seen in the Apadana procession of nation demonstrated on the Achaemenid Persian Apadana at Persepolis}

October 27, Monday
Arrival in the land of the Assacenians

Thence he marched towards the land of the Assacenians; for he received news that these people had made preparations to fight him, having 20,000 cavalry, more than 30,000 infantry, and 30 elephants.

{The land of the Assacenians may correspond to an area of the Afghanistan-Pakistan border between Peshawar and Chitral. This could correspond to the region around modern Asadabad or ancient Chughansuraee/ Chaga Serai (possibly just north of this area), Alexander had crossed the river Choes south of this a few weeks before}

October 29, Tuesday
Craterus arrives with military support

When Craterus had thoroughly fortified the city, for the founding of which he had been left behind, he brought the heavier armed men of his army for Alexander as well as the military engines, in case it might be necessary to lay siege to any place.

November 01, Saturday
March against the Assacenians

Alexander then marched against the Assacenians at the head of the Companion cavalry, the horse-archers, the brigades of Coenus and Polysperchon, the Agrianians, the light-armed troops,[594] and the archers.

November 02, Sunday
Passing through the land of the Gureans

Passing through the land of the Guraeans, he crossed the river Guraeus,[595] which gives its name to the land, with difficulty, both on account of its depth, and because its current is swift, and the stones in the river being round caused those who stepped upon them to stumble.[596]

{The author considers the river Gureans to correspond with the Panjkora River in the northern Khyber Pakhtunkhwa area of northwestern Pakistan. The land of the Gureans may have corresponded to the Gujar Kili emerald area of north-western Pakistan. The area is in the Swat valley and is well recognised for the uniqueness of its geology and stones (famed for its emeralds) which may fit well with the description of the stones here}

November 04, Tuesday
The Assacenians flee

When the barbarians perceived Alexander approaching, they durst not take their stand for a battle in close array, but dispersed one by one to their various cities with the determination of preserving these by resolute fighting.

November 06, Thursday
March Toward Massaga

Chapter 112: Siege of Massaga

In the first place Alexander led his forces against Massaga,[597] the largest of the cities in that district;

{The location Massaga is not known. According to the author's hypothesis Massaga AKA Mazaga would fit well with a location near the lower mid-section of the Panjkora River in northern Pakistan, possibly at the site of Zakhna/ Zakhna Kandao/ possibly (Ma)Zakhna, Khyber Pakhtunkhwa, Pakistan. Sir Olaf Kirkpatrick Kruuse Caroe has suggested a similar location at the Kat Kala Pass at the entrance to the Talash valley near the area of Upper Dir}

November 07, Friday
Approaching the walls of Massaga

and when he was approaching the walls, the barbarians being emboldened by the mercenaries whom they had obtained from the more distant Indians to the number of 7,000, when they saw the Macedonians pitching their camp, advanced against them with a run. Alexander, seeing that the battle was about to be fought near the city, was anxious to draw them further away from their walls, so that if they were put to rout, as he knew they would be, they might not be able easily to preserve themselves by fleeing for refuge into the city close at hand. When therefore he saw the barbarians running out, he ordered the Macedonians to turn round and retreat to a certain hill distant something about seven stades from the place where he had resolved to encamp. The enemy being emboldened, as if the

Macedonians had already given way, rushed upon them with a run and with no kind of order. But when the arrows began to reach them, Alexander at once wheeled round at the appointed signal, and led his plalanx against them with a run. His horse-lancers, Agrianians, and archers first ran forward and engaged with the barbarians, while he himself led the phalanx in regular order. The Indians were alarmed at this unexpected manoeuvre, and as soon as the battle became a hand-to-hand conflict, they gave way and fled into the city. About 200 of them were killed, and the rest were shut up within the walls. Alexander then led his phalanx up to the wall, from which he was soon after slightly wounded in the ankle with an arrow.

November 08, Saturday

On the next day he brought up his military engines and easily battered down a piece of the wall; but the Indians so gallantly kept back the Macedonians who were trying to force an entrance where the breach had been made, that he recalled the army for this day.

November 09, Sunday

But on the morrow the Macedonians themselves made a more vigorous assault, and a wooden tower was drawn up to the walls, from which the archers shot at the Indians, and missiles were hurled from the military engines which repulsed them to a great distance. But not even thus were they able to force their way within the wall.

November 10, Monday

On the third day he led the phalanx near again, and throwing a bridge from a military engine over to the part of the wall where the breach had been made, by this he led up the shield-bearing guards, who had captured Tyre for him in a similar way.[598] But as many were urged on by their ardour, the bridge received too great a weight, and was snapped asunder, so that, the Macedonians fell with it. The barbarians, seeing what was taking place, raised a great shout, and shot at them from the wall with stones, arrows, and whatever else any one happened to have at hand, or whatever any one could lay hold of at the time. Others issued forth by the small gates which they had between the towers in the wall, and at close quarters struck the men who had been thrown into confusion by the fall.

Chapter 113: Sieges of Massaga and Ora

Alexander now sent Alcetas with his own brigade to recover the men who had been severely wounded, and to recall to the camp those who were assailing the enemy.

November 11, Tuesday

On the fourth day he brought up another bridge against the wall in like manner upon another military engine. The Indians, as long as the ruler of the place survived, defended themselves gallantly; but when he was struck and killed with a missile hurled from an engine, and as some of their number had fallen in the siege, which had gone on without any cessation, while most of them were wounded and unfit for service, they sent a herald to Alexander. He was glad to preserve the lives of brave men; so he came to terms with the Indian mercenaries on this condition, that they should be admitted into the ranks with the rest of his army and serve as his soldiers. They therefore came out of the city with their arms, and encamped by themselves upon a hill which was facing the camp of the Macedonians; but they resolved to arise by night and run away to their own abodes, because they were unwilling to take up arms against the other Indians. When Alexander received intelligence of this, he placed the whole of his army round the hill in the night, and intercepting them in the midst of their flight, cut them to pieces.

November 12, Wednesday

He then took the city by storm, denuded as it was of defenders; and captured the mother and daughter of Assacenus.[599] In the whole siege five-and-twenty of Alexander's men were killed.

November 16, Sunday

Thence he despatched Coenus to Bazira,[600] entertaining an opinion that the inhabitants would surrender, when they heard of the capture of Massaga. He also despatched Attains, Alcetas, and Demetrius the cavalry officer to another city, named Ora, with instructions to blockade it until he himself arrived. The men of this city made a sortie against the forces of Alcetas; but the Macedonians easily routed them, and drove them into the city within the wall.

November 19, Wednesday
Coenus having difficulties at Bazira

But affairs at Bazira were not favourable to Coenus, for the inhabitants showed no sign of capitulating, trusting to the strength of the place, because not only was it situated on a lofty eminence, but it was also thoroughly fortified all round.

{Bazira possibly corresponds to Batrik in northern Pakistan}

November 20, Thursday
Alexander sets off to Bazira to support Coenus but changes Direction and sets off toward Ora

When Alexander learnt this, he started off to Bazira; but ascertaining that some of the neighbouring barbarians were about to get into the city of Ora by stealth, being despatched thither by Abisares[601] for that very purpose, he first marched to Ora. He ordered Coenus to fortify a certain strong position to serve as a basis of operations against the city of Bazira, and then to come to him with the rest of his army, after leaving in that place a sufficient garrison to restrain the men in the city from enjoying the free use of their land. But when the men of Bazira saw Coenus departing with the larger part of his army, they despised the Macedonians, as not being able to contend with them, and sallied forth into the plain. A sharply contested battle ensued, in which 500 of the barbarians fell, and over seventy were taken prisoners. But the rest, fleeing for refuge into the city,[602] were now more securely shut off from the country by the men in the fort.

{Ora likely corresponds to Arandu/Orandu or Arnawai in northern

Pakistan}

November 21, Friday
The siege of Ora

The siege of Ora proved an easy matter to Alexander, for he no sooner attacked the walls than at the first assault he got possession of the city, and captured the elephants which had been left there.

November 22, Saturday
The Bazirans escape to Aornus

Chapter 114: Capture of Bazira. — Advance to the Rock of Aornus

When the men in Bazira heard this news, despairing of their own affairs, they abandoned the city about the middle of the night, and fled to the rock as the other barbarians were doing. For all the inhabitants deserted the cities and began to flee to the rock which is in their land, and is called Aornus.[603] For stupendous is this rock in this land, about which the current report is, that it was found impregnable even by Heracles, the son of Zeus. I cannot affirm with confidence either way, whether the Theban, Tyrian, or Egyptian Heracles[604] penetrated into India or not ; but I am rather inclined to think that he did not penetrate so far; for men are wont to magnify the difficulty of difficult enterprises to such a degree as to assert that they would have been impracticable even to Heracles. Therefore, I am inclined to think, that in regard to this rock the name of Heracles was mentioned simply to add to the marvellousness of the tale. The circuit of the rock is said to be about 200 stades (i.e. about twenty-three miles), and its height where it is lowest, eleven stades (i.e., about a mile and a quarter). There was only one ascent, which was artificial and difficult; on the summit of the rock there was abundance of pure water, a spring issuing from the ground, from which the water flowed; and there was also timber, and sufficient good arable land for 1,000 men to till.[605]

{According to Aurel Stein Aornus corresponds to Pir Sar according. The author suggests that it corresponds to Ayun/Ayoun/Ayourn in Chitral, northern Pakistan}

November 23, Sunday

When Alexander heard this, he was seized with a vehement desire to capture this mountain also, especially on account of the legend which was current about Heracles. He then made Ora and Massaga fortresses to keep the land in subjection, and fortified the city of Bazira. Hephaestion and Perdiccas also fortified for him another city, named Orobatis, and leaving a garrison in it marched towards the river Indus.

November 28, Friday
Hephaestion and Perdiccas arrival at the Indus River

When they reached that river they at once began to carry out Alexander's instructions in regard to bridging it.

{The crossing of the Indus may have been in the region of Besham City area of Shangla District in the Khyber Pakhtunkhwa province of Pakistan through which the Karakram Highway passes}

November 24, Monday
Appoints Nicanor as viceroy of the area west of the Indus

Alexander then appointed Nicanor, one of the Companions, viceroy of the land on this side the river Indus;

November 29, Saturday
Nicanor subjugates the city of Peucelaotis

and in the first place leading his army towards that river, he brought over on terms of capitulation the city of Peucelaotis, which was situated not far from it. In this city he placed a garrison of Macedonians, under the command of Philip, and then reduced to subjection some other small towns situated near the same river, being accompanied by Cophaeus and Assagetes, the chieftains of the land.

{Peucelaotis has been suggested to correspond to Puskalavati in ancient Indian (City of Lotus Flowers) in the river Charsadda valley according to the Livius.org and Marco Prins although it does not fit directly with the location at the Indus River, according to the author it could correspond to the area near Bilkanai village of Shangla District, Khyber Pakhtunkhwa Province, Pakistan}

November 26, Wednesday
Arrival at Embolima

Arriving at the city of Embolima,[606] which was situated near the rock Aornus, he left Oraterus there with a part of the army, to gather as much corn as possible into the city, as well as all the other things requisite for a long stay, so that making this their base of operations, the Macedonians might be able by a long siege to wear out the men who were holding the rock, supposing it were not captured at the first assault.

{Embolima could correspond to a site near Kumrat Valley or the area of Kalam or Birmoghlasht near Chitral in northern Pakistan}

November 27, Thursday

He then took the bowmen, the Agrianians, and the brigade of Coenus, and selecting the lightest as well as the best-armed men from the rest of the phalanx, with 200 of the Companion cavalry and 100 horse-bowmen, he advanced to the rock. This day he encamped where it appeared to him convenient;

November 28, Friday

but on the morrow he approached a little nearer to the rock, and encamped again.

Chapter 115: Siege of Aornus

At this juncture some of the natives came to him, and surrendering themselves, offered to lead him to the part of the rock where it could be most easily assailed, and from which it would be easy for him to capture the place. With these he sent Ptolemy, son of Lagus, the confidential body-guard, in command of the Agrianians and the other light-armed troops, together with picked men from the shield-bearing guards. He gave this officer instructions, as soon as he had got possession of the place, to occupy it with a strong guard, and signal to him that it was held. Ptolemy proceeded along a road which was rough and difficult to pass, and occupied the position without the knowledge of the barbarians. After strengthening his position with a stockade and a ditch all round, he raised a beacon from the mountain, whence it was likely to be seen by Alexander. The flame was at once seen, and

November 29, Saturday

on the following day the king led his army forward; but as the barbarians disputed his advance, he could do nothing further on account of the difficult nature of the ground. When the barbarians perceived that Alexander could not make an assault, they turned round and attacked Ptolemy, and a sharp battle ensued between them and the Macedonians, the Indians making great efforts to demolish the stockade, and Ptolemy to preserve his position. But the barbarians, getting the worst of it in the skirmish, withdrew as the night came on. Alexander now selected from the Indian deserters a man who was not only devoted to him but acquainted with the locality,[607] and sent him by night to Ptolemy, carrying a letter, in which it was written that as soon as the king attacked the rock, Ptolemy was to come down the mountain upon the barbarians and not be contented with holding his position in guard; so that the Indians, being assailed from both sides at once, might be in perplexity what course to pursue.

November 30, Sunday

Accordingly, starting from his camp at daybreak, he led his army up the path by which Ptolemy had ascended by stealth, entertaining the opinion that if he could force his way in this direction and join his forces with those of Ptolemy, the work would no longer be difficult for him; and so it turned out. For until midday a smart battle was kept up between the Indians and the Macedonians, the latter striving to force a way of approach, and the former hurling missiles at them as they ascended. But as the Macedonians did not relax their efforts, advancing one after another, and those who were in advance rested till their comrades came up, after great exertions they gained possession of the pass early in the afternoon, and formed a junction with Ptolemy's forces. As the whole army was now united, Alexander led it thence against the rock itself. But the approach to it was still impracticable. Such then was the result of this day's labours.

December 01, Monday

At the approach of the dawn he issued an order that each soldier individually should cut 100 stakes; and when this had been done he heaped up a great mound against the rock, beginning from the top of the hill where they had encamped. From this mound he thought the arrows as well as the missiles launched from the military engines would be able to reach the defenders of the rock. Every one in the army assisted him in this work of raising the mound; while he himself superintended it, as an observer, not only, commending the man who completed his task with zeal and alacrity, but also chastising him who was dilatory in the pressing emergency.

Chapter 116: Capture of Aornus — Arrival at the Indus

On the first day his army constructed the mound the length of a stade;

December 02, Tuesday

and on the following day the slingers shooting at the Indians from the part already finished, assisted by the missiles which were hurled from the military engines, repulsed the sallies which they made against the men who were constructing the mound.

December 05, Friday

He went on with the work for three days without intermission,

December 06, Saturday
Alexander captures the city on the rock of Aornus

and on the fourth day a few of the Macedonians forcing their way occupied a small eminence which was on a level with the rock. Without taking any rest, Alexander went on with the mound, being desirous of connecting his artificial rampart with the eminence which the few men were now occupying for him. But then the Indians, being alarmed at the indescribable audacity of the Macedonians, who had forced their way to the eminence, and seeing that the mound was already united with it, desisted from attempting any longer to resist. They sent their herald to Alexander, saying that they were willing to surrender the rock, if he would grant them a truce. But they had formed the design of wasting the day by continually delaying the ratification of the truce, and of scattering themselves in the night with the view of escaping one by one to their own abodes. When Alexander discovered this plan of theirs, he allowed them time to commence their retreat, and to remove the guard which was placed all round the place. He remained quiet until they began their retreat; then taking 700 of the body-guards and shield-bearing infantry, he was the first to scale the rock at the part of it abandoned by the enemy; and the Macedonians ascended after him, one in one place another in another, drawing each other up. These men at the concerted signal turned themselves upon the retreating barbarians, and killed many of them in their flight. Others retreating with panic terror perished by leaping down the precipices; and thus the rook which had been inexpugnable to Heracles was occupied by Alexander. He offered sacrifice upon it, and arranged a fort, committing the superintendence of the garrison to Sisicottus, who long before had deserted from the Indians to Bessus in Bactra, and after Alexander had acquired possession of the country of Bactra, entered his army and appeared to be eminently trustworthy.

December 09, Tuesday

He now set out from the rock and invaded the land of the Assacenians; for he was informed that the brother of Assacenus, with his elephants and many of the neighbouring barbarians had fled into the mountains in this district.

December 10, Wednesday

When he arrived at the city of Dyrta,[608] he found none of the inhabitants either in it or in the land adjacent.

{Dyrta likely corresponds to an area near Besti in the region of North-West Frontier Province in Pakistan, approximately 33 miles from Ayun}

December 11, Thursday
Army split again into three segments

On the following day he sent out Nearchus and Antiochus, the colonels of the shield-bearing guards, giving the former the command of the Agrianians and the light-armed troops,[609] and the latter the command of his own regiments and two others besides. They were despatched both to reconnoitre the locality and to try if they could capture some of the barbarians anywhere in order to get information about the general affairs of the country; and he was especially anxious to learn news of the elephants. He now directed his march towards the river Indus,[610] the army going in advance to make a road for him, as otherwise this district would have been impassable. Here he captured a few of the barbarians, from whom he learnt that the Indians of that land had fled for safety to Abisares, but that they had left their elephants there to pasture near the river Indus. He ordered these men to show him the way to the elephants. Many of the Indians are elephant-hunters, and these Alexander kept in attendance upon him in high honour, going out to hunt the elephants in company with them. Two of these animals perished in the chase, by leaping down a precipice, but the rest were caught and being ridden by drivers were marshalled with the army. He also as he was marching along the river lighted upon a wood the timber of which was suitable for building ships; this was cut down by the army, and ships were built for him, which were brought down the river Indus to the bridge, which had long since been constructed by Hephaestion and Perdiccas at his command.

December 13, Saturday
Arrival at Nysa

Chapter 117 (Start of Book 5): Alexander at Nysa

In this country, lying between the rivers Cophen and Indus, which was traversed by Alexander, the city of Nysa[611] is said to be situated. The report is, that its foundation was the work of Dionysus, who built it after he had subjugated the Indians.[612] But it is impossible to determine who this Dionysus[613] was, and at what time, or from what quarter he led an army against the Indians. For I am unable to decide whether the Theban Dionysus, starting from Thebes or from the Lydian Tmolus[614] came into India at the head of an army, and after traversing the territories of so, many warlike nations, unknown to the Greeks of that time, forcibly subjugated none of them except that of the Indians. But I do not think we ought to make a minute examination of the legends which were promulgated in ancient times about the divinity; for things which are not credible to the man who examines them according to the rule of probability, do not appear to be wholly incredible, if one adds the divine agency to the story. When Alexander came to Nysa the citizens sent out to him their president, whose name was Acuphis, accompanied by thirty of their most distinguished men as envoys, to entreat Alexander to leave their city free for the sake of the god. The envoys entered Alexander's tent and found him seated in his armour still covered with dust from the journey, with his helmet on his head, and holding his spear in his hand. When they beheld the sight they were struck with astonishment, and falling to the earth remained silent a long time. But when Alexander caused them to rise, and bade them be of good courage, then at length Acuphis began thus to speak: "The Nysaeans beseech thee, king, out of respect for Dionysus, to allow them to remain free and independent; for when Dionysus had subjugated the nation of the Indians, and was returning to the Grecian sea, he founded this city from the soldiers who had become unfit for military service, and were under his inspiration as Bacchanals, so that it might be a monument both of his wandering and of his victory, to men of after times; just as thou also hast founded Alexandria near mount Caucasus, and another Alexandria in the country of the Egyptians. Many other cities thou hast already founded, and others thou wilt found hereafter, in the course of time, inasmuch as thou hast achieved more exploits than Dionysus. The god indeed called the city Nysa, and the land Nysaea after his nurse Nysa. The mountain also which is near the city he named Meros (i.e. thigh), because, according to the legend, he grew in the thigh of Zeus. From that time we inhabit Nysa, a free city, and we ourselves are independent, conducting our government with constitutional order. And let this be to thee a proof that our city owes its foundation to Dionysus; for ivy, which does not grow in the rest of the country of India, grows among us."

Chapter 118: Alexander at Nysa

All this was very pleasant to Alexander to hear; for he wished that the legend about the wandering of Dionysus should be believed, as well as that Nysa owed its foundation to that deity, since he had himself reached the place where Dionysus came, and had even advanced beyond the limits of the latter's march. He also thought that the Macedonians would not decline still to share his labours if he advanced further, from a desire to surpass the achievements of Dionysus. He therefore granted the inhabitants of Nysa the privilege of remaining free and independent; and when he inquired about their laws, he commended them because the government was in the hands of the aristocracy. He required them to send 300 of their horsemen to accompany him, and to select and send 100 of the aristocrats who presided over the government of the State, who also were 300 in number. He ordered Acuphis to make the selection, and appointed him governor of the land of Nysaea. When Acuphis heard this, he is said to have smiled at the speech; whereupon Alexander asked him why he laughed. Acuphis replied:— "How, king, could a single city deprived of 100 of its good men be still well governed? But if thou carest for the welfare of the Nysaeans, lead with thee the 300 horsemen, and still more than that number if thou wishest: but instead of the hundred of the best men whom thou orderest me to select lead with thee double the number of the others who are bad, so that when thou comest here again the city may appear[615] in the same good order in which it now is." By these remarks he persuaded Alexander; for he thought he was speaking with prudence. So he ordered them to send the horsemen to accompany him, but no longer demanded the hundred select men, nor indeed others in their stead. But he commanded Acuphis to send his own son and his daughter's son to accompany him.

{The author hypothesises that Nysa corresponds to Barenis/ Bare-nysa in northern Pakistan, this would fit with the Chitral, Kalash (and also Kafiristan-Nuristan) hypothesis where Alexander may have noted a similarity between the unique anthropological features of the populace here and those of the Greeks allowing him to accept the Dionysus theory of the people at that time. Whilst modern genetic analysis does not necessarily allude to Greek ancestry, the individuals do have a clear anthropological, linguistic and cultural characteristics associated with definable genetics that may have been adequate to corroborate their story. Barenis is approximately 26miles from Besti}

December 14, Sunday

He was now seized with a strong desire of seeing the place where the Nysaeans boasted to have certain memorials of Dionysus. So he went to Mount Merus with the Companion cavalry and the foot guard, and saw the mountain, which was quite covered with ivy and laurel and groves thickly shaded with all sorts of timber, and on it were chases of all kinds of wild animals.[616] The Macedonians were delighted at seeing the ivy, as they had not seen any for a long time; for in the land of the Indians there was no ivy, even where they had vines. They eagerly made garlands of it, and crowned themselves with them, as they were, singing hymns in. honour of Dionysus, and invoking the deity by his various names.[617] Alexander there offered sacrifice to Dionysus, and feasted in company with his companions.[618] Some authors have also stated, but I do not know if any one will believe it, that many of the distinguished Macedonians in attendance upon him, having crowned themselves with ivy, while they were engaged in the invocation of the deity, were seized with the inspiration of Dionysus, uttered cries of Evoi in honour of the god, and acted as Bacchanals.[619]

Chapter 119: Incredulity of Eratosthenes — Passage of the Indus

Any one who receives these stories may believe or disbelieve them as he pleases. But I do not altogether agree with Eratosthenes the Cyrenaean,[620] who says that everything which was attributed to the divine agency by the Macedonians was really said to gratify Alexander by their excessive eulogy. For he says that the Macedonians, seeing a cavern in the land of the Parapamisadians,[621] and hearing a certain legend which was current among the natives, or themselves forming a conjecture, spread the report that this forsooth was the cave where Prometheus had been bound, that an eagle frequented it to feast on his inward parts, that when Heracles arrived there he killed the eagle and set Prometheus free from his bonds. He also says that by their account the Macedonians transferred Mount Caucasus from the Euxine Sea to the eastern parts of the earth, and the land of the Parapamisadians to that of the Indians;[622] calling what was really Mount Parapaniisus by the name of Caucasus, in order to enhance Alexander's glory, seeing that he forsooth had gone over the Caucasus. He adds, that when they saw in India itself some oxen marked with the brand of a club, they concluded from this that Heracles had penetrated into India. Eratosthenes also disbelieves the similar tale of the wandering of Dionysus. Let me leave the stories about these matters undecided as far as I am concerned.

{The ivy on mount Merus was likely Hedera nepalensis (Himalayan ivy), is well recognised in the area. Mount Merus may correspond to Tirich Mir/ Tirich Meer and is both the highest Hindu Kush mountain and the highest mountain in the world outside of the Himalayas-Karakoram range}

December 18, Thursday
Alexander Arrives at the Indus

When Alexander arrived at the river Indus, he found a bridge made over it by Hephaestion, and two thirty- oared galleys, besides many smaller craft.[623] He moreover found that 200 talents of silver,[624] 3,000 oxen, above 10,000 sheep for sacrificial victims, and thirty elephants had arrived as gifts from Taxiles the Indian; 700 Indian horsemen also arrived from Taxiles as a reinforcement, and that prince sent word that he would surrender to him the city of Taxila,[625] the largest town between the rivers Indus and Hydaspes.[626]

{The distance from Barenis (possible region of Nysa) and Besham City (possible region of Alexander's Indus crossing) is approximately 90miles and Alexander would have likely passed an area near modern-day Shandur national park, famous for its polo and elephant polo matches}

December 20, Saturday
{Date of Winter Solstice in 327 BC}

Alexander there offered sacrifice to the gods to whom he was in the habit of sacrificing, and celebrated a gymnastic and horse contest near the river. The sacrifices were favourable to his crossing.

Chapter 120: Digression About India

The following are statements about the river Indus which are quite unquestionable, and therefore let me record them. The Indus is the largest of all the rivers in Asia and Europe, except the Ganges,[627] which is also an Indian river. It takes its rise on this side mount Parapamisus, or Caucasus, and discharges its water into the Great Sea which lies near India in the direction of the south wind. It has two mouths, both of which outlets are full of shallow pools like the five outlets of the Ister (or Danube).[628] It forms a Delta in the land of the Indians resembling that of Egypt[629]; and this is called Pattala in the Indian language. The Hydaspes, Acesines, Hydraotes, and Hyphasis are also Indian rivers[630] and far exceed the other rivers of Asia in size; but they are not only smaller but much smaller than the Indus, just as that river itself is smaller than the Ganges. Indeed Ctesias[631] says (if any one thinks his evidence to be depended upon), that where the Indus is narrowest, its banks are forty stades apart; where it is broadest, 100 stades; and most of it is the mean between these breadths.[632] This river Indus Alexander crossed at daybreak with his army into the country of the Indians; concerning whom, in this history I have described neither what laws they enjoy, nor what strange animals their land produces, nor how many and what sort of fish and water-monsters are produced by the Indus, Hydaspes. Granges, or the other rivers of India. Nor have I described the ants which dig up the gold for them,[633] nor the guardian griffins, nor any of the other tales that have been composed rather to amuse than to be received as

the relation of facts; since the falsity of the strange stories which have been fabricated about India cannot be exposed by any one.[634] However, Alexander and those who served in his army exposed the falsity of most of these tales; but there were even some of these very men who fabricated other stories. They proved that the Indians whom Alexander visited with his army, and he visited many tribes of them, were destitute of gold; and also that they were by no means luxurious in their mode of living. Moreover, they discovered that they were tall in stature, in fact as tall as any men throughout Asia, most of them being five cubits in height, or a little less. They were blacker than the rest of men, except the Ethiopians[635]; and in war they were far the bravest of all the races inhabiting Asia at that time. For I cannot with any justice compare the race of the ancient Persians with those of India, though at the head of the former Cyrus, son of Cambyses, set out and deprived the Medes of the empire of Asia, and subdued many other races partly by force and partly by voluntary surrender on their own part. For at that time the Persians were a poor people and inhabitants of a rugged land, having laws and customs very similar to the Laconian discipline.[636] Nor am I able with certainty to conjecture whether the defeat sustained by the Persians in the Scythian land was due to the difficult nature of the country invaded or to some other error on the part of Cyrus, or whether the Persians were really inferior in warlike matters to the Scythians of that district.

Chapter 121: Mountains and Rivers of Asia

But of the Indians I shall treat in a distinct work,[637] giving the most credible accounts which were compiled by those who accompanied Alexander in his expedition, as well as by Nearchus[638] who sailed right round the Great Sea which is near India. Then I shall add what has been compiled by Megasthenes[639] and Eratosthenes, two men of distinguished authority. I shall describe the customs peculiar to the Indians and the strange animals which are produced in the country, as well as the voyage itself in the external sea. But now let me describe so much only as appears to me sufficient to explain Alexander's achievements. Mount Taurus divides Asia, beginning from Mycale, the mountain which lies opposite the island of Samos; then, cutting through the country of the Pamphylians and Cilicians, it extends into Armenia. From this, country it stretches into Media and through the land of the Parthians and Chorasmians. In Bactria it unites with mount Parapamisus, which the Macedonians who served in Alexander's army called Caucasus, in order, as it is said, to enhance their king's glory; asserting that he went even beyond the Caucasus with his victorious arms. Perhaps it is a fact that this mountain range is a continuation of the other Caucasus in Scythia, as the Taurus[640] is of the same. For this reason I have on a previous occasion called this range Caucasus, and by the same name I shall continue to call it in the future. This Caucasus extends as far as the Great Sea which lies in the direction of India and the East. Of the rivers in Asia worth consideration which take their rise from the Taurus and Caucasus, some have their course turned towards the north, discharging themselves either into the lake Maeotis,[641] or into the sea called Hyrcanian, which in reality is a gulf of the Great Sea.[642] Others flow towards the south, namely, the Euphrates, Tigres, Indus, Hydaspes, Acesines, Hydraotes, Hyphasis, and all those that lie between these and the river Ganges. All these either discharge their water into the sea, or disappear by pouring themselves out into marshes, as the river Euphrates[643] does.

Chapter 122: General Description of India

Whoever arranges the position of Asia in such a way that it is divided by the Taurus and the Caucasus from the west wind to the east wind, will find that these two very large divisions are made by the Taurus itself, one of which is inclined towards the south and the south wind, and the other towards the north and the north wind. Southern Asia again may he divided into four parts, of which Eratosthenes and Megasthenes make India the largest. The latter author lived with Sibyrtius,[644] the viceroy of Arachosia, and says that he frequently visited Sandracotus, king of the Indians.[645] These authors say that the smallest of the four parts is that which is bounded by the river Euphrates and extends to our inland sea. The other two lying between the rivers Euphrates and Indus are scarcely worthy to be compared with India, if they were joined together. They say that India is bounded towards the east and the east wind as far as the south by the Great Sea, towards the north by mount Caucasus, as far as its junction with the Taurus; and that the river Indus cuts it off towards the west and the north-west wind, as far as the Great Sea. The greater part of it is a plain, which, as they conjecture, has been formed by the alluvial deposits of the rivers; just as the plains in the rest of the earth lying near the sea are for the most part due to the alluvial action of the rivers taken singly. Consequently, the names by which the countries are called were attached in ancient times to the rivers. For instance, a certain plain was called after the Hermus, which rises in the country of Asia from the mountain of Mother Dindymene,[646] and after flowing past the Aeolian city of Smyrna discharges its water into the sea. Another Lydian plain is named after the Cayster, a Lydian river ; another from the Caicus in Mysia; and the Carian plain, extending as far as the Ionian city of Miletus, is named from the Maeander. Both Herodotus and Hecataeus[647] the Iorians (unless the work about the Egyptian country is by another person, and not by Hecataeus) in like manner call Egypt a gift of the river[648]; and Herodotus has shown by no uncertain proofs that such is the case[649]; so that even the country itself perhaps received its name from the river. For that the river which both the Egyptians and men outside Egypt now name the Nile, was in ancient times called Aegyptus, Homer is sufficient to prove; since he says that Menelaus stationed his ships at the outlet of the river Aegyptus.[650] If therefore single rivers by themselves, and those not large ones, are sufficient to form an extensive tract of country, while flowing forward into the sea, since they carry down slime and mud from the higher districts whence they derive their sources, surely it is unbecoming to exhibit incredulity about India, how it has come to pass that most of it is a plain, which has been formed by the alluvial deposits of its rivers. For if the Hermus, the Cayster, the Caicus, the Maeander, and all the other[651] rivers of Asia which discharge their waters into the midland sea were all put together, they would not be worthy of comparison for volume of water with one of the Indian rivers. Not only do I mean the Ganges, which is the largest, and with which neither the water of the Egyptian Nile nor the Ister flowing through Europe is worthy to compare; but if all those rivers were mingled together they would not even then become equal to the river Indus, which is a large river as soon as it issues from its springs, and after receiving fifteen rivers,[652] all larger than those in the province of Asia, discharges its water into the sea, retaining its own name and absorbing those of its tributaries. Let these remarks which I have made about India suffice for the present, and let the rest be reserved for my "Description of India."

Chapter 123: Method of Bridging Rivers

How Alexander constructed his bridge over the river Indus, is explained neither by Aristobulus nor Ptolemy, authors whom I usually follow; nor am I able to form a decided opinion whether the passage was bridged with boats, as the Hellespont was by Xerxes and the Bosporus and the Ister were by Darius,[653] or whether he made a continuous bridge over the river. To me it seems probable that the bridge was made o- boats; for the depth of the water would not have admitted of the construction of a regular bridge, nor could so enormous a work have been completed in so short a time.[654] If the passage was bridged with boats, I cannot decide whether the vessels being fastened together with ropes and moored in a row were sufficient to form the bridge, as Herodotus the Halicarnassian says the Hellespont was bridged, or whether the work was effected in the way in which the bridge upon the Ister and that upon the Celtic Rhine[655] are made by the Romans, and in the way in which they bridged the Euphrates and Tigres, as often as necessity compelled them. However, as I know myself, the Romans find the quickest way of making a bridge to be with vessels; and this method I shall on the present occasion explain, because it is worth describing. At a preconcerted signal they let the vessels loose down the stream, not with their prows forward, but as if backing water.[656] As might naturally be expected, the stream carries them down, but a skiff furnished with oars holds them back, until it settles them in the place assigned to them. Then pyramidal wicker-baskets made of willow, full of unhewn stones, are let down into the water from the prow of each vessel, in order to hold it up against the force of the stream. As soon as any one of these vessels has been held fast, another is in the same way moored with its prow against the stream, distant from the first as far as is consistent with their supporting what is put upon them. On both of them are placed pieces of timber with sharp ends projecting out, on which cross-planks are placed to bind them together; and so proceeds the work through all the vessels which are required to bridge the river. At each end of this bridge firmly fixed gangways are thrown forward,[657] so that the approach may be safer for the horses and beasts of burden, and at the same time to serve as a bond to the bridge. In a short time the whole is finished with a great noise and bustle; but yet discipline is not relaxed while the work is going on. In each vessel the exhortations of the overseers to the men, or their censures of sluggishness, neither prevent the orders being heard nor impede the rapidity of the work.[658]

Chapter 124: March from the Indus to the Hydaspes

This has been the method of constructing bridges, practised by the Romans from olden times; but how Alexander laid a bridge over the river Indus I cannot say, because those who served in his army have said nothing about it. But I should think that the bridge was made as near as possible as I have described, or if it were effected by some other contrivance so let it be.

December 20, Saturday
Alexander Crosses the Indus

When Alexander had crossed to the other side of the river Indus, he again offered sacrifice there, according to his custom.[659]

December 27, Saturday
Alexander Arrives at Taxilla

Then starting from the Indus, he arrived at Taxila, a large and prosperous city, in fact the largest of those situated between the rivers Indus and Hydaspes. He was received in a friendly manner by Taxiles, the governor of the city, and by the Indians of that place; and he added to their territory as much of the adjacent country as they asked for.

326 BC

January 04, Sunday
Regional ambassadors visit Alexander

Thither also came to him envoys from Abisares, king of the mountaineer Indians, the embassy including the brother of Abisares as well as the other most notable men. Other envoys also came from Doxareus, the chief of the province, bringing gifts with them.

February 12, Thursday
{Date of January/February full moon Dionysus Day 326 BC}

Here again at Taxila, Alexander offered the sacrifices which were customary for him to offer, and celebrated a gymnastic and equestrian contest.

February 16, Monday

Having appointed Philip, son of Machatas, viceroy of the Indians of that district, he left a garrison in Taxila, as well as the soldiers who were invalided by sickness, and then

February 18, Wednesday

marched towards the river Hydaspes. For he was informed that Porus,[660] with the whole of his army was on the other side of that river, having determined either to prevent him from making the passage, or to attack him while crossing.

February 21, Saturday
Coenus sent to dismantle the ships at the Indus

When Alexander ascertained this, he sent Coenus, son of Polemocrates, back to the river Indus, with instructions to cut in pieces all the vessels which he had prepared for the passage of that river, and to bring them to the river Hydaspes.

March 02, Monday

Coenus cut the vessels in pieces and conveyed them thither, the smaller ones being cut into two parts, and the thirty-oared galleys into three.

April 06, Monday
Ship parts transported to the bank of the Hydaspes River (known today as the Jhelum River)

The sections were conveyed upon waggons, as far as the bank of the Hydaspes;

{The distance between the Indus River close to Taxila and the Jhelum (Hydaspes) is approximately 100miles}

April 15, Wednesday

and there the vessels were fixed together again, and seen as a fleet upon that river.

April 16, Thursday

Alexander took the forces which he had when he arrived at Taxila, and the 5,000 Indians under the command of Taxiles and the chiefs of that district, and marched towards the same river.

April 18, Saturday

Chapter 125: Porus obstructs Alexander's Passage

Alexander encamped on the bank of the Hydaspes, and Poras was seen with all his army and his large troop of elephants lining the opposite bank.[661] He remained to guard the passage at the place where he saw Alexander had encamped; and sent guards to all the other parts of the river which were easily fordable, placing officers over each detachment, being resolved to obstruct the passage of the Macedonians.

April 20, Monday

When Alexander saw this, he thought it advisable to move his army in various directions, to distract the attention of Porus, and render him uncertain what to do. Dividing his army into many parts,

April 21, Tuesday

he led some of his troops now in one direction and now in another, at one time ravaging the enemy's country, at another looking out for a place where the river might appear easier for him to ford it. The rest of his troops he entrusted[662] to his different generals, and sent them about in many directions. He also conveyed corn from all quarters into his camp from the land on this side the Hydaspes, so that it might be evident to Porus that he had, resolved to remain quiet near the bank until the water of the river subsided in the winter, and afforded him a passage in many places.

April 23, Thursday

As his vessels were sailing up and down the river, and skins were being filled with hay, and the whole bank appeared to be covered in one place with cavalry and in another with infantry, Porus was not allowed to keep at rest, or to bring his preparations together from all sides to any one point if he selected this as suitable for the defence of the passage. Besides at this season all the Indian rivers were flowing with swollen and turbid waters and with rapid currents; for it was the time of year when the sun is wont to turn towards the summer solstice.[663] At this season incessant and heavy rain falls in India; and the snows on the Caucasus, whence most of the rivers have their sources, melt and swell their streams to a great degree. But in the winter they again subside, become small and clear, and are fordable in certain places, with the exception of the Indus, Ganges, and perhaps one or two others. At any rate the Hydaspes becomes fordable.

{Summer solstice in 326BC is on June 22, so some time before this}

April 26, Sunday

Chapter 126: Alexander and Porus at the Hydaspes

Alexander therefore spread a report that he would wait for that season of the year, if his passage was obstructed at the present time; but yet all the time he was waiting in ambush to see whether by rapidity of movement he could steal a passage anywhere without being observed. But he perceived that it was impossible for him to cross at the place where Porus himself had encamped near the bank of the Hydaspes, not only on account of the multitude of his elephants, but also because his large army, arranged in order of battle and splendidly accoutred, was ready to attack his men as they emerged from the water. Moreover he thought that his horses would not be willing to mount the opposite bank, because the elephants would at once fall upon them and frighten them both by their aspect and trumpeting; nor even before that would they remain upon the inflated hides during the passage of the river; but when they looked across and saw the elephants they would become frantic and leap into the water. He therefore resolved to steal a crossing by the following manoeuvre:— In the night he led most of his cavalry along the bank in various directions, making a clamour and raising the battle-cry in honour of Enyalius.[664] Every kind of noise was raised, as if they were making all the preparations necessary for crossing the river. Porus also marched along the river at the head of his elephants opposite the places where the clamour was heard, and Alexander thus gradually got him into the habit of leading his men along opposite the noise. But when this occurred frequently, and there was merely a clamour and a raising of the battle-cry, Porus no longer continued to move about to meet the expected advance of the cavalry; but perceiving that his fear had been' groundless,[665] he kept his position in the camp. However he posted his scouts at many places along the bank.

May 13, Wednesday

When Alexander had brought it about that the mind of Porus no longer entertained any fear of his nocturnal attempts, he devised the following stratagem.

Chapter 127: Alexander's Strategem to Get Across

There was in the bank of the Hydaspes, a projecting headland, where the river makes a remarkable bend. It was densely covered by a grove,[666] containing all sorts of trees; and over against it in the river was an island full of trees and without a foot-track, on account of its being uninhabited. Perceiving that this island was right in front of the headland, and that both the spots were woody and adapted to conceal his attempt to cross the river, he resolved to convey his army over at this place. The headland and island were 150 stades distant from his great camp.[667] Along the whole of the bank, he posted sentries, separated as far as was consistent with keeping each other in sight, and easily hearing when any order should be sent along from any quarter. From all sides also during many nights clamours were raised and fires were burnt. But when he had made up his mind to undertake the passage of the river, he openly prepared his measures for crossing opposite the camp. Craterus had been left behind at the camp with his own division of cavalry, and the horsemen from the Arachotians and Parapamisadians, as well as the brigades of Alcetas and Polysperchon from the phalanx of the Macedonian infantry, together with the chiefs of the Indians dwelling this side of the Hyphasis, who had with them 5,000 men. He gave Craterus orders not to cross the river before Porus moved off with his forces against them, or before he ascertained that Porus was in flight and that they were victorious.[668] " If however," said he, "Porus should take only a part of his army and march against me, and leave the other part with the elephants in his camp, in that case do thou also remain in thy present position. But if he leads all his elephants with him against me, and a part of the rest of his army is left behind in the camp, then do thou cross the river with all speed. For it is the elephants alone," said he, "which render it impossible for the horses to land on the other bank. The rest of the army can easily cross."

Chapter 128: Passage of the Hydaspes

Such were the injunctions laid upon Craterus. Between the island and the great camp where Alexander had left this general, he posted Meleager,

Attains, and Gorgias, with the Grecian mercenaries, cavalry and infantry, giving them instructions to cross in detachments, breaking up the army as soon as they saw the Indians already involved in battle. He then picked the select body- guard called the Companions, as well as the cavalry regiments of Hephaestion, Perdiccas, and Demetrius, the cavalry from Bactria, Sogdiana, and Scythia, and the Daan horse-archers; and from the phalanx of infantry the shield-bearing guards, the brigades of Clitus and Coenus, with the archers and Agrianians, and made a secret march, keeping far away from the bank of the river, in order not to be seen marching towards the island and headland, from which he had determined to cross. There the skins were filled in the night with the hay which had been procured long before, and they were tightly stitched up. In the night a furious storm of rain occurred, by which his preparations and attempt to cross were rendered still more unobserved, since the noise of the thunder and the storm drowned with its din the clatter of the weapons and the noise which arose from the orders given by the officers. Most of the vessels, the thirty-oared galleys included with the rest, had been cut in pieces by his order and conveyed to this place, where they had been fixed together again[669] and hidden in the wood.

May 14, Thursday
Battle at the Hydaspes (likely before May18, Monday and soon after the full moon on May 11, Monday location likely a few miles downstream of modern-day Jhelum city in Pakistan, possibly near the town of Rasool)

At the approach of daylight, both the wind and the rain calmed down; and the rest of the army went over opposite the island, the cavalry mounting upon the skins, and as many of the foot soldiers as the boats would receive getting into them. They went so secretly that they were not observed by the sentinels posted by Porus, before they had already got beyond the island and were only a little way from the other bank.

Chapter 129: Passage of the Hydaspes

Alexander himself embarked in a thirty-oared galley and went over, accompanied by Perdiccas, Lysimachus, the confidential body-guards, Seleucus, one of the Companions, who was afterwards king,[670] and half of the shield-bearing guards; the rest of these troops being conveyed in

242

other galleys of the same size. When the soldiers got beyond the island, they openly directed their course to the bank; and when the sentinels perceived that they had started, they at once rode off to Porus as fast as each man's horse could gallop. Alexander himself was the first to land, and he at once took the cavalry as they kept on landing from his own and the other thirty-oared galleys, and drew them up in proper order. For the cavalry had received orders to land first; and at the head of these in regular array he advanced. But through ignorance of the locality he had effected a landing on ground which was not a part of the mainland, but an island, a large one indeed and where from the fact that it was an island, he more easily escaped notice. It was cut off from the rest of the land by a part of the river where the water was shallow. However, the furious storm of rain, which lasted the greater part of the night, had swelled the water so much that his cavalry could not find out the ford; and he was afraid that he would have to undergo another labour in crossing as great as the first. But when at last the ford was found, he led his men through it with much difficulty; for where the water was deepest, it reached higher than the breasts of the infantry; and of the horses only the heads rose above the river.[671] When he had also crossed this piece of water, he selected the choice guard of cavalry, and the best men from the other cavalry regiments, and brought them up from column into line on the right wing.[672] In front of all the cavalry he posted the horse-archers, and placed next to the cavalry in front of the other infantry the royal shield-bearing guards under the command of Seleucus. Near these he placed the royal foot-guard, and next to these the other shield-bearing guards, as each happened at the time to have the right of precedence. On each side, at the extremities of the phalanx, his archers, Agrianians and javelin-throwers were posted.

Chapter 130: The Battle at the Hydaspes

Having thus arranged his army, he ordered the infantry to follow at a slow pace and in regular order, numbering as it did not much under 6,000 men; and because he thought he was superior in cavalry, he took only his horse-soldiers, who were 5,000 in number, and led them forward with speed. He also instructed Tauron, the commander of the archers, to lead them on also with speed to back up the cavalry. He had come to the conclusion that if Porus should engage him with all his forces, he would easily be able to overcome him by attacking with his cavalry, or to stand on the defensive until his infantry arrived in the course of the action; but if the Indians should be alarmed at his extraordinary audacity in making the passage of the river and take to flight, he would be able to keep close to them in their flight, so that the slaughter of them in the retreat being greater, there would be only a slight work left for him. Aristobulus says that the son of Porus arrived with about sixty chariots, before Alexander made his later passage from the large island, and that he could have hindered Alexander's crossing (for he made the passage with difficulty even when no one opposed him); if the Indians had leaped down from their chariots and assaulted those who first emerged from the water. But he passed by with the chariots and thus made the passage quite safe for Alexander; who on reaching the bank discharged his horse-archers against the Indians in the chariots, and these were easily put to rout, many of them being wounded. Other writers say that a battle took place between the 'Indians who came with the son of Porus and Alexander at the head of his cavalry, that the son of Porus came with a greater force, that Alexander himself was wounded by him, and that his horse Bucephalas, of which he was exceedingly fond, was killed, being wounded, like his master by the son of Porus. Bat Ptolemy, son of Lagus, with whom I agree, gives a different account. This author also says that Porus despatched his son, but not at the head of merely sixty chariots; nor is it indeed likely that Porus hearing from his scouts that either Alexander himself or at any rate a part of his army had effected the passage of the Hydaspes, would despatch his son against him with only sixty chariots. These indeed were too many to be sent out as a reconnoitring party, and not adapted for speedy retreat; but they were by no means a sufficient force to keep back those of the enemy who had not yet got across, as well as to attack those who had already landed. Ptolemy says that the son of Porus arrived at the head of 2000 cavalry and 120 chariots; but that Alexander had already made even the last passage from the island before he appeared.

Chapter 131: Arrangements of Porus

Ptolemy also says that Alexander in the first place sent the horse-archers against these, and led the cavalry himself, thinking that Porus was approaching with all his forces, and that this body of cavalry was marching in front of the rest of his army, being drawn up by him as the vanguard. But as soon as he had ascertained with accuracy the number of the Indians, he immediately made a rapid charge upon them with the cavalry around him. When they perceived that Alexander himself and the body of cavalry around Mm had made the assault, not in line of battle regularly formed, bat by squadrons, they gave way; and 400 of their cavalry, including the son of Porus, fell in the contest. The chariots also were captured, horses and all, being heavy and slow in the retreat, and useless in the action itself on account of the clayey ground. When the horsemen who had escaped from this rout brought news to Porus that Alexander himself had crossed the river with the strongest part of his army, and that his son had been slain in the battle, he nevertheless could not make up his mind what course to take, because the men who had been left behind under Craterus were seen to be attempting to cross the river from the great camp which was directly opposite his position. However, at last he preferred to march against Alexander himself with all his army, and to come into a decisive conflict with the strongest division of the Macedonians, commanded by the king in person. But nevertheless he left a few of the elephants together with a small army there at the camp to frighten the cavalry under Craterus from the bank of the river. He then took all his cavalry to the number of 4,000 men, all his chariots to the number of 300, with 200 of his elephants and 30,000 choice infantry, and marched against Alexander. When he found a place where he saw there was no clay, but that on account of the sand the ground was all level and hard, and thus fit for the advance and retreat, of horses, he there drew up his army. First he placed the elephants in the front, each animal being not less than a plethrum[673] apart, so that they might be extended in the front before the whole of the phalanx of infantry, and produce terror everywhere among Alexander's cavalry. Besides he thought that none of the enemy would have the audacity to push themselves into the spaces between the elephants, the cavalry being deterred by the fright of their horses; and still less would the infantry do so, it being likely they would be kept off in front by the heavy-armed soldiers falling upon them, and trampled down by the elephants wheeling round against them. Near these he had posted the infantry, not occupying a line on a level with the beasts, but in a second line behind them, only so far distant that the companies of foot might be pushed forward a short distance into the spaces between them. He had also bodies of infantry standing beyond the elephants on the wings; and on both sides of the infantry he had posted the cavalry, in front of which were placed the chariots on both wings of his army.

Chapter 132: Alexander's Tactics

Such was the arrangement which Porus made of his forces. As soon as Alexander observed that the Indians were drawn up in order of battle, he stopped his cavalry from advancing farther, so that he might take up the infantry as it kept on arriving; and even when the phalanx in quick march had effected a junction with the cavalry, he did not at once draw it out and lead it to the attack, not wishing to hand over his men exhausted with fatigue and out of breath, to the barbarians who were fresh and untired. On the contrary, he caused his infantry to rest until their strength was recruited, riding along round the lines to inspect them.[674] When he had surveyed the arrangement of the Indians, he resolved not to advance against the centre, in front of which the elephants had been posted, and in the gaps between them a dense phalanx of men; for he was alarmed at the very arrangements which Porus had made here with that express design. But as he was superior in the number of his cavalry, he took the greater part of that force, and marched along against the left wing of the enemy for the purpose of making an attack in this direction. Against the right wing he sent Coenus with his own regiment of cavalry and that of Demetrius, with instructions to keep close behind the barbarians when they, seeing the dense mass of cavalry opposed to them, should ride out to fight them. Seleucus, Antigenes, and Tauron were ordered to lead the phalanx of infantry, but not to engage in the action until they observed[675] the enemy's cavalry and phalanx of infantry thrown into disorder by the cavalry under his own command. But when they came within range of missiles, he launched the horse-archers, 1000 in number, against the left wing of the Indians, in order to throw those of the enemy who were posted there into confusion by the incessant storm of arrows and by the charge of the horses. He himself with the Companion cavalry marched along rapidly against the left wing of the barbarians, being eager to attack them in flank while still in a state of disorder, before their cavalry could be deployed.

Chapter 133: Defeat of Porus

Meantime the Indians had collected their cavalry from all parts, and were riding along, advancing out of their position to meet Alexander's charge. Coenus also appeared with his men in their rear, according to his instructions. The Indians, observing this, were compelled to make the line of their cavalry face both ways[676]; the largest and best part against Alexander, while the rest wheeled round against Coenus and his forces. This therefore at once threw the ranks as well as the decisions of the Indians into confusion. Alexander, seeing his opportunity, at the very moment the cavalry was wheeling round in the other direction, made an attack on those opposed to him with such vigour that the Indians could not sustain the charge of his cavalry, but were scattered and driven to the elephants, as to a friendly wall, for refuge. Upon this, the drivers of the elephants urged forward the beasts against the cavalry; but now the phalanx itself of the Macedonians was advancing against the elephants, the men casting darts at the riders and also striking the beasts themselves, standing round them on all sides. The action was unlike any of the previous contests; for wherever the beasts could wheel round, they rushed forth against the ranks of infantry and demolished the phalanx of the Macedonians, dense as it was. The Indian cavalry also, seeing that the infantry were engaged in the action, rallied again and advanced against the Macedonian cavalry. But when Alexander's men, who far excelled both in strength and military discipline, got the mastery over them the second time, they were again repulsed towards the elephants and cooped up among them. By this time the whole of Alexander's cavalry had collected into one squadron, not by any command of his, but having settled into this arrangement by the mere effect of the struggle itself; and wherever it fell upon the ranks of the Indians they were broken up with great slaughter. The beasts being now cooped up into a narrow space, their friends were no less injured by them than their foes, being trampled down in their wheeling and pushing about. Accordingly there ensued a great slaughter of the cavalry, cooped up as it was in a narrow space around the elephants. Most of the keepers of the elephants had been killed by the javelins, and some of the elephants themselves had been wounded, while others no longer kept apart in the battle on account of their sufferings or from being destitute of keepers. But, as if frantic with pain, rushing forward at friends and foes alike, they pushed about, trampled down and killed them in every kind of way. However, the Macedonians retired whenever they were assailed, for they rushed at the beasts in a more open space, and in accordance with their own plan; and when they wheeled round to return, they followed them closely and hurled javelins at them; whereas the Indians retreating among them were now receiving greater injury from them. But when the beasts were tired out, and they were no longer able to charge with any vigour, they began to retire, facing the foe like ships backing water, merely uttering a shrill piping sound. Alexander himself surrounded the whole line with his cavalry, and gave the signal that the infantry should link their shields together so as to form a very densely closed body, and thus advance in phalanx. By this means the Indian cavalry, with the exception of a few men, was quite cut up in the action; as was also the infantry, since the Macedonians were now pressing upon them from all sides. Upon this, all who could do so turned to flight through the spaces which intervened between the parts of Alexander's cavalry.

Chapter 134: Losses Of the Combatants — Porus Surrenders

At the same time Craterus and the other officers of Alexander's army who had been left behind on the bank of the Hydaspes crossed the river, when they perceived that Alexander was winning a brilliant victory. These men, being fresh, followed up the pursuit instead of Alexander's exhausted troops, and made no less a slaughter of the Indians in their retreat. Of the Indians little short of 20,000 infantry and 3,000 cavalry were killed in this battle.[677] All their chariots were broken to pieces; and two sons of Porus were slain, as were also Spitaces, the governor of the Indians of that district, the managers of the elephants and of the chariots, find all the cavalry officers and generals of Porus's army. All the elephants which were not killed there, were captured. Of Alexander's forces, about 80 of the 6,000 foot-soldiers who were engaged in the first attack, were killed; 10 of the horse-archers, who were also the first to engage in the action; about 20 of the Companion cavalry, and about 200 of the other horsemen fell.[678] When Porus, who exhibited great talent in the battle, performing the deeds not only of a general but also of a valiant soldier, observed the slaughter of his cavalry, and some of his elephants lying dead, others destitute of keepers straying about in a forlorn condition, while most of his infantry had perished, he did not depart as Darius the Great King did, setting an example of flight to his men; but as long as any body of Indians remained compact in the battle, he kept up the struggle. But at last, having received a wound on the right shoulder, which part of his body alone was unprotected during the battle, he wheeled round. His coat of mail warded off the missiles from the rest of his body, being extraordinary both for its strength and the close fitting of its joints, as it was afterwards possible for those who saw him to observe. Then indeed he turned his elephant round and began to retire. Alexander, having seen that he was a great man and valiant in the battle, was very desirous of saving his life. He accordingly sent first to him Taxiles the Indian; who rode up as near to the elephant which was carrying Porus as seemed to him safe, and bade him stop the beast, assuring him that it was no longer possible for him to flee, and bidding him listen to Alexander's message. But when lie saw his old foe Taxiles, he wheeled round and was preparing to strike him with a javelin; and he would probably have killed him, if he had not quickly driven his horse forward out of the reach of Porus before he could strike him. But not even on this account was Alexander angry with Porus; but he kept on sending others in succession; and last of all Meroës an Indian, because he ascertained that he was an old friend of Porus. As soon as the latter heard the message brought to him by Meroës, being at the same time overcome by thirst, he stopped his elephant and dismounted from it. After he had drunk some water and felt refreshed, he ordered Meroës to lead him without delay to Alexander; and Meroës led him thither.[679]

Chapter 135: Alliance with Porus — Death of Buchephalas

When Alexander heard that Meroës was bringing Porus to him, he rode in front of the line with a few of the Companions to meet Porus; and stopping his horse, he admired his handsome figure and his stature,[680] which reached somewhat above five cubits. He was also surprised that he did not seem to be cowed in spirit,[681] but advanced to meet him as one brave man would meet another brave man, after having gallantly struggled in defence of his own kingdom against another king. Then indeed Alexander was the first to speak, bidding him say what treatment he would like to receive. The report goes that Porus replied: "Treat me, Alexander, in a kingly way!" Alexander being pleased at the expression, said: "For my own sake, Porus, thou shalt be thus treated; but for thy own sake do thou demand what is pleasing to thee!" But Porus said that everything was included in that, Alexander, being still more pleased at this remark, not only granted him the rule over his own Indians, but also added another country to that which he had before, of larger extent than the former.[682] Thus he treated the brave man in a kingly way, and from that time found him faithful in all things. Such was the result of Alexander's battle with Porus and the Indians living beyond the river Hydaspes, which was fought in the archonship of Hegemon at Athens, in the month Munychion[683]

{The archonship of Hegemon at Athens, in the month Munychion corresponds to the 18 April to 18 May, 326 BC alternatively Diodorus suggests the battle was fought after the summer solstice (22nd June 326 BC) in in the archonship of Chremes at Athens which corresponds to July 326 to June 325 BC. The dates used by Arrian (i.e. before the summer solstice are adopted here as subsequently Strabo is clear that the solstice was a date that he crossed the river Acesines)}

May 17, Sunday
After the battle at the Hydaspes

Alexander founded two cities, one where the battle took place, and the other on the spot whence he started to cross the river Hydaspes; the former he named Nicaea,[684] after his victory over the Indians, and the latter Bucephala in memory of his horse Bucephalas, which died there, not from having been wounded by any one, but from the effects of toil and old age; for he was about thirty years old, and quite worn out with toil.[685] This Bucephalas had shared many hardships and incurred many dangers with Alexander during many years, being ridden by none but the king, because he rejected all other riders. He was both of unusual size and generous in mettle. The head of an ox had been engraved upon him as a distinguishing mark, and according to some this was the reason why he bore that name; but others say, that though he was black he had a white mark upon his head which bore a great resemblance to the head of an ox. In the land of the Uxians this horse vanished from Alexander, who thereupon sent a proclamation throughout the country that he would kill all the inhabitants, unless they brought the horse back to him. As a result of this proclamation it was immediately brought back. So great was Alexander's attachment to the horse, and so great was the fear of Alexander entertained by the barbarians.[686] Let so much honour be paid by me to this Bucephalas for the sake of his master.

May 19, Tuesday

Chapter 136: Conquest of the Glausians — Embassy from Abisares — Passage of the Acesines

When Alexander had paid all due honours to those who had been killed in the battle, he offered the customary sacrifices to the gods in gratitude for his victory, and celebrated a gymnastic and horse contest upon the bank of the Hydaspes at the place where he first crossed with his army.[687]

May 21, Thursday

He then left Craterus behind with a part of the army, to erect and fortify the cities which he was founding there;

May 22, Friday

but he himself marched against the Indians conterminous with the dominion of Porus. According to Aristobulus the name of this nation was Glauganicians; but Ptolemy calls them Glausians. I am quite indifferent which name it bore. Alexander traversed their land with half the Companion cavalry, the picked men from each phalanx of the infantry, all the horse-bowmen, the Agrianians, and the archers. All the inhabitants came over to him on terms of capitulation; and he thus took thirty-seven cities, the inhabitants of which, where they were fewest, amounted to no less than 5,000, and those of many numbered above 10,000. He also took many villages, which were no less populous than the cities. This land also he granted to Porus to rule; and sent Taxiles back to his own abode after affecting a reconciliation between him and Porus.

June 14, Sunday

At this time arrived envoys from Abisares,[688] who told him that their king was ready to surrender himself and the land which he ruled. And yet before the battle which was fought between Alexander and Porus, Abisares intended to join his forces with those of the latter. On this occasion he sent his brother with the other envoys to Alexander, taking with them money and forty elephants as a gift.

June 15, Monday

Envoys also arrived from the independent Indians, and from a certain other Indian ruler named Porus.[689] Alexander ordered Abisares to come to him as soon as possible, threatening that unless he came he would see him arrive with his army at a place where he would not rejoice to see him.

June 17, Wednesday

At this time Phrataphernes, viceroy of Parthia and Hyrcania, came to Alexander at the head of the Thracians who had been left with him. Messengers also came from Sisicottus, viceroy of the Assacenians, to inform him that those people had slain their governor and revolted from Alexander.

June 18, Thursday

Against these he despatched Philip and Tyriaspes with an army, to arrange and set in order the affairs of their land. He himself advanced towards the river Acesines.[690]

June 22, Monday
Alexander crosses the River Acesines (modern day Chenab River) on the Summer Solstice in 326 BC according to Strabo

Ptolemy, son of Lagus, has described the size of this river alone of those in

India, stating that where Alexander crossed it with his army upon boats and skins, the stream was rapid and the channel was full of large and sharp rocks, over which the water being violently carried seethed and dashed. He says also that its breadth amounted to fifteen stades; that those who went over upon skins had an easy passage; but that not a few of those who crossed in the boats perished there in the water, many of the boats being wrecked upon the rocks and dashed to pieces. From this description then it would be possible for one to come to a conclusion by comparison, that the size of the river Indus has been stated not far from the fact by those who think that its mean breadth is forty stades, but that it contracts to fifteen stades where it is narrowest and therefore deepest; and that this is the width of the Indus in many places. I come then to the conclusion that Alexander chose a part of the Acesines where the passage was widest, so that he might find the stream slower than elsewhere.

{According to Srtrabo, this occurred at the Summer Solstice in 326 BC. Likely downstream of Wazirabad, approximately 40miles from the Jhelum River}

June 23, Tuesday

Chapter 137: Advance Beyond the Hydraotes

After crossing the river,[691] he left Coenus with his own brigade there upon the bank, with instructions to superintend the passage of the part of the army which had been left behind for the purpose of collecting[692] corn and other supplies from the country of the Indians which was already subject to him.

June 24, Wednesday

He now sent Porus away to his own abode, commanding him to select the most warlike of the Indians and take all the elephants he had and come to him. He resolved to pursue the other Porus, the bad one, with the lightest troops in his army, because he was informed that he had left the land which he ruled and had fled. For this Porus, while hostilities subsisted between Alexander and the other Porus, sent envoys to Alexander offering to surrender both himself and the land subject to him, rather out of enmity to Porus than from friendship to Alexander. But when he ascertained that the former had been released, and that he was ruling over another large country in addition to his own, then, fearing not so much Alexander as the other Porus, his namesake, he fled from his own land, taking with him as many of his warriors as he could persuade to share his flight. Against this man Alexander marched,

June 25, Thursday
Arrival at the Hydraotes River (modern-day Ravi River)

and arrived at the Hydraotes,[693] which is another Indian river, not less than the Acesines in breadth, but less in swiftness of current. He traversed the whole country as far as the Hydraotes, leaving garrisons in the most suitable places, in order that Craterus and Coenus might advance with safety, scouring most of the land for forage. Then he despatched Hephaestion into the land of the Porus who had revolted, giving him a part of the army, comprising two brigades of infantry, his own regiment of cavalry with that of Demetrius and half of the archers, with instructions to hand the country over to the other Porus, to subdue any independent tribes of Indians which dwelt near the banks of the river Hydraotes, and to give them also into the hands of Porus to rule.

{The Ravi River just downstream of Lahore is approximately 65miles away from Wazirabad-Chenab}

June 27, Saturday
Alexander crosses the Hydraotes (modern-day Ravi) River

He himself then crossed the river Hydraotes, not with difficulty, as he had crossed the Acesines.

June 28, Sunday
Date of the lunar eclipse in 326 BC

As he was advancing into the country beyond the Hydraotes, it happened that most of the people yielded themselves up on terms of capitulation; but some came to meet him with arms, while others who tried to escape he captured and forcibly reduced to obedience.

Chapter 138: Invasion of the Land of the Cathaeans

Meantime he received information that the tribe called Cathaeans and some other tribes of the independent Indians were preparing for battle, if he approached their land; and that they were summoning to the enterprise all the tribes conterminous with them who were in like manner independent. He was also informed that the city, Sangala by name,[694] near which they were thinking of having the struggle, was a strong one. The Cathaeans themselves were considered very daring and skilful in war; and two other tribes of Indians, the Oxydracians and Mallians, were in the same temper as the Oathaeans. For a short time before it happened that Porus and Abisares had marched against them with their own forces and had roused many other tribes of the independent Indians to arms, but were forced to retreat without effecting anything worthy of the preparations they had made.

When Alexander was informed of this,

{Strabo suggests that there was a lunar eclipse considered as a bad omen after crossing the Hydraotes a short time before the episode at Sangala.

Sangala has been suggested to correspond to modern-day Sialkot though this is unlikely as it doesn't fit with the side of the Ravi river on which Alexander had crossed. Sangala possibly corresponds somewhere downstream of Amritsar and Lahore, or possibly modern-day Shahpur Kanjra near Lahore}

June 29, Monday
Arrival at Pimprama

he made a forced march against the Cathaeans, and on the second day after starting from the river Hydraotes he arrived at a city called Pimprama, inhabited by a tribe of Indians named Adraistaeans, who yielded to him on terms of capitulation.
{Pimprama probably corresponds to an area now covered by the modern city of Lahore}

June 30, Tuesday

Giving his army a rest the next day,

July 01, Wednesday
Battle against the Cathaeans at Sangala

he advanced on the third day to Sangala, where the Oathaeans and the other neighbouring tribes had assembled and marshalled themselves in front of the city upon a hill which was not precipitous on all sides. They had posted their waggons all round this hill and were encamping within them in such, a way that they were surrounded by a triple palisade of waggons. When Alexander perceived the great number of the barbarians and the nature of their position, he drew up his forces in the order which seemed to him especially adapted to his present circumstances, and sent his horse-archers at once without any delay against them, ordering them to ride along and shoot at them from a distance; so that the Indians might not be able to make any sortie, before his army was in proper array, and that even before the battle commenced they might be wounded within their stronghold. Upon the right wing he posted the guard of cavalry and the cavalry regiment of Clitus; next to these the shield-bearing guards, and then the Agrianians. Towards the left he had stationed Perdiccas with his own regiment of cavalry, and the battalions of foot Companions. The archers he divided into two parts and placed them on each wing. While he was marshalling his army, the infantry and cavalry of the rear-guard came up. Of these, he divided the cavalry into two parts and led them to the wings, and with the infantry which came up he made the ranks of the phalanx more dense and compact. He then took the cavalry which had been drawn up on the right, and led it towards the waggons on the left wing of the Indians; for here their position seemed to him more easy to assail, and the waggons had not been placed together so densely.

Chapter 139: Assault upon Sangala

As the Indians did not run out from behind the waggons against the advancing cavalry, but mounted upon them and began to shoot from the top of them, Alexander, perceiving that it was not the work for cavalry, leaped down from his horse, and on foot led the phalanx of infantry against them. The Macedonians without difficulty forced the Indians from the first row of waggons; but then the Indians, taking their stand in front of the second row, more easily repulsed the attack, because they were posted in denser array in a smaller circle. Moreover the Macedonians were attacking them likewise in a confined space, while the Indians were secretly creeping under the front row of waggons, and without regard to discipline were assaulting their enemy through the gaps left between the waggons as each man found a chance.[695] But nevertheless even from these the Indians were forcibly driven by the phalanx of infantry. They no longer made a stand at the third row, but fled as fast as possible into the city and shut themselves up in it. During that day Alexander with his infantry encamped round the city, as much of it, at least, as his phalanx could surround; for he could not with his camp completely encircle the wall, so extensive was it. Opposite the part unenclosed by his camp, near which also was a lake, he posted the cavalry, placing them all round the lake, which he discovered to be shallow. Moreover, he conjectured that the Indians, being terrified at their previous defeat, would abandon the city in the night; and it turned out just as he had conjectured; for about the second watch of the night most of them dropped down from the wall, but fell in with[696] the sentinels of cavalry. The foremost of them were cut to pieces by these; but the men behind them perceiving that the lake was guarded all round, withdrew into the city again. Alexander now surrounded the city with a double stockade, except in the part where the lake shut it in, and round the lake he posted more perfect guards. He also resolved to bring military engines up to the wall, to batter it down. But some of the men in the city deserted to him, and told him that the Indians intended that very night to steal out of the city and escape by the lake, where the gap in the stockade existed. He accordingly stationed Ptolemy, son of Lagus, there, giving him three regiments of the shield-bearing guards, all the Agrianians, and one line of archers, pointing out to him the place where he especially conjectured the barbarians would try to force their way. "When thou perceivest the barbarians forcing their way here," said he, "do thou, with the army obstruct their advance, and order the bugler to give the signal. And do you, officers, as soon as the signal has been given, each being arrayed in battle order with your own men, advance towards the noise, wherever the bugle summons you. Nor will I myself withdraw from the action."

Chapter 140: Capture of Sangala

Such were the orders he gave; and Ptolemy collected there as many waggons as he could from those which had been left behind in the first flight, and placed them athwart, so that there might seem to the fugitives in the night to be many difficulties in their way; and as the stockade had been knocked down, or had not been firmly fixed in the ground, he ordered his men to heap up a mound of earth in various places between the lake and the wall. This his soldiers effected in the night.

July 02, Thursday
Victory at Sangala

When it was about the fourth watch,[697] the barbarians, just as Alexander had been informed, opened the gates towards the lake, and made a run in that direction. However they did not escape the notice of the guards there, nor that of Ptolemy, who had been placed behind them to render aid. But at this moment the buglers gave him the signal, and he advanced against the barbarians with his army fully equipped and drawn up in battle array. Moreover the waggons and the stockade which had been placed in the intervening space, were an obstruction to them. When the bugle sounded and Ptolemy attacked them, killing the men as they kept on stealing out through the waggons, then indeed they were driven back again into the city; and in their retreat 500 of them were killed. In the meanwhile Porus arrived, bringing with him the elephants that were left to -him, and 5,000 Indians. Alexander had constructed his military engines and they were being led up to the wall; but before any of it was battered down, the Macedonians took the city by storm, digging under the wall, which was made of brick, and placing scaling ladders against it all round. In the capture 17,000 of the Indians were killed, and above 70,000 were captured, besides 300 chariots and 500 cavalry. In the whole siege a little less than 100 of Alexander's army were killed; but the number of the wounded was greater than the proportion of the slain, being more than 1,200, among whom were Lysimachus, the confidential bodyguard, and other officers.

July 03, Friday

After burying the dead according to his custom,

July 04, Saturday

Alexander sent Eumenes, the secretary,[698] with 300 cavalry to the two cities which had joined Sangala in revolt, to tell those who held them about the capture of Sangala, and to inform them that they would receive no harsh treatment from Alexander if they stayed there and received him as a friend; for no harm had happened to any of the other independent Indians who had surrendered to him of their own accord. But they had become frightened, and had abandoned the cities and were fleeing; for the news had already reached them that Alexander had taken Sangala by storm.

July 06, Monday

When Alexander was informed of their flight he pursued them with speed;

July 08, Wednesday

but most of them were too quick for him, and effected their escape, because the pursuit began from a distant starting-place. But all those who were left behind in the retreat from weakness, were seized by the army and killed, to the number of about 500. Then, giving up the design of pursuing the fugitives any further,

July 11, Saturday

he returned to Sangala,

July 12, Sunday

and razed the city to the ground. He added the land to that of the Indians who had formerly been independent, but who had then voluntarily submitted to him.

July 14, Tuesday

He then sent Porus with his forces to the cities which had submitted to him, to introduce garrisons into them;

July 15, Wednesday
Arrival at the Hyphasis River (modern-day Beas River)

whilst he himself, with his army, advanced to the river Hyphasis,[699] to subjugate the Indians beyond it. Nor did there seem to him any end of the war, so long as anything hostile to him remained.

{The Hyphasis corresponds to the Beas River and Alexander possibly arrived to an area north of the town of Gowindwal, approximately 50miles from Lahore}

July 16, Thursday

Chapter 141: The Army Refuses to Advance — Alexander's Speech to the Officers

It was reported that the country beyond the river Hyphasis was fertile, and that the men were good agriculturists, and gallant in war; and that they conducted their own political affairs in a regular and constitutional manner. For the multitude was ruled by the aristocracy, who governed in no respect contrary to the rules of moderation. It was also stated that the men of that district possessed a much greater number of elephants than the other Indians, and that those men were of very great stature, and excelled in valour. These reports excited in Alexander an ardent desire to advance farther; but the spirit of the Macedonians now began to flag, when they saw the king raising one labour after another, and incurring one danger after another.

July 17, Friday

Conferences were held throughout the camp, in which those who were the most moderate bewailed their lot, while others resolutely declared that they would not follow Alexander any farther, even if he should lead the way.

July 18, Saturday
Alexander addresses his officers

When he heard of this, before the disorder and pusillanimity of the soldiers should advance to a great degree, he called a council of the officers of the brigades and addressed them as follows:— "Macedonians and Grecian allies, seeing that you no longer follow me into dangerous enterprises with a resolution equal to that which formerly animated you, I have collected you together into the same spot, so that I may either persuade you to march forward with me, or may be persuaded by you to return. If indeed the labours which you have already undergone up to our present position seem to you worthy of disapprobation, and if you do not approve of my leading you into them, there can be no advantage in my speaking any further. But, if as the result of these labours, you hold possession of Ionia,[700] the Hellespont, both the Phrygias, Cappadocia, Paphlagonia, Lydia, Caria, Lycia, Pamphylia, Phoenicia, Egypt together with Grecian Libya, as well as part of Arabia, Hollow Syria, Syria between the rivers,[701] Babylon, the nation of the Susians, Persia, Media, besides all the nations which the Persians and the Medes ruled, and many of those which they did not rule, the land beyond the Caspian Gates, the country beyond the Caucasus, the Tanais, as well as the land beyond that river, Bactria, Hyrcania, and the Hyrcanian Sea; if we have also subdued the Scythians as far as the desert; if, in addition to these, the river Indus flows through our territory, as do also the Hydaspes, the Acesines, and the Hydraotes, why do ye shrink from adding the Hyphasis also, and the nations beyond this river, to your empire of Macedonia? Do ye fear that your advance will be stopped in the future by any other barbarians? Of whom some submit to us of their own accord, and others are captured in the act of fleeing, while others, succeeding in their efforts to escape, hand over to us their deserted land, which we add to that of our allies, or to that of those who have voluntarily submitted to us.

Chapter 142: Alexander's Speech (continued)

"I, for my part, think, that to a brave man there is no end to labours except the labours themselves, provided they lead to glorious achievements. But if any one desires to hear what will be the end to the warfare itself, let him learn that the distance still remaining before we reach the river Ganges and the Eastern Sea is not great; and I inform you that the Hyrcanian Sea will be seen to be united with this, because the Great Sea encircles the whole earth. I will also demonstrate both to the Macedonians and to the Grecian allies, that the Indian Gulf is confluent with the Persian, and the Hyrcanian Sea with the Indian Gulf. From the Persian Gulf our expedition will sail round into Libya as far as the Pillars of Heracles.[702] From the pillars all the interior of Libya[703] becomes ours, and so the whole of Asia[704] will belong to us, and the limits of our empire, in that direction, will be those which God has made also the limits of the earth. But, if we now return, many warlike nations are left unconquered beyond the Hyphasis as far as the Eastern Sea, and many besides between these and Hyrcania in the direction of the north wind, and not far from these the Scythian races. Wherefore, if we go back, there is reason to fear that the races which are now held in subjection, not being firm in their allegiance, may be excited to revolt by those who are not yet subdued. Then our many labours will prove to have been in vain; or it will be necessary for us to. incur over again fresh labours and dangers, as at the beginning. But, O Macedonians and Grecian allies, stand firm! Glorious are the deeds of those who undergo labour and run the risk of danger; and it is delightful to live a life of valour and to die leaving behind immortal glory. Do ye not know that our ancestor[705] reached so great a height of glory as from being a man to become a god, or to seem to become one, not by remaining in Tiryns[706] or Argos, or even in the Pelopounese or at Thebes? The labours of Dionysus were not few, and he was too exalted a deity to be compared with Heracles. But we, indeed, have penetrated into regions beyond Nysa[707]; and the rock of Aornus, which Heracles was unable to capture, is in our possession. Do ye also add the parts of Asia still left unsubdued to those already acquired, the few to the many. But what great or glorious deed could we have performed, if, sitting at ease in Macedonia, we had thought it sufficient to preserve our own country without any labour, simply repelling the attacks of the nations on our frontiers, the Thracians, Illyrians, and Triballians, or even those Greeks who were unfriendly to our interests? If, indeed, without undergoing labour and being free from danger I were acting as your commander, while you were undergoing labour and incurring danger, not without reason would you be growing faint in spirit and resolution, because you alone would be sharing the labours, while procuring the rewards of them for others. But now the labours are common to you and me, we have an equal share of the dangers, and the rewards are open to the free competition of all. For the land is yours, and you act as its viceroys. The greater part also of the money now comes to you; and when we have traversed the whole of Asia, then, by Zeus, not merely having satisfied your expectations, but having even exceeded the advantages which each man hopes to receive, those of you who wish to return home I will send back to their own land, or I will myself lead them back; while those who remain here, I will make objects of envy to those who go back."[708]

Chapter 143: The Answer of Coenus

When Alexander had uttered these remarks, and others in the same strain, a long silence ensued, for the auditors neither had the audacity to speak in opposition to the king without constraint, nor did they wish to acquiesce in his proposal. Hereupon, he repeatedly urged any one who wished it, to speak, if he entertained different views from those which he had himself expressed. Nevertheless the silence still continued a long time; but at last, Coenus, son of Polemocrates, plucked up courage and spoke as follows[709]:— "O king, inasmuch as thou dost not wish to rule Macedonians by compulsion, but sayest thou wilt lead them by persuasion, or yielding to their persuasion wilt not use violence towards them, I am going to make a speech, not on my own behalf and that of my colleagues here present, who are held in greater honour than the other soldiers, and most of us have already carried off the rewards of our labours, and from our preeminence are more zealous than the rest to serve thee in all things; but I am going to speak on behalf of the bulk of the army. On behalf of this army I am not going to say what may be gratifying to the men, but what I consider to be both advantageous to thee at present, and safest for the future. I feel it incumbent upon me not to conceal what I think the best course to pursue, both on account of my age, the honour paid to me by the rest of the army at thy behest, and the boldness which I have without any hesitation displayed up to the present time in incurring dangers and undergoing labours. The more numerous and the greater the exploits have been, which were achieved by thee as our commander, and by those who started from home with thee, the more advantageous does it seem to me that some end should be put to our labours and dangers. For thou thyself seest how many Macedonians and Greeks started with thee, and how few of us have been left. Of our number thou didst well in sending back home the Thessalians at once from Bactra, because thou didst perceive that they were no longer eager to undergo labours.[710] Of the other Greeks, some have been settled as colonists in the cities which thou hast founded; where they remain not indeed all of them of their own free will. The Macedonian soldiers and the other Greeks who still continued to share our labours and dangers, have either perished in the battles, become unfit for war on account of their wounds, or been left behind in the different parts of Asia. The majority, however, have perished from disease, so that few are left out of many; and these few are no longer equally vigorous in body, while in spirit they are much more exhausted. AH those whose parents still survive, feel a great yearning to see them once more; they feel a yearning after their wives and children, and a yearning for their native land itself; which it is surely pardonable for them to yearn to see again with the honour and dignity they have acquired from thee, returning as great men, whereas they departed small, and as rich men instead of being poor. Do not lead us now against our will; for thou wilt no longer find us the same men in regard to dangers, since free-will will be wanting to us in the contests. But, rather, if it seem good to thee, return to thy own land, see thy mother, regulate the affairs of the Greeks, and carry to the home of thy fathers these victories so many and great. Then start afresh on another expedition, if thou wishest, against these very tribes of Indians situated towards the east; or, if thou wishest, into the Euxine Sea[711]; or else against Carchedon and the parts of Libya beyond the Carchedonians.[712] It is now thy business to manage these matters; and the other Macedonians and Greeks will follow thee, young men in place of old, fresh men in place of exhausted ones, and men to whom warfare has no terrors, because up to the present time they have had no experience of it; and they will be eager to set out, from hope of future reward. The probability also is, that they will accompany thee with still more zeal on this account, when they see that those who in the earlier expedition shared thy labours and dangers have returned to their own abodes as rich men instead of being poor, and renowned instead of being obscure as they were before. Self-control in the midst of success is the noblest of all virtues, king! For thou hast nothing to fear from enemies, while thou art commanding and leading such an army as this; but the visitations of the deity are unexpected, and consequently men can take no precautions against them."

Chapter 144: Alexander Resolves to Return

When Coenus had concluded this speech, loud applause was given to his words by those who were present; and the fact that many even shed tears, made it still more evident that they were disinclined to incur further hazards, and that return would be delightful to them. Alexander then broke up the conference, being annoyed at the freedom of speech in which Coenus indulged, and the hesitation displayed by the other officers.

July 19, Sunday

But the next day he called the same men together again in wrath, and told them that he intended to advance farther, but would not force any Macedonian to accompany him against his will; that he would have those only who followed their king of their own accord; and that those who wished to return home were at liberty to return and carry back word to their relations that they were come back, having deserted their king in the midst of his enemies. Having said this, he retired into his tent, and did not admit any of the Companions on that day, or until the third day from that, waiting to see if any change would occur in the minds of the Macedonians and Grecian allies, as is wont to happen as a general rule among a crowd of soldiers, rendering them more disposed to obey. But on the contrary, when there was a profound silence throughout the camp, and the soldiers were evidently annoyed at his wrath, without being at all changed by it, Ptolemy, son of Lagus, says that he none the less offered sacrifice there for the passage of the river, but the victims were unfavourable to him when he sacrificed.

July 22, Wednesday
Alexander Accedes to his officers

Then indeed he collected the oldest of the Companions and especially those who were friendly to him, and as all things indicated the advisability of returning, he made known to the army that he had resolved to march back again.

Chapter 145: Alexander Recrosses the Hydraotes and Acesines

Then they shouted as a mixed multitude would shout when rejoicing; and most of them shed tears of joy. Some of them even approached the royal tent, and prayed for many blessings upon Alexander; because by them alone he suffered himself to be conquered. Then he divided the army into brigades, and ordered twelve altars to be prepared, equal in height to very large towers, and in breadth much larger than towers, to serve as thank-offerings to the gods who had led him so far as a conqueror, and also to serve as monuments of his own labours.[713]

July 25, Saturday

When the altars were completed, he offered sacrifice upon them according to his custom, and celebrated a gymnastic and equestrian contest.

August 13, Thursday
Porus left in charge of the country as far as Hyphasis river (modern day Beas river)

After adding the country as far as the river Hyphasis to the dominion of Porus,

August 16, Sunday
Returns to the Hydraotes river (modern-day Ravi River)

he marched back to the Hydraotes.

{This may have corresponded to a journey from Goindwal [on the

Hyphasis/Beas river] to just south of Lahore [on the Hydraotes/Ravi river], a distance of approximately 80km}

August 18, Tuesday

Having crossed this river,

August 26, Wednesday
Arrival at the Acesines (modern-day Chenab)

he continued his return march to the Acesines, where he found the city which Hephaestion had been ordered to fortify, quite built. In this city he settled as many of the neighbouring people as volunteered to live in it, as well as those of the Grecian mercenaries who were now unfit for military service; and then began to make the necessary preparations for a voyage down the river into the Great Sea.

{Likely downstream of Wazirabad, approximately 100km from Lahore}

September 03, Thursday
Visited by Arsaces

At this time Arsaces, the ruler of the land bordering on that of Abisares, and the brother of the latter, with his other relations, came to Alexander, bringing the gifts which are reckoned most valuable among the Indians, including some elephants from Abisares, thirty in number. They declared that Abisares himself was unable to come on account of illness; and with these men the ambassadors sent by Alexander to Abisares agreed. Readily believing that such was the case, he granted that prince the privilege of ruling his own country as his viceroy, and placed Arsaces also under his power.

September 06, Sunday

After arranging what tribute they were to pay,

September 10, Thursday
he again offered sacrifice near the river Acesines.

September 13, Sunday
Crosses Acesines (modern-day Chenab) river again

He then crossed that river again,

September 21, Monday
Comes back to Hydaspes (according to Strabo, specifically before the rising (first visibility) of Arcturus AKA Alpha Boötis occurring approximately on September 24,)

and came to the Hydaspes, where he employed the army in repairing the damage caused to the cities of Nicaea and Bucephala by the rain, and put the other affairs of the country in order.

{This may have been near Rasool/ Rasul just south of Jhelum, modern-day Punjab, approximately 60km from Wazirabad}

Chapter 146 (Start of Book 6): Preparations for a Voyage down the Indus

Alexander now resolved to sail down the Hydaspes to the Great Sea, after he had prepared on the banks of that river many thirty-oared galleys and others with one and a half bank of oars, as well as a number of vessels for conveying horses, and all the other things requisite for the easy conveyance of an army on a river. At first he thought he had discovered the origin of the Nile, when he saw crocodiles in the river Indus, which he had seen in no other river except the Nile,[714] as well as beans growing near the banks of the Acesines of the same kind as those which the Egyptian land produces.[715] This conjecture was confirmed when he heard that the Acesines falls into the Indus. He thought the Nile rises somewhere or other in India, and after flowing through an extensive tract of desert country loses the name of Indus there; but afterwards when it begins to flow again through the inhabited land, it is called Nile both by the Aethiopians of that district and by the Egyptians, and finally empties itself into the Inner Sea.[716] In like manner Homer made the river Egypt give its name to the country of Egypt.[717] Accordingly when he wrote to Olympias about the country of India, after mentioning other things, he said that he thought he had discovered the sources of the Nile, forming his conclusions about things so great from such small and trivial premisses. However, when he had made a more careful inquiry into the facts relating to the river Indus, he learned the following details from the natives: — That the Hydaspes unites its water with the Acesines, as the latter does with the Indus, and that they both yield up their names to the Indus; that the last-named river has two mouths, through which it discharges itself into the Great Sea; but that it has no connection with the Egyptian country. He then removed from the letter to his mother the part he had written about the Nile.[718] Planning a voyage down the rivers as far as the Great Sea, he ordered ships for this purpose to be prepared for him. The crews of his ships were fully supplied from the Phoenicians, Cyprians, Carians, and Egyptians who accompanied the army.

September 28, Monday
Death of Coenus

Chapter 147: Voyage down the Hydaspes

At this time Coenus, who was one of Alexander's most faithful Companions, fell ill and died, and

October 01, Thursday
Burial of Coenus

the king buried him with as much magnificence as circumstances allowed.

October 28, Wednesday
Meeting with Indian Viceroys

Then collecting the Companions and the Indian envoys who had come to him, he appointed Porus king of the part of India which had already been conquered, seven nations in all, containing more than 2,000 cities.

November 04, Wednesday
Distribution of the army before the journey down the Hydaspes

After this he made the following distribution of his army.[719] With himself he placed on board the ships all the shield-bearing guards, the archers, the Agrianians, and the body-guard of cavalry.[720] Craterus led a part of the infantry and cavalry along the right bank of the Hydaspes, while along the other bank Hephaestion advanced at the head of the most numerous and efficient part of the army, including the elephants, which now numbered about 200. These generals were ordered to march as quickly as possible to the place where the palace of Sopeithes was situated,[721] and Philip, the viceroy of the country beyond the Indus[722] extending to Bactria, was ordered to follow them with his forces after an interval of three **day**s. He sent the Nysaean cavalry back to Nysa.[723] The whole of the naval force was under the command of Nearchus; but the pilot of Alexander's ship was Onesicritus, who, in the narrative which he composed of Alexander's campaigns, falsely asserted that he was admiral, while in reality he was only a pilot.[724] According to Ptolemy, son of Lagus, whose statements I chiefly follow, the entire number of the ships was about eighty thirty-oared galleys; but the whole number of vessels, including the horse transports and boats, and all the other river craft, both those previously plying on the rivers and those built at that time, fell not far short of 2,000.[725]

November 7, Saturday
Commencement the journey down the Hydaspes (Strabo identifies that the commencement took place before the setting of the Pleiades, which in 326 BC is the November 9, Monday (cosmic setting))

Chapter 148: Voyage down the Hydaspes (continued)

When he had made all the necessary preparations the army began to embark at the approach of the dawn; while according to custom he offered sacrifice to the gods and to the river Hydaspes, as the prophets directed.[726] When he had embarked he poured a libation into the river from the prow of the ship out of a golden goblet, invoking the Acesines as well as the Hydaspes, because he had ascertained that it is the largest of all the rivers which unite with the Hydaspes, and that river confluence was not far off. He also invoked the Indus, into which the Acesines flows after its junction with the Hydaspes. Moreover he poured out libations to his forefather Heracles, to Ammon,[727] and the other gods to whom he was in the habit of sacrificing, and then he ordered the signal for starting seawards to be given with the trumpet. As soon as the signal was given they commenced the voyage in regular order; for directions had been given at what distance apart it was necessary for the baggage vessels to be arranged, as also for the vessels conveying the horses and for the ships of war; so that they might not fall foul of each other by sailing down the channel at random. He did not allow even the fast-sailing ships to get out of rank by outstripping the rest. The noise of the rowing was never equalled on any other occasion, inasmuch as it proceeded from so many ships rowed at the same time; also the shouting of the boatswains giving the time for beginning and stopping the stroke of the oars, and the clamour of the rowers, when keeping time all together with the dashing of the oars made a noise like a battle-cry. The banks of the river also, being in many places higher than the ships, and collecting the sound into a narrow space, sent back to each other an echo which was very much increased by its very compression. In some parts too the groves of trees on each side of the river helped to swell the sound, both from the solitude and the reverberation of the noise. The horses which were visible on the decks of the transports struck the barbarians who saw them with such surprise that those of them who were present at the starting of the fleet accompanied it a long way from the place of embarkation. For horses had never before been seen on board ships in the country of India; and the natives did not call to mind that the expedition of Dionysus into India was a naval one. The shouting of the rowers and the noise of the rowing were heard by the Indians who had already submitted to Alexander, and these came running down to the river's bank and accompanied him singing their native songs. For the Indians have been eminently fond of singing and dancing since the time of Dionysus and those who under his bacchic inspiration traversed the land of the Indians with him.[728]

November 09, Monday

Chapter 149: Voyage down the Hydaspes into the Acesines

Sailing thus, he stopped on the third day at the spot where he had instructed Hephaestion and Craterus to encamp on opposite banks of the river at the same place. Here he remained two **day**s, until Philip with the rest of the army came up with him.

November 11, Wednesday

He then sent this general with the men he brought with him to the river Acesines, with orders to march along the bank of that river. He also sent Craterus and Hephaestion off again with instructions how they were to conduct the march. But he himself continued his voyage down the river Hydaspes, the channel of which is nowhere less than twenty stades broad. Mooring his vessels near the banks wherever he could he received some of the Indians dwelling near into allegiance by their voluntary surrender, while he reduced by force those who came into a trial of strength with him.

November 21, Saturday

Then he sailed rapidly towards the country of the Mallians and Oxydracians, having ascertained that these tribes were the most numerous and the most warlike of the Indians in that region; and having been informed that they had put their wives and children for safety into their strongest cities, with the resolution of fighting a battle with him, he made the voyage with the greater speed with the express design of attacking them before they had arranged their plans, and while there was still lack of preparation and a state of confusion among them.

November 22, Sunday

Thence he made his second start,

November 26, Thursday
Arrival at the Hydaspes and Acesines confluence (corresponding to the Jhelum-Chenab confluence at Timmu in the Jhang District of modern-day Pakistan)

and on the fifth day reached the junction of the Hydaspes and Acesines. Where these rivers unite, one very narrow river is formed out of the two; and on account of its narrowness the current is swift. There are also prodigious eddies in the whirling stream, and the water rises in waves and plashes exceedingly, so that the noise of the swell of waters is distinctly heard by people while they are still far off. These things had previously been reported to Alexander by the natives, and he had told his soldiers; and yet, when his army approached the junction of the rivers, the noise made by the stream produced so great an impression upon them that the sailors stopped rowing, not from any word of command, but because the very boatswains who gave the time to the rowers became silent from astonishment and stood aghast at the noise.

Chapter 150: Voyage down the Acesines

When they came near the junction of the rivers, the pilots passed on the order that the men should row as hard as possible to get out of the narrows, so that the ships might not fall into the eddies and be overturned by them, but might by the vigorous rowing overcome the whirlings of the water. Being of a round form, the merchant vessels which happened to be whirled round by the current received no damage from the eddy, but the men who were on board were thrown into disorder and fright. For being kept upright by the force of the stream itself, these vessels settled again into the onward course. But the ships of war, being long, did not emerge so scatheless from the whirling current, not being raised aloft in the same way as the others upon the plashing swell of water. These ships had two ranks of oars on each side, the lower oars being only a little out of the water. These vessels getting athwart in the eddies, their oars could not be raised aloft in proper time and were consequently caught by the water and came into collision with each other. Thus many of the ships were damaged; two indeed fell foul of each other and were destroyed, and many of those sailing in them perished.[729] But when the river widened out, there the current was no longer so rapid, and the eddies did not whirl round with so much violence.

{Timmu is approximately 360km by river from Jhelum}

November 27, Friday

Alexander therefore moored his fleet on the right bank, where there was a protection from the force of the stream and a roadstead for the ships. A certain promontory also in the river jutted out conveniently for collecting the wrecks. He preserved the lives of the men who still being conveyed upon them; and

December 06, Sunday

when he had repaired the damaged ships, he ordered Nearchus to sail down the river until he reached the confines of the nation called Mallians.

December 08, Tuesday
Leaves ships to fight land battles

He himself made an inroad into the territories of the barbarians who would not yield to him, and

December 17, Thursday

after preventing them from succouring the Mallians,

December 22, Tuesday
Reunited with the navy

he again formed a junction with the naval armament.[730] Hephaestion, Craterus, and Philip had already united their forces here.

December 26, Saturday
Troops divided in to 5 parts (one of which was a navy)

Alexander then transported the elephants, the brigade of Polysperchon, the horse-archers, and Philip with his army, across the river Hydaspes, and instructed Craterus to lead them. He sent Nearchus with the fleet with orders to set sail three days before the army started. He divided the rest of his army into three parts, and ordered Hephaestion to go five days in advance, so that if any should flee before the men under his own command and go rapidly forward they might fall in with Hephaestion's brigade and thus be captured. He also gave a part of the army to Ptolemy, son of Lagus, with orders to follow him after the lapse of three days, so that all those who fled from him and turned, back again might fall in with Ptolemy's brigade. He ordered those in advance to wait, when they arrived at the confluence of the rivers Acesines and Hydraotes, until he himself came up; and he instructed Craterus and Ptolemy also to form a junction with him at the same place.

325 BC (LEAP YEAR)

January 02, Saturday
Marches toward the land of the Mallians

Chapter 151: Campaign against the Mallians

He then took the shield-bearing guards, the bowmen, the Agrianians, Peithon's brigade of men, who were called foot Companions, all the horse bowmen and half the cavalry Companions, and marched through a tract of country destitute of water against the Mallians, a tribe of the independent Indians.[731]

January 03, Sunday

On the first day he encamped near a small piece of water which was about 100 stades distant from the river Acesines. Having dined there and caused his army to rest a short time, he ordered every man to fill whatever vessel he had with water. After travelling the remaining part of that day and all the ensuing night a distance of about 400 stades,

January 04, Monday
Attack on a Mallian city (possibly near Dab Kalān in Multan Province, Pakistan) and the Mallian escape to the Hydraotes/ Ravi river

he at **day**break reached the city into which many of the Mallians had fled for refuge. Most of them were outside the city and unarmed, supposing that Alexander would never come against them through the waterless country. It was evident that he led his army by this route for this very reason, because it was difficult to lead an army this way, and consequently it appeared incredible to the enemy that he would lead his forces in this direction. He therefore fell upon them unexpectedly, and killed most of them without their even turning to defend themselves, since they were unarmed. He cooped the rest up in the city, and posted his cavalry all round the wall, because the phalanx of infantry had not yet[732] come up with him. He thus made use of his cavalry in place of a stockade. As soon as the infantry arrived, he sent Perdiccas with his own cavalry regiment and that of Clitus, as well as the Agrianians, against another city of the Mallians, whither many of the Indians of that region had fled for refuge. He ordered Perdiccas to blockade the men in the city, but not to commence the action until he himself should arrive, so that none might escape from this city and carry news to the rest of the barbarians that Alexander was already approaching; He then began to assault the wall; but the barbarians abandoned it, finding that they were no longer able to defend it, since many had been killed in, the capture, and others had been rendered unfit for fighting on account of their wounds. Fleeing for refuge into the citadel, they defended themselves for some time from a position commanding from its height and difficult of access. But as the Macedonians pressed on vigorously from all sides, and Alexander himself appeared now in this part of the action and now in that, the citadel was taken by storm, and all the men who had fled into it for refuge were killed, to the number of 2,000. Perdiccas also reached the city to which he had been despatched and found it deserted; but learning that the inhabitants had fled from it not long before, he made a forced march on the track of the fugitives. The light-armed troops followed him as quickly as they could on foot, so that he took and massacred as many of the fugitives as could not outstrip him and flee for safety into the river-marshes.

Chapter 152: Campaign against the Mallians (continued)

After dining and causing his men to rest until the first watch of the night, Alexander marched forward; and travelling a great distance through the night, he arrived at the river Hydraotes[733]

{Dab Kalān (the possible location of the Malian city) is approximately 55km from Timmu Bridge (confluence of the Jhelum and Chenab rivers)}

January 05, Tuesday
Attack on the Mallian fortress

at daybreak. There he ascertained that most of the Mallians had already crossed the river; but coming upon those who were still in the act of crossing, he slew many of them in their passage. Having crossed with them in pursuit without any delay by the same ford, he kept close up with those who had out- stripped him in their retreat. Many also of these he slew; some he took prisoners; but the majority of them escaped into a place strong by nature and made more so by fortifications. When the infantry reached him, Alexander despatched Peithon against the men in the fortress, giving him the command of his own brigade of infantry and two regiments of cavalry. These, attacking the place, took it at the first assault, and made slaves of all those who had fled thither for safety, at least as many of them as had not perished in the attack. After accomplishing this, Peithon returned again to the camp. Alexander in person led his forces against a certain city of the Brachmans,[734] because he ascertained that some of the Mallians had fled for refuge into it. When he reached it, he led his phalanx in serried ranks close up to the wall on all sides. The enemy seeing that their walls were being undermined, and being themselves repulsed by the missiles, abandoned the walls, and having fled for safety into the citadel, began to defend themselves from thence. A few Macedonians having rushed in with them, turning round and drawing together into a close body, drove some of them back and killed five-and-twenty of them in their retreat. Hereupon Alexander ordered the scaling-ladders to be placed against the citadel on all sides, and the wall to be undermined; and when one of the towers, being undermined, fell down, and a part of the wall between two towers was breached, and thus rendered the citadel more accessible to assault in this quarter, he was seen to be the first man to scale the wall and get hold of it. The other Macedonians seeing him were ashamed of themselves and mounted the ladders in various places. The citadel was soon in their possession. Some of the Indians began to set fire to the houses and being caught in them were killed; bat most of them were slain fighting. About 5,000 in all were killed; and on account of their valour, only a few were taken prisoners.

January 06, Wednesday

Chapter 153: Defeat of the Mallians at the River Hydraotes

Having remained there one day to give his army rest,

January 07, Thursday

he advanced on the morrow against the other Mallians. He found the cities abandoned, and ascertained that the men had fled into the desert.

January 08, Friday

There he again gave the army one day's rest, and

January 09, Saturday
Crossing the Hydraotes river (modern day Ravi river), possibly near modern-day Qatal Pur in Multan Province

on the next day sent Peithon and Demetrius the cavalry general back to the river, in command of their own troops, giving them in addition as many battalions of the light-armed infantry as were sufficient for the enterprise. Their instructions were to go along the bank of the river, and if they met any of those who had fled for safety into the woods, of which there were many near the river's bank, to kill all who refused to surrender. Peithon and Demetrius captured many of these in the woods and killed them. He himself led his forces against the largest city of the Mallians, whither he was informed many from the other cities had taken refuge. But this also the Indians abandoned when they heard that Alexander was marching against it. Crossing the river Hydraotes, they remained with their forces drawn up upon its bank, because it was high, and they thought they could obstruct Alexander's passage. When he heard this, he took all the cavalry which he had with him, and went to the part of the river where he was informed that the Mallians had drawn themselves up for battle; and the infantry was ordered to follow. When he reached the river and beheld the enemy drawn up on the opposite bank, he made no delay, but instantly plunged into the ford with the cavalry alone. When they saw that lie was now in the middle of the river, though they were drawn up ready for battle, they withdrew from the bank with all speed; and Alexander followed them with his cavalry alone. But when the Indians perceived only cavalry, they wheeled round and fought with desperate valour, being about 50,000 in number. When Alexander perceived that their phalanx was densely compact, and that his own infantry was absent, he rode right round their army and made charges upon them, but did not come to close fighting with them. Meanwhile the archers, the Agrianians and the other battalions of light-armed infantry, being picked men whom he was leading with him, arrived, and his phalanx of infantry was seen not far off. As all kinds of danger were threatening them at once, the Indians now wheeled round again and began to flee with headlong speed into the strongest of their adjacent cities; but Alexander followed them and slew many, while those who escaped into the city were cooped up within it. At first indeed he surrounded the city with the horse-soldiers as they came up from the march; but when the infantry arrived, he encamped all round the wall for this day, because not much of it was left for making the assault, and his army had been exhausted, the infantry by the long march, and the cavalry by the uninterrupted pursuit, and especially by the passage of the river.

January 10, Sunday
Alexander badly injured during attack on the Mallian Stronghold traditionally considered near Multan City/ Multan Citadel, though due to its proximity to the Hydraotes (Ravi river) more likely near Kabirwala and Sarai Sidhu in Pakistan (north of Multan City)

Chapter 154: Storming of the Mallian Stronghold

On the following day, dividing the army into two parts, he himself assaulted the wall at the head of one, and Perdiccas led on the other. Upon this the Indians did not wait to receive the attack of the Macedonians, but abandoned the walls of the city and fled for safety into the citadel. Alexander and his troops therefore split open a small gate, and got within the city long before the others; for those who had been put under Perdiccas were behind time, having experienced difficulty in scaling the walls, as most of them did not bring ladders, thinking that the city had been captured, when they observed that the walls were deserted by the defenders. But when the citadel was seen to be still in the possession of the enemy, and many of them were observed drawn up in front of it to repel attacks, some of the Macedonians tried to force an entry by undermining the wall, and others by placing scaling ladders against it, wherever it was practicable to do so. Alexander, thinking that the men who carried the ladders were too slow, snatched one from a man who was carrying it, placed it against the wall, and began to mount it, crouching under his shield. After him mounted Peucestas, the man who carried the sacred shield which Alexander took from the temple of the Trojan Athena and used to keep with him, and have it carried before him in all his battles.[735] After Peucestas, by the same ladder ascended Leonnatus the confidential body-guard; and up another ladder went Abreas, one of the soldiers who received double pay for distinguished services.[736] The king was now near the battlement of the wall, and leaning his shield against it was pushing some of the Indians within the fort, and had cleared that part of the wall, by killing others with his sword. The shield-bearing guards becoming very anxious for the king's safety, pushed each other with ardour up the same ladder and broke it; so that those who were already mounting fell down and made the ascent impracticable for the rest. Alexander then, standing upon the wall, was being assailed all round from the adjacent towers; for none of the Indians dared approach him. He was also being assailed by the men in the city, who were throwing darts at him from no great distance; for a mound of earth happened to have been heaped up there opposite the wall. Alexander was conspicuous both by the brightness of his weapons and by his extraordinary display of audacity. He therefore perceived that if he remained where he was, he would be incurring danger without being able to perform anything at all worthy of consideration; but if he leaped down within the fort he might perhaps by this very act strike the Indians with terror, and if he did not, but should only thereby be incurring danger, at any rate he would die not ignobly after performing great deeds of valour worthy of recollection by men of after times.[737] Forming this resolution, he leaped down from the wall into the citadel; where, supporting himself against the wall, he struck with his sword and killed some of the Indians who came to close quarters with him, including their leader, who rushed upon him too boldly. Another man who approached him he kept in check by hurling a stone at him, and a third in like manner. Those who advanced nearer to him he again kept off with his sword; so that the barbarians were no longer willing to approach him, but standing round him cast at him from all sides whatever any one happened to have or could get hold of at the time.

Chapter 155: Alexander Dangerously Wounded

Meantime Peucestas and Abreas, the soldier entitled to double pay, and after them Leonnatus, being the only men who happened to have scaled the wall before the ladders were broken, had leaped down and were fighting in front of the king. Abreas, the man entitled to double pay, fell there, being shot with an arrow in the forehead. Alexander himself also was wounded with an arrow under the breast through his breastplate into the chest, so that Ptolemy says air was breathed oat from the wound together with the blood. But although he was faint with exhaustion, he defended himself, as long as his blood was still warm. But the blood streaming out copiously and without ceasing at every expiration of breath, he was seized with a dizziness and swooning, and bending over fell upon his shield. After he had fallen

Peucestas defended him, holding over him in front the sacred shield brought from Troy; and on the other side he was defended by Leonnatus. But both these men were themselves wounded, and Alexander was now nearly fainting away from loss of blood. For the Macedonians had experienced great difficulty in the assault also on this account, because those who saw Alexander being shot at upon the wall and then leaping down into the citadel within, in their ardour arising from fear lest their king should meet with any mishap by recklessly exposing himself to danger, broke the ladders. Then some began to devise one plan and others another to mount upon the wall, as well as they could in their state of embarrassment, some fixing pegs into the wall, which was made of earth, and suspending themselves from these hoisted themselves up with, difficulty by their means; others got up by mounting one upon the other. The first man who got up threw himself down from the wall into the city, and so on in succession; and when they saw the king lying there on the ground they all raised a loud lamentation and howl of grief. Now ensued a desperate conflict around his fallen body, one Macedonian after another holding his shield in front of him. In the meantime some of the soldiers having shivered in pieces the bar by which the gate in the space of wall between the towers was secured, entered the city a few at the time while others, inasmuch as a gap had been made in the gate, put their shoulders under it and forced it into the space inside the wall, and thus laid the citadel open in that quarter.

Chapter 156: Alexander Wounded

Hereupon some of them began to kill the Indians, all of whom they slew, sparing not even a woman or child. Others carried off the king, who was lying in a faint condition, upon his shield ; and they could not yet tell whether he was likely to survive. Some authors have stated that Critodemus, a physician of Cos, an Asclepiad by birth[738] made an incision into the injured part and drew the weapon out of the wound. Other authors say that as there was no physician present at the critical moment, Perdiccas, the confidential body-guard, at Alexander's bidding, made an incision with his sword into the wounded part and removed the weapon. On its removal there was such a copious effusion of blood that Alexander swooned again; and the effect of the swoon was, that the effusion of blood was stanched.[739] Many other things concerning this catastrophe have been recorded by the historians; and Rumour having received the statements as they were given by the first falsifiers of the facts, still preserves them even to our times, nor will she desist from handing the falsehoods on to others also in regular succession, unless a stop is put to it by this history.[740] For example, the common account is, that this calamity befell Alexander among the Oxydracians; whereas, it really occurred among the Mallians, an independent tribe of Indians; the city belonged to the Mallians,[741] and the men who wounded him were Mallians. These people, indeed, had resolved to join their forces with the Oxydracians and then to make a desperate struggle; but he forestalled them by marching against them through the waterless country, before any aid could reach them from the Oxydracians, or they could render any help to the latter. Moreover, the common account is, that the last battle fought with Darius was near Arbela, at which battle he fled and did not desist from flight until he was arrested by Bessus and put to death at Alexander's approach; just as the battle before this was at Issus, and the first cavalry battle near the Granicus. The cavalry battle did really take place near the Granicus, and the next battle with Darius near Issus; but those authors who make Arbela most distant say that it is 600[742] stades distant from the place where the last battle between Alexander and Darius was fought, while those who make it least distant, say that it is 500 stades off. Moreover, Ptolemy and Aristobulus say that the battle was fought at Gaugamela near the river Bumodus. But as Gaugamela was not a city, but only a large village, the place is not celebrated, nor is the name pleasing to the ear; hence, it seems to me, that Arbela, being a city, has carried off the glory of the great battle. But if it is necessary to consider that this engagement took place near Arbela, being in reality so far distant from it, then it is allowable to say that the sea-battle fought at Salainis occurred near the isthmus[743] of the Corinthians, and that fought at Artemisium, in Euboea, occurred near Aegina or Sunium. Moreover, in regard to those who covered Alexander with their shields in his peril, all agree that Peucestas did so; but they no longer agree in regard to Leonnatus or Abreas, the soldier in receipt of double pay for his distinguished services. Some say that Alexander, having received a blow on the head with a piece of wood, fell down in a fit of dizziness; and that having risen again he was wounded with a dart through the corselet in the chest. But Ptolemy, son of Lagus, says that he received only this wound in the chest. However, in my opinion, the greatest error made by those who have written the history of Alexander is the following. There are some who have recorded[744] that Ptolemy, son of Lagus, in company with Peucestas, mounted the ladder with Alexander; that Ptolemy held his shield over him when he lay wounded, and that he was called Soter (the preserver) on that account.[745] And yet Ptolemy himself has recorded that he was not even present at this engagement, but was fighting battles against other barbarians at the head of another army. Let me mention these facts as a digression from the main narrative, so that the correct account of such great deeds and calamities may not be a matter of indifference to men of the future.[746]

January 12, Tuesday

Chapter 157: Anxiety of the Soldiers about Alexander

While Alexander was remaining in this place until his wound was cured, the first news which reached the camp from which he had set out to attack the Mallians was that lie had died of the wound; and at first there arose a sound of lamentation from the entire army, as one man handed the rumour on to another. When they ceased their lamentation, they became spiritless, and felt perplexed as to the man who was to become the leader of the army; for many of the officers seemed to have stood in equal rank and merit, both in the opinion of Alexander and in that of the Macedonians. They were also in a state of perplexity how to get back in safety to their own country, being quite enclosed by so many warlike nations, some of whom had not yet submitted, and who they conjectured would fight stoutly for their freedom; while others would no doubt revolt as soon as they were relieved of their fear of Alexander. Besides, they seemed at that time to be in the midst of impassable rivers, and all things appeared to them uncertain and impracticable now that they were bereft of Alexander. But when at length the news came that he was still alive, they with difficulty acquiesced in it; and did not yet believe that he was likely to survive. Even when a letter came from the king, saying that he was coming down to the camp in a short time, this did not appear to most of them worthy of credit, on account of their excessive fear; for they conjectured that the letter was concocted by his confidential body-guards and generals.

January 13, Wednesday

Chapter 158: Joy of the Soldiers at Alexander's Recovery

When Alexander became acquainted with this, for fear some attempt at a revolution might be made in the army,

January 17, Sunday
Alexander sails to his camp at the confluence of the Hydraotes (Ravi) and Acesines (Chenab) rivers (near modern day Timmu bridge/ Athara Hazari in Pakistan)

he had himself conveyed, as soon as it could be done with safety, to the bank of the river Hydraotes, and placed in a boat to sail down the river.

{The distance between the Mallian stronghold (possibly Sarai Sidhu and alexander's camp at the river confluence (possibly Timmu bridge/ Athara Hazari) is approximately 80km by river}

January 18, Monday
Alexander demonstrates he is alive at his camp

For the camp was at the confluence of the Hydraotes and Acesines, where Hephaestion was at the head of the army, and Nearchus of the fleet. When the ship bearing the king approached the camp, he ordered the tent covering to be removed from the stern, that he might be visible to all. But they were still incredulous, thinking, forsooth, that Alexander's corpse was being conveyed on the vessel; until at length he stretched out his hand to the multitude, when the ship was nearing the bank. Then the men raised a cheer, lifting their hands, some towards the sky and others to the king himself. Many even shed involuntary tears at the unexpected sight. Some of the shield-bearing guards brought a litter for him when he was conveyed out of the ship; but he ordered them to fetch his horse. When he was seen again mounting his horse, the whole army re-echoed with loud clapping of hands, so that the banks of the river and the groves near them reverberated with the sound. On approaching his tent he dismounted from his horse, so that he might be seen walking. Then the men came near, some on one side, others on the other, some touching his hands, others his knees, others only his clothes. Some only came close to get a sight of him, and went away having chanted his praise, while others threw garlands upon him, or the flowers which the country of India supplied at that season of the year. Nearchus says that some of his friends incurred his displeasure, reproaching him for exposing himself to danger in the front of the army in battle; which they said was the duty of a private soldier, and not that of the general.[747] It seems to me that Alexander was offended at these remarks, because he knew that they were correct, and that he deserved the censure. However, like those who are mastered by any other pleasure, lie had not sufficient self-control to keep aloof from danger, through his impetuosity in battle and his passion for glory. Nearchus also says that a certain old Boeotian, whose name he does not mention, perceiving that Alexander was offended at the censures of his friends and was looking sullenly at them, came near him, and speaking in the Boeotian dialect, said: "Alexander, it is the part of heroes to perform great deeds!" and repeated a certain Iambic verse, the purport of which is, that the man who performs anything great is destined also to suffer.[748] This man was not only acceptable to Alexander at the time, but was afterwards received into his more intimate acquaintance.

January 22, Friday
Submission of the Mallians and Oxydracians

Chapter 159: Voyage down the Hydraotes and Acesines into the Indus

At this time arrived envoys from the Mallians who still survived, offering the submission of the nation; also from the Oxydracians came both the leaders of the cities and the governors of the provinces, accompanied by the other 150 most notable men, with full powers to make a treaty, bringing the gifts which are considered most valuable among the Indians, and also, like the Mallians, offering the submission of their nation. They said that their error in not having sent an embassy to him before was pardonable, because they excelled other races in the desire to be free and independent, and their freedom had been secure from the time Dionysus came into India until Alexander came; but if it seemed good to him, inasmuch as there was a general report that he also was sprung from gods, they were willing to receive whatever viceroy he might appoint, pay the tribute decreed by him, and give him as many hostages as he might demand. He therefore demanded the thousand best men of the nation, whom he might hold as hostages, if he pleased; and if not, that he might keep them as soldiers in his army, until he had finished the war which he was waging against the other Indians.

January 26, Tuesday

They accordingly selected the thousand best and tallest men of their number, and sent them to him, together with 500 chariots and charioteers, though these were not demanded. Alexander appointed Philip viceroy over these people and the Mallians who were still surviving. He sent back the hostages to them, but retained the chariots.

January 30, Saturday

When he had satisfactorily arranged these matters, since many vessels had been built during the delay arising from his being wounded,[749] he embarked 1,700 of the cavalry Companions, as many of the light-armed troops as before, and 10,000 infantry, and sailed a short distance down the river Hydraotes.

February 12, Friday
Arrival at another confluence of the Hydraotes river (Ravi) and The Acesines river (Chenab), likely near Samandwāna in modern-day Pakistan

But when that river mingled its waters with the Acesines, the latter giving its name to the united stream, he continued his voyage down the Acesines,

February 27, Saturday
Arrival at the confluence of the Acesines river (Chenab) with the Indus, likely just south of Seetpur in modern-day Pakistan

until he reached its junction with the Indus. For these four large rivers,[750] which are all navigable, discharge their water into the river Indus, though each does not retain its distinct name, for the Hydaspes discharges itself into the Acesines, and after the junction the whole stream forms what is called the Acesines. Again this same river unites with the Hydraotes, and after absorbing this river, still retains its own name. After this the Acesines takes in the Hyphasis, and finally flows into the Indus under its own name; but after the junction it yields its name to the Indus. From this point I have no doubt that the Indus proceeds 100 stades,[751] and perhaps more, before it is divided so as to form the Delta ; and there it spreads out more like a lake than a river.

{The Acesines-Hydraotes (Chenab-Ravi) confluence is approximately 220 km upstream of the Acesines-Indus (Chenab-Indus) confluence}

March 06, Sunday

Chapter 160: Voyage down the Indus to the Land of Musicanus

There at the confluence of the Acesines and Indus, he waited until Perdiccas with the army arrived, after having routed on his way the independent tribe of the Abastanians.[752] Meantime, he was joined by other thirty-oared galleys and trading vessels which had been built for him among the Xathrians, another independent tribe of Indians who had yielded to him. From the Ossadians, who were also an independent tribe of Indians, came envoys to offer the submission of their nation. Having fixed the confluence of the Acesines and Indus as the limit of Philip's viceroyalty, he left with him all the Thracians and as many men from the infantry regiments as appeared to him sufficient to provide for the security of the country. He then ordered a city to be founded there at the very junction of the two rivers, expecting that it would become large and famous among men.[753] He also ordered a dockyard to be made there. At this time the Bactrian Oxyartes, father of his wife Roxana, came to him, to whom he gave the viceroyalty over the Parapamisadians, after dismissing the former viceroy, Tiryaspes, because he was reported to be exercising his authority improperly.[754] Then he transported Craterus with the main body of the army and the elephants to the left bank of the river Indus, both because it seemed easier for a heavy-armed force to march along that side of the river, and the tribes dwelling near were not quite friendly. He himself sailed down to the capital of the Sogdians; where he fortified another city, made another dockyard, and repaired his shattered vessels. He appointed Oxyartes viceroy, and Peithon general of the land extending from the confluence of the Indus and Acesines as far as the sea, together with all the coastland of India.

March 08, Tuesday

He then again despatched Craterus with his army through the country of the Arachotians and Drangians; and himself sailed down the river into the dominions of Musicanus, which was reported to be the most prosperous part of India. He advanced against this king because he had not yet come to meet him to offer the submission of himself and his land, nor had he sent envoys to seek his alliance. He had not even sent him the gifts which were suitable for a great king, or asked any favour from him.

March 09, Wednesday

He accelerated his voyage down the river to such a degree that he succeeded in reaching the confines of the land of Musicanus before he had even heard that Alexander had started against him.

March 10, Thursday
Muscicanus Capitulates to Alexander

Musicanus was so greatly alarmed that he went as fast as he could to meet him, bringing with him the gifts valued most highly among the Indians, and taking all his elephants.

March 12, Saturday

He offered to surrender both his nation and himself, at the same time acknowledging his error, which was the most effectual way with Alexander for any one to get what he requested.

March 13, Sunday

Accordingly for these considerations Alexander granted him an indemnity for his offences. He also granted him the privilege of ruling the city and country, both of which Alexander admired. Craterus was directed to fortify the citadel in the capital; which was done while Alexander was still present. A garrison was also placed in it, because he thought the place suitable for keeping the circumjacent tribes in subjection.

March 15, Tuesday

Chapter 161: Campaign against Oxycanus and Sambus

Then he took the archers, Agrianians, and cavalry sailing with him, and marched against the governor of that country, whose name was Oxycanus,[755] because he neither came himself nor did envoys come from him, to offer the surrender of himself and his land.

March 18, Friday

At the very first assault he took by storm the two largest cities under the rule of Oxycanus; in the second of which that prince himself was captured. The booty he gave to his army, but the elephants he led with himself. The other cities in the same land surrendered to him as he advanced, nor did any one turn to resist him; so cowed in spirit[756] had all the Indians now become at the thought of Alexander and his fortune.

March 25, Friday

He then marched back against Sambus, whom he had appointed viceroy of the mountaineer Indians and who was reported to have fled, because he learned that Musicanus had been pardoned by Alexander and was ruling over his own land. For he was at war with Musicanus.

March 27, Sunday
Arrival at Sindimana (possibly capital of the Sindhi people and may correspond to Hyderabad or its region)

But when Alexander approached the city which the country of Sambas held as its metropolis, the name of which was Sindimana, the gates were thrown open to him at his approach, and the relations of Sambus reckoned up his money and went out to meet him, taking with them the elephants also. They assured him that Sambus had fled, not from any hostile feeling towards Alexander, but fearing on account of the pardon of Musicanus.[757]

April 02, Saturday

He also captured another city which had revolted at this time, and slew as many of the Brachmans[758] as had been instigators of this revolt. These men are the philosophers of the Indians, of whose philosophy, if such it may be called, I shall give an account in my book descriptive of India.[759]

Chapter 162: Musicanus Executed — Capture of Patala

April 04, Monday

Meantime he was informed that Musicanus had revolted.

April 06, Wednesday

He despatched the viceroy, Peithon, son of Agenor, with a sufficient army against him, while he himself marched against the cities which had been put under the rule of Musicanus. Some of these he razed to the ground, reducing the inhabitants to slavery; and into others he introduced garrisons and fortified the citadels.

April 17, Sunday

After accomplishing this, he returned to the camp and fleet. By this time Musicanus had been captured by Peithon, who was bringing him to Alexander. The king ordered him to be hanged in his own country, and with him as many of the Brachmans as had instigated him to the revolt.

April 23, Saturday

Then came to him the ruler of the land of the Patalians,[760] who said that the Delta formed by the river Indus was still larger than the Egyptian Delta.[761] This man surrendered to him the whole of his own land and entrusted both himself and his property to him.

April 25, Monday

Alexander sent him away again in possession of his own dominions, with instructions to provide whatever was needful for the reception of the army. He then sent Craterus into Carmania with the brigades of Attains, Meleager, and Antigenes, some of the archers, and as many of the Companions and other Macedonians as, being now unfit for military service, he was despatching to Macedonia by the route through the lands of the Arachotians and Zarangians. To Craterus he also gave the duty of leading the elephants; but the rest of the army, except the part of it which was sailing with himself down to the sea, he put under the command of Hephaestion.

May 01, Sunday
Recommencement of the Voyage by water

He transported Peithon with the cavalry-lancers and Agrianians to the opposite bank of the Indus, not the one along which Hephaestion was about to lead the army. Peithon was ordered to collect men to colonize the cities which had just been fortified, and to form a junction with the king at Patala, after having settled the affairs of the Indians of that region, if they attempted any revolutionary proceedings.

May 03, Tuesday

On the third day of his voyage, Alexander was informed that the governor of the Patalians[762] had collected most of his subjects and was going away by stealth, having left his land deserted. For this reason Alexander sailed down the river with greater speed than before[763];

May 07, Saturday
Arrival at Patala (likely corresponds to modern-day Thatta in Pakistan), this date corresponds with two time corroborations. (i) Strabo suggests that this arrival corresponded to the time of the setting of the dog star Sirius, the last visibility of this star occurred at around this date in 325 BC. (ii) Plutarch suggests that the journey down the river took 8 months which fits very well here (considering the start date was also marked by a known astronomical point – the setting of the Pleiades in 326 BC), Although Strabo suggests that this was the 9th month from the beginning of his river journey down the Hydaspes, this may possibly have been based on the Attic month rather than time length (e.g. a journey from January 01 to October 01

is a 9 month journey in terms of days, but as is falls on the beginning of the 10th month, it may be mis-calculated/ rounded up to a 10 month journey)

and when he arrived at Patala, he found both the country and the city deserted by the inhabitants and tillers of the soil.

{Patala likely corresponds to modern-day Thatta in Pakistan}

May 09, Monday

He however despatched the lightest; troops in his army in pursuit of the fugitives;

May 11, Wednesday

and when some of them were captured, he sent them away to the rest, bidding them be of good courage and return, for they might inhabit the city and till the country as before.

May 16, Monday

Most of them accordingly returned.

May 19, Thursday

Chapter 163: Voyage down the Indus

After instructing Hephaestion to fortify the citadel in Patala,

May 21, Saturday

he sent men into the adjacent country, which was waterless, to dig wells and to render the land fit for habitation. Certain of the native barbarians attacked these men, and falling upon them unawares slew some of them; but having lost many of their own men, they fled into the desert. The work was therefore accomplished by those who had been sent out, another army having joined them, which

May 26, Thursday

Alexander had despatched to take part in the work, when he heard of the attack of the barbarians.

May 30, Monday

Near Patala the water of the Indus is divided into two large rivers, both of which retain the name of Indus as far as the sea. Here Alexander constructed a harbour and dockyard; and when his works had advanced towards completion he resolved to sail down as far as the mouth of the right branch of the river.[764]

June 06, Monday
Sends Leonnatus to explore around Patala

He gave Leonnatus the command of 1,000 cavalry and 8,000 heavy and light-armed infantry, and sent him to march through the island of Patala opposite the naval expedition;

June 08, Wednesday
Commences expeditionary sail around Patala

while he himself took the fastest sailing vessels, having one and a half bank of oars, all the thirty-oared galleys, and some of the boats, and began to sail down the right branch of the river. The Indians of that region bad fled, and consequently he could get no pilot for the voyage, and the navigation of the river was very difficult.

June 09, Thursday
Ships damaged

On the day after the start a storm arose, and the wind blowing right against the stream made the river hollow[765] and shattered the hulls of the vessels violently, so that most of his ships were injured, and some of the thirty-oared galleys were entirely broken up. But they succeeded in running them aground before they quite fell to pieces in the water;

June 25, Saturday

and others were therefore constructed.

June 26, Sunday

He then sent the quickest of the light-armed troops into the land beyond the river's bank and

June 29, Wednesday

captured some Indians, who from this time

July 02, Saturday

piloted him down the channel.

July 07, Thursday

But when they arrived at the place where the river expands, so that where it was widest it extended 200 stades, a strong wind blew from the outer sea, and the oars could hardly be raised in the swell; they therefore took refuge again in a canal into which his pilots conducted them.

July 08, Friday

Chapter 164: Voyage down the Indus into the Sea

While their vessels were moored here, the phenomenon of the ebb and flow of the tide in the great sea occurred, so that their ships were left upon dry ground. This caused Alexander and his companions no small alarm, inasmuch as they were previously quite unacquainted with it. But they were much more alarmed when, the time coming round again, the water approached and the hulls of the vessels were raised aloft.[766] The ships which it caught settled in the mud were raised aloft without any damage, and floated again without receiving any injury; but those that had been left on the drier land and had not a firm settlement, when an immense compact wave advanced, either fell foul of each other or were dashed against the land and thus shattered to pieces.

July 13, Wednesday

When Alexander had repaired these vessels as well as his circumstances permitted, he sent some men on in advance down the river in two boats to explore the island at which the natives said he must moor his vessels in his voyage to the sea.

July 22, Friday
Report from the island of Cilluta (possibly corresponds to modern-day Keti/ Keti Bandar)

They told him that the name of the island was Cilluta.[767] As he was informed that there were harbours in this island, that it was a large one and had plenty of water in it, he made the rest of his fleet put in there; but

July 26, Tuesday

he himself with the best sailing ships advanced beyond, to see if the mouth of the river afforded an easy voyage out into the open sea.

August 01, Monday
Arrival at island off the coast of modern-day Sindh (possibly Churna/ Charna)

After advancing about 200 stades from the first island, they described another which was quite out in the sea.

{200 stades approximately equals 31.5km according to Firsov conversion and fits in terms of approximate distance from Keti Bandar}

August 09, Tuesday
Return to Cilluta (Keti / Ket-bandar)

Then indeed they returned to the island in the river; and having moored his vessels near the extremity of it,

August 11, Thursday
Sacrifices according to Ammon. Alexander may have felt he was near the Nile based on previous geographical misinterpretations of the era. Clear mentions of sacrifice to Ammon would likely correspond to a prominent time in the ancient Egyptian calendar. The author hypothesises that a corresponding time here would be the ancient Egyptian New Year/ the birth of Ammon or the hybrid Ra-Horakhty deity. We can identify this time as the Thoth festival (Day 19 of the new year month) festival fell on the new moon in August, which was August 30 in 325 BC, as a result the Egyptian New Year would have been on August 11.

Alexander offered sacrifice to those gods to whom he said he had been directed by Ammon to sacrifice.

August 12, Friday

On the following day he sailed down to the other island which was in the deep sea; and having come to shore here also, he offered other sacrifices to other gods and in another manner. These sacrifices he also offered according to the oracular instructions of Ammon.

August 15, Monday

Then having gone beyond the mouths of the river Indus, he sailed out into the open sea, as he said, to discover if any land lay anywhere near in the sea; but in my opinion, chiefly that he might be able to say that he had navigated the great outer sea of India.

August 17, Wednesday
Likely sea journey along the coast of Sindh and Gujarat

There he sacrificed some bulls to Poseidon and cast them into the sea; and having poured out a libation after the sacrifice, he threw the goblet and bowls, which were golden, into the deep as thank offerings, praying the god to escort safely for him the fleet, which he intended to despatch to the Persian Gulf and the mouths of the Euphrates and Tigres.[768]

August 21, Sunday
Return to Patala

Chapter 165: Exploration of the Mouths of the Indus

Returning to Patala, he found that the citadel had been fortified and that Peithon had arrived with his army, having accomplished everything for which he was despatched.

August 22, Monday

He ordered Hephaestion to prepare what was needful for the fortification of a naval station and the construction of dockyards; for he resolved to leave behind here a fleet of many ships near the city of Patala, where the river Indus divides itself into two streams.

August 24, Wednesday
Inspects the best route of the Indus to the sea

He himself sailed down again into the Great Sea by the other mouth of the Indus, to ascertain which branch of the river is easier to navigate. The mouths of the river Indus are about 1800 stades distant from each other.[769] In the voyage down he arrived at a large lake in the mouth of the river, which the river makes by spreading itself out; or perhaps the waters of the surrounding district draining into it make it large, so that it very much resembles a gulf of the sea.[770]

August 25, Thursday

For in it were seen fish like those in the sea, larger indeed than those in our sea. Having moored his ships then in this lake, where the pilots directed, he left there most of the soldiers and all the boats with Leonnatus; but he himself with the thirty-oared galleys and the vessels with one and a half row of oars passed beyond the mouth of the Indus, and advancing into the sea also this way, ascertained that the outlet of the river on this side (i.e. the west) was easier to navigate than the other.

August 26, Friday

He moored his ships near the shore, and taking with him some of the cavalry went along the sea-coast three days' journey, exploring what kind of country it was for a coasting voyage, and ordering wells to be dug, so that the sailors might have water to drink.

August 29, Monday

He then returned to the ships and

August 31, Wednesday
Returns to Patala

sailed back to Patala;

September 01, Thursday
Sends troops off to gather four months worth of provisions for the imminent journey back toward Persia. Splits troops into two groups, an army (under himself) and a navy (under Nearchus) for the journey

but he sent a part of his army along the sea-coast to effect the same thing, instructing them to return to Patala when they had dug the wells. Sailing again down to the lake, he there constructed another harbour and dockyard; and leaving a garrison for the place, he collected sufficient food to supply the army for four months, as well as whatever else he could procure for the coasting voyage.

Chapter 166: Campaign against the Oritians

The season of the year was then unfit for voyaging; for the periodical winds prevailed, which at that season do not blow there from the north, as with us, but from the Great Sea, in the direction of the south wind.[771] Moreover it was reported that there the sea was fit for navigation after the beginning of winter, from the setting of the Pleiades[772] until the winter solstice; for at that season mild breezes usually blow from the land drenched as it has been with great rains; and these winds are convenient on a coasting voyage both for oars and sails. Nearchus, who had been placed in command of the fleet, waited for the coasting season;

{Setting of the Pleiades in 325 was on November 08 and the winter solstice occurred on December 19 in 325BC}

September 18, Sunday
Alexander leaves Patala
According to (i) Strabo, Admiral Nearchus sailed away after Alexander's march just after the achronical rising of the Pleiades rising of the Pleiades, falling on the September 26 according to astronomical charts. (ii) Arrian however states that Alexander left Patala on Boedromion 20, this is one of the few times we have an actual date from classical authors. Boedromion actually begins on the third new moon after the Summer Solstice, which took place on June 21 in 325. The 3rd new moon after summer solstice was August 30, so 20th Boedromion corresponds to September 18 (which also fits well with the date before Nearchus left)

but Alexander, starting from Patala,

September 28, Wednesday
Arrival at the Arabius river (modern day Hub River in Balochistan province of Pakistan, near the town of Phull)

advanced with all his army as far as the river Arabius.[773]

{The distance between Keti/ Keti Bandar (Indus) and Phull (Arabius) along the coast is approximately 200km}

September 29, Thursday

He then took half of the shield-bearing guards and archers, the infantry regiments called foot Companions, the guard of the Companion cavalry, a squadron of each of the other cavalry regiments, and all the horse-bowmen, and turned away thence on the left towards the sea to dig wells, so that there might be abundance, of them for the fleet sailing along on the coasting voyage; and at the same time to make an unexpected attack upon the Oritians,[774] a tribe of the Indians in this region, which had long been independent. This he meditated doing because they had performed no friendly act either to himself or his army. He placed Hephaestion in command of the forces left behind. The Arabitians,[775] another independent tribe dwelling near the river Arabius, thinking that they could not cope with Alexander in battle, and yet being unwilling to submit to him, fled into the desert when they heard that he was approaching. But crossing the river Arabius, which was both narrow and shallow, and travelling by night through the greater part of the desert,

September 30, Friday

he came near the inhabited country at daybreak. Then ordering the infantry to follow him in regular line, he took the cavalry with him, dividing it into squadrons, that it might occupy a very large part of the plain, and thus marched into the land of the Oritians. All those who turned to defend themselves were cut to pieces by the cavalry, and many of the others were taken prisoners. He then encamped near a small piece of water; but when Hephaestion formed a junction with him, he advanced farther. Arriving at the largest village of the tribe of the Oritians, which was called Rhambacia,[776] he commended the place and thought that if he colonized a city there it would become great and prosperous.

October 02, Sunday

He therefore left Hephaestion behind to carry out this project.[777]

{The Oritians likely had their capital at Ora, which in turn possibly corresponds to the ancient coastal town Ormara in modern-day Pakistan. According to legend, one of Alexander's generals named Ormoz, died here so that the town is named after him, although this would not fit with Alexander arriving at a place already named Ora. {The distance between Phull (Arabius) and Ormara along the coast is approximately 360km}

October 03, Monday

Chapter 167: March through the Desert of Gadrosia

Again he took half of the shield-bearing guards and Agrianians, the guard of cavalry and the horse-bowmen, and marched forward to the confines of the Gadrosians and Oritians, where he was informed that the passage was narrow, and the Oritians were drawn up with the Gadrosians and were encamping in front of the pass, with the purpose of barring Alexander's passage. They had indeed marshalled themselves there; but when it was reported that he was already approaching, most of them fled from the pass, deserting their guard.

October 04, Tuesday

The chiefs of the Oritians, however, came to him, offering to surrender both themselves and their nation. He instructed these to collect the multitude of their people together and send them to their own abodes, since they were not about to suffer any harm.

October 07, Friday
Finalises plans in Ora (possibly corresponding to Ormara in Pakistan)

Over these people he placed Apollophanes as viceroy, and with him he left Leonnatus the confidential body-guard in Ora,[778] at the head of all the Agrianians, some of the bowmen and cavalry, and the rest of the Grecian mercenary infantry and cavalry. He instructed him to wait until the fleet had sailed round the land, to colonize the city, and to regulate the affairs of the Oritians so that they might pay the greater respect to the viceroy.

October 09, Sunday
Leaves Ora (possibly corresponding to Ormara in Pakistan)

He himself, with the main body of the army (for Hephaestion had arrived at the head of the men who had been left behind), advanced

October 10, Monday
Arrives on the border of Gadrosia (corresponds to modern-day coastal Baluchistan and the Makran on the Iran-Pakistan Border). According to Curtius, this took 22 days after leaving Patala

into the land of the Gadrosians by a route most of which was desert. Aristobulus says that in this desert many myrrh-trees grew, larger than the ordinary kind; and that the Phoenicians, who accompanied the army for trafficking, gathered the gum of myrrh, and loading the beasts of burden, carried it away.[779] For there was a great quantity of it, inasmuch as it exuded from large stems and had never before been gathered. He also says that this desert produces many odoriferous roots of nard,[780] which the Phoenicians likewise gathered; but much of it was trampled down by the army, and a sweet perfume was diffused far and wide over the land by the trampling; so great was the abundance of it. In the desert there were also other kinds of trees, one of which had foliage like that of the bay-tree, and grew in places washed by the waves of the sea. These trees were on ground which was left dry by the ebb-tide; but when the water advanced they looked as if they had grown in the sea. Of others the roots were always washed by the sea, because they grew in hollow places, from which the water could not retire; and yet the trees were not destroyed by the sea. Some of these trees in this region were even thirty cubits high. At that season they happened to be in bloom; and the flower was very much like the white violet,[781] but the perfume was far superior to that of the latter. There was also another thorny stalk growing out of the earth, the thorn on which was so strong that, piercing the clothes of some men just riding past, it pulled the horseman down from his horse rather than be itself torn off the stalk. It is also said that when hares run past these bushes, the thorns cling to their fur; and thus these animals are caught, as birds are with bird-lime, or fish with hooks. However they were easily cut through with steel; and when the thorns are cut the stalk gives forth much juice, still more abundantly than fig-trees do in the springtime, and more pungent.[782]

{30 cubits = 1.37m, The author suggests that the trees described here correspond very well with Avicennia marina, also known as Grey Mangrove or White Mangrove. Whilst these plants have been considered to be mangroves, the first attribution of the Avicennia marina was suggested to be that by Alexander's admiral Nearchus on his sea voyage on the Arabian coast rather than the land description here (see Schneider P, The Journal of the Hakluyt Society, The Discovery of Tropical Mangroves in Graeco-Roman Antiquity: Science and Wonder, 2011). The author suggests that this attribution is now pertinent as it can substantiate Alexander's journey season in the winter of 325 BC rather than the traditional late summer/autumn time in 325 BC that has been prominent. The author's reasoning is as follows: (1) The flowers of Avicennia marina can be white and very similar to white violet, (2) Their location fits as they can be found on coastal Balochistan and southern Iran (corresponding to Alexander's location), (3) They thrive in salty sea regions which fits the coastal location, (4) They exist at the height described in Arrian, (5) They are considered to have a distinctive sweet / pungent banana-like smell and (6) importantly regarding timing and season, they are quite distinct in that they bloom/flower in November-December in northern tropical sites (see Duke NC, Journal of Ecology, Phenological Trends With Latitude in The Mangrove Tree Avicennia Marina, 1990; 78, 113-133) which specifically offers the timing with Alexander}

November 20, Sunday
Commences march across the Gadrosian/ Gedrosian desert (corresponding to modern day Makran on the coast of the Persian Gulf and the Gulf of Oman at the Iran/ Pakistan border

Chapter 168: March through the Desert of Gadrosia

Thence Alexander marched through the land of the Gadrosians, by a difficult route, which was also destitute of all the necessaries of life; and in many places there was no water for the army. Moreover they were compelled to march most of the way by night, and a great distance from the sea. However he was very desirous of coming to the part of the country along the sea, both to see what harbours were there, and to make what preparations he could on his march for the fleet, either by employing his men in digging wells, or by making arrangements somewhere for a market and anchorage. But the part of the country of the Gadrosians near the sea was entirely desert. He therefore sent Thoas, son of Mandrodorus, with a few horsemen down to the sea, to reconnoitre and see if there happened to be any haven anywhere near, or whether there was water or any other of the necessaries of life not far from the sea. This man returned and reported that he found some fishermen upon the shore living in stifling huts, which were made by putting together mussel-shells, and the back-bones of fishes were used to form the roofs.[783] He also said that these fishermen used little water, obtaining it with difficulty by scraping away the gravel, and that what they got was not at all fresh. When Alexander reached a certain place in Gadrosia, where corn was more abundant, he seized it and placed it upon the beasts of burden; and marking it with his own seal, he ordered it to be conveyed down to the sea. But while he was marching to the halting stage nearest to the sea, the soldiers paying little regard to the seal, the guards made use of the corn themselves, and gave a share of it to those who were especially pinched with hunger. To such a degree were they overcome by their misery that after mature deliberation' they resolved to take account of the visible and already impending destruction rather than the danger of incurring the king's wrath, which was not before their eyes and still remote. When Alexander ascertained the necessity which constrained them so to act, he pardoned those who had done the deed. He himself hastened forward to collect from the land all he could for victualling the army which was sailing round with the fleet; and sent Cretheus the Callatian[784] to convey the supplies to the coast. He also ordered the natives to grind as much corn as they could and convey it down from the interior of the country, together with dates[785] and sheep for sale to the soldiers. Moreover he sent Telephus, one of the confidential Companions, down to another place on the coast with a small quantity of ground corn.

Chapter 169: March through Gadrosia

He then advanced towards the capital of the Gadrosians, which was named Pura[786]; and he arrived there in sixty days after starting from Ora. Most of the historians of Alexander's reign assert that all the hardships which his army suffered in Asia were not worthy of comparison with the labours undergone here. Nearchus alone asserts that Alexander pursued this route, not from ignorance of the difficulty of the journey, but because he heard that no one had ever hitherto passed that way with an army and emerged in safety from the desert, except Semiramis, when she fled from India. The natives said that even she emerged with only twenty men of her army; and that Gyrus, son of Cambyses, escaped with only seven of his men.[787] For they say that Cyrus also marched into this region for the purpose of invading India; but that he did not effect his retreat before losing the greater part of his army, from the desert and the other difficulties of this route. When Alexander received this information he was seized with a desire of excelling Cyrus and Semiramis. Nearchus says that he turned his march this way, both for this reason and at the same time for the purpose of conveying provisions near the fleet. The scorching heat and lack of water destroyed a great part of the army, and especially the beasts of burden; most of which perished from thirst and some of them even from the depth and heat of the sand, because it had been thoroughly scorched by the sun. For they met with lofty ridges of deep sand, not closely pressed and hardened, but such as received those who stepped upon it just as if they were stepping into mud, or rather into untrodden snow. At the same time too the horses and mules suffered still more, both in going up and coming down the hills, from the unevenness of the road as well as from its instability. The length of the marches between the stages also exceedingly distressed the army; for the lack of water often compelled them to make the marches of unusual length.[788] When they travelled by night on a journey which it was necessary to complete, and at **day**break came to water, they suffered no hardship at all; but if, while still on the march, on accouiit of the length of the way, they were caught by the heat, then they did indeed suffer hardships from the blazing sun, being at the same time oppressed by unassuageable thirst.[789]

Chapter 170: Sufferings of the Army

The soldiers killed many of the beasts of burden of their own accord; for when provisions were lacking, they came together, and slaughtered most of the horses and mules. They ate the flesh of these, and said that they had died of thirst or had perished from the heat. There was no one who divulged the real truth of their conduct, both on account of the men's distress and because all alike were implicated in the same offence. What was being done had not escaped Alexander's notice; but he saw that the best cure for the present state of affairs would be to pretend to be ignorant of it, rather than to permit it as a thing known to himself. The consequence was, that it was no longer easy to convey the soldiers who were suffering from disease, or those who were left behind on the roads on account of the heat, partly from the want of beasts of burden and partly because the men themselves were knocking the waggons to pieces, not being able to draw them on account of the depth of the sand. They did this also because in the first stages they were compelled on this account to go, not by the shortest routes, but by those which were easiest for the carriages. Thus some were left behind along the roads on account of sickness, others from fatigue or the effects of the heat, or from not being able to bear up against the drought; and there was no one either to show them the way or to remain and tend them in their sickness. For the expedition was being made with great urgency; and the care of individual persons was necessarily neglected in the zeal displayed for the safety of the army as a whole. As they generally made the marches by night, some of the men were overcome by sleep on the road; afterwards rousing up again, those who still had strength followed upon the tracks of the army; but only a few out of many overtook the main body in safety. Most of them perished in the sand, like men shipwrecked on the sea.[790] Another calamity also befell the army, which greatly distressed men, horses, and beasts of burden; for the country of the Gadrosians is supplied with rain by the periodical winds, just as that of the Indians is; not the plains of Gadrosia, but only the mountains where the clouds are carried by the wind and are dissolved into rain without passing beyond the summits of the mountains. On one occasion, when the army bivouacked, for the sake of its water, near a small brook which was a winter torrent, about the second watch of the night the brook which flowed there was suddenly swelled by the rains in the mountains which had fallen unperceived by the soldiers. The torrent advanced with so great a flood as to destroy most of the wives and children of the men who followed the army, and to sweep away all the royal baggage as well as all the beasts of burden still remaining. The soldiers, after great exertions, were hardly able to save themselves together with their weapons, many of which they lost beyond recovery. When, after enduring the burning heat and thirst, they lighted upon abundance of water, many of them perished from drinking to excess, not being able to check their appetite for it. For this reason Alexander generally pitched his camp, not near the water itself, but at a distance of about twenty stades from it, to prevent the men and beasts from pressing in crowds into the river and thus perishing, and at the same time to prevent those who had no control over themselves from fouling the water for the rest of the army by stepping into the springs or streams.

Chapter 171: Alexander's Magnanimous Conduct.

Here I have resolved not to pass over in silence the most noble deed perhaps ever performed by Alexander, which occurred either in this land or, according to the assertion of some other authors, still earlier, among the Parapamisadians.[791] The army was continuing its march through the sand, though the heat of the sun was already scorching, because it was necessary to reach water before halting. They were far on the journey, and Alexander himself, though oppressed with thirst, was nevertheless with great pain and difficulty leading the, army on foot, so that his soldiers, as is usual in such a ease, might more patiently bear their hardships by the equalization of the distress. At this time some of the light-armed soldiers, starting away from the army in quest of water, found some collected in a shallow cleft, a small and mean spring. Collecting this water with difficulty, they came with all speed to Alexander, as if they were bringing him some great boon. As soon as they approached the king, they poured the water into a helmet and carried it to him. He took it, and commending the men who brought it, immediately poured it upon the ground in the sight of all. As a result of this action, the entire army was re-invigorated to so great a degree that any one would have imagined that the water poured away by Alexander had furnished a draught to every man. This deed beyond all others I commend as evidence of Alexander's power of endurance and self-control, as well as of his skill in managing an army. The following adventure also occurred to the army in that country. At last the guides declared that they no longer remembered the way, because the tracks of it had been rendered invisible by the wind blowing the sand over them. Moreover, in the deep sand which had been everywhere reduced to one level, there was nothing by which they could conjecture the right way, not even the usual trees growing along it, nor any solid hillock rising up; and they had not practised themselves in making journeys by the stars at night or' by the sun in the daytime, as sailors do by the constellations of the Bears — the Phoenicians by the Little Bear, and other men by the Greater Bear.[792] Then at length Alexander perceived that it was necessary for him to lead the way by declining to the left; and taking a few horsemen with him he advanced in front of the army. But when the horses even of these were exhausted by the heat, he left most of these men behind, and rode away with only five men and found the sea. Having scraped away the shingle on the sea-beach, he found water fresh and pure, and then went and fetched the whole army. For seven days they marched along the sea-coast, supplying themselves with water from the shore. Thence he led his expedition into the interior, for now the guides knew the way.

December 08, Thursday
Arrival at Pura, the Capital of Gadrosia (likely corresponds to

modern-day Fahraj in Kerman Province, Iran, having taken 60 days to arrive there from Ora)

Chapter 172: March through Carmania — Punishment of Viceroys

When he arrived at the capital of Gadrosia, he there gave his army a rest. He deposed Apollophanes from the viceroyalty,[793] because he discovered that he had paid no heed to his instructions. Thoas was appointed viceroy over the people of this district; but as he fell ill and died, Sibyrtius succeeded to the office. The same man had also lately been appointed by Alexander viceroy of Carmania; but now the rule over the Arachotians and Gadrosians was given to him, and Tlepolemus, son of Pythophanes, received Carmania.

{This passage suggests Gadrosia was crossed in the winter, which corresponds to the rain mentioned here as winter in the Makran area is when the rainy season occurs. Pura possibly corrponds to Bampur, but more likely ancient Pahura also known as Fahraj in Kerman Province modern-day Iran. Pura/ Fahraj is approximately 1200Km Ora/ Ormara. The author approximates that Alexander left Pura on December 13}

December 15, Thursday
En-route to Carmania

The king was already advancing into Carmania, when news was brought to him that Philip, the viceroy of the country of the Indians, had been plotted against by the mercenaries and treacherously killed; but that Philip's Macedonian bodyguards had caught some of the murderers in the very act and others afterwards, and had pat them to death. When he had ascertained this, he sent a letter into India to Eudemus and Taxiles, ordering them to administer the affairs of the land which had previously been subordinated to Philip until he could send a viceroy for it.

December 18, Sunday
Arrival at Carmania (in the region of modern-day province of Kerman, the author suggests this could be in the Jiroft city area, a prominent area from the Bronze age onward, possibly near the Konar Sandal archaeological sites)

When he arrived in Carmania, Craterus effected a junction with him, bringing with him the rest of the army and the elephants. He also brought Ordanes, whom he had arrested for revolting and trying to effect a revolution.[794] Thither also came Stasanor, the viceroy of the Areians[795] and Zarangians, accompanied by Pharismanes, son of Phrataphernes, the viceroy of the Parthians and Hyrcanians. There came also the generals who had been left with Parmenio over the army in Media, Oleander, Sitalces, and Heracon, bringing with them the greater part of their army. Both the natives and the soldiers themselves brought many accusations against Oleander and Sitalces, as for example, that the temples had been pillaged by them, old tombs rifled, and other acts of injustice, recklessness, and tyranny perpetrated against their subjects. As these charges were proved,[796] he put them to death, in order to inspire others who might be left as viceroys, governors, or prefects of provinces with the fear of suffering equal penalties with them if they swerved from the path of duty.[797] This was one of the chief means by which Alexander kept in subordination the nations which he had conquered in war or which had voluntarily submitted to him, though they were so many in number and so far distant from each other; because under his regal sway it was not allowed that those who were ruled should be unjustly treated by those who ruled. At that time Heracon was acquitted of the charge, but soon after, being convicted by the men of Susa of having pillaged the temple in that city, he also suffered punishment. Stasanor and Phrataphernes came to Alexander bringing a multitude of beasts of burden and many camels, when they learnt that he was marching by the route to Gadrosia, conjecturing that his army would suffer the very hardships which it did suffer. Therefore these men arrived just at the very time they were required, as also did their camels and beasts of burden. For Alexander distributed all these animals to the officers man by man, to all the various squadrons and centuries of the cavalry, and to the various companies of the infantry, as their number allowed him.

{Konar Sandal (Carmania) is approximately 120km from Fahraj (Pura)}

Chapter 173: Alexander in Carmania.

Certain authors have said (though to me the statement seems incredible) that Alexander led his forces through Carmania lying extended with his Companions upon two covered waggons joined together, the flute being played to him; and that the soldiers followed him wearing garlands and sporting. Food was provided for them, as well as all kinds of dainties which had been brought together along the roads by the Carmanians. They say that he did this in imitation of the Bacchic revelry of Dionysus, because a story was told about that deity, that after subduing the Indians he traversed the greater part of Asia in this manner and received the appellation of Thriambus.[798] For the same reason the processions in honour of victories after war were called thriambi. This has been recorded neither by Ptolemy, son of Lagus, nor by Aristobulus, son of Aristobulus, nor by any other writer whose testimony on such points any one would feel to be worthy of credit. It is sufficient therefore for me to record it as unworthy of belief.[799] But as to what I am now going to describe I follow the account of Aristobulus.

December 19, Monday
Celebrated completion of journey through Gadrosia

In Carmania Alexander offered sacrifices to the gods as thank-offerings for his victory over the Indians, and because his army had been brought in safety out of Gadrosia. He also celebrated a musical and gymnastic contest.

{Usual celebration of winter solstice, which in 325 BC fell on December 19}

December 21, Wednesday

He then appointed Peucestas one of his confidential body-guards, having already resolved to make him viceroy of Persis. He wished him, before being appointed to the viceroyalty, to experience this honour and evidence of confidence, as a reward for his exploit among the Mallians. Up to this time the number of his confidential body-guards had been seven:— Leonnatus, son of Anteas, Hephaestion, son of Amyntor, Lysimachus, son of Agathocles, Aristonous, son of Pisaeus, these four being Pellaeans; Perdiccas, son of Orontes, from Orestis, Ptolemy, son of Lagus, and Peithon, son of Crateas, the Heordaeans. Peucestas, who had held the shield over Alexander, was now added to them as an eighth.

December 22, Thursday
Nearchus arrives at the coast of Carmania (possibly at Hormirzad or modern-day Bandar Abbas, as this was a well-known port in Achaemenid times)

At this time Nearchus, having sailed round the coast of Ora and Gadrosia and that of the Ichthyophagi, put into port in the inhabited part of the coastland of Carmania,[800] and

December 27, Tuesday
Nearchus reports on his voyage to Alexander

going up thence into the interior with a few men he reported to Alexander the particulars of the voyage which he had made along the coasts of the external sea.

{Nearchus likely landed his boats on the Minab river or further north on the Rudan river on his route to Alexander}

324 BC

January 02, Monday
Nearchus sent back down to complete and expedition in the Persian Gulf

Nearchus was then sent down to the sea again to sail round as far as the country of Susiana, and the outlets of the river Tigres.[801] How he sailed from the river Indus to the Persian Sea and the mouth of the Tigres, I shall describe in a separate book, following the account of Nearchus himself.[802] For he also wrote a history of Alexander in Greek. Perhaps I shall be able to compose this narrative in the future, if inclination and the divine influence urge me to it.

January 03, Tuesday
Hephaestion sent to Persis for provisions

Alexander now ordered Hephaestion to march into Persis[803] from Carmania along the sea-shore with the larger division of the army and the beasts of burden, taking with him also the elephants; because, as he was making the expedition in the season of winter,[804] the part of Persis near the sea was warm and possessed abundant supplies of provisions.

{Other sources also suggest that Alexander commissioned Alexandria Carmania as one of his now growing 70+ number of cities. This city was founded with some of his veterans on the Carmania coastline corresponding to the coastline of modern-day Kerman/ Hormozgan Provinces. During this time, Cleander and several other Median generals attended the king, but were accused of immoral conduct and conspiracy and were executed. The location of Alexandria Carmania remains debated, and is associated with the mouth of the Minab River, as Nearchus' men landed their boats on visiting Alexander. Possibly at Gulishkird. The author suggests that there was already well established ports on the Persian coastline, however a possible explanation would therefore be that Alexander would have picked an inland location with direct river access to the coast as a location for a city. Hence linking the central, land-locked and well-farmed area of Carmania with the Persian Gulf, the Gulf of Oman and the Indian Ocean. Such a location, with similar principles to the islands at the mouth of the Indus feeding to the sea, could correspond to an area near an inland area of the Rudan river as it feeds to the Minab and thence the sea. An area near Ziarat-e Ali or close to the river up- or down-stream could correspond to this}

January 04, Wednesday
Leaves Carmania

Chapter 174: Alexander in Persis — Tomb of Cyrus Repaired

He himself then marched to

January 29, Sunday
Arrival at Pasargadae

Pasargadae in Persis, with the lightest of his infantry, the Companion cavalry and a part of the archers; but he sent Stasanor down to his own land.[805] When he arrived at the confines of Persis, he found that Phrasaortes was no longer viceroy, for he happened to have died of disease while Alexander was still in India. Orxines was managing the affairs of the country, not because he had been appointed ruler by Alexander, but because he thought it his duty to keep Persia in order for him, as there was no other ruler.[806]

{Pasargadae is approximately 495km from Konar Sandal (Carmania)}

February 26, Sunday
Atropates arrives from Media

Atropates, the viceroy of Media, also came to Pasargadae, bringing Baryaxes, a Mede, under arrest, because he had assumed the upright head-dress and called himself king of the Persians and Medes.[807] With Baryaxes he also brought those who had taken part with him in the attempted revolution and revolt. Alexander put these men to death.

{Atropates journey from Media (approximately modern Azarbaijan (capital at Tabriz) and Iranian Kurdistan) is approximately 1250km from Pasargadae}

February 28, Tuesday
Management of the Tomb of Cyrus

He was grieved by the outrage committed upon the tomb of Cyrus, son of Cambyses; for according to Aristobulus, he found it dug through and pillaged. The tomb of the famous Cyrus was in the royal park at Pasargadae, and around it a grove of all kinds of trees had been planted. It was also watered by a stream, and high grass grew in the meadow. The base of the tomb itself had been made of squared stone in the form of a rectangle. Above there was a stone building surmounted by a roof, with a door leading within, so narrow that even a small man could with difficulty enter, after suffering much discomfort.[808] In the building lay a golden coffin, in which the body of Cyrus had been buried, and by the side of the coffin was a couch, the feet of which were of gold wrought with the hammer. A carpet of Babylonian tapestry with purple rugs formed the bedding upon it were also a Median coat with sleeves and other tunics of Babylonian manufacture. Aristobulus adds that Median trousers and robes dyed the colour of hyacinth were also lying upon it, as well as others of purple and various other colours; moreover there were collars, sabres, and earrings of gold and precious stones soldered together, and near them stood a table. On the middle of the couch lay the coffin[809] which contained the body of Cyrus. Within the enclosure, near the ascent leading to the tomb, there was a small house built for the Magians who guarded the tomb; a duty which they had discharged ever since the time of Cambyses, son of Cyrus, son succeeding father as guard. To these men a sheep and specified quantities of wheaten flour and wine were given daily by the king; and a horse once a month as a sacrifice to Cyrus. Upon the tomb an inscription in Persian letters had been placed, which bore the following meaning in the Persian language: " man, I am Cyrus, son of Cambyses, who founded the empire of the Persians, and was king of Asia. Do not therefore grudge me this monument." As soon as Alexander had conquered Persia, he was very

313

desirous of entering the tomb of Cyrus; but he found that everything else had been carried off except the coffin and couch. They had even maltreated the king's body; for they had torn off the lid of the coffin and cast out the corpse. They had tried to make the coffin itself of smaller bulk and thus more portable, by cutting part of it off and crushing part of it up; but as their efforts did not succeed, they departed, leaving the coffin in that state. Aristobulus says that he was himself commissioned by Alexander to restore the tomb for Cyrus, to put in the coffin the parts of the body still preserved, to put the lid on, and to restore the parts of the coffin which had been, defaced. Moreover he was instructed to stretch the couch tight with bands, and to deposit all the other things which used to lie there for ornament, both resembling the former ones and of the same number. He was ordered also to do away with the door, building part of it up with stone and plastering part of it over with cement, and finally to put the royal seal upon the cement. Alexander arrested the Magians who were the guards of the tomb, and put them to the torture to make them confess who had done the deed; but in spite of the torture they confessed nothing either about themselves or any other person. In no other way were they proved to have been privy to the deed; they were therefore released by Alexander.[810]

March 19, Sunday
Arrival in Persepolis approximately 40km from Pasargadae (possibly to coincide with the Vernal Equinox/ Persian Spring arrival festival in 324 BC, as he was adopting Persian customs [see entry below])

Chapter 175: Peucestas Appointed Viceroy of Persis

Thence he proceeded to the royal palace of the Persians, which he had on a former occasion himself burnt down, as I have previously related, expressing my disapprobation of the act[811]; and on his return Alexander himself did not commend it. Many charges were brought by the Persians against Orxines, who ruled them after the death of Phrasaortes. He was convicted of having pillaged temples and royal tombs, and of having unjustly put many of the Persians to death. He was therefore hanged by men acting under Alexander's orders[812]; and Peucestas the confidential body-guard was appointed viceroy of Persis. The king placed special confidence in him both for other reasons, and especially on account of his exploit among the Mallians, where he braved the greatest dangers and helped to save Alexander's life. Besides this, he did not refuse to accommodate himself to the Asiatic mode of living; and as soon as he was appointed to the position of viceroy of Persis, he openly assumed the native garb, being the only man among the Macedonians who adopted the Median dress in preference to the Grecian.[813] He also learnt to speak the Persian language correctly, and comported himself in all other respects like a Persian. For this conduct he was not only commended by Alexander, but the Persians also were highly delighted with him, for preferring their national customs to those of his own forefathers.

Chapter 176 (Start of Book 7): Alexander's Plans — The Indian Philosophers

When Alexander arrived at Pasargadae and Persepolis,[814] he was seized with an ardent desire to sail down the Euphrates and Tigres[815] to the Persian Sea, and to see the mouths of those rivers as he had already seen those of the Indus as well as the sea into which it flows. Some authors[816] also have stated that he was meditating a voyage round the larger portion of Arabia, the country of the Ethiopians, Libya (i.e. Africa), and Numidia beyond Mount Atlas to Gadeira (i.e. Cadiz),[817] inward into our sea (i.e. the Mediterranean); thinking that after he had subdued both Libya and Carchedon (i.e. Carthage), he might with justice be called king of all Asia.[818] For he said that the kings of the Persians and Medes called themselves Great Kings without any rights since they did not rule the larger part of Asia. Some say that he was meditating a voyage thence into the Baxine Sea, to Scythia and the Lake Maeotis (i.e. the Sea of Azov); while others assert that he intended to go to Sicily and the Iapygian Cape,[819] for the fame of the Romans spreading far and wide was now exciting his jealousy. For my own part I cannot conjecture with any certainty what were his plans; and I do not care to guess. But this I think I can confidently affirm, that he meditated nothing small or mean; and that he would never have remained satisfied with any of the acquisitions he had made, even if he had added Europe to Asia, or the islands of the Britons to Europe; but would still have gone on seeking for unknown lands beyond those mentioned. I verily believe that if he had found no one else to strive with, he would have striven with himself. And on this account I commend some of the Indian philosophers, who are said to have been caught by Alexander as they were walking in the open meadow where they were accustomed to spend their time.[820] At the sight of him and his army they did nothing else but stamp with their feet on the earth, upon which they were stepping. When he asked them by means of interpreters what was the meaning of their action, they replied as follows: "King Alexander, every man possesses as much of the earth as this, upon which we have stepped; but thou being only a man like the rest of us, except in being meddlesome and arrogant, art come over so great a part of the earth from thy own land, giving trouble both to thyself and others.[821] And yet thou also wilt soon die, and possess only as much of the earth as is sufficient for thy body to be buried in."

Chapter 177: Alexander's Dealings with the Indian Sages

On this occasion Alexander, commended both the words and the men who spoke them; but nevertheless he did just the opposite to that which he commended. When also in the Isthmus he met Diogenes of Sinope, lying in the sun, standing near him with his shield-bearing guards and foot Companions, he asked if he wanted anything. But Diogenes said that he wanted nothing else, except that he and his attendants would stand out of the sunlight. Alexander is said to have expressed his admiration of Diogenes's conduct.[822] Thus it is evident that Alexander was not entirely destitute of better feelings, but he was the slave of his insatiable ambition. Again, when he arrived at Taxila and saw the naked sect of Indian philosophers, he was exceedingly desirous that one of these men should live with him; because he admired their power of endurance.[823] But the oldest of the philosophers, Dandamis by name, of whom the others were disciples, refused to come himself to Alexander, and would not allow the others to do so.[824] He, is said to have replied that he was himself a son of Zeus, if Alexander was[825]; and that he wanted nothing from him, because he was quite contented with what he had. And besides he said that he saw his attendants wandering over so much of the land and sea to no advantage and that there was no end to their many wanderings. Therefore he had no desire that Alexander should give him anything which was in his own possession, nor on the other hand was he afraid that he should be excluded from anything which Alexander ruled over. For while he lived the country of India, which produces the fruits in their season, was sufficient for him; and when he died he should be released from the body, an unsuitable associate. Alexander then did not attempt to force him to come with him, considering that the man was free to do as he pleased. But Megasthenes has recorded that Calanus, one of the philosophers of this region, who had very little power over his desires, was induced to do so; and that the philosophers themselves reproached him, for having deserted the happiness existing among them, and serving another lord instead of the God.[826]

April 15, Saturday
Calanus' ritual suicide (Agnipravesa, Sanskrit term for 'voluntary

death by fire')

Chapter 178: Self-sacrifice or the Indian Calanus

This I have recorded, because in a history of Alexander it is necessary also to speak of Calanus; for when he was in the country of Persis his health became delicate, though he had never before been subject to illness.[827] Accordingly, not being willing to lead the life of a man in infirm health, he told Alexander that in such circumstances he thought it best for him to put an end to his existence, before he came into experience of any disease which might compel him to change his former mode of living. For a long time the king tried to dissuade him; however, when he saw that he was not to be overcome, but would find some other way of release, if this were not yielded to him, he ordered a funeral pyre to be heaped up for him, in the place where the man himself directed, and gave instructions that Ptolemy, son of Lagus, the confidential body-guard, should have the charge of it. They say that a solemn procession, consisting both of horses and men, advanced before him, some of the latter being armed and others carrying all kinds of incense for the pyre. They also say that they were carrying gold and silver goblets and royal apparel; and because he was unable to walk through illness, a horse was prepared for him. However, not being able to mount the horse, he was conveyed stretched out upon a litter, crowned with a garland after the custom of the Indians, and singing in the Indian language. The Indians say that he sang hymns to the gods and eulogiums on his countrymen.[828] Before he ascended the funeral-pyre he presented the horse which he should himself have mounted, being a royal steed of the Nisaean breed,[829] to Lysimachus, one of those who attended him to learn his philosophy. He distributed among his other disciples the goblets and rugs which Alexander had ordered to be cast into the pyre as an honour to him. Then mounting the pyre he lay down upon it in a becoming manner, and was visible to the whole army. To Alexander the spectacle appeared unseemly, as it was being exhibited at the cost of a friend; but to the rest it was a cause of wonder that he did not move any part of his body in the fire.[830] As soon as the men to whom the duty had been assigned set fire to the pyre, Nearchus says the trumpets sounded, in accordance with Alexander's order, and the whole army raised the war-cry as it was in the habit of shouting when advancing to battle. The elephants also chimed in with their shrill and warlike cry, in honour of Calanus. Authors upon whom reliance may be placed, have recorded these and such-like things, facts of great import to those who are desirous of learning how steadfast and immovable a thing the human mind is in regard to what it wishes to accomplish.

May 22, Monday
Sends Atropates to Media,

Chapter 179: Marriages between Macedonians and Persians

At this time Alexander sent Atropates away to his own viceroyalty,[831]

July 11, Tuesday
Arrival at Susa, Pliny suggests it took seen months (lunar months) for Alexander to get there from Pura/Fahraj (having left on December 13, 325 BC)

after advancing to Susa; where

July 13, Thursday

he arrested Abulites and his son Oxathres, and, put them to death on the ground that they were governing the Susians badly.[832] Many outrages upon temples, tombs, and the subjects themselves had been committed by those who were ruling the countries conquered by Alexander in war; because the king's expedition into India had taken a long time, and it was not thought credible that he would ever return in safety from so many nations possessing so many elephants, going to his destruction beyond the Indus, Hydaspes, Acesines, and Hyphasis.[833] The calamities that befell him among the Gadrosians were still greater inducements to those acting as viceroys in this region to be free from apprehension of his return to his dominions. Not only so, but Alexander himself is said to have become more inclined at that time to believe accusations which were plausible in every way, as well as to inflict very severe punishment upon those who were convicted even of small offences, because with the same disposition he thought they would be likely to perform great ones.[834]

August 04, Friday
Mass Wedding (on a full moon, as it was customary to this in the ancient era)

In Susa also he celebrated both his own wedding and those of his companions. He himself married Barsine, the eldest daughter of Darius,[835] and according to Aristobulus, besides her another, Parysatis, the youngest daughter of Ochus.[836] He had already married Roxana, daughter of Oxyartes the Bactrian.[837] To Hephaestion he gave Drypetis, another daughter of Darius, and his own wife's sister; for he wished Hephaestion's children to be first cousins to his own. To Craterus he gave Amastrine, daughter of Oxyartes the brother of Darius; to Perdiccas, the daughter of Atropates, viceroy of Media; to Ptolemy the confidential body-guard, and Eumenes the royal secretary, the daughters of Artabazus, to the former Artacama, and to the latter Artonis. To Nearchus he gave the daughter of Barsine and Mentor; to Seleucus the daughter of Spitamenes the Bactrian. Likewise to the rest of his Companions he gave the choicest daughters of the Persians and Medes, to the number of eighty. The weddings were celebrated after the Persian manner, seats being placed in a row for the bridegrooms; and after the banquet the brides came in and seated themselves, each one near her own husband. The bridegrooms took them by the right hand and kissed them; the king being the first to begin, for the weddings of all were conducted in the same way. This appeared the most popular thing which Alexander ever did; and it proved his affection for his Companions. Each man took his own bride and led her away; and on all without exception Alexander bestowed dowries.[838] He also ordered that the names of all the other Macedonians who had married any of the Asiatic women should be registered. They were over 10,000 in number; and to these Alexander made presents on account of their weddings.

August 10, Thursday

Chapter 180: The Soldiers Rewarded

He now thought it a favourable opportunity to liquidate the debts of all the soldiers who had incurred them[839]; and for this purpose he ordered that a register should be made of how much each man owed, in order that they might receive the money. At first only a few registered their names, fearing that this was being instituted as a test by Alexander, to discover which of the soldiers found their pay insufficient for their expenses, and which of them were extravagant in their mode of living. When he was informed that most of them were not registering their names, but that those who had borrowed money on bonds were concealing the fact, he reproached them for their distrust of him. For he said that it was not right either that the king should deal otherwise than sincerely with his subjects, or that any of those ruled by him should think that he would deal otherwise than sincerely with them. Accordingly, he had tables placed in the camp with money upon them; and he appointed men to manage the distribution of it. He ordered the debts of all who showed a money-bond to be liquidated without the debtors' names being any longer registered. Consequently, the men believed that Alexander was dealing sincerely with them; and the fact that they were not known was a greater pleasure to them than the fact that they ceased to be in debt. This presentation to the army is said to have amounted to 20,000 talents.[840] He also gave presents to particular individuals, according as each man was held in honour for his merit or valour, if he had become conspicuous in crises of danger. Those who were distinguished for their personal gallantry he crowned with golden chaplets:—first, Peucestas, the man who had held the shield over him; second, Leonnatus, who also had held his shield over him, and moreover had incurred dangers in India and won a victory in Ora.[841] For he had posted himself with the forces left with him against the Oritians and the tribes living near them, who were trying to effect a revolution, and had conquered them in battle. He also seemed to have managed other affairs in Ora with great success. In addition to these, he crowned Nearchus for his successful voyage round the coast from the land of the Indians through the Great Sea; for this officer had now arrived at Susa. Besides these three, he crowned Onesicritus, the pilot of the royal ship; as well as Hephaestion and the rest of the confidential bodyguards.

August 15, Tuesday

Chapter 181: An Army of Asiatics Trained under the Macedonian Discipline

The viceroys from the newly-built cities and the rest of the territory subdued in war came to him bringing with them youths just growing into manhood to the number of 30,000, all of the same age, whom Alexander called Epigoni (successors).[842] They were accoutred with Macedonian arms, and exercised in military discipline after the Macedonian system. The arrival of these is said to have vexed the Macedonians, who thought that Alexander was contriving every means in his power to free himself from his previous need of their services. For the same reason also the sight of his Median dress was. no small cause of dissatisfaction to them; and the weddings celebrated in the Persian fashion were displeasing to most of them, even including some of those who married, although they had been greatly honoured by the king putting himself on the same level with them in the marriage ceremony. They were offended at Peucestas, the viceroy of

Persis, on account of his Persianizing both in dress and in speech, because the king was delighted by his adopting the Asiatic customs. They were disgusted that the Bactrian, Sogdianian, Arachotian, Zarangian, Arian, and Parthian horsemen, as well as the Persian horsemen called the Evacae, were distributed among the squadrons of the Companion cavalry; as many of them at least as were seen to excel in reputation, fineness of stature, or any other good quality; and that a fifth cavalry division was added to these troops, not composed entirely of foreigners; but the whole body of cavalry was increased in number, and men were picked from the foreigners and put into it. Oophen, son of Artabazus,, Hydarnes and Artiboles, sons of Mazaeus, Sisines and Phradasmenes, sons of Phrataphernes, viceroy of Parthia and Hyrcania, Histanes, son of Oxyartes and brother of Alexander's wife, Roxane, as well as Autobares and his brother Mithrobaeus were picked out and enrolled among the foot-guard in addition to the Macedonian officers. Over these Hystaspes the Bactrian was placed as commander; and Macedonian spears were given to them instead of the barbarian javelins which had thongs attached to them.[843] All this offended the Macedonians, who thought that Alexander was becoming altogether Asiatic in his ideas, and was holding the Macedonians themselves as well as their customs in a position of contempt.[844]

August 23, Wednesday

Chapter 182: Navigation of the Tigres
Alexander now ordered Hephaestion to lead the main body of the infantry as far as the Persian Sea,

August 27, Sunday
Sails down the Eulaeus river (modern-day Dez river that then joins the Karun river)

while he' himself, his fleet having sailed up into the land of Susiana, embarked, with the shield-bearing guards and the body-guard of infantry; and having also put on board a few of the cavalry Companions, he sailed down the river Eulaeus

September 04, Monday
Arrival at the Persian Gulf (from the Dez river to the Karun river and then via the Bulaeus river [modern day Bahmanshir channel] to the sea)

to the sea.[845] When he was near the place where the river discharges itself into the deep, he left there most of his ships, including those which were in need of repair, and with those especially adapted for fast sailing he coasted along out of the river Bulaeus through the sea

September 09, Saturday
Arrival at the Tigris

to the mouth of the Tigres.

September 10, Sunday
Journey of the remaining ships. The text is clear that the ships went down the Eulaeus river (Dez-Karen river) and entered a 'man-made' canal joining this to the Tigris. To-date the only recognised canal linking the Karun to the Tigris has been the 'Haffar' or 'dug out' canal linking these two rivers, ascribed to the reign of Panah Khusraw AKA Adud ad-Dawlah in the late 10th century AD. The author hypothesis that such a clear description of a man-made canal pre-dating the Haffar by 13 centuries, suggests that the canal may have been in some existence in the Achaemenid era (and possibly built by them), but may have been modified or re-inforced by the he Daylamite Buwayhid king who may have subsequently taken credit for it

The rest of the ships were conveyed down the Eulaeus as far as the canal which has been cut from the Tigres into the Eulaeus, and by this means they were brought into the Tigres. Of the rivers Euphrates and Tigres which enclose Syria between them, whence also its name is called by the natives Mesopotamia,[846] the Tigres flows in a much lower channel than the Euphrates, from which it receives many canals; and after taking up many tributaries and its waters being swelled by them, it falls into the Persian Sea.[847] It is a large river and can be crossed on foot nowhere as far as its mouth,[848] inasmuch as none of its water is used up by irrigation of the country. For the land through which it flows is more elevated than its water, and it is not drawn off into canals or into another river, but rather receives them into itself. It is nowhere possible to irrigate the land from it. But the Euphrates flows in an elevated channel, and is everywhere on a level with the land through which it passes. Many canals have been made from it, some of which are always kept flowing, and' from which the inhabitants on both banks supply themselves with water; others the people make only when requisite to irrigate the land, when they are in need of water from drought.[849] For this country is usually free from rain. The consequence is, that the Euphrates at last has only a small volume of water, which disappears into a marsh. Alexander sailed over the sea round the shore of the Persian Gulf lying between the rivers Eulaeus and Tigres;

September 11, Monday
Meets with Hephaestion on the Tigris

and thence he sailed up the latter river as far as the camp where Hephaestion had settled with all his forces.

September 14, Thursday
Arrival at Opis (southeast of modern Baghdad [and north of ancient Babylon] possibly at Tall al-Mujailat)

Thence he sailed again to Opis, a city situated on that river.[850] In his voyage up he destroyed the weirs which existed in the river, and thus made the stream quite level. These weira had been constructed by the Persians, to prevent any enemy having a superior naval force from sailing up from the sea into their country. The Persians had had recourse to these contrivances because they were not a nautical people; and thus by making an unbroken succession of weirs they had rendered the voyage up the Tigres a matter of impossibility. But Alexander said that such devices were unbecoming to men who are victorious in battle; and therefore he considered this means of safety unsuitable for him; and by easily demolishing the laborious work of the Persians, he proved in fact that what they thought a protection was unworthy of the name.

September 16, Saturday
Announcement of re-organisation of the army

Chapter 183: The Macedonians Offended at Alexander

When he arrived at Opis, he collected the Macedonians and announced that he intended to discharge from the army those who were useless for military service either from age or from being maimed in the limbs; and he said he would send them back to their own abodes. He also promised to give those who went back as much as would make them special objects of envy to those at home and arouse in the other Macedonians the wish to share similar dangers and labours. Alexander said this, no doubt, for the purpose of pleasing the Macedonians; but on the contrary they were, not without reason, offended by the speech which he delivered, thinking that now they were despised by him and deemed to be quite useless for military service. Indeed, throughout the whole of this expedition they had been offended at many other things; for his adoption of the Persian dress, thereby exhibiting his contempt for their opinion, caused them grief, as did also his accoutring the foreign soldiers called Epigoni in the Macedonian style, and the mixing of the alien horsemen among the ranks of the Companions. Therefore they could not remain silent and control themselves, but urged him to dismiss all of them from his army; and they advised him to prosecute the war in company with his father, deriding Ammon by this remark.

September 17, Sunday
Alexander's speech to his army

When Alexander heard this (for at that time he was more hasty in temper than heretofore, and no longer, as of old, indulgent to the Macedonians from having a retinue of foreign attendants), leaping down from the platform with his officers around him, he ordered the most conspicuous of the men who had tried to stir up the multitude to sedition to be arrested. He himself pointed out with his hand to the shield-bearing guards those whom they were to arrest, to the number of thirteen; and he ordered these to be led away to execution.[851] When the rest, stricken with terror, became silent, he mounted the platform and spoke as follows:—

Chapter 184: Alexander's Speech

"The speech which I am about to deliver will not be for the purpose of checking your start homeward, for, so far as I am concerned, you may depart wherever you wish; but because I wish you to know what kind of men you were originally and how you have been transformed since you came into our service. In the first place, as is reasonable, I shall begin my speech from my father Philip. For he found you vagabonds and destitute of means, most of you clad in hides, feeding a few sheep up the mountain sides, for the protection of which you had to fight with small success against Illyrians, Triballians, and the border Thracians.[852] Instead of the hides he gave you cloaks to wear, and from the mountains he led you down into the plains, and made you capable of fighting the neighbouring barbarians, so that you were no longer compelled to preserve yourselves by trusting rather to the inaccessible strongholds than to your own valour. He made you colonists of cities, which he adorned with useful laws and customs; and from being slaves and subjects, he made you rulers over those very barbarians by whom you yourselves, as well as your property, were previously liable to be plundered and ravaged. He also added the greater part of Thrace to Macedonia, and by seizing the most conveniently situated places on the sea-coast, he spread abundance over the land from commerce, and made the working of the mines a secure employment.[853] He made you rulers over the Thessalians, of whom you had formerly been in mortal fear[854]; and by humbling the nation of the Phocians, he rendered the avenue into Greece broad and easy for you, instead of being narrow and difficult.[855] The Athenians and Thebans who were always lying in wait to attack Macedonia, he humbled to such a degree,—I also then rendering him my personal aid in the campaign,[856]—that instead of paying tribute to the former[857] and being vassals to the latter,[858] those States in their turn procure security to themselves by our assistance. He penetrated into the Peloponnese, and after regulating its affairs, was publicly declared commander-in-chief of all the rest of Greece in the expedition against the Persian, adding this glory not more to himself than to the commonwealth of the Macedonians. These were the advantages which accrued to you from my father Philip; great indeed if looked at by themselves, but small if compared with those you have obtained from me. For though I inherited from my father only a few gold and silver goblets, and there were not even sixty talents in the treasury, and though I found myself charged with a debt of 500 talents owing by Philip,[859] and I was obliged myself to borrow 800 talents in addition to these, I started from the country which could not decently support you, and forthwith laid open to you the passage of the Hellespont, though at that time the Persians held the sovereignty of the sea. Having overpowered the viceroys of Darius with my cavalry, I added to your empire the whole of Ionia,[860] the whole of Aeolis, both Phrygias[861] and Lydia, and I took Miletus by siege. All the other places I obtained by voluntary surrender, and I granted you the privilege of appropriating the wealth found in them. The chest of Egypt and Cyrene, which I acquired without fighting a battle, have come to you. Coele-Syria, Palestine, and Mesopotamia are your property. Babylon, Bactria, and Susa are yours. The wealth of the Lydians, the treasures of the

Persians, and the riches of the Indians are yours; and so is the External Sea. You are viceroys, you are generals, you are captains. What then have I reserved to myself after all these labours, except this purple robe and this diadem?[862] I have appropriated nothing myself, nor can any one point out my treasures, except these possessions of yours or the things which I am guarding on your behalf.[863] Individually, however, have no motive to guard them, since I feed on the same fare as you do, and I take only the same amount of sleep. Nay, I do not think that my fare is as good as that of those among you who live luxuriously; and I now that I often sit up at night to watch for you, that you may be able to sleep.

Chapter 185: Alexander's Speech (continued)

"But some one may say, that while you endured toil and fatigue, I have acquired these things as your, leader without myself sharing the toil and fatigue. But who is there of you who" knows that he has endured greater toil for me than I have for him? Come now! whoever of you has wounds, let him strip and show them, and I will show mine in turn; for there is no part of my body, in front at any rate, remaining free from wounds; nor is there any kind of weapon used either for close combat or for hurling at the enemy, the traces of which I do not bear on my person. For I have been wounded with the sword in close fight, I have been shot with arrows, and I have been struck with missiles projected from engines of war; and though oftentimes I have been hit with stones and bolts of wood for the sake of your lives, your glory, and your wealth, I am still leading you as conquerors over all the land and sea, all rivers, mountains, and plains. I have celebrated your weddings with my own, and the children of many of you will be akin to my children. Moreover I have liquidated the debts of all those who had incurred them, without inquiring too closely for what purpose they were contracted, though you receive such high pay, and carry off so much booty whenever there is booty to be got after a siege. Most of you have golden crowns, the eternal memorials of your valour and of the honour you receive from me. Whoever has been killed, has met with a glorious end and has been honoured with a splendid burial. Brazen statues of most of the slain have been erected at home,[864] and their parents are held in honour, being released from all public service and from taxation. But no one of you has ever been killed in flight under my leadership. And now I was intending to send back those of you who are unfit for service, objects of envy to those at home; but since you all wish to depart, depart all of you! Go back and report at home that your king Alexander, the conqueror of the Persians, Medes, Bactrians, and Sacians[865]; the man who has subjugated the Uxians, Arachotians, and Drangians; who has also acquired the rule of the Parthians, Chorasmians, and Hyrcanians, as far as the Caspian Sea; who has marched over the Caucasus, through the Caspian Gates; who has crossed the rivers Oxus and Tanais, and the Indus besides, which has never been crossed by any one else except Dionysus; who has also crossed the Hydaspes, Acesines, and Hydraotes, and who would have crossed the Hyphasis, if you had not shrunk back with alarm; who has penetrated into the Great Sea by both the mouths of the Indus; who has marched through the desert of Gadrosia, where no one ever before marched with an army; who on his route acquired possession of Carmania and the land of the Oritians, in addition to his other conquests, his fleet having in the meantime already sailed round the coast of the sea which extends from India to Persia—report that when you returned to Susa you deserted him and went away, handing him over to the protection of conquered foreigners. Perhaps this report of yours will be both glorious to you in the eyes of men and devout forsooth in the eyes of the gods. Depart!"

Chapter 186: Reconciliation between Alexander and his Army

Having thus spoken, he leaped down quickly from the platform, and entered the palace, where he paid no attention to the decoration of his person, nor was any of his Companions admitted to see him. Not even on the morrow was any one of them admitted to an audience;

September 20, Wednesday
Selects Persian officers for military command and the Macedonian soldiers react

but on the third day he summoned the select Persians within, and among them he distributed the commands of the brigades, and made the rule that only those whom he had proclaimed his kinsmen,[866] should have the honour of saluting him with a kiss.[867] But the Macedonians who heard the speech were thoroughly astonished at the moment, and remained there in silence near the platform; nor when he retired did any of them accompany the king, except his personal Companions and the confidential body-guards. Though they remained, most of them had nothing to do or say; and yet they were unwilling to retire. But when the news was reported to them about the Persians and Medes, that the military commands were being given to Persians, that the foreign soldiers were being selected and divided into companies, that a Persian footguard, Persian foot Companions, a Persian regiment of men with silver shields,[868] as well as the cavalry Companions, and another royal regiment of cavalry distinct from these, were being called by Macedonian names, they were no longer able to restrain themselves; but running in a body to the palace, they cast their weapons there in front of the gates as a sign of supplication to the king. Standing in front of the gates, they shouted, beseeching to be allowed to enter, and saying that they were willing to surrender the men who had been the instigators of the disturbance on that occasion, and those who had begun the clamour. They also declared they would not retire from the gates either **day** or night, unless Alexander would take some pity upon them. When he was informed of this, he came out without delay; and seeing them lying on the ground in humble guise, and hearing most of them lamenting with loud voice, tears began to flow also from his own eyes. He made an effort to say something to them, but they continued their importunate entreaties.[869] At length one of them, Callines by name, a man conspicuous both for his age and because he was captain of the Companion cavalry, spoke as follows:—"O king, what grieves the Macedonians is, that thou hast already made some of the Persians kinsmen to thyself, and that Persians are called Alexander's kinsmen, and have the honour of saluting thee with a kiss; whereas none of the Macedonians have as yet enjoyed this honour." Then Alexander interrupting him, said:—" But all of you without exception I consider my kinsmen, and so from this time I shall call you." When he had said this, Callines advanced and saluted him with a kiss, and so did all those who wished to salute him. Then they took up their weapons and returned to the camp, shouting and singing a song of thanksgiving to Apollo.

September 22, Friday

Banquet of reconciliation and joint Greek-Persian ceremony (attended by Greek prophets and Persian Magians, possibly Zoroastrian priests). In Alexander's journey, the only other mention of ancient Persian priests/ Magians was negative regarding the tomb of Cyrus, as a result, this is the first positive mention of them, suggesting a possible strategic or bona-fide acceptance of the Persian religion as part of his increasing adoption of Persian culture. The author suggests that this date was therefore one well recognised by both Greek and Persian priest, namely the Autumn Equinox. The festival Mehregan remains celebrated in the Zoroastian calendar to the current era as the 'festival of friendship' which fits well here. Although modern calendars suggest this takes place on day 196 of the Persian calendar (195 days after the Spring Equinox or Noruz), in ancient times, this was also known as the feast of Mithra and was likely celebrated at the Autumn Equinox (Boyce, A History of Zoroastrianism, The Early Period). This date would have been on

September 22nd, and would have been well recognised by the Greek and specifically the Macedonians; who's New Year followed this date on the first new moon.

After this Alexander offered sacrifice to the gods to whom it was his custom to sacrifice, and gave a public banquet, over which he himself presided, with the Macedonians sitting around him; and next to them the Persians; after whom came the men of the other nations, honoured for their personal rank or for some meritorious action. The king and his guests drew wine from the same bowl and poured out - the same libations, both the Grecian prophets and the Magians commencing the ceremony. He prayed for other blessings, and especially that harmony and community of rule might exist between the Macedonians and Persians. The common account is, that those who took part in this banquet were 9,000 in number, that all of them poured out one libation, and after it sang a song of thanksgiving to Apollo.[870]

September 26, Tuesday
Older soldiers arranged to go back home to Macedonia

Chapter 187: Ten Thousand Macedonians Sent Home with Craterus — Disputes between Antipater and Olympias

Then those of the Macedonians who were unfit for service on account of age or any other misfortune, went back of their own accord, to the number of about 10,000. To these Alexander gave the pay not only for the time which had already elapsed, but also for that which they would spend in returning home. He also gave to each man a talent in addition to his pay.[871] If any of them had children by Asiatic wives, he ordered them to leave them behind with him, lest they should introduce into Macedonia a cause of discord, taking with them children by foreign women who were of a different race from the children whom they had left behind at home born of Macedonian mothers. He promised to take care that they should be brought up as Macedonians, educating them not only in general matters but also in the art of war. He also undertook to lead them into Macedonia when they arrived at manhood, and hand them over to their fathers. These uncertain and obscure promises were made to them as they were departing; and he thought he was giving a most indubitable proof of the friendship and affection he had for them by sending with them, as their guardian and the leader of the expedition, Craterus, the man most faithful to him, and whom he valued equally with himself.[872]

October 02, Monday
Ceremony of goodbye to some of his soldiers

Then, having saluted them all, he with tears dismissed them likewise weeping from his presence.

October 06, Friday
Craterus leads men back to Macedonia and Antipater ordered back due to conflicts with Olympias

He ordered Craterus[873] to lead these men back, and when he had done so, to take upon himself the government of Macedonia, Thrace, and Thessaly, and to preside over the freedom of the Greeks. He also ordered Antipater to bring to him the Macedonians of manly age as successors to those who were being sent back. He despatched Polysperchon also with Craterus, as his second in command, so that if any mishap befell Craterus on the march (for he was sending him back on account of the weakness of his health), those who were going might not be in need of a general.[874] A secret report was also going about that Alexander was now overcome by his mother's accusations of Antipater, and that he wished to remove him from Macedonia.[875] This report was current among those who thought that royal actions are more worthy of honour in proportion to their secrecy, and who were inclined to impute what is worthy of belief to a bad motive rather than to attribute it to the real one; a course to which they were led by appearances and their own depravity. But probably this sending for Antipater was not designed for his dishonour, but rather to prevent any unpleasant consequences to Antipater and Olympias from their quarrel which he might not himself be able to rectify. For they were incessantly writing to Alexander, the former saying that the arrogance, acerbity, and meddlesomeness of Olympias was exceedingly unbecoming to the king's mother; insomuch that Alexander was related to have used the following remark in reference to the reports which he received about his mother:— that she was exacting from him a heavy house-rent for the ten months.[876] The queen wrote that Antipater was overweeningly insolent in his pretensions and in the service of his court, no longer remembering the one who had appointed him, but claiming to win and hold the first rank[877] among the Macedonians and Greeks. These slanderous reports about Antipater appeared to have more weight with Alexander, since they were more formidable in regard to the regal dignity. However no overt act or word of the king was reported, from which any one could infer that Antipater was in any way less in favour with him than before.[878]

October 20, Friday
Hephaestion reconciled with Eumenes over an argument. Plutarch suggests that they had a history of rowing; specifically over Eumenes' apartments who Hephaestion had bestowed to Evius the flute player. This personal feud had been escalated to Alexander who had initially taken the side of Eumenes (seemingly on logical grounds), but he subsequently rebuked Eumenes in favour of Hephaestion (seemingly on emotional grounds for his closest friend or 'second-self'). The argument described here may also have been on something else such as management strategy for Antipater and Craterus. Alexander who have left Opis at this time or a few days after the Macedonian new year on October 18.

Chapter 188: The Nisaean Plain — The Amazons

It is said that Hephaestion much against his will yielded to this argument and was reconciled to Eumenes, who on his part wished to settle the dispute.[879]

November 08, Wednesday
Meets female Amazons whilst passing through the Nisaean Plain in Media, home of the large Nisaean horses, likely near ancient Nisaea near modern-day Behistun, somewhere between Behistun and Hamadan (Ecbatana) at the foot of the southern Zagros mountains. The author associates this area with modern-day Borujerd, an ancient region near Hamadan, well-known for its special horses. The Nisaean Plain would therefore correspond to the modern-day Silakhor Plain

In this journey[880] Alexander is said to have seen the plain which was devoted to the royal mares. Herodotus says that the plain itself was named Nisaean, and that the mares were called Nisaean[881]; adding that in olden times there were 150,000 of these horses. But at this time Alexander found not many above 50,000; for most of them had been carried off by robbers. They say that Atropates, the viceroy of Media, gave him a hundred women, saying that they were of the race of Amazons.[882] These had been equipped with the arms of male horsemen, except that they carried axes instead of spears and targets instead of shields. They also say that they had the right breast smaller than the left, and that they exposed it in battle. Alexander dismissed them from the army, that no attempt to violate them might be made by the Macedonians or barbarians; and he ordered them to carry word to their queen that he was coining to her in order to procreate children by her.[883] But this story has been recorded neither by Aristobulus nor Ptolemy, nor any other writer who is a trustworthy authority on such matters. I do not even think that the race of Amazons was surviving at that time; for before Alexander's time they were not mentioned even by Xenophon,[884] who mentions the Phasians, Colchians, and all the other barbaric races which the Greeks came upon, when they started from Trapezus or before they marched down to Trapezus. They would certainly have fallen in with the Amazons if they were still in existence. However it does not seem to me credible that this race of women was altogether fictitious, because it has been celebrated by so many famous poets. For the general account is, that Heracles, marched against them and brought the girdle of their queen Hippolyte into Greece.[885] The Athenians also under Theseus were the first to conquer and repulse these women as they were advancing into Europe[886]; and the battle of the Athenians and Amazons has been painted by Micon,[887] no less than that of the Athenians and Persians. Herodotus also has frequently written about these women[888]; and so have the Athenian writers who have honoured the men who perished in war with funeral orations. They have mentioned the exploit of the Athenians against the Amazons as one of their special glories.[889] If therefore Atropates showed any equestrian women to Alexander, I think he must have shown him some other foreign women trained in horsemanship, and equipped with the arms which were said to be those of the Amazons.[890]

{The distance from Opis (south of Baghdad) and the Nisaean plane east of Behistun at around Borujerd is approximately 400km}

November 22, Wednesday
Arrives at modern-day Ecbatana (modern-day Hamadan in Iran). Possibly at the winter solstice as he celebrated this in previous years

Chapter 189: Death of Hephaestion

In Ecbatana Alexander offered sacrifice according to his custom, for good fortune; and he celebrated a gymnastic and musical contest. He also held drinking parties with his Companions.

{The distance from the Nisaean plane east of Behistun at around Borujerd to Ecbatana (modern-day Hamadan) is approximately 100km}

December 13, Wednesday
Hephaestion becomes unwell

At this time Hephaestion fell sick;

December 19, Tuesday
Hephaestion dies (on a day of a gymnastic contest, corresponds to the Winter Solstice that Alexander had celebrated in previous years)

and they say that the stadium was full of people on the seventh day of his fever, for on that day there was a gymnastic contest for boys. When Alexander was informed that Hephaestion was in a critical state, he went to him without delay, but found him no longer alive.[891] Different authors have given different accounts of Alexander's grief on this occasion; but they agree in this, that his grief was great. As to what was done in honour of Hephaestion, they make diverse statements, just as each writer was actuated by good-will or envy towards him, or even towards Alexander himself. Of the authors who have made these reckless statements, some seem to me to have thought that whatever Alexander said or did to show his excessive grief for the man who was the dearest to him in the world, redounds to his own honour; whereas others seem to have thought that it rather tended to his disgrace, as being conduct unbecoming to any king and especially to Alexander. Some say that he lay prostrate on his companion's body for the greater part of that day, bewailing him and refusing to depart from him, until he was forcibly carried away by his Companions. Others that he lay upon the body the whole day and night. Others again say that he hanged the physician Glaucias, for having indiscreetly given the medicine[892]; while others affirm that he, being a spectator of the games, neglected Hephaestion, who was filled with wine. That Alexander should have cut off his hair in honour of the dead man, I do not think improbable, both for other reasons and especially from a desire to imitate Achilles, whom from his boyhood he had an ambition to rival.[893] Others also say that Alexander himself at one time drove the chariot on which the body was borne; but this statement I by no means believe. Others again affirm that he ordered the shrine of Asclepius in Ecbatana to be razed to the ground; which was an act of barbarism, and by no means in harmony with Alexander's general behaviour, but rather in accordance with the arrogance of Xerxes in his dealings with the deity, who is said to have let fetters down into the Hellespont, in order to punish it forsooth.[894] But the following statement, which has been recorded, does not seem to me entirely beyond the range of probability:—that when Alexander was marching to Babylon, he was met on the road by many embassies from Greece, among which were some Epidaurian envoys, who obtained from him their requests.[895] He also gave them an offering to be conveyed to Asclepias, adding this remark:—" Although Asclepius has not treated me fairly, in not saving the life of my Companion, whom I valued equally with my own head."[896] It has been stated by most writers that he ordered honours to be always paid to Hephaestion as a hero; and some say that he even sent men to Ammon's temple to ask the god if it were allowable to offer sacrifice to Hephaestion as a god; but Ammon replied that it was not allowable. All the authorities, however, agree as to the following facts:—that

December 22, Friday
Publishes a decree of public mourning and orders a funeral Pyre after 3 days of personal mourning for the death of Hephaestion (at a cost of several billion dollars by current currency standards)

until the third day after Hephaestion's death, Alexander neither tasted food nor paid any attention to his personal appearance, but lay on the ground either bewailing or silently mourning; that he also ordered a funeral pyre to be prepared for him in Babylon at the expense of 10,000 talents; some say at a still greater cost[897]; that a decree was published throughout all the barbarian territory for the observance of a public mourning.[898] Many of Alexander's Companions dedicated themselves and their arms to the dead Hephaestion in order to show their respect to him; and the first to begin the artifice was Eumenes, whom we a short time ago mentioned as having been at variance with him.[899] This he did that Alexander might not think he was pleased at Hephaestion's death. Alexander did not appoint any one else to be commander of the Companion cavalry in the place of Hephaestion, so that the name of that general might not perish from the brigade; but that division of cavalry was still called Hephaestion's and the figure made from Hephaestion went in front of it. He also resolved to celebrate a gymnastic and musical contest, much more magnificent than any of the preceding, both in the multitude of competitors and in the amount of money expended upon it. For he provided 3,000 competitors in all; and it is said that these men a short time after also competed in the games held at Alexander's own funeral.

323 BC

January 28, Sunday

Chapter 190: Subjugation of the Cossaeans — Embassies from Distant Nations

The mourning was prolonged for many days; and as he was now beginning to recall himself from it, under such circumstances his Companions had less difficulty in rousing him to action.

February 03, Saturday
Winter expedition against the Cosseans (Likely the Kassites in modern mountainous Luristan and the modern-day city of Khorramabad)

Then at length he made an expedition against the Cossaeans,[900] a warlike race bordering on the territory of the Uxians. They are mountaineers, inhabiting strong positions in separate villages. Whenever a force approached them, they were in the habit of retiring to the summits of their mountains, either in a body or separately as each man found it practicable; and thus they escaped, making it difficult for those who attacked them with their forces to come near them. After the enemy's departure, they used to turn themselves again to marauding, by which occupation they supported themselves. But Alexander subdued this race, though he marched against them in the winter; for neither winter nor ruggedness of ground was any impediment either to him or to Ptolemy, son of Lagus, who led a part of the army in the campaign against them. Thus no military enterprise which Alexander undertook was ever unsuccessful.

{The distance between Ecbatana (Hamedan) and the mountainous Cossaean area (Khorramabad) is approximately 150km}

February 27, Tuesday
International news en-route in returning to Babylon

As he was marching back to Babylon, he was met by embassies from the Libyans, who congratulated him and crowned him as conqueror of the kingdom of Asia.[901] From Italy also came Bruttians, Lucanians, and Tyrrhenians[902] as envoys, for the same purpose. The Carthaginians are said to have sent an embassy to him at this time[903]; and it is also asserted that envoys came to request his friendship from the Ethiopians, the Scythians of Europe, the Gauls, and Iberians—nations whose names were heard and their accoutrements seen then for the first time by Greeks and Macedonians. They are also said to have entrusted to Alexander the duty of settling their disputes with each other. Then indeed it was especially evident both to himself and to those about him that he was lord of all the land and sea.[904] Of the men who have written the history of Alexander, Aristus and Asclepiades[905] alone say that the Romans also sent an embassy to him, and that when he met their embassy, he predicted something of the future power of Rome, observing both the attire of the men, their love of labour, and their devotion to freedom. At the same time he made urgent inquiries about their political constitution. This incident I have recorded neither as certainly authentic nor as altogether incredible; but none of the Roman writers have made any mention of this embassy having been despatched to Alexander; nor of those who have written an account of Alexander's actions, has either Ptolemy, son of Lagus, or Aristobulus mentioned it. With these authors I am generally inclined to agree. Nor does it seem likely that the Roman republic, which was at that time remarkable for its love of liberty, would send an embassy to a foreign king, especially to a place so far away from their own land, when they were not compelled to do so by fear or any hope of advantage, being possessed as they were beyond any other people by hatred to the very name and race of despots.[906]

March 02, Friday
Sent Heraclides to collect ship-building wood from the mountains (likely in early spring as otherwise the weather would not have permitted this)

Chapter 191: Exploration of the Caspian — The Chaldaean Sooth-sayers

After this, Alexander sent Heraclides, son of Argaeus, into Hyrcania in command of a company of shipwrights, with orders to cut timber from the Hyrcanian mountains and with it to construct a number of ships of war, some without decks and others with decks after the Grecian fashion of ship-building.[907] For he was very desirous of discovering with what sea the one called the Hyrcanian or Caspian unites; whether it communicates with the water of the Euxine Sea, or whether the Great Sea comes right round from the Eastern Sea, which is near India and flows up into the Hyrcanian Gulf; just as he had discovered that the Persian Sea, which was called the Red Sea, is really a gulf of the Great Sea.[908] For the sources of the Caspian Sea had not yet been discovered, although many nations dwell around it, and navigable rivers discharge their waters into it. From Bactria, the Oxus, the largest of Asiatic rivers, those of India excepted, discharges itself into this sea[909]; and through Scythia flows the Jaxartes.[910] The general account is, that the Araxes also, which flows from Armenia, falls into the same sea.[911] These are the largest; but many others flow into these, while others again discharge themselves directly into this sea. Some of these were known to those who visited these nations with Alexander; others are situated towards the farther side of the gulf, as it seems, in the country of the Nomadic Scythians, a district which is quite unknown.

March 05, Monday
Crosses Tigris river (possibly near modern-day Numaniyah in modern-day Iraq)

When Alexander had crossed the river Tigres with his army and

{The distance from the Cossaean area (Khorramabad) to the Tigris (Numaniyah) is approximately 300km}

March 07, Wednesday
Met by the Chaldean philosophers/ priests between the Tigris and Babylon (modern-day Al-Hillah, Iraq) requesting him not to enter Babylon

was marching to Babylon, he was met by the Chaldaean philosophers[912]; who, having led him away from his Companions, besought him to suspend his march to that city. For they said that an oracular declaration had been made to them by the god Belus, that his entrance into Babylon at that time would not be for his good. But he answered their speech with a line from the poet Euripides to this effect: He the best prophet is that guesses well."[913] But said the Chaldaeans:—"O king, do not at any rate enter the city looking towards the west nor leading the army advancing in that direction; bat rather go right round towards' the east." But this did not turn out to be easy for him, on account of the difficulty of the ground; for the deity was leading him to the place where entering he was doomed soon to die. And perhaps it was better for him to be taken off in the very acme of his glory as well as of the affection entertained for him by men, before any of the vicissitudes natural to man befell him. Probably this was the reason Solon advised Croesus to look at the end of a long life, and not before pronounce any man happy.[914] Yea indeed, Hephaestion's death had been no small misfortune to Alexander; and I think he would rather have departed before it occurred than have been alive to experience it; no less than Achilles, as it seems to me, would rather have died before Patroclus than have been the avenger of his death.

Chapter 192: The Advice of the Chaldees Rejected

But he had a suspicion that the Chaldaeans were trying to prevent his entrance into Babylon at that time with reference rather to their own advantage than to the declaration of the oracle. For in the middle of the city of the Babylonians was the temple of Belus,[915] an edifice very great in size, constructed of baked bricks which were cemented together with bitumen. This temple had been razed to the ground by Xerxes, when he returned from Greece; as were also all the other sacred buildings of the Babylonians. Some say that Alexander had formed the resolution to rebuild it upon the former foundations ', and for this reason he ordered the Babylonians to carry away the mound. Others say that he intended to build a still larger one than that which formerly existed.[916] But after his departure, the men who had been entrusted with the work prosecuted it without any vigour, so that he determined to employ the whole of his army in completing it. A great quantity of land as well as gold had been dedicated to the god Belus, by the Assyrian kings; and in olden times the temple was kept in repair and sacrifices were offered to the god. But at that time the Chaldaeans were appropriating the property of the god, since nothing existed upon which the revenues could be expended. Alexander suspected that they did not wish him to enter Babylon for this reason, for fear that in a short time the temple would be finished, and they should be deprived of the gains accruing from the money. And yet, according to Aristobulus, he was willing to yield to their persuasions so far at least as to change the direction of his entry into the city.

{The distance from the Tigris (Numaniyah) to Babylon (modern-day Al-Hillah) is approximately 100km}

March 08, Thursday
Encamps near the Euphrates river near Babylon (Al-Hillah) on the north side of the city.

For this purpose, on the first day he encamped near the river Euphrates;

March 09, Friday
Enters Babylon against the requests of the Chaldeans and is met by Greek ambassadors. Marches south along the river (with it on the right) and turns left to to the west of the city and enters the city.

and on the next day he marched along the bank, keeping the river on his right hand, with the intention of passing beyond the part of the city turned towards the west, and there wheeling round to lead his army towards the east. But on account of the difficulty of the ground he could not march with his army in this direction; because if a man who is entering the city from the west, here changes his direction eastward, he comes upon ground covered with marshes and shoals. Thus, partly by his own will and partly against his will, he disobeyed the god.

Chapter 193: Predictions of Alexander's Death

Moreover Aristobulus has recorded the following story. Apollodorus the Amphipolitan, one of Alexander's Companions, was general of the army which the king left with Mazaeus, the viceroy of Babylon.[917] When he joined his forces with the king's on the return of the latter from India, and observed that he was severely punishing the viceroys who had been placed over the several countries, he sent to his brother Peithagoras and asked him to divine about his safety. For Peithagoras was a diviner who derived his knowledge of the future from the inspection of the inward parts of animals. This man sent back to Apollodorus, inquiring of whom he was so especially afraid, as to wish to consult divination. The latter wrote back: "The king himself and Hephaestion." Peithagoras therefore in the first place offered sacrifice with reference to Hephaestion. But as there was no lobe visible upon the liver of the sacrificial victim,[918] he stated this fact in a letter, which he sealed and sent to his brother from Babylon to Ecbatana, explaining that there was no reason at all to be afraid of Hephaestion, for in a short time he would be out of their way. And Aristobulus says that Apollodorus received this epistle only one day before Hephaestion died. Then Peithagoras again offered sacrifice in respect to Alexander, and the liver of the victim consulted in respect to him was also destitute of a lobe. He therefore wrote to Apollodorus to the same purport about Alexander as about Hephaestion. Apollodorus did not conceal the information sent to him, but told Alexander, in order the more to show his good-will to the king, if he urged him to be on his guard lest some danger might befall him at that time. And Aristobulus says that the king commended Apollodorus, and when he entered Babylon, he asked Peithagoras what sign he had met with, to induce him to write thus to his brother. He said that the liver of the victim sacrificed for him was without a lobe. When Alexander asked what the sign portended, he said that it was a very disastrous one. The king was so far from being angry with him, that he even treated him with greater respect, for telling him the truth without any disguise. Aristobulus says that he himself heard this story from Peithagoras; and adds that the same man acted as diviner for Perdiccas and afterwards for Antigonus, and that the same sign occurred for both. It was verified by fact; for Perdiccas lost his life leading an army against Ptolemy,[919] and Antigonus was killed in the battle fought by him at Ipsus against Seleucus and Lysimachus.[920] Also concerning Calanus, the Indian philosopher, the following story has been recorded. When he was going to the funeral pyre to die, he gave the parting salutation to all his other companions; but he refused to approach Alexander to give him the salutation, saying lie would meet him at Babylon and there salute him. At the time indeed this remark was treated with neglect; but afterwards, when Alexander had died at Babylon, it came to the recollection of those who had heard it, and they thought forsooth that it was a divine intimation of Alexander's approaching end.

Chapter 194: Embassies from Greece — Fleet Prepared for Invading Arabia

As he was entering Babylon, he was met by embassies from the Greeks; but for what purpose each embassy was sent has not been recorded. [921] To me indeed it seems probable that most of them came to crown and eulogize him on account of his victories, especially the Indian ones, as well as to say that the Greeks rejoiced at his safe return from India. It is said that he greeted these men with the right hand, and after paying them suitable honour sent them back. He also gave the ambassadors permission to take with them all the statues of men and images of gods and the other votive offerings which Xerxes had carried off from Greece to Babylon, Pasargadae, Susa, or any other place in Asia. In this way it is said that the brazen statues of Harmodius and Aristogeiton,[922] as well as the monument of the Celcaean Artemis, were carried back to Athens.[923]

March 14, Wednesday
Nearchus arrives from his Arabian journey

Aristobulus says that he found at Babylon the fleet with Nearchus, which had sailed from the Persian Sea up the river Euphrates; and another which had been conveyed from Phoenicia, consisting of two Phoenician quinqueremes, three quadriremes, twelve triremes, and thirty triacontors. These had been taken to pieces and conveyed to the river Euphrates from Phoenicia to the city of Thapsacus. There they were joined together again and sailed down to Babylon. The same writer says that he cut down the cypresses in Babylonia and with them built another fleet; for in the land of the Assyrians these trees alone are abundant, but of the other things necessary for ship-building this country affords no supply. A multitude of purple-fishers and other sea-faring men came to him from Phoenicia and the rest of the sea-board to serve as crews for the ships and perform the other services on board. Near Babylon he made a harbour by excavation large enough to afford anchorage to 1,000 ships of war; and adjoining the harbour he made dockyards. Miccalus the Clazomenian[924] was despatched to' Phoenicia and Syria with 500 talents[925] to enlist some men and to purchase others who were experienced in nautical affairs. For Alexander designed to colonize the sea-board near the Persian Gulf, as well as the islands in that sea. For he thought that this land would become no less prosperous than Phoenicia. He made these preparations of the fleet to attack the main body of the Arabs,[926] under the pretext that they were the only barbarians of this region who had not sent an embassy to him or done anything else becoming their position and showing respect to him. But the truth was, as it seems to me, that Alexander was insatiably ambitious of acquiring fresh territory.[927]

Chapter 195: Description of Arabia — Voyage of Nearchus

The common report is, that he heard that the Arabs venerated only two gods, Uranus and Dionysus[928]; the former because he is visible and contains in himself the heavenly luminaries, especially the sun, from which emanates the greatest and most evident benefit to all things human; and the latter on account of the fame he acquired by his expedition into India. Therefore he thought himself quite worthy to be considered by the Arabs as a third god, since he had performed deeds by no means inferior to those of Dionysus. If then he could conquer the Arabs, he intended to grant them the privilege of conducting their government according to their own customs, as he had already done to the Indians. The fertility of the land was a secret inducement to him to invade it; because he heard that the people obtained cassia from the lakes, and myrrh and frankincense from the trees; that cinnamon was cut from the shrubs, and that the meadows produce spikenard without any cultivation.[929] As to the size of the country, he was informed that the seaboard of Arabia was not less in extent than that of India; that near it lie many islands; that in all parts of the country there were harbours sufficiently commodious to provide anchorage for his fleet, and that it supplied sites for founding cities, which would become flourishing. He was also informed that there were two islands in the sea facing the mouth of the Euphrates, the first of which was not far from the place where the waters of that river are discharged into the sea, being about 120 stades[930] distant from the shore and the river's mouth. This is the smaller of the two, and was densely covered with every kind of timber. In it was also a temple of Artemis, around which the inhabitants themselves spent their lives. The island was devoted to the use of wild goats and stags, which were allowed to range at large as being dedicated to Artemis. It was unlawful to chase them unless any one wished to offer sacrifice to the goddess; and for this purpose alone it was lawful to chase them. Aristobulus says that Alexander ordered this island to be called Icarus, after the island so named in the Aegean Sea,[931] on which, as the report goes, Icarus, son of Daedalus fell, when the wax, by which the wings had been fastened to him, melted. For he did not fly near the earth, according to his father's injunctions, but senselessly flying far aloft, he allowed the sun to soften and loosen the wax. Icarus left his name to the island and the sea, the former being called Icarus and the latter the Icarian. The other island was said to be distant from, the mouth of the Euphrates about a day and night's voyage for a ship running before the breeze. Its name was Tylus[932]; it was large and most of it neither rugged nor woody, but suitable for producing cultivated fruits and all things in due season. Some of this information was imparted to Alexander by Archias, who was sent with a triacontor to investigate the course of the coasting voyage to Arabia, and who went as far as the island of Tylus, but durst not pass beyond that point. Androsthenes[933] was despatched with another triacontor and sailed to a part of the peninsula of Arabia. Hieron of Soli the pilot also received a triacontor from Alexander and advanced farthest of those whom he despatched to this region; for he had received instructions to sail round the whole Arabian peninsula as far as the Arabian Gulf near Egypt over against Heroopolis.[934] Although he coasted along the country of the Arabs to a great distance he durst not go as far as he was ordered; but returning to Alexander he reported that the size of the peninsula was marvellous, being only a little smaller than the country of the Indians, and its extremity projected far into the Great Sea.[935] Nearchus indeed in his voyage from India had seen this stretching out a little, before he turned aside into the Persian Gulf, and he was almost induced to cross over to it. The pilot Onesicritus thought they ought to have gone thither; but Nearchus says that he himself prevented it, so that after sailing right round the Persian Gulf he might be able to give a report to Alexander that he had accomplished the voyage on which he had sent him. For Nearchus said he had not been despatched to navigate the Great Sea, but to explore the land bordering on the sea, to find out what men inhabit it, to discover the harbours and rivers in it, to ascertain the customs of the people, and to see if any of the country was fertile and if any was sterile. This was the reason why Alexander's naval expedition returned in safety; for if it had sailed beyond the deserts of Arabia, it would not have returned in safety. This is said also to have been the reason why Hieron turned back.[936]

March 26, Monday
Sails from Babylon down the Euphrates

Chapter 196: Description of the Euphrates and the Pallacopas

While the triremes were being built for him, and the harbour near Babylon was being excavated, Alexander sailed from Babylon down the Euphrates

April 07, Saturday
Arrives at the port of Pallacopas (Nearchus called this Salmus), feeds into the Mesopotamian Marshes on the Euphrates side. The author suggests this could correspond with the area of the Al Chabaish marshland (near modern-day Hammar lake)

to what was called the river Pallacopas, which is distant from Babylon about 800 stades.[937] This Pallacopas is not a river rising from springs, but a canal cut from the Euphrates. For that river flowing from the Armenian mountains,[938] proceeds within its banks in the season of winter, because its water is scanty; bub when the spring begins to make its appearance, and especially just before the summer solstice, it pours along with mighty stream and overflows its banks into the Assyrian country.[939] For at that season the snow upon the Armenian mountains melts and swells its water to a great degree; and as its stream flows high above the level of the country, it would flow over the land if some one had not furnished it with an outlet along the Pallacopas and turned it aside into the marshes and pools, which, beginning from this canal, extend as far as the country contiguous to Arabia. Thence it spreads out far and wide into a shallow lake, from which it falls into the sea by many invisible mouths. After the snow has melted, about the time of the setting of the Pleiades, the Euphrates flows with a small stream; but none the less the greater part of it discharges itself into the pools along the Pallacopas. Unless, therefore, some one had dammed up the Pallacopas again, so that the water might be turned back within the banks and carried down the channel of the river, it would hare drained the Euphrates into itself, and consequently the Assyrian country would not be watered by it. But the outlet of the Euphrates into the Pallacopas was dammed up by the viceroy of Babylonia with great labour (although it was an easy matter to construct the outlet), because the ground in this region is slimy and most of it mud, so that when it has once received the water of the river it is not easy to turn it back. But more than 10,000 Assyrians were engaged in this labour even until the third month. When Alexander was informed of this, he was induced to confer a benefit upon the land of Assyria. He determined to shut up the outlet where the stream of the Euphrates was turned into the Pallacopas.

{The distance from the Babylon (modern-day Al-Hillah) and the Al Chabaish marshland (near modern-day Hammar lake) is approximately 310km}

April 09, Monday
Travels 30 stades (5.55km) from Pallacopas

When he had advanced about thirty stades, the earth appeared to be somewhat rocky, so that if it were' cut through and a junction made with the old canal along the Pallacopas, on account of the hardness of the soil, it would not allow the water to percolate, and there would be no difficulty in turning it back at the appointed season.

April 11, Wednesday
Returns to Pallacopas

For this purpose he sailed to the Pallacopas, and then continued his voyage down that canal into the pools towards the country of the Arabs.

April 18, Wednesday
Founds a city on the coastal river leading to the Persian Gulf (the author suggest this to be near modern-day Basra)

There seeing a certain admirable site, he founded a city upon it and fortified it. In it he settled as many of the Grecian mercenaries as volunteered to remain, and such as were unfit for military service by reason of age or wounds.

May 04, Friday
Returns toward Babylon through the marshes near the city

Chapter 197: An Omen of Alexander's Approaching Death

Having thus proved the falsity of the prophecy of the Chaldaeans, by not having experienced any unpleasant fortune in Babylon,[940] as they had predicted, but having marched out of that city without suffering any mishap, he grew confident in spirit and sailed again through the marshes, having Babylon on his left hand. Here a part of his fleet lost its way in the narrow branches of the river through want of a pilot, until he sent a man to pilot it and lead it back into the channel of the river. The following story is told. Most of the tombs of the Assyrian kings had been built among the pools and marshes.[941] When Alexander was sailing through these marshes, and, as the story goes, was himself steering the trireme, a strong gust of wind fell upon his broadbrimmed Macedonian hat, and the fillet which encircled it. The hat, being heavy, fell into the water; but the fillet, being carried along by the wind, was caught by one of the reeds growing near the tomb of one of the ancient kings.[942] This incident itself was an omen of what was about to occur, and so was the fact that one of the sailors[943] swam off towards the fillet and snatched it from the reed. But he did not carry it in his hands, because it would have been wetted while he was swimming; he therefore put it round his own head and thus conveyed it to the king. Most of the biographers of Alexander say that the king presented him with a talent as a reward for his zeal, and then, ordered his head to be cut off; as the prophets had directed him not to permit that head to be safe which had worn the royal fillet. However, Aristobulus says that the man received a talent; but afterwards also received a scourging for placing the fillet round his head. The same author says that it was one of the Phoenician sailors who fetched the fillet for Alexander; but there are some who say it was Seleucus, and that this was an omen to Alexander of his death and to Seleucus of his great kingdom. For that of all those who succeeded to the sovereignty after Alexander, Seleucus became the greatest king, was the most kingly in mind, and ruled over the greatest extent of land after Alexander himself, does not seem to me to admit of question.[944]

{The distance from Alexander's city near the Persian Gulf (likely near Basra) and Babylon (Al-Hillah) is approximately 390km}

May 05, Saturday
Return to Babylon

Chapter 198: The Army Recruited from the Persians — Hephaestion's Memory Honoured

When he returned to Babylon he found that Peucestas had arrived from Persis, bringing with him 20,000 Persians, as well as many Cossaeans and Tapurians, because these races were reported to be the most warlike of those bordering on Persis. Philoxenus also came to him, bringing an army from Caria; Menander, with another from Lydia, and Menidas with the cavalry which had been put under his command.[945] At the same time arrived embassies from Greece, the members of which, with crowns upon their own heads, approached Alexander and crowned him with golden crowns, as if forsooth they came to him as special envoys deputed, to pay him divine honours; and his end was not far off. Then he commended the Persians for their great zeal towards him, which was shown by their obedience to Peucestas in all things, and Peucestas himself for the prudence which he had displayed in ruling them. He distributed these foreign soldiers among the Macedonian ranks in the following way. Each company was led by a Macedonian decurion, and next to him was a Macedonian receiving double pay for distinguished valour; and then came one who received ten staters,[946] who was so named from the pay he received, being less than that received by the man with double pay, but more than that of the men who were serving as soldiers without holding a position of honour. Next to these came twelve Persians, and last in the company another Macedonian,

346

who also received the pay of ten staters; so that in each company there were twelve Persians and four Macedonians, three of whom received higher pay, and the fourth was in command of the company.[947] The Macedonians were armed in their hereditary manner; but of the Persians some were archers, while others had javelins furnished with straps, by which they were held.[948]

May 07, Monday
Reviews his fleet

At this time Alexander often reviewed his fleet, had many sham-fights with his triremes and quadriremes in the river, and contests both for rowers and pilots, the winners receiving crowns.

May 12, Saturday
Return of envoys from the Oracle at Siwah

Now arrived the special envoys whom he had despatched to Ammon to inquire how it was lawful for him to honour Hephaestion. They told him that Ammon said it was lawful to offer sacrifice to him as to a hero. Rejoicing at the response of the oracle, he paid respect to him as a hero from that time.

May 16, Wednesday
Dispatch of letter to Cleomenes

He also despatched a letter to Cleomenes, who was a bad man and had committed many acts of injustice in Egypt.[949] For my own part I do not blame him for his friendship to Hephaestion and for his recollection of him even when dead; but I do blame him for many other acts. For the letter commanded Cleomenes to prepare chapels for the hero Hephaestion in the Egyptian Alexandria, one in the city itself and another in the island of Pharos, where the tower is situated.[950] The chapels were to be exceedingly large and to be built at lavish expense. The letter also directed that Cleomenes should take care that Hephaestion's name should be attached to them; and moreover that his name should be engraved on all the legal documents with which the merchants entered into bargains with each other.[951] These things I cannot blame, except that he made so much ado about matters of trifling moment. But the following I must blame severely: "If I find," said the letter, "the temples and chapels of the hero Hephaestion in Egypt well completed, I will not only pardon, you any crimes you may have committed in the past, but in the future you shall suffer no unpleasant treatment from me, however great may be the crimes you have committed." I cannot commend this message sent, from a great king to a man who was ruling a large country and many people, especially as the man was a wicked one.[952]

May 24, Thursday
Non-sensical occupation of Alexander's throne

Chapter 199: Another Omen of Alexander's Death

But Alexander's own end was now near. Aristobulus says that the following occurrence was a prognostication of what was about to happen. He was distributing the army which came with Peucestas from Persia, and that which came with Philoxenus and Menander from the sea,[953] among the Macedonian lines, and becoming thirsty he retired from his seat and thus left the royal throne empty. On each side of the throne were couches with silver feet, upon which his personal Companions were sitting. A certain man of obscure condition (some say that he was even one of the men kept under guard without being in chains), seeing the throne and the couches empty, and the eunuchs standing round the throne (for the Companions also rose up from their seats with the king when he retired), walked through the line of eunuchs, ascended the throne, and sat down upon it.[954] According to a Persian law, they did not make him rise from the throne; but rent their garments and beat their breasts and faces as if on account of a great evil. When Alexander was informed of this, he ordered the man who had sat upon his throne to be put to the torture, with the view of discovering whether he had done this according to a plan concerted by a conspiracy.

May 25, Friday
Torture of the throne-sitter

But the man confessed nothing, except that it came into his mind at the time to act thus. Even more for this reason the diviners explained that this occurrence boded no good to him.

June 01, Friday
Festivities at Medius' residence, Daisios 21 (in the ancient Macedonian calendar, 1st Daisios is May 12th on a new moon)

A few days after this, after offering to the gods the customary sacrifices for good success, and certain others also for, the purpose of divination, he was feasting with his friends, and was drinking far into the night.[955] He is also said to have distributed the sacrificial victims as well as a quantity of wine to the army throughout the companies and centuries. There are some who have recorded that he wished to retire after the drinking party to his bed-chamber; but Medius, at that time the most influential of the Companions, met him and begged him to join a party of revellers at his residence, saying that the revel would be a pleasant one.

Chapter 200: Alexander Seized with Fever

The Royal Diary gives the following account,[956] to the effect that he revelled and drank at the dwelling of Medius;

June 02, Saturday
Drinking at Medius' residence, Daisios 22 (in the ancient Macedonian calendar)

then rose up, took a bath, and slept; then again supped at the house of Medius and again drank till far into the night.

June 03, Sunday
Develops a fever and crosses the river to the park, Daisios 23 (in the ancient Macedonian calendar)

After retiring from the drinking party he took a bath; after which he took a little food and slept there, because he already felt feverish. He was carried out upon a couch to the sacrifices, in order that he might offer them according to his daily custom. After performing the sacred rites he lay down

in the banqueting hall until dusk. In the meantime he gave instructions to
the officers about the expedition and voyage, ordering those who were
going on foot to be ready on the fourth day, and those who were going to
sail with him to be ready to sail on the fifth day. From this place he was
carried upon the couch to the river, where he embarked in a boat and sailed
across the river to the park. There he again took a bath and went to rest.

June 04, Monday
Bathed to cool down, Daisios 24 (in the ancient Macedonian calendar)

On the following day he took another bath and offered the customary
sacrifices. He then entered a tester bed, lay down, and chatted with Medius.
He also ordered his officers to meet him at daybreak. Having done this he
ate a little supper and was again conveyed into the tester bed. The fever
now raged the whole night without intermission.

June 05, Tuesday
Fever rages, makes a sacrifice, Daisios 25 (in the ancient Macedonian calendar)

The next day he took a bath; after which he offered sacrifice, and gave
orders to Nearchus and the other officers that the voyage should begin on
the third day.

June 06, Wednesday
Third day of bathing to cool down, Daisios 26 (in the ancient Macedonian calendar)

The next day he bathed again and offered the prescribed sacrifices. After
performing the sacred rites, he did not yet cease to suffer from the fever.
Notwithstanding this, he summoned the officers and gave them
instructions to have all things ready for the starting of the fleet. In the
evening he took a bath, after which he was very ill.

June 07, Thursday
New instructions to officers, Daisios 27 (in the ancient Macedonian calendar)

The next day he was transferred to the house near the swimming-bath, where he offered the prescribed sacrifices. Though he was now very dangerously ill, he summoned the most responsible of his officers and gave them fresh instructions about the voyage.

June 08, Friday
Carried to perform sacrifices, Daisios 28 (in the ancient Macedonian calendar). Demonstration of peripheral muscle weakness

On the following day he was with difficulty carried out to the sacrifices, which he offered; and none the less gave other orders to the officers about the voyage.

June 09, Saturday
Deteriorates further, Daisios 29 (in the ancient Macedonian calendar). Weakness clearly affecting central nervous system as he could not speak, according to the author this progression could represent a nervous system/ neurological infection. Please see the authors work, ascribing this illness to an ascending meningitis likely secondary to a congenital scoliotic syndrome (Ashrafian H, The death of Alexander the Great--a spinal twist of fate, J Hist Neurosci. 2004 Jun;13(2):138-42.)

The next day, though he was now very ill, he offered the prescribed sacrifices. He now gave orders that the generals should remain in attendance in the hall,[957] and that the colonels and captains should remain before the gates. But being now altogether in a dangerous state, he was conveyed from the park into the palace. When his officers entered the room, he knew them indeed, but could no longer utter a word, being speechless. During the ensuing night and

June 10, Sunday
Deteriorates further, Panemos 01 (in the ancient Macedonian calendar). Further deterioration. New moon

day and the next night and

June 11, Monday
Alexander dies in the late afternoon according to the Babylonian Astronomical diary, Panemos 02 (in the ancient Macedonian calendar).

day he was in a very high fever.

Chapter 201: Alexander's Death

Such is the account given in the Royal Diary. In addition to this, it states that the soldiers were very desirous of seeing him; Some, in order to see him once more while still alive; others, because there was a report that he was already dead, imagined that his death was being concealed by the confidential body-guards, as I for my part suppose. Most of them through grief and affection for their king forced their way in to see him. It is said that when his soldiers passed by him he was unable to speak; yet he greeted each of them with his right hand, raising his head with difficulty and making a sign with his eyes. The Royal Diary also says that Peithon, Attains, Demophon, and Peucestas, as well as Cleomenes, Menidas, and Seleucus, slept in the temple of Serapis,[958] and asked the god whether it would be better and more desirable for Alexander to be carried into his temple, in order as a suppliant to be cured by him. A voice issued from the god saying that he was not to be carried into the temple, but that it would be better for him to remain where he was. This answer was reported by the Companions; and soon after Alexander died, as if forsooth this were now the better thing. Neither Aristobulus nor Ptolemy has given an account differing much from the preceding. Some authors, however, have related that his Companions asked him to whom he left his kingdom; and that he replied: " To the best."[959] Others say, that in addition to this remark, he told them that he saw there would be a great funeral contest held in his honour.[960]

Chapter 202: Rumour that Alexander was Poisoned

I am aware that many other particulars have been related by historians concerning Alexander's death, and especially that poison was sent for him by Antipater, from the effects of which he died.[961] It is also asserted that the poison was procured for Antipater by Aristotle, who was now afraid of Alexander on account of Callisthenes.[962] It is said to have been conveyed by Cassander, the son of Antipater,[963] some recording that he conveyed it in the hoof of a mule, and that his younger brother Iollas gave it to the king.[964] For this man was the royal cup-bearer, and he happened to have received some affront from Alexander a short time before his death. Others have stated that Medius, being a lover of Iollas, took part in the deed; for he it was who induced the king to hold the revel. They say that Alexander was seized with an acute paroxysm of pain over the wine-cup, on feeling which he retired from the drinking bout.[965] One writer has not even been ashamed to record that when Alexander perceived he was unlikely to survive, he was going out to throw himself into the river Euphrates, so that he might disappear from men's sight, and leave among the men of after-times a more firmly-rooted opinion that he owed his birth to a god, and had departed to the gods. But as he was going out he did not escape the notice of his wife Roxana, who restrained him from carrying out his design. Whereupon he uttered lamentations, saying that she forsooth envied him the complete glory of being thought the offspring of the god. These statements I have recorded rather that I may not seem to be ignorant that they have been made, than because I consider them worthy of credence or even of narration.

Chapter 203: Character of Alexander

Alexander died in the hundred and fourteenth Olympiad, in the archonship of Hegesias at Athens.[966] According to the statement of Aristobulus, he lived thirty- two years, and had reached the eighth month of his thirty-third year. He had reigned twelve years and these eight months.[967] He was very handsome in person, and much devoted to exertion, very active in mind, very heroic in courage, very tenacious of honour, exceedingly fond of incurring danger, and strictly observant of his duty to the gods. In regard to the pleasures of the body, he had perfect self-control; and of those of the mind, praise was the only one of which he was insatiable. He was very clever in recognising what was necessary to be done, even when it was still a matter unnoticed by others; and very successful in conjecturing from the observation of facts what was likely to occur. In marshalling, arming, and ruling an army, he was exceedingly skilful; and very renowned for rousing the courage of his soldiers, filling them with hopes of success, and dispelling their fear in the midst of danger by his own freedom from fear. Therefore even what he had to do in secret he did with the greatest boldness. He was also very clever in getting the start of his enemies, and snatching from them their advantages by secretly forestalling them, before any one even feared what was about to happen. He was likewise very steadfast in keeping the agreements and settlements which he made, as well as very secure from being entrapped by deceivers. Finally, he was very sparing in the expenditure of money for the gratification of his own pleasures; but he was exceedingly bountiful in spending it for the benefit of his associates.

Chapter 204: Apology for Alexander's Errors

That Alexander should have committed errors in his conduct from quickness of temper or from wrath,[968] and that he should have been induced to comport himself like the Persian monarchs to an immoderate degree, I do not think remarkable if we fairly consider both his youth[969] and his uninterrupted career of good fortune; likewise that kings have no associates in pleasure who aim at their best interests, but that they will always have associates urging them to do wrong. However, I am certain that Alexander, was the only one of the ancient kings who, from nobility of character, repented of the errors which he had committed. The majority of men, even if they have become conscious that they have committed an error, make ttg mistake of thinking that they can conceal their sin by defending their error as if it had been a just action. But it seems to me that the only cure for sin is for the sinner to confess it, and to be visibly repentant in regard to it. Thus the suffering will not appear altogether intolerable to those who have undergone unpleasant treatment, if the person who inflicted it confesses that he has acted dishonourably; and this good hope for the future is left to the man himself, that he will never again commit a similar sin, if he is seen to be vexed at his former errors. I do not think that even his tracing his origin to a god was a great error on Alexander's part, if it was not perhaps merely a device to induce his subjects' to show him reverence.[970] Nor does he seem to me to have been a less renowned king than Minos, Aeacus, or Rhadamanthus, to whom no insolence is attributed by the men of old, because they traced their origin to Zeus. Nor does he seem at all inferior to Theseus or Ion, the former being the reputed son of Poseidon, and the latter of Apollo. His adoption of the Persian mode of dressing also seems to me to have been a political device in regard to the foreigners, that the king might not appear altogether an alien to them; and in regard to the Macedonians, to show them that he had a refuge from their rashness of temper and insolence. For this reason I think, he mixed the Persian royal guards, who carried golden apples at the end of their spears,[971] among the ranks of the Macedonians, and the Persian peers[972] with the Macedonian body-guards. Aristobulus also asserts that Alexander used to have long drinking parties, not for the purpose of enjoying the wine, as he was not a great wine-drinker, but in order to exhibit his sociality and friendly feeling to his Companions.[973]

Chapter 205: Eulogy of Alexander

Whoever therefore reproaches Alexander as a bad man, let him do so; but let him first not only bring before his mind all his actions deserving reproach, but also gather into one view all his deeds of every kind. Then, indeed, let him reflect who he is himself, and what kind of fortune he has experienced; and then consider who that man was whom he reproaches as bad, and to what a height of human success he attained, becoming without any dispute king of both continents,[974] and reaching every place by his fame; while he himself who reproaches him is of smaller account, spending his labour on petty objects, which, however, he does not succeed in effecting, petty as they are. For my own part, I think there was at that time no race of men, no city, nor even a single individual to whom Alexander's name and fame had not penetrated. For this reason it seems to me that a hero totally unlike any other human being could not have been born without the agency of the deity. And this is said to have been revealed after Alexander's death by the oracular responses, by the visions which presented themselves to various people, and by the dreams which were seen by different individuals. It is also shown by the honour paid to him by men up to the present time, and by the recollection which is still held of him as more than human. Even at the present time, after so long an interval, other oracular responses in his honour have been received by the nation of the Macedonians. In relating the history of Alexander's achievements, there are some things which I have been compelled to censure; but I am not ashamed to admire Alexander himself. Those actions I have branded as bad, both from a regard to my own veracity, and at the same time for the benefit of mankind.[975] For this reason I think that I undertook the task of writing this history not without the divine inspiration.

The End of the History of Alexander's Deeds.

ORIGINAL REFERENCES

[1] Ptolemaeus, surnamed Soter, the Preserver, but more commonly known as the Son of Lagus, a Macedonian of low birth. Ptolemy's mother, Arsinoe, had been a concubine of Philip of Macedon, for which reason it was generally believed that Ptolemy was the offspring of that king. Ptolemy was one of the earliest friends of Alexander before his accession to the throne, and accompanied him throughout his campaigns, being one of his most skilful generals and most intimate friends. On the division of the empire after Alexander's death, Ptolemy obtained the kingdom of Egypt, which he transmitted to his descendants. After a distinguished reign of thirty-eight years, he abdicated the throne to his youngest son, Ptolemy Philadelphus. He survived this event two years, and died B.C. 283. He was a liberal patron of literature and the arts, and wrote a history of the wars of Alexander, which is one of the chief authorities on which Arrian composed his narrative. For his beneficence, see Aelian (Varia Historia, xiii. 12). Not only Arrian, but Plutarch and Strabo, derived much information from Ptolemy's work, which is highly commended by Athenaeus.

[2] Aristobulus of Potidaea, a town in Macedonia, which was afterwards called Cassandrea, served under Alexander, and wrote a history of his wars, which, like that of Ptolemy, was sometimes more panegyrical than the facts warranted. Neither of these histories has survived, but they served Arrian as the groundwork for the composition of his own narrative. Lucian in his treatise, Quomodo historia sit conscribenda, ch. 12, accuses Aristobulus of inventing marvellous tales of Alexander's valour for the sake of flattery. Plutarch based his Life of Alexander chiefly on the work of this writer. We learn from Lucian (Macrobioi, c. 22), that Aristobulus wrote his history at the advanced age of eighty-four. He was employed by Alexander to superintend the restoration of Cyrus's tomb (Arrian, vi. 30).

[3] ἀναλέγομαι in the sense of reading through = ἀναγιγνώσκειν, is found only in the later writers, Arrian, Plutarch, Dion, Calllmachus, etc.

[4] B.C. 336. He was murdered by a young noble named Pausanias, who stabbed him at the festival which he was holding to celebrate the marriage of his daughter with Alexander, king of Epirus. It was suspected that both Olympias and her son Alexander were implicated in the plot. At the time of his assassination Philip was just about to start on an expedition against Persia, which his son afterwards so successfully carried out. See Plutarch (Alex., 10); Diod., xvi. 93, 94; Aristotle (Polit., v. 8, 10).

[5] It was the custom of the Athenians to name the years from the president of the college of nine archons at Athens, who were elected annually. The Attic writers adopted this method of determining dates. See Smith's Dictionary of Antiquities.

[6] Alexander the Great was the son of Philip II. and Olympias, and was born at Pella B.C. 356. In his youth he was placed under the tuition of Aristotle, who acquired very great influence over his mind and character, and retained it until his pupil was spoiled by his unparalleled successes. See Aelian (Varia Historia, xii. 54). Such was his ability, that at the age of 16 he was entrusted with the government of Macedonia by his father, when he marched

against Byzantium. At the age of 18 by his skill and courage he greatly assisted Philip in gaining the battle of Chaeronea. When Philip was murdered, Alexander ascended the throne, and after putting down rebellion at home, he advanced into Greece to secure the power which his father had acquired. See Diod., xvii. 4; Arrian, vii. 9.

[7] See Justin, xi. 2.

[8] "Arrian speaks as if this request had been addressed only to the Greeks within Peloponnesus; moreover he mentions no assembly at Corinth, which is noticed, though with some confusion, by Diodorus, Justin, and Plutarch. Cities out of Peloponnesus, as well as within it, must have been included; unless we suppose that the resolution of the Amphictyonic assembly, which had been previously passed, was held to comprehend all the extra-Peloponnesian cities, which seems not probable."—Grote.

[9] Justin (ix. 5) says: "Soli Lacedaemonii et legem et regem contempserunt." The king here referred to was Philip.

[10] See Justin, xi. 3; Aeschines, Contra Ctesiphontem, p. 564.

[11] The Triballians were a tribe inhabiting the part of Serbia bordering on Bulgaria. The Illyrians inhabited the eastern coast of the Adriatic Sea, the districts now called North Albania, Bosnia, Dalmatia and Croatia.

[12] We learn from Thucydides, ii. 96, that these people were called Dii.

[13] The Nessus, or Nestus, is now called Mesto by the Greeks, and Karasu by the Turks.

[14] Now known as the Balkan. The defiles mentioned by Arrian are probably what was afterwards called Porta Trajani. Cf. Vergil (Georg., ii. 488); Horace (Carm., i. 12, 6).

[15] πεποιηντο:—Arrian often forms the pluperfect tense without the augment. διασκεδάσουσι:—The Attic future of this verb is διασκεδῶ, Cf. Aristoph. (Birds, 1053).

[16] The Agrianes were a tribe of Eastern Paeonia who lived near the Triballians. They served in the Macedonian army chiefly as cavalry and light infantry.

[17] Perhaps Neapolis and Eion, which were the harbours of Philippi and Amphipolis.

[18] This officer was commander of the royal body-guard. His father was Parmenio, the most experienced of Alexander's generals.

[19] Thucydides says (Bk. ii. 96): "On the side of the Triballians, who were also independent, the border tribes were the Trerians and the Tilataeans, who live to the north of mount Scombrus, and stretch towards the west as far as the river Osoius. This river flows from the same mountains as the Nestus and the Hebrus, an uninhabited and extensive range, joining on to Rhodope." The Osoius is now called Isker. It is uncertain which river is the Lyginus; but perhaps it was another name for the Oscius.

[20] Also named Danube. Cf. Hesiod (Theog., 339); Ovid (Met., ii. 249); Pindar (Olym. iii. 2i).

[21] It is uncertain in what part of the Danube this island was. It cannot be the Pence of Strabo (vii, 8). Cf. Apullonius Rhodius (iv. 809); Martialis (vii. 84); Valerius Flaccus (viii. 217).

[22] These two generals are mentioned (iii. 11 infra) as being present at the battle of Arbela. Sopolis is also mentioned (iv. 13 and 18 infra).

[23] Bottiaea was a district of Macedonia on the right bank of the Axius.

[24] The classical writers have three names to denote this race:—Celts, Galatians, and Gauls. These names were originally, given to all the people of the North and West of Europe; and it was not till Caesar's time that the Romans made any distinction between Celts and Germans. The name of Celts was then confined to the people north of the Pyrenees and west of the Rhine. Cf. Ammianus (xv. 9); Herodotus (iv. 49); Livy (v. 33, 34); Polybius (iii. 39).

[25] Arrian is here speaking, not of Alexander's time, but of his own, the second century of the Christian era. The Quadi were a race dwelling in the south-east of Germany. They are generally mentioned with the Marcomanni, and were formidable enemies of the Romans, especially in the reign of Marcus Aurelius, when Arrian wrote. This nation disappears from

history about the end of the fourth century.

[26] The Marcomanni, like the Quadi, were a powerful branch of the Suevic race, originally dwelling in the south-wesb of Germany; but in the reign of Tiberius they dispossessed the Boii of the country now called Bohemia. In conjunction with the Quadi, they were very formidable to the Romans until Commodus purchased peace from them. The name denotes "border men." Cf. Caesar (Bel. Gal., i. 51).

[27] The Iazygians were a tribe of Sarmatians, who migrated from the coast of the Black Sea, between the Dnieper and the Sea of Azov, in the reign of Claudius, and settled in Dacia, near the Quadi, with whom they formed a close alliance. They were conquered by the Goths in the fifth century. Cf. Ovid (Tristia, ii. 191).

[28] Called also Sarmatians. Herodotus (iv. 21) says that these people lived east of the Don, and were allied to the Scythians. Subsequent writers understood by Sarmatia the east part of Poland, the south of Russia, and the country southward as far as the Danube.

[29] These people were called Dacians by the Romans. They were Thracians, and are said by Herodotus and Thucydides to have lived south of the Danube, near its mouths. They subsequently migrated north of this river, and were driven further west by the Sarmatians. They were very formidable to the Romans in the reigns of Augustus and Domitian. Dacia was conquered by Trajan ; but ultimately abandoned by Aurelian, who made the Danube the boundary of the Roman Empire. About the Getae holding the doctrine of immortality, see Herodotus (iv. 94). Cf. Horace (Carm., iii. 6, 13; Sat., ii. 6, 53).

[30] The Scythians are said by Herodotus to have inhabited the south of Russia. His supposition that they came from Asia is doubtless correct. He gives ample information about this race in the fourth book of his History.

[31] Herodotus (iv. 47) says the Danube had five mouths; but Strabo (vii. 3) says there were seven. At the present time it has only three mouths. The Greeks called the Black Sea πόντος εὔξεινος, the sea kind to strangers. Cf. Ovid (Tristia, iv. 4, 55):—"Frigida me cohibent Euxini litora Ponti, Dictus ab antiquis Axenus ille fuit."

[32] The sarissa, or more correctly sarisa, was a spear peculiar to the Macedonians. It was from fourteen to sixteen feet long. See Grote's Greece, vol. xi. ch. 92, Appendix.

[33] Son of Parmenio and brother of Philotas.

[34] The parasang was a Persian measure, containing thirty stades, nearly three and three-quarter English miles. It is still used by the Persians, who call it ferseng. See Herodotus (vi. 42) and Grote's History of Greece, vol. viii. p. 316.

[35] Son of Neoptolemus. After Alexander's death Meleager resisted the claim of Perdiccas to the regency, and was associated with him in the office. He was, however, soon afterwards put to death by the order of his rival.

[36] Son of Machatas, was an eminent general, slain in India. See vi. 27 infra.

[37] The Macedonian kings believed they were sprung from Hercules. See Curtius, iv. 7.

[38] The Adriatic Sea.

[39] Cf. Aelian (Varia Historia, xii. 23); Strabo, vii. p. 293; Aristotle (Nicom. Ethics, iii. 7; Eudem. Eth., iii. 1):—οἶον οἱ Κελτοὶ πρὸς τὰ κύματα ὅπλα ἀπαντῶσι λαβόντες; Ammianus, xv. 12.

[40] The Paeonians were a powerful Thracian people, who in early times spread over a great part of Thrace and Macedonia. In historical times they inhabited the country on the northern border of Macedonia. They were long troublesome to Macedonia, but were subdued by Philip the father of Alexander, who, however, allowed them to retain their own chiefs. The Agrianians were the chief tribe of Paeonians, from whom Philip and Alexander formed a valuable body of light-armed troops.

[41] Bardylis was a chieftain of Illyria who carried on frequent wars with the Macedonians, but was at last defeated and slain by Phillip, B.C. 359. Clitus had been subdued by Phillip in 249 B.C.

[42] This Glaucias subsequently afforded asylum to the celebrated Pyrrhus, King of Epirus, when an infant of two years of age. He took the child into his own family and

brought him up with his own children. He not only refused to surrender Pyrrhus to Cassander, but marched into Epirus and placed the boy, when twelve years of age, upon the throne, leaving him under the care of guardians, B.C. 307.

[43] The Taulantians were a people of Illyria in the neighbourhood of Epidamnus, now called Durazzo.

[44] These were an Illyrian people in the Dalmatian mountains.

[45] Cyna was the daughter of Philip, by Audata, an Illyrian woman. See Athenæus, p. 557 D. She was given in marriage to her cousin Amyntas, who had a preferable claim to the Macedonian throne as the son of Philip's elder brother, Perdiccas. This Amyntas was put to death by Alexander soon after his accession. Cyna was put to death by Alcetas, at the order of Perdiccas, the regent after Alexander's death. See Diodorus, xix. 52.

[46] The capital of Macedonia. On its site stands the modern village of Neokhori, or Yenikiuy. Philip and Alexander were born here.

[47] A tributary of the Axius, called Agrianus by Herodotus. It is now called Tscherna.

[48] This city was situated south of lake Lychnitis, on the west side of the chain of Scardus and Pindus. The locality is described in Livy, xxxi. 39, 40.

[49] Now called Devol.

[50] The use of καίτοι with a participle instead of the Attic καίπερ is frequent in Arrian and the later writers.

[51] The Hypaspists—shield-bearers, or guards—were a body of infantry organized by Philip, originally few in number, and employed as personal defenders of the king, but afterwards enlarged into several distinct brigades. They were hoplites intended for close combat, but more lightly armed and more fit for rapid evolutions than the phalanx. Like the Greeks, they fought with the one-handed pike and shield. They occupied an intermediate position between the heavy infantry of the phalanx, and the peltasts and other light troops. See Grote's Greece, vol. xi. ch. 92.

[52] The heavy cavalry, wholly or chiefly composed of Macedonians by birth, was known by the honourable name of ἑταῖροι, Companions, or Brothers in Arms. It was divided, as it seems, into 15 Ἴλαι, which were named after the States or districts from which they came. Their strength varied from 150 to 250 men. A separate one, the 16th Ἴλη, formed the so-called agema, or royal horse-guard, at the head of which Alexander himself generally charged. See Arrian, iii. 11, 13, 18.

[53] In addition to his other military improvements, Philip had organized an effective siege-train with projectile and battering engines superior to anything of the kind existing before. This artillery was at once made use of by Alexander in this campaign against the Illyrians.

[54] Perdiccas, son of Orontes, a Macedonian, was one of Alexander's most distinguished generals. The king is said on his death-bed to have taken the royal signet from his finger and to have given it to Perdiccas. After Alexander's death he was appointed regent; but an alliance was formed against him by Antipater, Craterus, and Ptolemy. He marched into Egypt against Ptolemy. Being defeated in his attempts to force the passage of the Nile, his own troops mutinied against him and slew him (B.C. 321). See Diodorus, xviii. 36. For his personal valour see Aelian (Varia Historia, xii. 39).

[55] Coenus, son of Polemocrates, was a son-in-law of Parmenio, and one of Alexander's best generals. He violently accused his brother-inlaw Philotas of treason, and personally superintended the torturing of that famous officer previous to his execution (Curtius, vi. 36, 42). He was put forward by the army to dissuade Alexander from advancing beyond the Hyphasis (Arrian, v. 27). Soon after this he died and was "buried with all possible magnifioenoe near that river, B.C. 327 (Arrian, Ti. 2)."

[56] The Cadmea was the Acropolis of Thebes, an oval eminence of no great height, named after Cadmus, the leader of a Phoenician colony, who is said to have founded it. Since the battle of Chaeronea, this citadel had been held by a Macedonian garrison.

[57] Amyntas was a Macedonian officer, and Timolaus a leading Theban of the Macedonian faction.

[58] Cf. Aelian (Varia Historia, xii. 57).

[59] These were two provinces in the west of Macedonia.

[60] Two divisions of Epirus.

[61] A town on the Penēus in Hestiacotis.

[62] A town in Boeotia, on the lake Copais, distant 50 stades north-west of Thebes.

[63] It seems from Plutarch, that Alexander was really wounded in the head by a stone, in a battle with the Illyrians.

[64] This Alexander was also called Lyncestes, from being a native of Lyncestis, a district of Macedonia. He was an accomplice in Philip's murder, but was pardoned by his successor. He accompanied Alexander the Great into Asia, but was put to death in B.C. 330, for having carried on a treasonable correspondence with Darius. See Arrian, i. 25.

[65] The friend and charioteer of Hercules.

[66] He sent to demand the surrender of the anti-Macedonian leaders, Phoenix and Prothytes, but offering any other Thebans who came out to him the terms agreed upon in the preceding year. See Plutarch (Life of Alexander, 11); and Diodorus, xvii. 9.

[67] The Boeotarchs were the chief magistrates of the Boeotian confederacy, chosen annually by the different States. The number varied from ten to twelve. At the time of the battle of Delium, in the Peloponnesian war, they were eleven in number, two of them being Thebans. See Grote, History of Greece, vol. ii. p. 296.

[68] Arrian says that the attack of the Macedonians upon Thebes was made by Perdiccas, without orders from Alexander; and that the capture was effected in a short time and with no labour on the part of the captors (ch. ix.). But Diodorus says that Alexander ordered and arranged the assault, that the Thebans made a brave and desperate resistance for a long time, and that not only the Boeotian allies, but the Macedonians themselves committed great slaughter of the besieged (Diod. xvii. 11-14). It is probable that Ptolemy, who was Arrian's authority, wished to exonerate Alexander from the guilt of destroying Thebes.

[69] Amyntas was one of Alexander's leading officers. He and his brothers were accused of being accomplices in the plot of Philotas, but were acquitted. He was however soon afterwards killed in a skirmish (Arrian, iii. 27).

[70] The mythical founder of the walls of Thebes. See Pausanias (ix. 17).

[71] The Thebans had incurred the enmity of the other Boeotians by treating them as subjects instead of allies. They had destroyed the restored Plataea, and had been the chief enemies of the Phocians in the Sacred War, which ended in the subjugation of that people by Philip, See Smith's History of Greece, pp. 467, 473, 506.

[72] More than 500 Macedonians were killed, while 6,000 Thebans were slain, and 30,000 sold into slavery. See Aelian (Varia Historia, xiii. 7); Diodorus (xvii. 14); Pausanias (viii. 30); Plutarch (Life of Alexander, 11). The sale of the captives realized 440 talents, or about £107,000; and Justin (xi. 4) says that large sums were offered from feelings of hostility towards Thebes on the part of the bidders.

[73] B.C. 415-413. See Grote's Greece, vol. vii.

[74] B.C. 405. See Thucydides (ii. 13); Xenophon (Hellenics, ii. 2).

[75] By Conon's victory at Cnidus, B.C. 394.

[76] At Leuctra they lost 400 Spartans and 1,000 other Lacedaemonians. See Xen. (Hellen., vi. 4).

[77] The Achaeans, Eleans, Athenians, and some of the Arcadians, were allies of Sparta at this crisis, B.C. 369. See Xen. (Hellen., vii. 5) Diodorus (xv. 85).

[78] B.C. 426. See Thuc., iii. 52, etc.

[79] B.C. 416 and 421. See Thuc., v. 32, 84, etc.

[80] These persons must have forgotten that Alexander's predecessor and namesake had served in the army of Xerxes along with the Thebans. See Herodotus vii. 173.

[81] Plutarch (Lysander, 15) says that the Theban Erianthus moved that Athens should

be destroyed.

[82] See Aelian (Varia Historia, xii. 57).

[83] Plutarch (Alexander, 13) tells us that Alexander was afterwards sorry for his cruelty to the Thebans. He believed that he had incurred the wrath of Dionysus, the tutelary deity of Thebes, who incited him to kill his friend Clitus, and induced his soldiers to refuse to follow him into the interior of India.

[84] Orchomenus was destroyed by the Thebans B.C. 364. See Diod., xv. 79; Demosthenes (Contra Leptimem, p. 489). It was restored by Philip, according to Pausanias, iv. 27.

[85] The Great Mysteries of Demeter were celebrated at Eleusis, from the 15th to the 23rd of the month Boedromion, our September.

[86] All these nine men were orators except Chares, Charidemus, and Ephialtes, who were military men. Plutarch (Life of Demosthenes, 23) does not mention Chares, Diotimus, and Hyperides, but puts the names of Callisthenes and Damon in the list.

[87] See Aeschines (Adversus Ctesiphontem, pp. 469, 547, 551, 603, 633); Plutarch (Demosthenes, 22; Phocion, 16); Diodorus, xvii. 5.

[88] At the head of this embassy was Phocion.

[89] He was put to death by Darius shortly before the battle of Issus, for advising him not to rely on his Asiatic troops in the contest with Alexander, but to subsidize an army of Grecian mercenaries. See Curtius, iii. 5; Diodorus, xvii. 30.

[90] Archelaus was king of Macedonia from B.C. 413-399. He improved the internal arrangements of his kingdom, and patronised art and literature. He induced the tragic poets, Euripides and Agathon, as well as the epic poet Choerilus, to visit him; and treated Euripides especially with favour. He also invited Socrates, who declined the invitation.

[91] Aegae, or Edessa, was the earlier capital of Macedonia, and the burial place of its kings. Philip was murdered here, B.C. 336.

[92] A narrow strip of land in Macedonia, between the mouths of the Haliaomon and Penēus, the reputed home of Orpheus and the Muses.

[93] Cf. Apollonius Rhodius, iv. 1284; Livy, xxii. i.

[94] This man was the most noted soothsayer of his time. Telmissus was a city of Caria, celebrated for the skill of its inhabitants in divination. Cf. Arrian (Anab. i. 25, ii. 18, iii. 2, iii. 7, iii. 15, iv. 4, iv. 15); Herodotus, i. 78; and Cicero (De Divinatione, i. 41)

[95] Diodorus (xvii. 17) says that there were 30,000 infantry and 4,500 cavalry. He gives the numbers in the different brigades as well as the names of the commanders. Plutarch (Life of Alexander, 15) says that the lowest numbers recorded were 30,000 infantry and 5,000 cavalry; and the highest, 34,000 infantry and 4,000 cavalry.

[96] This lake is near the mouth of the Strymon. It is called Prasias by Herodotus (v. 16). Its present name is Tak-hyno.

[97] This mountain is now called Pirnari. Xerxes took the same route when marching into Greece. See Herodotus, v. 16, vii; 112; Aeschylus (Persae, 494); Euripides (Rhesus, 922, 972).

[98] Now called Maritza. See Theocritus, vii. 110.

[99] Cf. Homer (Iliad, ii. 701); Ovid (Epistolae Heroidum, xiii. 93); Herodotus (ix. 116).

[100] The Athenians supplied twenty ships of war. See Diodorus, xvii. 22.

[101] A landing-place in the north-west of Troas, near Cape Sigacum.

[102] Cf. Diodorus, xvii. 17; Justin, xi. 5.

[103] The celebrated general, mentioned already in chap. 10.

[104] Son of Amyntas, a Macedonian of Pella. He was the most intimate friend of Alexander, with whom he had been brought up. Cf. Aelian (Varia Historia, xii. 7).

[105] Plutarch (Life of Alex., 15), says that Alexander also went through the ceremony, still customary in his own day, of anointing himself with oil and running up to the tomb naked. Cf. Aelian (Varia Historia, x. 4) Cicero (Pro Archia, oh. 10).

[106] By Pindar and Bacchylides.

[107] See Xenophon's Anabasis, Book ii.

[108] A town in the Macedonia district of Mygdonia, south of Lake Bolbe. It is now called Polina.

[109] We find from Diodorus (xvii. 7), that the Persian king had subsidized this great general and 5,000 Greek mercenaries to protect his seaboard from the Macedonians. Before the arrival of Alexander, he had succeeded in checking the advance of Parmenio and Callas. If Memnon had lived and his advice been adopted by Darius, the fate of Persia might have been very different. Cf. Plutarch (Life of Alex., 18).

[110] Diodorus (xvii. 18) says that Memnon, while advising the Persian generals to lay waste the country, and to prevent the Macedonians from advancing through scarcity of provisions, also urged them to carry a large force into Greece and Macedonia, and thus transfer the war into Europe.

[111] The Granicus rises in Mount Ida, and falls into the Propontis near Cyzicus. Ovid (Metam., xi. 763) calls it Granicus bicornis.

[112] This was a brigade of about 1,000 men. See Livy, xxxvii. 42.

[113] ἱποφθάσομεν. This future is used by the later writers for the Attic ἱποφθήσομαι. It is found however in Xenophon.

[114] Craterus was one of Alexander's best generals. On the death of the king he received the government of Macedonia and Greece in conjunction with Antipater, whose daughter he married. He fell in battle against Eumenes (B.C. 321).

[115] Calas was appointed viceroy of Phrygia. He Consequently took no further part in Alexander's campaigns after this.

[116] Alexander had three generals named Philip, two of whom are mentioned here as sons of Amyntas and Menelaus. The third was son of Machatas, and was left in India as viceroy.

[117] Son of Tyrimmas, was commander of the Odrysian cavalry. See iii. 12 infra.

[118] Diadorus (xvii. 19) says that the Persian cavalry numbered 10,000 and their infantry 100,000. Both these numbers are inaccurate. We know from Arrian (chaps. 12 and 13) that the Persian infantry was inferior in number to that of Alexander.

[119] This is an Homeric name for Mars the war-god. In Homer Ares is the Trojan and Enyalius the Grecian war-god. Hence they are mentioned as different in Aristophanes (Pax, 457). See Paley's note on Homer (vvi. 166). As to the practice of shouting the war-cry to Mars before battle, see Xenophon (Anab., i. 8, 18; v. 2, 14). The Scholiast on Thucydides (i. 50) says that the Greeks used to sing two paeans, one to Mars before battle, another to Apollo after it.

[120] ὡς ἀνυστόν=ὡς δυνατόν Cf. Arrian, iv. 12, 6; Xenophon (Anab., i, 8, 11; Res. Laced., i. 3).

[121] ξυνειστήκει μάχη. This is a common expression with Arrian, copied from Herodotus (i. 74, et passim).

[122] Plutarch (Alex., 16); Diodorus (xvii. 20).

[123] Diodorus (xvii. 21) says that more than 10,000 of the Persian infantry were killed, and 2,000 cavalry; and that more than 20,000 were made prisoners.

[124] Her name was Statira.

[125] An important city in Macedonia on the Thermaic gulf, named after a temple of Zeus.

[126] Lysippus of Sicyon was one of the most famous of Greek statuaries. None of his works remain, inasmuch as they were all executed in bronze. Alexander published an edict that no one should paint his portrait but Apelles, and that no one should make a statue of him but Lysippus. When Metellus conquered Macedonia, he removed this group of bronze statues to Rome, to decorate his own portico. See Pliny (Nat. Hist., xxxiv. 19); Velleius Paterculus (i. 11).

[127] As most of the infantry on the Persian side were Grecian mercenaries, frho, according to Plutarch, fought with desperate valour, and, according to Arrian himself, all the

infantry were killed except 2,000, the riumber of Alexander's slain must have been larger than Arrian here states.

[128] At Corinth, B.C. 336.

[129] For the fact that the Acropolis of Athens was often called simply polis, see Thucydides, ii. 15; Xenophon (Anab. vii. 1, 27); Antiphon (146, 2); Aristophanes (Equites, 1093; Lysistrata, 758).

[130] A city at the foot of Mount Ida.

[131] A city of Bithynia, on the Propontis.

[132] About eight miles.

[133] This river flows through Phrygia and Lydia, and falls into the gulf of Smyrna. Its present name is Kodus-Chai. See Vergil (Georg., ii. 137); Silius, i. 159; Claudian (Raptus Proserpinae, ii. 67).

[134] Nearly two-and-a-half miles.

[135] For a description of this fortress, see Herodotus, i. 84.

[136] Memnon had succeeded his brother Mentor as governor for the Persian king of the territory near the Hellespont. See Diodoras, xvii. 7.

[137] This man took refuge with Darius, and distinguished himself at the battle of Issus. See Plutarch (Alex., 20); Curtius, iii. 28. He met with his death soon after in Egypt. See Arrian, ii. 6 and 13; Diod., xvii. 48.

[138] The temple of Artemis at Ephesus had been burnt down by Herostratus in the night on which Alexander was born (Oct. 13-14, B.C. 356), and at this time was being restored by the joint efforts of the Ionian cities. See Strabo, xiv. 1. Heropythus and Syrphax are not mentioned by any other writers.

[139] This was the Carian Magnesia, situated on the Lethaeus, a tributary of the Maeander. Tralles was on the Eudon, another tributary of the Maeander. See Juxenal, iii. 70.

[140] Lysimachus was of mean origin, his father having been a serf in Sicily. He was one of Alexander's confidential body-guards, and on the death of the great king obtained Thrace as his portion of the dismembered empire. In conjunction with Seleuous he won the battle of Ipsus, by which he obtained a great part of Asia Minor. He ultimately acquired all the European dominions of Alexander in addition to Asia Minor; but in his eightieth year he was defeated and slain by Seleuous at the battle of Corus, B.C. 281. Sintenis was the first to substitute Lysimachus for Antimachus, the reading of the MSS. Cf. vi. 28 infra.

[141] Eleven in number. See Herodotus, i. 149-151.

[142] Thirteen in number, of which Miletus and Ephesus were the chief in importance.

[143] For the celebrated interview of Alexander with Apelles at Ephesus, see Aelian (Varla Historia, ii. 3).

[144] Cf. Herodotus, vi. 7. Here the Persians destroyed the Ionic fleet, B.C. 497.

[145] Famous for the victory won near it by Leotychides and Xanthippusover the Persians, B.C. 479.

[146] Cf. Vergil (Aeneid, vi. 3). Obvertunt pelago proras. See Conington's note.

[147] Strabo (xiv. 1) says that Miletus had four harbours.

[148] ἐφομαρτούντων. This word is rare in prose. See Homer (Iliad, viii. 191); Apollonius Rhodius, i. 201.

[149] Miletus lay nearly ten miles south of the mouth of the Maeander.

[150] A similar stratagem was used by Lysander at Aegospotami, B.C. 405. See Xenophon (Hellenics, ii. 1).

[151] Iassus was a city in Caria on the Iassian Gulf, founded by the Argives and further colonized by the Milesians.

[152] Caria formed the south-west angle of Asia Minor. The Greeks asserted that the Carians were emigrants from Crete. We learn from Thucydides and Herodotus that they entered the service of foreign rulers. They formed the body-guard of queen Athaliah, who had usurped the throne and stood in need of foreign mercenaries. The word translated in our Bible in 2 Kings xi. 4, 19 as captains, ought to be rendered Carians. See Fuerst's Hebrew

Lexicon, sub voce יָרַב.

[153] Now called Budrum. It was the birthplace of the historians Herodotus and Dionysius.

[154] Little more than half a mile.

[155] Now called Melasso, a city of Caria, about ten miles from the Gulf of Iassus.

[156] A colony of Troezen, on the western extremity of the same peninsula on which stood Halicarnassus.

[157] Diodorus (xvii. 25) says that this incident occurred in the night, which is scarcely probable. Compare the conduct of the two centurions Pulfio and Varenus in the country of the Nervii. Caesar (Gallic War, v. 44).

[158] Compare the sieges of Avaricum, Gergovia, and Alesia by Caesar (Gallic War, lib. vii.); and that of Saguntum by Hannibal. See Livy, xxi. 7-15.

[159] This use of ἀμφί with the Dative, is poetical. The Attic writers use περί with the Accusative. Cf. ii. 3, 8; iii. 30, 1.

[160] There were at least four generals in Alexander's army of this name. The one here mentioned was probably not the famous son of Lagus.

[161] Diodorus (xvii. 25-27) gives a very different account of the last struggle of the besieged in Halicarnassus. When the leaders saw that they must eventually succumb, they made a last desperate effort to destroy Alexander's military engines. Ephialtes, the eminent Athenian exile, headed the sally, which vfas effected by troops simultaneously issuing from all the gates at daybreak. The advanced guard of the Macedonians, consisting of young troops, vrere put to rout; but the veterans of Philip restored the battle under a man named Atharrias. Ephialtes was slain, and his men driven back into the city.

[162] Hecatomnus, king of Caria, left three sons, Mausolus, Hidrieus, and Pixodarus; and two daughters, Artemisia and Ada. Artemisia married Mausolus, and Ada married Hidrieus. All these children succeeded their father in the sovereignty, Pixodarus being the last surviving son.

[163] Amyntas, king of Macedonia, grandfather of Alexander the Great, adopted the celebrated Athenian general Iphicrates, in gratitude to him as the preserver of Macedonia. See Aeschines (De Falsa Legatione, pp. 249, 250).

[164] See Arrian, ii. 20 infra.

[165] The Marmarians alone defended their city with desperate valour. They finally set fire to it, and escaped through the Macedonian camp to the mountains. See Diodorus (xvii. 28). As to Xanthus the river, see Homer (Iliad, ii. 877; vi. 172); Horace (Carm., iv. 6, 26).

[166] Lycia was originally called Milyas; but the name was afterwards applied to the high table in the north of Lycia, extending into Pisidia. See Herodotus, i. 173.

[167] Phaselis was a seaport of Lyoia on the Gulf of Pamphylia. It is now called Tekrova.

[168] He also crowned with garlands the statue of Theodectes the rhetorician, which the people of Phaselis, his native city, had erected to his memory. This man was a friend and pupil of Aristotle, the tutor of Alexander. See Plutarch (Life of Alex., 17); Aristotle (Nicom. Ethics, vii. 7).

[169] Philip was murdered by Pausanias. Three only of his reputed accomplices are known by name, and they were Alexander, Heromenes, and Arrhabaeus, sons of Aëropus. The two latter were put to death; but the first named was not only spared, but advanced to high military command for being the first to salute Alexander as king. Compare Curtius (vii. 1); Justin (xi. 2). Alexander was accused by some of forgiving his father's murderers. Probably the reference was to his kind treatment of Olympias and this Alexander. See Curtius, vi. 43.

[170] That of the Hellespontine Phrygia. See chap. xvii. supra

[171] See chap. xvii. supra.

[172] Nearly £250,000.

[173] See chap. xi. supra.

[174] Compare Plutarch (Alex., 17). Just as the historians of Alexander affirmed that the

sea near Pamphylia providientially made way for him, so the people of Thapsacus, when they saw the army of Cyrus cross the Euphrates on foot, said that the river made way for him to come and take the sceptre (Xen., Anab., i. 4). So also the inhabitants prostrated themselves before Lucullus when the same river subsided and allowed his army to cross (Plutarch, Lucullus, chap. xxiv.). There was the same omen in the reign of Tiberius, when Vitellius, with a Roman army, crossed the Euphrates to restore Tiridates to the throne of Parthia (Tacitus, Annals, vi. 37). Cf. Strabo, xiv. 3.

[175] Aspendus was on the Eurymedon.

[176] About £12,000.

[177] Sidē was on the coast of Pamphylia, a little west of the river Melas.

[178] Syllium was about five miles from the coast, between Aspendus and Side.

[179] This river is celebrated for the double victory of Cimon the Athenian over the Persians, in B.C. 466. See Smith's Greece, p. 252; Grote, vol. v. p. 163.

[180] This lake is mentioned by Herodotus (vii. 30), as being near the city of Anava. It is now called Burdur.

[181] Here Cyrus the Younger reviewed his Grecian forces and found them to be 11,000 hoplites and 2,000 peltasts. Here that prince had a palace and park, in which rose the river Maeander, close to the source of the Marsyas. See Xenophon (Anab., i. 2); compare Curtius (iii. 1).

[182] Curtius (iii. 1) says they made a truce with Alexander for sixty days.

[183] Antigonus, called the One-eyed, was father of Demetrius Poliorcetes. On the division of Alexander's empire he received Phrygia, Lycis, and Pamphylia. He eventually acquired the whole of Asia Minor; but was defeated and slain at the battle of Ipsus by the allied forces of Cassander, Lysimachus, Ptolemy, and Seleucus (B.C. 301). When he was slain he was in his eighty-first year.

[184] Balacrus was left by Alexander to command in Egypt. See Arrian (iii. 5).

[185] The capital of the old Phrygian kings. It was rebuilt in the time of Augustus, and called Juliopolis.

[186] This Ptolemy was killed at the battle of Issus (Arrian, ii. 110).

[187] We learn from Curtius (iv. 34) that Alexander released these prisoners at the request of ambassadors from Athens, who met him in Syria after his return from Egypt.

[188] The other cities of Lesbos were Methymna, Antissa, Eresus, and Pyrrha.

[189] Now called Cape Sigri, the west point of the island.

[190] The southern point of Euboea, now called Cape Mandili. Cf. Homer (Odyss., iii. 177).

[191] The south-eastern point of Laconia, now called Cape Malia di St. Angelo. It was dreaded by ancient mariners: see Homer (Odyssey, ix. 80); Ovid (Armores, ii. 16, 24); Vergil (Aeneid, v. 193). There was a saying;—Μαλέας δέ Κάμψας των οίκαδε (Strabo viii. p. 250).

[192] In accordance with the convention of Corinth. Compare next chapter. For the pillars compare Herodotus (ii. 102, 106); Thucydides v. 18, 47, 56); Aristophanes (Acharnians, 727; Lysistrata, 513).

[193] This treaty was concluded by the Spartans with the king of Persia, B.C. 387. It was designed to break up the Athenian supremacy. It stipulated that all the Grecian colonies in Asia were to be given to the Persian king; the Athenians were to retain only Imbros, Lesbos, and Scyros; and all the other Grecian cities were to be autonomous. See Xenophon (Hellenics, iv. 8; v.1).

[194] Cf. ii. 13 infra.

[195] "Cyclades ideo sio appellatae, quod omnes ambiunt Delon partu deorum insignem."—Ammianus, xxii. 8, 2. Cf. Horace (Carm.,i. 14, 19; iii. 28, 14).

[196] Cf. Vergil (Aeneid, ii. 21).

[197] The regent of Macedonia and Greece during Alexander's absence.

[198] One of the Cyclades, a little to the north-east of Melos. It was noted for the low morality of its inhabitants. See Aristophanes (Fragment, 558; on the authority of Suidas).

[199] Euripus properly means any narrow sea, where the ebb and flow of the tide is violent. The name was especially applied to the strait between Boeotia and Euboea, where the ancients asserted the sea ebbed and flowed seven times in the day (Strabo, ix. 1). Modern observers have noticed these extraordinary tides. The present name of the island, Negropont, is the Italian name formed from Egripo, the modern corruption of Euripus. Cf. Cicero, pro Muraena, xvii.:—Quod fretum, quem Euripum tot motus, tantas, tam varias habere putatis agitationes fluctuum, quantas perturbationes et quantos aestus habet ratio comitiorum. Aristotle, Ethica Nicomachea, ix. 6:—τῶν τοιούτων γὰρ μένει τὰ βουλήματα, καὶ οὐ μεταῤῥεῖ ὥσπερ Εὔριπος.

[200] One of the Cyclades, about half-way between Attica and Siphnus.

[201] ἐπιπτῆναι, a poetical form for ἐπιπτέσθαι.

[202] Cf. Justin, xi. 7.

[203] Cf. Curtius, iii. 2 (Zumpt's edition); Plutarch (Alexander, 18).

[204] Now called Angora. In the time of Alexander the country was named Great Phrygia, the term Galatia being afterwards applied to it, from the fact that it was conquered by the Gauls in the 3rd century B.C.

[205] Now called Kizil-Irmak, i.e. the Red River. It is the largest river in Asia Minor, and separated the empires of Persia and Lydia, until the conquest of the latter by Cyrus.

[206] The chief pass over the Taurus between Cappadocia and Cilicia. It is more than 3,600 feet above the sea-level. Its modern name is Golek-Boghaz. Cf. Curtius, iii. 9-11. It is called Tauri Pylae by Cicero (Epistolae ad Atticum, v. 20, 2).

[207] See Xenophon (Anabasis, i. 2, 20, 21).

[208] Curtius (iii. 11) says, that Alexander wondered at his own good fortune, when he observed how easily Arsames might have blocked up the pass. Cyrus the Younger was equally fortunate in finding this impregnable pass abandoned by Syennesis, king of Cilicia. See Xenophon (Anabasis, i. 2, 21).

[209] Now called Tersoos-Chai: See Curtius, iii. 12; Justin, xi. 8; and Lucian (De Domo, i.). At Tarsus the emperor Julian was buried. See Ammianus, xxv. 10, 5.

[210] Probably none of the physicians would venture to prescribe, for fear of being held responsible for his death, which seemed likely to ensue. Nine years after, when Hephaestion died of fever at Ecbatana, Alexander the physician who had attended him to be crucified. See Arrian, vii. 14; Plutarch (Alexander, 72).

[211] Cf. Curtius, iii. 14-16; Diodorus, xvii. 31; Justin, xi. 8; Plutarch (Alex., 19). The barbarous conduct of Alexander towards Philotas four years after, when contrasted with his noble confidence in Philip, shows the bad effect of his unparalleled success, upon his moral character.

[212] This pass was called the Syrian Gates, lying between the shore of the Gulf of Issus and Mount Amanus. Cyrus the Younger was six days marching from Tarsus through this pass. See Xenophon (Anab., i. 4). The Greeks often gave the name of Assyria to the country usually called by them Syria. The Hebrew name for it is Aram (high-land). Cf. Cicero (ad Diversos, xv. 4, 4); Diod., xiv. 21.

[213] A city of Cilicia on the coast, a Little west of the mouth of the Cydnus.

[214] Said to have been the last of the Assyrian kings.

[215] Cf. Strabo (xiv. 5) for a description of this statue.

[216] This was, doubtless, the arrow-headed writing which has been deciphered by Sir Henry Rawlinson. Cf. Herodotus, iv. 87; Thucydides, iv. 50.

[217] Now called Mezetlu. It was a Rhodian colony on the coast of Cilicia, between the rivers Cydnus and Lamus. It was afterwards re-named Pompeiopolis. The birthplace of Philemon, Aratus, and Chrysippus.

[218] About £49,000.

[219] Asander was a nephew of Parmenio. He afterwards brought a reinforcement to Alexander from Greece (Arrian, iv. 7). After the king's death he obtained the rule of Caria, but joining the party of Ptolemy and Cassander, he was defeated by Antigonus, B.C. 313.

The Diary of Alexander the Great

[220] These were Carian cities.

[221] Cos, the birthplace of Apelles and Hippocrates, is one of the group of islands called Sporades, off the coast of Caria. Triopium is the promontory terminating the peninsula of Cnidus, the south-west headland of Asia Minor, Cf. Tibullus, ii. 3, 57; Propertius, i. 2, 1; ii. 1, 5; Herodotus, i. 174.

[222] Called by the Romans, Aesculapius. He was the god of the medical art, and no doubt Alexander sacrificed to him, and celebrated the games, in gratitude for his recovery from the fever he had had at Tarsus.

[223] This plain is mentioned in Homer, vi. 201; Herodotus, vi. 95. The large river Pyramus, now called Jihan, falls into the sea near Mallus.

[224] Mallus was said to have been founded by Amphilochus after the fall of Troy. This hero was the son of Amphiaraus, the great prophet of Argos, whom Zeus is said to have made immortal. Magarsus, of Megarsa, was the port of Mallus. The difference of meaning between θύειν and ἐναγίζειν is seen from Herodotus, ii. 44; Plutarch (Moralia, ii. p. 857 D).

[225] Usually called the Syrian Gates. See chap. v. note ¹ supra.

[226] A city on the Gulf of Issus, being a settlement of the Phoenicians. Herodotus (iv. 38) calls the gulf the Myriandric Gulf. Cf. Xenophon (Anab., i. 4).

[227] Cf. Arrian, vii. 29; Curtius, viii. 17.

[228] Aeschines tells us in his speech against Ctesiphon (p. 552), that the anti-Macedonian statesmen at Athens at this time received letters from their friends, stating that Alexander was caught and pinned up in Cilicia. He says Demosthenes went about showing these letters and boasting of the news. Josephus (Antiquities of the Jews, xi. 7, 3) says that "not only Sanballat at Samaria but all those that were in Asia also were persuaded that the Macedonians would not so much as come to a battle with the Persians, on account of their multitude."

[229] There are two passes by which the eastern countries are entered from Cilicia; one on the south, near the sea, leads into Syria. The other pass lies more to the north, and leads to the country near the Euphrates. The latter was called the Amanic, and the former the Syrian gate. Alexander had just passed through the Syrian gate in order to march against Darius, at the very time that Darius was descending into Cilicia by the Amanic gate, and occupying Issus with his advanced guard. Alexander, who had reached Myriandrus in Syria, made a countermarch to meet Darius. Plutarch (Alex., 20) says that they missed each other in the night, which is quite a mistake

[230] Cf. Sallust (Catilina, 59); Caesar (Bell. Gall., ii. 25).

[231] See Xenophon (Anab., iii. 3).

[232] At Cunaxa. Xenophon (ii. 2, 6) does not mention the name of the place where the battle was fought, but says that he was informed it was only 360 stadia (about 40 miles) from Babylon. We get the name Cunaxa from Plutarch (Life of Artaxerxes, c. 8), who says it was 500 stadia (about 58 miles) from Babylon.

[233] Callisthenes the historian, who accompanied Alexander into Asia, states that the breadth of the plain between the mountain and the sea was not more than fourteen stadia, or a little more than one English mile and a half. See Polybius, xii. 17.

[234] These seem to have been foreign mercenaries. See Polybius, v. 79, 82; Strabo, xv. 3. Hesychius says that they were not a nation, but foreigners serving for pay.

[235] Callisthenes—as quoted in Polybius, xii. 18—reckoned the Grecian mercenaries of Darius at 30,000, and the cavalry at 30,000. Arrian enumerates 90,000 heavy-armed, not including the cavalry. Yet Polybius tries to prove that there was not room even for the 60,000 troops mentioned by Callisthenes,

[236] "The depth of this single phalanx is not given, nor do we know the exact width of the ground which it occupied. Assuming a depth of sixteen, and one pace in breadth to each soldier, 4,000 men would stand in the breadth of a stadium of 250 paces; and therefore 80,000 men in a breadth of twenty stadia. Assuming a depth of twenty-six, 6,500 men would stand in the breadth of the stadium, and therefore 90,000 in a total breadth of 14 stadia,

which is that given by Kallisthenes. Mr. Kinneir states that the breadth between Mount Amanus and the sea varies between one and a half mile and three miles."—Grote.

|237| Diodorus (xvii. 31), and Plutarch (Alex., 18), give the same number; but Justin (xi. 9) says the Persians numbered 400,000 infantry and 100,000 cavalry. It took five days for them to cross the Euphrates, over bridges of boats (Curtius, iii. 17). The money alone of the king required 600 mules and 300 camels to convey it (Curtius, iii. 8).

|238| Cf. Arrian, iii. 11; and Xenophon (Anab., i. 8, 21, 22).

|239| See Donaldson's New Cratylus, sect. 178.

|240| Cf. Xenophon (Cyropaedia, vii. 1, 6).

|241| In describing the battle of Arbela, Arrian mentions eight distinct squadrons of Macedonian heavy cavalry, which was known by the name of the Companions. Among the squadrons several, if not all, were named after particular towns or districts of Macedonia, as here, Anthemus, and Leuge. We also find mention of the squadrons of Bottiaca, Amphipolis, and Apollonia. See also Arrian.i. 2; i. 12; iii. 11.

|242| τῇ γνώμῃ δεδουλωμένος. An expression imitated from Thucydides, iv. 34; compare Arrian, iii. 11; v. 19; vi. 16, where the same words are used of Porus and the Indians.

|243| κυμῆναν τῆς φάλαγγος. An expression imitated from Xenophon (Anab., i. 8, 18). It is praised by Demetrius (De Elocutione, 84). Krüger reads ἐκκυμῆναν. Cf. Plutarch (Pompey, 69).

|244| Curtius (iii. 29) says that on Alexander's side 504 were wounded, and 182 killed. Diodorus (xvii. 36) says, that 450 Macedonians were killed. Justin (xi. 9) states that 280 were slain.

|245| Polybius, who lived nearly three centuries before Arrian, censures Callisthenes for asserting that the Persian cavalry crossed the river Pinarus and attacked the Thessalians. No doubt Arrian received this information from the lost works of Ptolemy and Aristobulus (Poly., xii. 18).

|246| ἀμπάτης is the poetical form of ἀναβάτης, the word used by Xenophon, Plato, and other Attic writers. The latter is found only once in Arrian (III. xiii. 5).

|247| ἢ τῶν πεζῶν is Martin's emendation for ἢ ὡς πεζῶν.

|248| Curtius (iii. 27) and Diodorus (xvii. 34) give a graphic description of a direct charge made by Alexander upon Darius, and a sanguinary conflict between Alexander's body-guard and the Persian nobles, in which the Great King's horses were wounded and became unmanageable, whereupon Darius got out, mounted a horse, and fled. We learn from Plutarch (Alex., 20) that Chares affirmed Alexander came into hand-to-hand conflict with Darius, and that he received a wound in the thigh from that king's sword. Plutarch says that Alexander wrote to Antipater that he had been wounded in the thigh with a dagger, but did not say by whom. He also wrote that nothing serious had resulted from the wound. The account of Arrian is far the most trustworthy. Callisthenes stated that Alexander made a direct attack upon Darius (Polybius, xii. 22). We know from Xenophon that the Persian kings were in the habit of occupying the centre, and that Cyrus directed Clearchus to make the attack against the person of his brother Artaxerxes at the battle of Cunaxa. Polybius seems to have been ignorant of this custom of the Persian kings when he wrote his criticism on the statement of Callisthenes.

|249| ἀφείλετο. On this word see Donaldson (New Cratylus, sect. 315). Cf. Aeschylus (Persae, 428); Thucydides (iv. 134); Xenophon (Hellenics, i. 2, 16).

|250| The victories of the Greeks and Macedonians over the Persians were materially aided by the pusillanimity of Xerxes and Darius. Compare the conduct of Xerxes at Salamis (Herodotus, viii. 97; Aeschylus, Persae, 465-470, with Mr. Paley's note) and that of Darius at Arbela (Arrian, iii. 14).

|251| Diodorus (xvii. 36) and Curtius (iii. 29) agree with Arrian as to the number of slain in the army of Darius. Plutarch (Alex., 20) gives the number as 110,000.

[252] Justin (xi. 9) agrees with Arrian, that the wife of Darius was also his sister. Grote speaks of the mother, wife, and sister of Darius being captured, which is an error. Diodorus (xvii. 38) and Curtius (iii. 29) say that the son was about six years of age.

[253] Cf. Xenophon (Cyropaedia,ii. 1, 3; vii, 5, 85).

[254] Damascus,—the Hebrew name of which is Dammesek,—a very ancient city in Syria, at the foot of the Antilibanus, at an elevation of 220 feet above the sea, in a spacious and fertile plain about 30 miles in diameter, which is watered by three rivers, two of which are called in the Bible Abana and Pharpar. It has still a population of 150,000. The emperor Julian, in one of his letters, calls it " the Eye of all the East."

[255] About £730,000.

[256] B.C. 333; end of October or beginning of November.

[257] Alexander erected three altars on the bank of the Pinarus, to Zeus, Heracles, and Athena (Curtius, iii. 33). Cicero, who was proconsul of Cilicia, speaks of "the altars of Alexander at the foot of Amanus," and says that he encamped there four days (Epistolae ad Diversos, xv. 4).

[258] About £12,000.

[259] This distinguished general saved Alexander's life in India, in the assault on the city of the Mallians. After the king's death, he received the rule of the lesser or Hellespontine Phrygia. He was defeated and slain by the Athenians under Antiphilus, against whom he was fighting in alliance with Antipater, B.C. 323. See Diodorus, xviii. 14, 15; Plutarch (Phocion, 25).

[260] Compare Diodorus, xvii. 37, 38; Curtius, iii. 29-32.

[261] Named Sisygambis.

[262] In a letter written by Alexander to Parmenio, an extract from which is preserved by Plutarch (Alex., 22), he says that he never saw nor entertained the desire of seeing the wife of Darius, who was said to be the most beautiful woman in Asia; and that he would not allow himself to listen to those who spoke about her beauty. Cf. Ammianus (xxiv. 4, 27), speaking of Julian: "Ex virginibus autem, quae speciosae sunt captae, ut in Perside, ubi feminarum pulchritudo excellit, nec contrectare aliquam voluit, nec videre: Alexandrum imitatus et Africanum, qui haec declinabant, ne frangeretur cupiditate, qui se invictos a laboribus ubique praestiterunt."

[263] Thapsacus is understood to be identical with the city called Tiphsach (passage) in 1 Kings iv. 24; which is there said to have been the eastern boundary of Solomon's empire. It is generally supposed that the modern Deir occupies the site of the ancient Thapsacus; but it has been discovered that the only ford in this part of the river is at Suriyeh, 165 miles above Deir. This was probably the site of Thapsacus. From the time of Seleucus Nicator the city was called Amphipolis (Pliny, v. 21). See Stephanus of Byzantium, sub voce Amphipolis. Cf . Xenophon (Anabasis, i. 4, 11).

[264] The Euphrates is the largest river of western Asia, and rises in the mountains of Armenia. It unites with the Tigris, and after a course of 1,780 miles flows into the Persian Gulf. It is navigable by boats for 1,200 miles. The annual inundation, caused by the melting of the snow in the mountains of Armenia, takes place in the month of May. The Euphrates, Tigris, and Eulaeus had formerly three separate outlets into the Persian Gulf; but the three now unite in a single stream, which is called Shat-el-Arab, The Hebrew name for the river which the Greeks called Euphrates, was Pĕrath (rapid stream). It is called in the Bible, the Great River, and the River (Gen. xv. 18; Exod. xxiii. 31; et passim). In Jeremiah xiii. 4-7, the word Pĕrath stands for Ephrath, another name for Bethlehem; in our Bible it is mis-translated. See Fürst's Hebrew Lexicon.

[265] The term Cĕnaan was applied to the lowland plain from Aradus to Gaza. The northern portion, from Aradus to Carmel, is known to as under its Grecian name of Phoenicia, which is probably derived front the Greek phoinix (a palm-tree), which grew abundantly in the country, and was the emblem of some of its towns. Others derive it from

another Greek word phoinix (red dye), which formed one of its most important manufactures. The Phoenicians applied the term Cenaan to their land in contrast to the highlands to the west, which they called Aram (highland), the Hebrew name for Syria. The country of Phoenicia was 120 miles long and with an average breadth of 12 miles, never exceeding 20 miles. The chief cities of Phoenicia were Tyre, Sidon, Aradus, Byblus, Berytus, Tripolis, and Accho or Ptolemais. Its central position between the eastern and western countries, early developed its commercial power, and its intercourse with foreign nations at an early period produced an advanced state of civilization and refinement. The Phoenicians were a Semitic nation like the Israelites; and their language bears a remarkable affinity with the Hebrew, as is seen by fragments of the Carthaginian language preserved in Plautus. In an inscription discovered at Marseilles in 1845, out of 94 words 74 were found in the Hebrew Bible. The Phoenicians were asserted by the Greeks to have communicated to them the knowledge of letters; and this statement is corroborated by the similarity of the Hebrew and ancient Greek letters. Their colonies spread from Cyprus to Crete and the Cyclades, thence to Euboea, Greece, and Thrace. The coasts of Asia Minor and Bithynia were dotted with their settlements, and they carried their commerce into the Black Sea. They also had colonies in Sicily, Sardinia, Ivica, and Spain, where they founded Cadiz. The northern coast of Africa was lined with their colonies, the most flourishing of which was Carthage, which rose to be one of the great powers of the world. Strabo says that they had 300 colonies on the western coast of Africa. They visited the coasts of England for tin; and thus, to quote the words of Humboldt, "the Tyrian flag waved at the same time in Britain and the India Ocean." Herodotus (iv. 42, 43) says that under the patronage of Necho, king of Egypt, they circumnavigated Africa; but he states that he does not believe it was a fact. The reason which he assigns for his disbelief is, that the navigators alleged that the sun was on their right hand, which is the strongest argument in favour of the truth of their statement. In Isaiah xxiii. 11, Phoenicia is called Cĕnaan, where the English Bible has erroneously, the merchant city. In the Bible the word Cĕnaanim is frequently used for merchants, because the Phoenicians were the principal commercial people of antiquity (Job xli. 6; Prov. xxxi. 24; Isaiah xxiii. 8; Hos. xii. 7; Zeph. i. 11; Zech. xiv. 21). Tripolis consisted of three distinct cities, 600 feet apart, each having its own walls, but all united in a common constitution with one place of assembly. These cities were colonies respectively of Sidon, Tyre, and Aradus. Tripolis was a flourishing port on a headland whioh is a spur of Lebanon. It is now called Tripoli, and is still a large town. See Dr. Smith's Dictionary of Classical Geography.

[266] The oldest towns in Cyprus,—Citium, Amathus, and Paphus,—were Phoenician colonies. These were afterwards eclipsed by the Greek colonies, Salamis, Soli, and New Paphus. In Hebrew the island is called Ceth, and the inhabitants Cittim. Gesenius says, that upon a Sidonian coin Ceth in Cyprus, which the Greeks called Citium, is described as a Sidonian colony. Diodorus (xvi. 42) says there were nine kings in Cyprus. It is probable that the kings of the Hittites mentioned in 1 Kings x. 29, were from Cyprus. Also the Hittite women whom Solomon married were probably Cyprians (1 Kings xi. 1). The kings of the Hittites of whom the Syrians were afraid were also Cypriotes (2 Kings Tii. 6); and the land of the Hittites mentioned in Judges i. 26, probably means Cyprus. Josephus, Eusebius, and Jerome understand these passages to refer to Cyprus. In Isaiah xxiii. 1, the land of Cittim refers to Cyprus, which belonged to Tyre, the revolt of which the prophet announced. This revolt is confirmed by Menander (Josephus, ix. 14, 9).

[267] Agis III. was ultimately defeated and slain by Antipater, B.C. 330. See Curtius, vi. 1 and 2; Grote's Greece, vol. xii. pp. 102-106.

[268] About £7,300.

[269] Now Cape Matapan. Cf. Propertius, iii. 2, 11; Tibullus, iii. 3, 13; Homer (Hymn to Apollo, 411).

[270] The Cretans were very early civilized and powerful, for we read in Homer of their 100 cities. Before the Trojan war lived the famous king Minos, who is said to have given

laws to Crete, and to have been the first potentate who possessed a navy, with which he suppressed piracy in the Aegean Sea. The Cretans gradually degenerated, so that we find in the New Testament St. Paul quoting from their own poet, Epimenides: "Always liars and beasts are the Cretans, and inwardly sluggish" (Titus i. 12). The lying propensity of the Cretans is proved from the fact that the verb to Cretize, was used in Greek with the meaning "to speak falsely." In Hebrew, Crete is called Caphtor (cypress). It is mentioned in Jer. xlvii. 4. It was the native land of a tribe of Philistines called Caphtorim (Gen. x. 14; Deut. ii. 23; 1 Chron. i. 12). The fact that the Philistines came partly from Crete is also affirmed in Amos ix. 7. Another branch of the Philistines came from Casloach in Egypt. The Caphtorim emigrated originally from Egypt to Crete, from which island they were probably driven by the Greeks. Tacitus asserts that the inhabitants of Palestine came from Crete (Historiae, v. 2); and the early name of Gaza was Minoa, after the famous king of Crete. Another Hebrew name for Crete is Cĕrēth, whence the inhabitants were called Cĕrēthim. They are mentioned in Ezek. xxv. 16, and Zeph. ii. 5; where the Septuagint and the Syriac have Cretans. We find the Philistines, who were partly emigrants from Crete, called Cerethim in 1 Sam. xxx. 14. From among these Cerethim and Philistines David chose his body-guard, which was composed of men skilled in shooting and slinging (2 Sam. viii. 18, xv. 18, xx. 7, 23; 1 Kings i. 38, 44; 1 Chron. xviii. 17).

[271] From Diodorus (xvii. 48) it appears that Agis went personally to Crete, and compelled most of the cities to join the Persian side. We also learn that the deputies of the Greeks assembled at the Isthmian games at Corinth sent an embassy to Alexander to congratulate him on his victory at Issus, and to present him with a golden wreath. (See also Curtius, iv. 22.)

[272] Coele-Syria, or Hollow Syria, is, in its more limited sense, the country between the ranges of Libanus and Anti-Libanus, in which Damascus and Baalbek are situated; in its wider meaning, it comprises the whole of Northern Syria, in opposition to- the countries of Phoenicia and Palestine.

[273] Aradus is an island lying two or three miles from the mainland of Phoenicia. According to Strabo, a State was founded in it by refugees from Sidon. For a long time the island was independent, under its own kings; and even after it fell under the sway of the Macedonian kings of Syria, and subsequently under that of the Romans, it retained a great deal of its commercial prosperity. Aradus appears in Hebrew under the form Arvad. It is evident from Ezek. xxvii. 8, 11, that its inhabitants were skilful sailors and brave warriors. They sent out colonies to Aradus south of Carmel, the island of Aradus near Crete, and the islands in the Persian gulf. The present name of this island is Ruad. The Aradians inhabited the mainland opposite the island, as well as the island itself.

[274] Artaxerxes Ochus reigned B.C. 359-338.

[275] Perinthus was a Samian colony on the Propontis. For the siege by Philip, see Diodorus, xvi. 74-76.

[276] Impartial historians deny that Philip's murderers were bribed; they committed the murder from private resentment.

[277] Ochus was poisoned about B.C. 338, by the eunuch Bagoas, who placed upon the throne Arses, one of the king's sons, killing all the rest. Cf. Aeliau (Varia Historia, vi. 8). Two years afterwards, Bagoas put Arses and all his children to death; thus leaving no direct heir of the regal family alive. He then placed upon the throne one of his adherents, named Darius Codomannus, a descendant of one of the brothers of Artaxerxes Mnemon. Bagoas soon afterwards tried to poison this Darius; but the latter, discovering his treachery, forced him to drink the deadly draught himself (Diod., xvii. 5; Justin., x. 3). From Arrian, iii. 19, we learn that Bistanes, a son of Ochus, was alive after the battle of Arbela.

[278] Aeschines, in his speech against Ctesiphon (p. 634), asserts that Darius sent 300 talents to Athens, that the Athenians refused them, and that Demosthenes took them, reserving 70 talents for his own private use. Deinarchus repeats this statement in his speech against Demosthenes. (pp. 9-14). If Demosthenes had really acted thus, it is strange

Alexander knew nothing about it.

[279] This statement of Arrian is confirmed by Curtius (iii. 34), who says that Parmenio captured the treasure, not in the city, but from fugitives who were conveying it away.

[280] In giving the names of the captured Grecian envoys, Curtius (iii. 35) seems to have confounded this with a future occasion, mentioned in Arrian (iii. 24).

[281] The great Iphicrates had been adopted by Alexander's grandfather, as is stated in a note on Book I. chap. 23.

[282] Byblus is said by Strabo (xvi. 2) to have been situated on a height not far from the sea. It was reported to be the oldest city in the world. It possessed a considerable extent of territory, including Berytus, and was an independent State for a long period, the last king being deposed by Pompey. On a Byblus coin of Alexander's time appears the name Einel, which is the king Enylus mentioned by Arrian (ii. 20). Byblus was the chief seat of the worship of Adonis, or Thammuz, who was supposed to have been born there. In the Bible it appears under its Hebrew name Gebal (mountain-district). The inhabitants of Gebal are said in Ezek. xxvii. 9 to have been skilled in building ships. In Josh, xiii. 5 the northern boundary of the Holy Land is said to reach as far as the land of the Giblite, or inhabitant of Gebal. In 1 Kings v. 18 the word translated in our Bible stone-squarers ought to be rendered Giblites. The Arabs still call the place Jebail. Cf. Milton (Paradise Lost, i. 446).

[283] Sidon, or in Hebrew Tsidon (fortress), is called in Gen. x. 15, 19 the firstborn son of Canaan, i.e. it was the first city founded by the Canaanites or Phoenicians. It lay about twenty miles south of Tyre, on a small promontory two miles south of the river Bostremus. We read in Homer that it was famous for its embroidered robes and metal utensils, and from other ancient writers we find that it manufactured glass and linen and also prepared dye's. Before the time of David it fell under the rule of Tyre; but when Shalmaneser, king of Assyria, invaded Phoenicia, it revolted from Tyre and submitted to the invader. It was governed by its own kings under the Babylonian and Persian empires; and under the latter power it reached its highest prosperity, surpassing Tyre in wealth and importance. In the expedition of Xerxes against Greece, the Sidonians furnished the best ships in the whole fleet, and their king obtained the highest place under Xerxes in the council. But they revolted against Ochus, king of Persia, and being betrayed to him by their own king Tennes, they burnt their city and ships. It is said that 40,000 persons perished in the fire and by the sword, B.C. 351. (Diodorus, xvi. 43-45). No doubt this barbarous treatment of Ochus induced the Sidonians to take the side of Alexander. The city was already built and again flourishing when that king appeared on the scene. Near the site of the ancient city is the present town of Saida, with a population of about 5,000. Cf. Homer (Iliad, vi. 289; xxiii. 741); Lucan, iii. 217.

[284] At Sidon, Alexander deposed the reigning king Strato, a friend of the Persians; and a poor man, named Abdalonymus, distantly related to the regal family, was put into his place (Curtius, iv. 3, 4). Diodorus (xvii. 47) tells the same story, but applies it to Tyre, probably by mistake.

[285] The Hebrew name for Tyre is Tsor (rock). In Isa. xxiii. 4 it is called the fortress of the sea; and in ver. 8, "Tsor, the crowning one," because Tyre gave rulers to the Phoenician cities and colonies. Valuable information about the power, trade, and customs of Tyre is derived from Ezek. xxvi-xxviii.; and we learn the fact that she employed mercenaries like her colony Carthage (Ezek. zxvii. 10, 11). In the classical writers the name is corrupted into Tyrus, and sometimes into Sarra. Tyre was unsuccessfully besieged for five years by Shalmaneser. It was also besieged for thirteen years by Nebuchadnezzar, and in the end an alliance was formed, by which the Tyrians retained their own king as a vassal of the king of Babylon. This arrangement was continued under the kings of Persia.

[286] Curtius (iv. 7) tells us that the envoys also brought to Alexander a golden wreath, together with abundant supplies for his army.

[287] This king must have brought home his ships for the defence of Tyre, for he was in the city when it was captured. See chap. 24.

[288] The Phoenician god Melkarth (lord of the city), whom the Syrians called Baal

(lord), was supposed to be identical with the Grecian Heracles, or Hercules, who was the mythical ancestor of the Macedonian kings. Curtius (iv. 7) tells us that Alexander affirmed he had been ordered by an oracle to sacrifice in Tyre to Heracles. Gesenius informs us that a Maltese inscription identifies the Tyrian Melkarth with Heracles.

[289] Who was the son of Labdacus.

[290] See Herodotus, ii. 43, 44.

[291] The district comprising all the south-west of Spain outside the pillars of Heracles, or Straits of Gibraltar, was called Tartessus, of which the chief city was Tartessus. Here the Phoenicians planted colonies, one of which still remains under the name of Cadiz. The Romans called the district Baetica, from the principal river, the Baetis or Guadalquivir. The Hebrew name for this region is Tarshish, of which Tartessus is the Greek form. Tarshish was the station for the Phoenician trade with the West, which extended as far as Cornwall. The Tyrians fetched from this locality silver, iron, lead, tin, and gold (Isa. xxiii. 1, 6, 10, lxvi. 19; Jer. x. 9; Ezek. xxvii. 12, xxxviii. 13). Martial, Seneca, and Avienus, the first two of whom were Spaniards, understood Tartessus to stand for the south-west of Spain and Portugal. The word Tarshish probably means sea-coast, from the Sanscrit tarischa, the sea. Ovid (Met., xiv. 416); Martial, viii. 28; Silius, xiii. 673.

[292] Of Miletus. Herodotus knew his writings well, but they have not come down to us. See Herod, (ii. 143; v. 36 and 125).

[293] The Iberians were originally called Tibarenes, or Tibari. They dwelt on the east of the Black Sea, and west of Colchis, whence they emigrated to Spain. This nation is called Tubal in the Hebrew Bible; in Isa.', lxvi. 19 the Iberians of western Europe are referred to.

[294] An island near Cadiz, now called Leon. Cf. Hesiod (Theogonia, . 287-294); Herodotus, iv. 8.

[295] Now called Arta.

[296] Arrian omits to mention that the Tyrians pointed out to him that his wish to sacrifice to Hercules might be gratified without entering their city, since at Palaetyrus, on the mainland, separated from Tyre only by a narrow strait, was a temple of that deity more ancient than that in Tyre. See Curtius, iv. 7; Justin, xi. 10. We learn from Arrian, i. 18, that when Alexander offered sacrifice to the Ephesian Diana he marched to the temple with his whole army in battle array. No doubt it was this kind of thing the Tyrians objected to. Alexander actually did the same at Tyre after its capture. (See chapter 24.)

[297] For this use of ἐνύπνιον, cf. Homer (Iliad, ii. 56); Aristophanes (Wasps, 1218).

[298] Cf. Arrian, i. 11 and 25 supra.

[299] The island was about half a mile from the mainland, and about a mile in length.

[300] We learn from Diodorus (xvii. 40) that the breadth of this mole was about 200 feet.

[301] Curtius (iv. 10) says that the timber was procured from Lebanon, and the stones from Old Tyre on the mainland.

[302] Cf. Polyaenus (iy. 3).

[303] Cf. Cæsar (Bell. Gall., vii 24)—reliquasque res, quibus ignis excitari potest, fundebant. Krüger has unnecessarily altered ἐπὶ ταύτῃ into ἐπ' αὐτήν (i.e. πρῷραν).

[304] Curtius (iv. 12) says that the stern was loaded with stones and sand.

[305] Diodorus (xvii. 42) and Curtius (iv. 12) say that a great tempest helped to demolish the palisade.

[306] We learn from Josephus (Antiquities of the Jews, ix, 14), on the authority of Menander, that when Shalmaneser, king of Assyria, four centuries before Alexander's time, besieged Tyre, the other Phoenicians supplied him with ships in like manner.

[307] This was a state vessel, or guardship, similar to the Paralus and Salaminia at Athens. See Alciphron, Bk. I. Epistle 11, with Bergler's note.

[308] See Arrian, ii. 2 supra.

[309] Curtius (iv. 11) says that about thirty of the Macedonians collecting timber in Lebanon were killed by a party of wild Arabs, and that a few were also captured by them.

Lebanon is a Hebrew word meaning white, like Alpes. It was so called on account of its white cliffs, just as Britain is called by Aristotle, Albion, the Celtic for white.

[310] Plutarch (Life of Alexander, 24) gives us, on the authority of Chares, some details of daring valour on the part of Alexander in this expedition.

[311] Cleander was put to death by Alexander for oppression in exercising his duties as governor of Media. See Arrian, vi. 27 infra.

[312] In regard to this manoeuvre, see Herodotus, yi. 12; Thucydides, i. 49, with Arnold's note.

[313] συμπεπηγμέναι:—"In the best authors πέπηγα, is used as the perf. pass, of πήγνυμι" (Liddell & Scott). Cf. v. 12, 4; 24, 4, infra.

[314] Cf. Plautus (Mercator, iv. 2, 5), hortator remigum.

[315] Amathus was a town on the south coast of Cyprus. It is now called Limasol. Cf. Herodotus, v. 104–115; Tacitas (Ann., iii. 62); Vergil (Aeneid, x. 51).

[316] Curium was also a town on the south coast of Cyprus.

[317] Diodorus (xvii. 45) says, that after Admetus was killed, Alexander recalled his men from the assault that night, but renewed it next day.

[318] Agenor, the father of Cadmus, was the reputed founder of Tyre and Sidon. See Curtius, iv. 19.

[319] The Tyrians had been encouraged in their resistance by the promise of aid from their colony Carthage. But the Carthaginians excused themselves on the ground of their own difficulties in contending with the Greeks. The Tyrians however despatched their women, children, and old men to Carthage for safety. See Diodorus, xvii. 40, 41; Curtius, iv. 8 and 15. We learn from Diod., xx. 14, that the Carthaginians were in the habit of sending to the Tyrian Hercules the tenth of their revenues.

[320] Diodorus (xvii. 46) and Curtius (iv. 19) state that 2,000 Tyrians who had escaped the massacre were hanged on the sea-shore by Alexander's order.

[321] The end of July and beginning of August B.C. 332. Diodorus (xvii. 46) tells us that the siege lasted seven months. See also Curtius (iv. 20) and Plutarch (Life of Alexander, 24). We find from Strabo (xvi. 2) that Tyre again became a flourishing city.

[322] About £2,440,000 <this is the calculated estimation in 1884, in current terms this is approximately £300,000,000 >

[323] Diodorus (xvii. 54) puts the arrival of this embassy after Alexander's conquest of Egypt. Curtius (iv. 21) says that the name of the daughter whom Darius offered to Alexander was Statira.

[324] The term Palestine is derived from Pĕleshieth, the name given in Hebrew to the coast district in the south-west of Palestine, the inhabitants of which were called Pĕlishtim, or Philistines. As this tract of country lay directly between Phoenicia and Egypt, it became known to the Greeks sooner than the rest of the Holy Land, and they called it Syria Palaestinē. The name was gradually extended until it became the usual one for all the Holy Land among Greek and Latin writers. An interesting account of Alexander's visit to Jerusalem and his dealings with the Jews is found in Josephus (Antiquities, xi. 8).

[325] Nearly two miles and a half. Strabo (xvi. 2) says that the city was only seven stades from the sea.

[326] Gaza is the Greek form of the Hebrew name Azzah (fortress). Its position on the border of Egypt and Palestine has given it importance from the earliest times. It was one of the five cities of the Philistines; and retained its own king till a late period, as we learn from Zechariah ix. 5. It was the scene of a battle between Richard I. and the Saracens. It is now called Guzzeh, with a population of 15,000.

[327] Compare Arrian, i. 11 and 25; ii. 18. Plutarch (Alex., 25) says that the bird was entangled and caught among the nets and cords. See also Curtius, iv. 26.

[328] A stadium equalled 606.75 feet.

[329] Cf. Thucydides, ii. 76 (description of the siege of Plataeae).

[330] Diodorus (xvii. 48) says that the siege of Gaza lasted two months. Polybius (xvi. 40) speaks of the resolution and valour of the Gazaeans. We learn from Curtius (iv. 28) and from Dionysius of Halicarnassus (De Compositione Verborum, pp. 123-125) that Alexander treated the brave Batis with horrible cruelty. He ordered his feet to be bored and brazen rings to be put through them, after which the naked body was tied to the back of a chariot which was driven by Alexander himself round the city, in imitation of the treatment of Hector by Achilles at Troy. Cf. Arrian, vii. 14. Dionysius quotes from Hegesias of Magnesia, who wrote a history of Alexander, not now extant. Curtius says that nearly 10,000 of the Persians and Arabs were slain at Gaza. Strabo (xvi. 2) says that in his time (i.e. in the reign of Augustus) the city still remained desolate, as it was left by Alexander.

[331] Pelusium is identical with the Hebrew Sin (a marsh) the most easterly city of Egypt, which is called in Ezekiel xxx. 15, the strength of Egypt, because it was the key to that country from its frontier position. Cf. Herodotus, iii. 5. Strabo (xvii. 1) says it was situated near marshes. It stood east of the Pelusiac branch of the Nile, about 2.5miles from the sea. This mouth of the river was choked up with sand as early as the first century of the Christian era (Lucan, viii. 465). Sennacherib advanced as far as this city, and here Cambyses defeated the Egyptians, B.C. 525. Iphicrates the Athenian advanced to Pelusium with the satrap Pharnabazus, B.C. 373. Cf. Vergil (Georic, i. 228); Martial, xiii. 9; Silius, iii. 375.

[332] Curtius (iv. 22) says that this fleet was under the command of Hephaestion.

[333] His predecessor, Sabaces, was slain at Issus. See Arrian, ii. 11 supra.

[334] Curtius (iv. 29) says that Mazaces surrendered to Alexander treasure to the amount of 800 talents, nearly £200,000. <this is the calculated estimation in 1884, in current terms this is approximately £25,000,000 >

[335] Memphis, the capital of Egypt, is called in the Hebrew Bible, Noph. In Hosea ix. 6 it is called Moph. The Egyptian name was Mĕnoph, of which both Moph and Noph are contractions. The name signifies place of Ftah, the Egyptian name for Vulcan. Memphis stood on the west bank of the Nile, and is said by Herodotus (ii. 99) to have been founded by Menes. It had a circumference of fifteen miles. Its numerous temples were famous and are mentioned in the poems of Martial, Ovid, and Tibullus. It never recovered the devastation committed by Cambyses, who was exasperated by its resistance. The rise of Alexandria as the capital under the Ptolemies, hastened the decline of Memphis. At Gizeh, near Memphis, are the three great pyramids, being of the height respectively of 460, 446, and 203 feet. Not far off are six smaller ones. Near the second pyramid is the Sphinx, cut out of the solid rook, which was probably an object of worship. Cf. Apollodorus, ii. 4.

[336] Heliopolis is known in Hebrew as On, which is an Egyptian word meaning Sun. It is mentioned in Gen. xli. 45, 50; xlvi. 20. In Ezek. XXX. 17, it is called Aven, which is the same word in Hebrew as On, with a variation of the vowels. In Jer. xliii. 13 it is called Beith-Shemesh, which in Hebrew means House of the Sun, a translation of the Egyptian name. The Greeks called it Heliopolis, City of the Sun. The great temple of the Sun and its priesthood are described by Herodotus and Strabo. There are still remaining a beautiful obelisk of red granite nearly 70 feet high, and the brick wall of the temple 3,750 feet long by 2,370 feet broad. Cf. Apollodorus, ii. 4.

[337] The word Nile never occurs in the Hebrew Bible; but that river is called Yeor (river). In Amos viii. 8 it is called Yeor Mitsraim, the river of Egypt; but it is usually called simply Yeor, the river. In Isa. xxiii. 3 the corn of Egypt is called the harvest of Yeor, or the Nile. In like manner Avon, Ganges, Rhine, mean river. The Greek name Neilos, or Nile, means a bed with a stream, and was originally applied to the land of Egypt, as the valley of the Nile. It rises in the lake Victoria Nyanza, and has a course of 3,300 miles. In Isa. xxiii. 3 and Jer. ii. 18 the Nile is called Shichor (turbid). In Homer (Odys., iv. 477, etc.) the river is called Egypt as well as the country. Cf. Ammianus, xxii. 15.

[338] The Bull of Memphis, sacred to Ftah, the god of fire. See Herodotus, iii. 27, 28; Strabo, xvii. 1; Ammianus, xxii. 14; Ovid (Met., ix. 690).

[339] Now Aboukir, about 13 miles north-east of Alexandria, near the westernmost

mouth of the Nile. Cf. Aeschylus (Supp., 311; Prom., 846); Strabo, xvii. 1, 17; Tacitus (Ann., ii. 60).

[340] Usually called Lake Mareotis, now Mariût. Cf . Vergil (Georgic, ii. 91).

[341] We learn, from Curtius (iv. 38), that Alexander at first resolved to build the city on the island of Pharos, but finding it too small, built it on the mainland.

[342] A goddess representing the moon, and wife of Osiris the sun-god.

[343] Cf. Strabo (xvii. 1); Plutarch (Alex., 26); Diodorus (xvii. 52); Curtius (iv. 33); Ammianus (xxii. 16).

[344] We find from Valerius Maximus (i. 4) and Ammianus, l.c., that his name was Dinocrates.

[345] Krüger substitutes ἐπενόει for ἐποίει, comparing iv. 1, 3, and 4, 1 infra.

[346] See Arrian, ii. 2 supra.

[347] Methymna was, next to Mitylene, the most important city in Lesbos.

[348] Chares was an Athenian who had been one of the generals at the fatal battle of Chaeronea. Curtius (iv. 24) says that he consented to evacuate Mitylene with his force of 2,000 men on condition of a free departure.

[349] On an island in the Nile, of the same name, opposite Syene. It served as the southern frontier garrison station.

[350] The temple of Jupiter Ammon was in the oasis of Siwah, to the west of Egypt. Its ruins were discovered by Browne in 1792. This oasis is about 6 miles long and 3 broad. The people called Libyans occupied the whole of North Africa excluding Egypt. In Hebrew they are called Lubim (sunburnt). See 2 Chron. xii. 3; xvi. 8; Dan. xi. 43; Nah. iii. 9. Cf. Herodotus, ii. 32; iv. 168-199.

[351] King of the island Seriphus. Cf. Herodotus, ii. 91.

[352] The gigantic son of Poseidon and Ge.

[353] King of Egypt, who was said to have sacrificed all foreigners that visited the land.

[354] Perseus was the grandfather of Alemena, the mother of Hercules.

[355] About 183 miles. This city lay at the extreme west of Egypt, in Marmarica.

[356] "For some distance onward the engineers had erected a line of telegraph poles to guide us, but after they ceased the desert was absolutely trackless. Our guides were the stars—had the night been overcast the enterprise would have been impossible—and we were steered by a naval officer, Lieutenant Rawson, who had doubtless studied on previous nights the relation of these celestial beacons to the course of our march. The centre of the line was the point of direction; therefore he rode between the centre battalions (75th and 79th) of the Highland Brigade. Frequently in the course of the night, after duly ascertaining what dark figure I was addressing, I represented to him that his particular star was clouded over; but he always replied that he had another in view, a second string to his bow, which he showed me, and that he was convinced he had not deviated in the least from the proper direction. And he was right, his guidance was marvellously correct; for his reward, poor fellow, he was shot down in the assault, mortally wounded. Here we were adrift, but for the stars, in a region where no token existed on the surface by which to mark the course—any more than on the ocean without a compass—and the distance to be traversed was many miles."—Sir Edward Hamley: " The Second Division at Tel-el-Kebir," Nineteenth Century, December, 1882.

[357] Strabo (xvii. 1) quotes from Callisthenes, whose work on Alexander is lost. He agrees with Aristobulus about the two ravens. Callisthenes is also quoted by Plutarch (Alex., 27) in regard to this prodigy. Curtius (iv. 30) says that there were several ravens; and Diodorus (xvii. 49) speaks of ravens.

[358] Nearly five miles. Cf. Lucan, ix. 511-543.

[359] This Fountain of the Sun, as it is called, is 30 paces long and 20 broad; 6 fathoms deep, with bubbles constantly rising from the surface. Cf. Herodotus, iv. 181; Lucretius, vi. 849-878; Ptolemy, iv. 5, 37.

[360] This is what we call sal ammoniac, known to chemists as hydrochlorate of

ammonia. The dactylos was the smallest Greek measure of length, about 0.7 of an inch.

[361] We learn from Strabo (xvii. 1), on the authority of Callisthenes, that the declaration of the oracle of Ammon was confirmed by those of Apollo at Branchidae near Miletus, and of Athena at Erythrae in Ionia. Plutarch (Alex., 28) and Arrian (vii. 29) assert that Alexander set afloat the declaration that he was the son of Zeus to overawe the foreigners over whom he was extending his rule.

[362] Ewald and others think that Heroöpolis was identical with the Raamses of the Bible. Raamses, or Rameses, is a Coptic word meaning "the son of the sun."

[363] A city founded by the Milesians on the Canopic branch of the Nile. It remained a purely Greek city, being the only place where Greeks were allowed to settle and trade in Egypt. Cf. Herodotus, ii. 97, 135, 178, 179.

[364] Cf. Tacitus (Historiae, i. 11).

[365] We learn, from Curtius (iv. 34), that Alexander went to Samaria to chastise the inhabitants, who had burnt his deputy, Andromachus, to death.

[366] From early times the Athenians kept two sacred vessels for state purposes, the one called the Paralus and the other Salaminia. In the earliest times the former was used for coasting purposes, and the latter for the journey to Salamis. Hence their respective names. See Dr. Smith's Dict. of Antiquities. Aeschines, in his oration against Ctesiphon (p. 550), asserts that he was informed by the seamen of the Paralus that Demosthenes on this occasion sent a letter to Alexander soliciting pardon and favour.

[367] Cf. Aelian, Varia Historia, i. 25; Curtius, iv. 34.

[368] Beroea was a city of Macedonia, on the Astraeus, a tributary of the Haliacmon, about 20 miles from the sea.

[369] Other historians call this queen Cleopatra. She was the daughter of a Macedonian named Attalus. Plutarch (Alex., 9 and 10) says that she was cruelly put to death by Olympias during Alexander's absence. Justin (ix. 7; xi. 2) states that Olympias first slew her daughter on her mother's bosom and then had Cleopatra hanged; while Alexander put to death Caranus, the infant son of Philip and Cleopatra. Pausanias (viii. 7) says that Olympias caused Cleopatra and her infant son to be roasted on a brazen vessel. Cf. Aelian (Varia Historia, xiii. 35).

[370] This king was brother of Alexander's mother Olympias, and husband of Cleopatra the daughter of Philip and Olympias. He crossed over into Italy to aid the Tarentines against the Lucanians and Bruttians, but was eventually defeated and slain near Pandosia, B.C. 326.

[371] June-July, B.C. 331.

[372] We learn, from Curtius (iv. 37), that Alexander took eleven days to march from Phoenicia to the Euphrates.

[373] Curtius (iv. 37) says that Tigris is the Persian word for arrow; and that the river was so named on account of the swiftness of its current. The Hebrew name is Chiddekel, which means arrow. See Gen. ii. 14; and Dan. i. 4, where it is called the great river. The name Tigris is derived from the Zend Tighra, which comes from the Sanscrit Tig, to sharpen. It is now called Dijleh. It joins the Euphrates 90 miles from the sea, and the united stream is called Shat-el-Arab. Its entire length is 1,146 miles. In ancient times the two rivers had distinct mouths. So the Rhon formerly had several mouths. See Livy, xxi. 26. Strabo (iv. 1, 8) says that Timaeus gave it five mouths; Polybius gives it two; others give seven.

[374] This eclipse occurred September 20th, B.C. 331.

[375] The part of Assyria lying between the Upper Tigris and the Lycus was called Aturia.

[376] Called Carduchi by Xenophon. These mountains separate Assyria and Mesopotamia from Media and Armenia

[377] Cf. Aelian (Varia Historia, xii. 38).

[378] Arachosia comprised what is now the south-east part of Afghanistan and the north-east part of Beloochistan.

[379] Aria comprised the west and north-west part of Afghanistan and the east part of

Khorasan.

[380] Parthia is the modern Khorasan. Hyrcania was the country south and south-east of the Caspian Sea. The Tapurians dwelt in the north of Media, on the borders of Parthia between the Caspian passes. Cf. Ammianus, xxiii. 6.

[381] The Cadusians lived south-west of the Caspian, the Albanians on the west of the same sea, in the south-east part of Georgia, and the Sacesinians in the north-east of Armenia, on the river Kur.

[382] "The Red Sea was the name originally given to the whole expanse of sea to the west of India as far as Africa. The name was subsequently given to the Arabian Gulf exclusively. In Hebrew it is called Yam-Suph (Sea of Sedge, or a seaweed resembling wool). The Egyptians called it the Sea of Weeds.

[383] The Uxians occupied the north-west of Persis, and Susiana was the country to the north and west of Persis.

[384] The Sitacenians lived in the south of Assyria. ἐτετάχατο. is the Ionic form for τεταγμένοι ἦσαν.

[385] The Greeks called this country Mesopotamia because it lies between the rivers Euphrates and Tigris. In the Bible it is called Paddan-Aram (the plain of Aram, which is the Hebrew name of Syria). In Gen. xlviii. 7 it is called merely Paddan, the plain. In Hos. xii. 12, it is called the field of Aram, or, as our Bible has it, the country of Syria. Elsewhere in the Bible it is called Aram-naharaim, Aram of the two rivers, which the Greeks translated Mesopotamia. It is called "the Island," by Arabian geographers.

[386] Curtius (iv. 35 and 45) states that Darius had 200,000 infantry, 45,000 cavalry, and 200 scythed chariots; Diodorus (xvii. 53) says, 800,000 infantry, 200,000 cavalry, and 200 scythed chariots; Justin (xi. 12) gives 400,000 foot and 100,000 horse; and Plutarch (Alex., 31) speaks of a million of men. For the chariots cf. Xenophon (Anab., i 8, 10); Livy, xxxvii. 41.

[387] This is the first instance on record of the employment of elephants in battle.

[388] This river is now called Ghasir, a tributary of the Great Zab. The village Gaugamela was in the district of Assyria called Aturia, about 69 miles from the city of Arbela, now called Erbil.

[389] About 7 miles.

[390] Xenophon (Anab., iii. 4, 35) explains why this was so.

[391] σφεῖς here stands for αὐτοί.

[392] See note 1 to ii. 10 supra.

[393] These people were a Scythian tribe leading a nomadic life east of the Caspian. They are called Daoi by Herodotus, i. 125; Dahae by Ammianus, xxii. 8, 21; Livy, xxxv. 48; xxxvii. 38; Vergil (Aeneid, viii. 728); Pliny, vi. 19; Strabo, xi. 7. They are mentioned in Ezra iv. 9 as subjects of Persia. The district is now called Daikh. See Früst's Hebrew Lexicon, sub voce דָּהָ.

[394] A title of honour. Curtius says that they numbered 15,000.

[395] Cf. Herodotus, vii. 41.

[396] This people lived to the south of the Caspian.

[397] "Several names of various contingents stated to have been present in the field are not placed in the official return— thus the Sogdiani, the Arians, and the Indian mountaineers are mentioned by Arrian as having joined Darius (iii. 8); the Kossaeans by Diodorus (xvii. 59); the Sogdiani, Massagatae, Belitae, Kossaeans, Gortyae, Phrygians, and Kataonians, by Curtius (iv. 12)."—Grote.

[398] This distinguished general succeeded Antipater as regent of Macedonia, but was overcome by Cassander, the son of the former, and became subordinate to him.

[399] There were thus six taxeis, or brigades of foot Companions, as they were called, in the phalanx of infantry at the battle of Arbela. Arrian's description of the battle at the Granicus (i. 14) seems to be erroneous in some of the words of the text; yet it may be

gathered from it that there were also six taxeis in Alexander's phalanx on that occasion also.

[400] See Arrian's Tactics, 29.

[401] Cf. Diodorus (xvii. 57).

[402] See Donaldson's New Cratylus, sect. 178.

[403] Cf. Curtius, iv. 35. "Equitibus equisque tegumenta erant ex ferreis laminis serie inter se connexis."

[404] Compare the uselessness of the Persian scythed chariots at the battle of Cunaxa. See Xenophon (Anabasis, i. 8). So also at the battle of Magnesia between Scipio and Antiochus. See Livy, xxxvii. 41.

[405] πεφρικυῖα, imitated from Homer (Iliad, iv. 282). Cf. Vergil (Aeneid, x. 178, horrentibus hastis); Livy, xliv. 41 (horrendis hastis).

[406] Curtius (iv. 58, 59) and Diodorus (xvii. 60) describe quite an Homeric battle, Darius hurling a spear at Alexander, and Alexander hurling his at Darius and killing his charioteer. They say that the Persians mistook the fall of the charioteer for that of the king, and fled, carrying Darius with them.

[407] Curtius (iv. 59) and Diodorus (xvii. 60) say that so thick a cloud of dust was raised by the mighty mass of fugitives, that nothing could be clearly distinguished, and that thus the Macedonians lost the track of Darius. The noise of the shouting and the cracking of whips served as guides to the pursuers.

[408] Sisygambis, the mother of Darius, whom these Persians were especially anxious to liberate from the custody of the Macedonians, refused to go with them. See Diodorus and Curtius.

[409] Arrian does not say much about this vigorous charge of Mazaeus, the commander of the Persian right wing. See Curtius (iv. 60); Diodorus (xvii. 60).

[410] We learn from Diodorus and Curtius that Parmenio had driven Mazaeus back before Alexander's arrival.

[411] The Lycus, now called the Great Zab, is a tributary of the Tigris. Xenophon calls it Zabatus (Anab., ii. 5). The Greek Lycus is a translation of the Syrian Zaba (wolf).

[412] About sixty-nine miles. Cf. Strabo (xvi. 1, 3).

[413] ἐλνύσας. This is an Ionic word used by Herodotus (viii. 71, etc.), and rarely in Attic poets and later prose writers.

[414] See Arrian, ii. 11 supra.

[415] Curtius (iv. 63) says that 40,000 of the Persians were slain, and that less than 300 Macedonians were killed. Diodorus (xvii. 61) states that more than 90,000 Persians and 500 Macedonians were slain.

[416] September 331 B.C. Cf. Plutarch (Alex., 31).

[417] For this prediction, see iii. 7 supra.

[418] As to the kinsmen and apple-bearers, see iii. 11 supra.

[419] Diodorus (xvii. 63) and Curtius (v. 6) state that from the treasure captured in Babylon, Alexander distributed to each Macedonian horseman about £24, to each of the Grecian horsemen £20, to each of the Macedonian infantry £8, and to the allied infantry two months' pay.

[420] Belus, or Bel, the supreme deity of the Babylonians, was identical with the Syrian Baal. The signification of the name is mighty. Cf. Herodotus (i. 181); Diodorus (ii. 9); Strabo (xvi. 1).

[421] See i. 17 supra.

[422] The Chaldees appear in Hebrew under the name of Casdim, who seem to have originally dwelt in Carduchia, the northern part of Assyria. The Assyrians transported these rude mountaineers to the plains of Babylonia (Isa. xxiii. 13). The name of Casdim, or Chaldees, was applied to the inhabitants of Mesopotamia (Gen. xi. 28); the inhabitants of the Arabian desert in the vicinity of Edom (Job i. 17); those who dwelt near the river Chaboras (Ezek. i. 3; xi. 24); and the priestly caste who had settled at a very early period in Babylon, as we are informed by Diodorus and Eusebius. Herodotus says that these priests were

dedicated to Belus. It is proved by inscriptions that the ancient language was retained as a learned and religious literature. This is probably what is meant in Daniel i. 4 by "the book and tongue of the Casdim." Cf. Diodorus (ii. 29-31); Ptolemy (v. 20, 3); and Cicero (De Divinatione, i. 1). See Fürst's Hebrew Lexicon, sub voce כַּשְׂדָּי.

[423] In the Bible this city is called Shushan. Near it was the fortress of Shushan, called in our Bible the Palace (Neb. i. 2; Esth. ii. 8). Susa was situated on the Choaspes, a river remarkable for the excellence of its water, a fact referred to by Tibullus (iv. 1, 140) and by Milton (Paradise Reg., iii. 288). The name Shushan is derived from the Persian word for lily, which grew abundantly in the vicinity. The ruins of the palace mentioned in Esther i. have recently been explored, and were found to consist of an immense hall, the roof of which was supported by a central group of thirty-six pillars arranged in the form of a square. This was flanked by three porticoes, each containing two rows of six pillars. Cf. Strabo (xv. 7, 28).

[424] The name of the viceroy was Abulites (Curtius, v. 8).

[425] If these were Attic talents, the amount would be, equivalent to £11,600,000; but if they were Babylonian or Aeginetan talents, they were equal to £19,000,000. Cf. Plutarch (Alex., 36, 37); Justin (xi. 14); and Curtius (v. 8). Diodorus (xvii. 66) tells us that 40,000 talents were of uncoined gold and silver, and 9,000 talents of gold bearing the effigy of Darius.

[426] Cf. Arrian (vii. 19); Pausanias (i. 8, 5); Pliny (Nat. Hist., xxxiv. 9); Valerius Maximus (ii. 10, 1). For Harmodius and Aristogeiton see Thucydides, vi. 56-58.

[427] Polis meant in early times a particular part of Athens, viz. the citadel, usually called the Acropolis. Cf. Aristophanes (Lysistrata, 245 et passim).

[428] Demeter and Persephone.

[429] About £730,000.

[430] Antipater had been left by Alexander regent of Macedonia. Agis III., king of Sparta, refused to acknowledge Alexander's hegemony, and after a hard struggle was defeated and slain by Antipater at Megalopolis, B.C. 330. See Diodorus, xvii. 63; Curtius, vi. 1 and 2.

[431] According to Curtius (v. 6) these forces amounted to nearly 15,000 men. Amyntas also brought with him fifty sons of the chief laen in Macedonia, who wished to serve as royal pages. Cf. Diodorus, xvii. 64.

[432] A river flowing through Susiana, formed by the junction of the Eulaeus and Coprates.

[433] Cf. Strabo, xv. 3.

[434] πλεονεκτούμενοι, with dative, defrauded of. Cf. Demosthenes, 1035, 26.

[435] γέρα. An Homeric expression.

[436] Named Sisygambis (Curtius, v. 11).

[437] This was the Araxes. See Strabo, xv. 3.

[438] Notice the use of the adverb πρίν with the genitive, instead of the preposition πρό. Cf. Pindar (Pythia, iv. 76) πρίν ὥρας

[439] Curtius (v. 16) says that Ariobarzanes after a bloody contest got away through the Macedonian lines, with about 40 horsemen and 5,000 foot, and made for Persepolis. Being shut out of that fortress, he was overtaken and slain with all his companions. Cf. Diodorus (xvii. 68).

[440] Diodorus (xvii. 69) and Justin (xi. 14) state that on approaching Persepolis, Alexander met 800 Grecian captives, mutilated by loss of arms, legs, eyes, ears, or other members. Curtius (v. 17-19) says there were 4,000 of them. Alexander offered to send these men home, with means of future support; but they preferred to remain in Persis. The king gave them money, clothing, cattle, and land.

[441] Diodorus (xvii. 71) and Curtius (v. 20) both state that the amount of treasure captured at Persepolis was 120,000 talents, or £27,600,000. In his own letter Alexander stated that there was sufficient treasure and valuable property to load 10,000 mule carts and

5,000 camels (Plutarch, Alex., 37). Curtius tells us that 6,000 talents were captured at Pasargadae.

|442| Pasargadae was the old capital of Persia, founded by Cyrus; but its place was afterwards taken by Persepolis.

|443| Diodorus (xvii. 70, 71) and Curtius (v. 20, 22) say that Alexander delivered Persepolis to his soldiers to pillage, and that he ordered a general massacre of the inhabitants. These authors agree with Plutarch (Alex., 38) in asserting that in a drunken revel he was instigated by the courtesan Thais to set fire to the palace, and accompanied her to commence the act of destruction. See Dryden's famous ode. But Arrian's account establishes the fact that the fire was the result of a deliberate plan. As regards the massacre, Plutarch (37) expressly states that Alexander wrote home that he ordered it from motives of policy.

|444| This was the principal pass through the Elburz mountains from Media into Hyrcania and Parthia.

|445| This was the capital of Media, called in Chaldee Achmetha (Ezra vi. 2). The present city of Hamadan is on the same site. It is situated at the foot of Mount Orontes, and was used by the Persian and Parthian kings as their summer residence. It was surrounded by seven walls, each overtopping the one before it, from the outer to the inner, crowned with battlements of different colours. Its citadel was used as a royal treasury. Below it stood a splendid palace, with silver tiles, and adorned with wainscotings, capitals, and entablatures of gold and silver. These treasures, to the value of 4,000 talents, were coined into money by Antiochus the Great of Syria. See Herodotus, i. 98; Polybius, x. 27.

|446| This tribe lived in the mountains between Media and Persis.

|447| £1,700,000.

|448| Curtius (v. 23) says that 6,000 Grecian mercenaries under Plato the Athenian met Alexander in Media, having marched up from Cilicia.

|449| Diodorus (xvii. 80) says that the amount of treasure deposited at Ecbatana was 180,000 talents or £41,400,000.

|450| A large city in the extreme north of Media, mentioned in the Book of Tobit. It was famous in the Middle Ages under the name of Rai. The ruins of Rai lie south-east of Teheran.

|451| ἔστε generally means until. In its present use cf. ii. 11 supra, ἔστε μὲν φάος ἦν.

|452| The Drangians lived in a part of Ariana west of Arachosia.

|453| Justin (xi. 15) and Curtius (v. 34) state that Darius was bound in chains of gold. The former says that the name of the place was Thara in Parthia, where the king was arrested. Probably these chains were those worn by the king or his nobles, according to the Persian custom. This is the only sentence in Arrian where περì suffers anastrophe, coming after the noun.

|454| Plutarch (Alex., 42) says that Alexander rode 3,300 stades, or about 400 miles, in eleven days. In the next chapter he says that only sixty of his men were able to keep up with him in the pursuit.

|455| Curtius (v. 24-38) gives very ample details of what occurred during the last days of Darius. Cf. Diodorus (xvii. 73); Justin (xi. 15).

|456| The Persian kings were buried at Persepolis. See Diodorus, xvii. 71. Plutarch (Alex., 43) says that Alexander sent the corpse of Darius to his mother.

|457| In the year B.C. 330, the first of Hecatombaion fell on the first of July.

|458| Darius came to the throne B.C. 336.

|459| In 2 Kings xi. 4, 19 the word translated captains in our Bible is Carim, the Carians. These men formed the body-guard of the usurper Athaliah, who stood in need of foreign mercenaries. David had a bodyguard of Philistines and Cretans. The Carians served as mercenaries throughout the ancient world, as we learn from Thucydides, i. 8; Herodotus, i. 171; ii. 152; v. 111; Strabo, xiv. 2. The Lydians appear in the Bible under the name of Lud (Isa. lxvi. 19). Herodotus (i. 94) gives an account of the colonization of Umbria by the Lydians, from which sprung the state of the Etruscans. Hence Vergil (Aeneid, ii. 782) speaks

of the "Lydius Tybris." See also Aeneid, viii. 479; Horace (Satires, i. 6, 1); Tacitus (Annals, iv. 55); Dionysius (Archaeologia Romana, i. 28).

[460] He married Barsine, eldest daughter of Darius (Arrian, vii. 4 infra). She was also called Arsinoe and Stateira.

[461] According to Curtius (vi. 6-10) the soldiers were very desirous of returning home; but Alexander made an harangue and induced them to advance into Hyrcania.

[462] The modern Balkh.

[463] The Caspian.

[464] Diodorus (xvii. 75) calls this river Stiboetis; Curtius (vi. 10) calls it Ziobetis.

[465] Krüger has ἐνταῦθα instead of ἐν τούτῳ.

[466] Curtius (vi. 14) says Artabazus had nine sons, one of whom, Pharnabazus, was the admiral of the Persian fleet. See Arrian (ii. 1; ii. 2; iii. 2 supra).

[467] Cf. Curtius, vi. 16.

[468] Sinope was a prosperous colony of Miletus on the Euxine. It is still called Sinoub. It was the birthplace of Diogenes.

[469] Chalcedon was a colony of Megara, situated on the Propontis at the entrance of the Bosporus, nearly opposite Byzantium.

[470] Areia occupied what is now the east part of Khorasan, and the west and north-west of Afghanistan. Susia is the modern Tus.

[471] Compare the words of Tissaphernes to Clearchus (Xenophon, Anabasis, ii. 6): "Though the king is the only man who can wear the tiara erect upon his head, I shall be able to wear mine erect upon my heart in, full confidence, when you are in my service." Cf. Curtius (iii. 8); Aristophanes (Birds, 487). The cap of the ordinary Persians was low, loose, and clinging about the head in folds; whereas that of the king was high and erect above the head. From Xenophon (Cyropaedia, viii. 3, 13) we learn that the Persian king's, vest was of a purple colour, half mixed with white, and that no one else was allowed to wear this mixture of white. He had loose trousers of a scarlet colour, and a robe entirely purple. Cf. also Strabo (xv. 3), where the tiara is said to be in the shape of a tower; and Seneca (De Beneficiis, vi. 31); Ammianus, xviii. 8, 5.

[472] See Xenophon (Anab., i. 2, 27; Cyropaedia, viii. 3); Curtius (iii. 8).

[473] These people are also called Drangians. They lived west of Aiaohosia in Diangiana.

[474] According to Plutarch (Alex., 48, 49) Alexander suborned Antigone, the mistress oi Philotas, to reveal his secret conversation.

[475] Cf. Gurtim, yi. 32.

[476] The word ἐπιμηνυτής is found nowhere else in any Greek author.

[477] Full details of the conspiracy and trial of Philotas are given hy Curtius (vi. 25-44).

[478] Arrian says nothing about Philotas being put to the torture; but this fast is asserted with ample details by Plutarch (Alex., 49); Diodorut (xvii. 80); Curtive (vi. 42, 43); and JusHn (xii. 5).

[479] Full particulars of the murder of Parmenio are given by Curtius (vii. 7-9).

[480] For the trial of Amyntas, cf. Curtius, vii. 2-6.

[481] Alexander also formed a separate cohort of the men who were pronounced sympathisers with Parmenio, and this cohort afterwards greatly distinguished itself. See Diodorus, xvii. 80; Curtius, vii. 10; Justin, xii. 5.

[482] The Ariaspians inhabited the south part of Drangiana on the borders of Gadrosia. The river Etymander, now known as the Hilmend, flowed through their territories. Cf. Curtius, vii. 11; Diodorus, xvii. 81.

[483] Gadrosia was the furthest province of the Persian empire on the south-east It comprised the south-east part of Beloochistan.

[484] This was not the range usually so called, but what was known as the Indian Caucasus, the proper name being Paropanisus. It is now called Hindu-Koosh.

[485] This city was probably on the site of Beghram, twenty-five miles north-east of Cabul. See Grote's Greece, vol. xii. ch. 94.

[486] There are two kinds of silphium of laserpitium, the Cyrenaic, and the Persian. The latter is usually called asafœtida. See Herodotus (iv. 169); Pliny (Historia Naturalis, xix. 15; xxiii. 48); Aelian (Varia Historia, xii. 37); Aristophanes (Plutus, 925); Plautus (Rud., iii. 2, 16); Catullus (vii. laserpitiferis Cyrenis).

[487] Cyrene was a colony founded by Battus from Thera, an island colonized by the Spartans. The territory of Cyrenaica is now a part of Tripoli. Cf. Pindar (Pyth., iv. 457); Herodotus (iv. 159-205)

[488] This Tanais was usually called Jaxartes, now Sir, flowing into the sea of Aral.

[489] The Oxus, now called Jihoun or Amou, flows into the sea of Aral, but formerly flowed into the Caspian.

[490] Some think this town stood where Naksheh now is, and others think it was at Kesch.

[491] Cf. Xenophon, Anab., i. 5, 10.

[492] Curtius (vii. 24) follows the account of Aristobulus, and so does Diodorus (xvii. 83) in the main. Cf. Aelian (Varia Historia, xii. 37).

[493] The modern Samarcand.

[494] Arrian and Strabo are wrong in stating that the Jáxartes rises in the Caucasus, or Hindu-Koosh. It springs from the Comedae Montes, now called Moussour. It does not flow into the Hyrcanian, or Caspian Sea but into the Sea of Aral. It is about 900 miles long.

[495] The river Tanais, of which Herodotus speaks (iv. 45, 57), is the Don; and the Lake Maeotis, is the Sea of Azov. Cf. Strabo (vii. cc. 3 and 4).

[496] Euxeinos (kind to strangers); called before the Greeks settled upon it Axenos (inhospitable). See Ovid (Tristia, iv.. 4). Cf. Ammianus (xxii. 8, 33): " A contrario per oavillationem Pontus Euxinus adpellatur, et euethen Graeoi dicimus stultum, et nootem euphronen et furias Eumenidas."

[497] So Gurtivs (vi. 6) makes the Don the boundary of Etirope and Asia. "Tanais Europam et Asiam medius interfuit." Ammianus says: "Tanais inter Caucasias oriens rupes, per sinuosos labitur circumflexus, Asiamque disterminans ab Europa, in stagnis Maeoticis deliteseit." The Eha, or Volga, is first mentioned by Ptolemy in the second century of the Christian era.

[498] Gadeira is now called Cadiz. The Greeks called the continent of Africa by the name of Libya. So Polybius (iii. 37) says that the Don is the boundary of Europe, and that Libya is separated from Asia and Europe respectively by the Nile and the Straits of Gibraltar, or, as he calls the latter, " the mouth at the pillars of Hercules." Arrian here, like many ancient authors, considers Libya a part of Asia. Of. Juvenal, x. i.

[499] Curtius (vii. 23) gives an account of the massacre by Alexander of the descendants of the Branchidae, who had surrendered to Xerxes the treasures of the temple of Apollo near Miletus, and who, to escape the vengeance of the Greeks, had accompanied Xerxes into the interior. They had been settled in Sogdiana, and their descendants had preserved themselves distinct from the barbarians for 150 years, till the arrival of Alexander. We learn from the table of contents of the 17th book of Diodorus, that that historian also gave an account of this atrocity of Alexander in the part of his history, now lost, which came after the 83rd chapter. Cf. Herodotus (i. 92, 157; v. 36); Strabo (xi. 11; xiv. 1).

[500] See Homer's Iliad, xiii. 6. Cf. Curtius, vii. 26; Ammianus, xxiii. 6.

[501] Cf. Thucydides, ii. 97.

[502] Curtius (vii 26) says, he sent one of his friends named Berdes on this mission. 205

[503] This was called Alexandria Ultima, on the Jaxartes, probably the modem Khojend.

[504] Of. Gwrtius (vii. 26). Zariaspa was another name for Bactra. See Pliny (vi. 18) and Straho (xi. 11).

[505] This city was also called Cyreaohata, because it was the furthest city founded by Cyrus, and the extreme city of the Persian empire.

[506] δυσί was not used in Attic Greek, or but seldom. It became common after the time of Alexander.

[507] Instead of ἡμέρᾳ μιᾷ, Siutenis reads ἡμέραν μίαν.

[508] This city was called by the Greeks, Alexandria on the Tanais. See Curtius, vii. 28.

[509] Cf. Livy, xxi. 27:— Hispani sine ulla mole in utres vestimentis oonjectis ipsi caetris superpositis inoubautes flumen tranavere.

[510] See Herodotus, iv. 122-142.

[511] This was Maracanda, according to iii. 30 supra. There is an error in the text; Abicht proposes to read ἐπὶ τὰ ὅρια, instead of ἐς τὰ βασίλεια.

[512] This river is now called Sogd, or Kohik. The Greek name signifies "very precious," a translation of the native name. Cf. Strabo, p. 518.

[513] Curtius (Tii. 32) says that Spitamenes laid an ambush for the Macedoniana, and slew 300 cavalry and 2,000 infantry.

[514] About 170 miles.

[515] Curtius (vii. 40) says that Alexander founded six cities in Bactria and Sogdiana. Justin (xii. 5) says there were twelve.

[516] This is a mistake; for it ends in a lake Dengiz near Karakoul.

[517] The Areius is now called Heri-rud. The Etymander is the modem Hilmend. Nothing is known of the Epardus.

[518] The Peneius is now called Salambria. It forces its way through the Tale of Tempe, between mounts Olympus and Ossa, into the sea. Cf. Ovid (Met., i. 568-576).

[519] On the analogy of πρὶν the later prose-writers use ἔστε with the infinitive. Cf. Arrian, ii. 1, 3; v. 16, 1.

[520] See Bk. iii. ch. 29 supra.

[521] See Bk. iii. ch. 19 stpra.

[522] See Bk. iii. ch. 16 supra.

[523] Curtius (vii. 40) says that the reinforcement was 19,000 men.

[524] Cf. Plutarch (Alex., 43); Diodorus (xvii. 83).

[525] I.e. non-Hellenic.

[526] Cf. Diodorus, xvii. 77; Justin, xii. 3. We learn from Plutarch (Alex., 45), that he did not assume the tiaia of the Persian kings. Cf. Arrian, vii. 9; vii. 29 infra. The Medio robe was a long silken garment reaching to the feet, and falling round the body in many deep folds.

[527] Caranus, a descendant of Temenus, king of Argos, is said to have settled in Macedonia, and to have become the founder of the dynasty of Macedonian kings. Temenus was a descendant of Heracles. Cf. ii. 5; iv. 10. One of the chief causes of disgust which the Greeks felt at the conduct of Pausanias, the conqueror at Plataea, was, that he adopted the Persian attire. " This pedigree from Temenus and Hercules may be suspicious; yet it was allowed, after a strict inquiry by the judges of the Olympic games (Herodotus, v. 22), at a time when the Macedonian kings were obscure and unpopular in Greece. When the Achaean league declared against Phllip, it was thought decent that the deputies of Argos should retire (T. Liv., xxxii. 22)."—Gibbon. Cf. Herodotus, viii. 137; Thucydides, ii. 99, 100; v. 80.

[528] Cf. Curtius, viii. 6.

[529] The sons of Jove, Castor and Pollux. ἐπιφρασθέντα is a word borrowed from Homer and Herodotus.

[530] Cf. Curtius, viii. 17: "Non deerat talia concupiscenti perniciosa adulatio perpetuum malum regum, quorum opes saepius assentatio quam hostis evertit."

[531] Curtius (viii. 3 and 4) says that it was Alexander himself that spoke depreciatingly of Philip, and that Clitus even dared to defend the murdered Farmenio.

[532] Instead of the usual reading from καὶ ταύτῃ to καὶ ταύτην, Sintenis reads οἱ δὲ σάρισαν παρὰ τῶν φυλάκων τινὸς καὶ ταύτῃ παίσαντα τὸν Κλεῖτον ἀποκτεῖναι.

[533] Cf. Curtius (viii. 3 and 6), who calls the sister of Clitus, Hellauioe.

[534] From Plutarch (Alex., 13) we learn that Alexander imagined he had incurred the avenging wrath of Bacchus hy destroying Thebes, the birthplace of that deity, on which account it was supposed to be under his tutelary care.

|535| Curtius (viii. 6) says, that in order to console the king, the Macedonian army passed a vote that Clitus had been justly slain, and that his corpse should not be buried. But the king ordered its burial.

|536| A philosopher of Abdera, and pupll of Democritus. After Alexander's death, Anaxarchus was thrown by shipwreck into the hands of Nioocreon, king of Cyprus, to whom he had given offence, and who had him pounded to death in a mortar.

|537| Cf. Sophocles (Oedipus Co?., 1382; Antigone, 451);; Hesiod (Opera et Diet, 254-257); Pindar (Olympia, viii. 28); Demosthenes |Advert. Arittogiton, p. 772); Herodotus, iii. 31.

|538| Plutarch (Alex., 52) tells us that Callisthenes the philosopher was also summoned with Anaxarchus to administer consolation, but he adopted such a different tone that Alexander was displeased with him.

|539| Curtius (viii. 17) says that Agis was the composer of very poor poems.

|540| Justin (xii. 6) says that Callisthenes was a fellow-student with Alexander under Aristotle. He composed three historical works: I. Hellenica, from B.C. 387 to 337; II. The History of the Sacred War, from B.C. 357 to 346; III. The History of Alexander. Cf. Diodorus, xiv. 117. According to Polybius (xii. 23), he was accused by Timaeus of having flattered Alexander in his History.

|541| Hipparchus was slain B.C. 514, and Hippias was expelled from Athens B.C. 510. See Thucydides, vi. 53-59.

|542| Eurystheus was king over Argos and Mycenae alone.

|543| When Conon the famous Athenian visited Babylon, he would not see Artaxerxes, from repugnance to the ceremony of prostration, which was required from all who approached the Great King. We are also informed by Plutarch (Artaxerxes, 22), that Pelopidas declined to perform this ceremony, so degrading in the eyes of the Greeks. His colleague, Ismenias, however, dropped his ring in front of the king, and then stooped to pick it up, thus going through the act of prostration. Cf. Aelian (Varia Historia, i. 21). Xenophon said to his soldiers:—οὐδένα γὰρ ἄνθρωπον δεσπότην ἀλλὰ τοὺς θεοὺς προσκυνεῖτε γὰρ. (Anab., iii. 13).

|544| Curtius (viii. 18) says that the speech proposing to honour Alexander as a god was made by Cleon, a Sicilian Greek.

|545| ἀχθομένους. The usual reading is μαχομένους

|546| Cf. Xenophon (Cyrop., i. 4, 27): λέγεται τοὺς συγγενεῖς φιλοῦντας ἀποπέμπεσθαι αὐτὸν νόμῳ Περσικῷ

|547| πρόσκεινται. Cf. Herodutus, i. 118:-τοῖσι θεῶν τιμὴ αὕτη προσκέεται.

|548| Alexander's mother Olympias was daughter of Neoptolemus, king of Epirus, who traced his descent from Neoptolemus, son of Achilles, the grandson of Aeacus.

|549| οι λόγοι γίγνονται. There is another reading, ολίγοι γίγνωνται.

|550| Cf. Herodutus, i. 214, with Dean Blakesley's note.

|551| Curtius (viii. 20) says, that it was Polysperchon who made sport of the Persian, and incurred the king's wrath.

|552| Ammianus (xviii. 3) says: "Ignorans profecto vetus Aristotelis sapiens dictum, qui Callisthenem sectatorem et propinquum suum ad regem Alexandrum mittens, ei saepe mandabat, ut quam rarissime et jucunde apud hominem loqueretur, vitae potestatem et necis in acie linguae portantem."

|553| Cf. Curtius (viii. 21); Aelian (Varia Historia, xiv. 49). After the battle of Pydna, where the Romans conquered the Macedonians, the pueri regii followed the defeated king Perseus to the sanctuary at Samothrace, and never quitted him till he surrendered to the Romans. See Livy, xiv. 6.

|554| For this use of διαπίπτειν, cf. Aristophanes (Knights, 695); Polybius (v.26, 16); διαπεσούσης αυτω της επιβουλής.

|555| Alexander wrote to Craterus, Attalus, and Acletas, that the pages, though put to

the torture, asserted that no one but themselves was privy to the conspiracy. In another letter, written to Antipater the regent of Macedonia, he says that the pages had been stoned to death by the Macedonians, but he himself whould punish the Sophist, and those who sent him put, and those who harboured in their cities conspirators against him.Aristotle had sent Callisthene out. Alexander refers to him and the Athenians. See Plutarch (Alex., 55).

[556] Cf. Arrian (vii. 29).

[557] Curtius (viii. 29) says that Alexander afterwards repented of his guilt in murdering the philosopher. His tragical death excited great indignation among the ancient philosophers. See Seneca (Naturales Quaestiones, vi. 23) ; Cicero (Tusc. Disput., iii. 10), speaking of Theophrastus, the friend of Callistheues.

[558] We find from chapter xxii. that these events occurred at Bactra.

[559] The Chorasmians were a people who inhabited the country near the lower part of the river Oxus, between the Caspian and Aral Seas.

[560] This mythical race of warlike females is said to have come from the Caucasus and to have settled near the modern Trebizond, their original abode being in Colchis. Cf. Arrian (vii. 13); Strabo(xi. 5); Diod. (xvii. 77); Curt. (vi. 19); Justin (xii· 3); Homer; (Iliad, iii. 189); Aeschylus (Eumenides, 655); Herod (iv. 110-116; ix. 27).

[561] See iii. 29 supra.

[562] Propontis means the sea before the Pontus. Compare Ovid (Tristia, i. 10, 31):— "Quaque tenent Ponti Byzantia littora fauces."

[563] We learn, from Curtius (viii. 3), that it was at this place that Clitus was murdered.

[564] These were a people dwelling to the north-east of the Caspian, who were chiefly remarkable for having defeated and killed Cyrus the Great. See Herodotus, i. 201-216.

[565] There were two other generals named Peithon; one the son of Agenor, and the other the son of Crateas. See Arrian, vi. 15, 28, etc.

[566] Curtius (viii. 1) says that the name of the defeated general was Attinas.

[567] Artabazus was in his 95th year when he joined Alexander with the Grecian troops of Darius in B.C. 330. See Curtius, vi. 14. His viceroyalty was destined for Clitus; but on the death of that general it was conferred on Amyntas. See Curtius, viii. 3.

[568] Curtius (viii. 11 and 12) says that the wife of Spitamenes murdered him and carried his head to Alexander.

[569] The Hebrew name for Media is Madai, which means middle-land. The Greeks called the country Media, according to Polybius (v. 44), because it lies near the middle of Asia.

[570] Of the year 327 B.C.

[571] ωρα, akin to Latin cura, a poetical and Ionic word, often found in Herodotus.

[572] About £2,700.

[573] About £327. Curtius (vii. 41) says that the first prize was 10 talents, the second 9 talents, and the same proportion for the eight others, so that the tenth man who mounted received one talent. The stater of Darius, usually called a daricus, was a gold coin of Persia, See Smith's Dictionary of Antiquities.

[574] Cf. Curtius (vii. 43), vela, signum capti verticis.

[575] Roxana and her son Alexander Aegus were put to death by Cassander, B.C. 311.

[576] Statira. She died shortly before the battle of Arbela.

[577] καρτερος αυτου. Cf. Theocritus, xv. 94, αμων καρτερος.

[578] After the capture of Damascus, Alexander married Barsine, the widow of his rival Memnon, and daughter of Artabazus. She was distinguished for her beauty and accomplishments, having received a Grecian education. By her he had a son named Heracles. See Plutarch (Alex., 21). She and her son were put to death by Polysperchon, B.C.309.

[579] Cf. Herodotus, i. 131; Curtius, iv. 42. The Persians called this god Ormuzd.

[580] Curtius (viii. 16) says that Alexander saw Roxana at a banquet given by Oxyartes in his honour.

|581| Krüger substituted περιειργε for περιέργει.

|582| βατά. Cf. Xenophon (Anab., iv. 6, 17).

|583| Arrian imitates Hepodotus in the use of ως with the infinitive instead of ωστε.

|584| This term is a Persian word meaning mountaineers. The tribe mentioned here lived between the rivers Oxus and Jaxartes, on the borders of Bactria and Sogdiana.

|585| Curtius (viii. 17) says Alexander took with him 30,000 select troops from all the conquered provinces, and that the army which he led against the Indians numbered 120,000 men.

|586| This is the Indian Caucasus, or mount Parapamisus, now called Hindu-Koosh.

|587| The Cophen is now called Cabul. Nicaea was probably on the same site as the city of Cabul. Others say it is Beghram. The Greek word Satrapes denotes a Persian viceroy. It is a corruption of a word meaning court-guardian, in the Behistun Inscriptions written Khshatrapa. See Rawlinson's Herod., i. 192.

|588| Curtius (viii. 43) says that Taxiles was the title which the king of this district received. His name was Omphis.

|589| A district between the rivers Indus and Attock. Its capital, Peucela, is the modern Pekheli.

|590| The brigade of Clitus still bore the name of its commander after his death. Cf. Arrian, vii. 14 infra.

|591| These were tribes liviiig in the north-west of the Punjab.

|592| Probably the modern Kama, a tributary of the Cabul.

|593| Supposed to be another name for the Choes.

|594| και τους ψιλους. The usual reading is τους χιλίους, 1,000 Agrianians.

|595| A tributary of the Cophen, probably what is now called the Lundye, running parallel with the Kama.

|596| Cf. Livy, xxi. 31:— "Amnis saxa glareosa volvens, nihil stabile nectutum ingredienti praebet."

|597| This was the capital of the Assacenians. Curtius (viii. 37) calls it Mazagae, and describes its strong position.

|598| See Bk. ii. 23 supra.

|599| Curtius (viii. 37, 38) says that the name of the queen was Cleophis, and that after the surrender she gained Alexander's favour. He also informs us that the king died just before Alexander's arrival.

|600| Probably Bajour, north-west of Peshawur. The position of Ora cannot be fixed.

|601| This was the king of the Indian mountaineers. See Arrian, v. 8 infra.

|602| On the ground of εν τη πόλει ξυμφυγόντες not being classical Greek, Krüger has substituted εν τη πόλη ξυμπεθευγόντες, and Sintenis εις την πόλιν ξυμφυγόντες. No one however ought to expect Arrian to be free from error, writing, as he did, in the middle of the second century of the Christian era.

|603| This seems to be the Greek translation of the native name, meaning the place to which no bird can rise on account of its height. Cf. Strabo, xv. 1. This mountain was identified by Major Abbot, in 1854, as Mount Mahabunn, near the right bank of the Indus, about 60 miles above its confluence with the Cabul.

|604| Cf. Arrian, ii. 16 supra.

|605| Curtius (viii. 39) says that the river Indus washed the base of the rock, and that it^ shape resembled the meta or goal in a race-course, which was a stone shaped like a sugar-loaf. Arrian's description is more likely to be correct as he took it from Ptolemy, one of Alexander's generals.

|606| Near mount Mahabunn are two places called Umb and Balimah, the one in the valley of the river and the other on the mountain above it. See Major Abbot's Gradus ad Aornon.

|607| δαήμων, a poetical word. Cf. Homer (Odyssey, viii. 159).

|608| Probably Dyrta was at the point where the Indus issues from the Hindu-Koosh.

|609| Grovovius first introduced και before τους ψιλους.

|610| The name Indus is derived from the Sanscrit appellation Sindhu, from a root Syandh, meaning to flow. The name Indians, or Sindians, was originally applied only to the dwellers on the banks of this river. Hindustan is a Persian word meaning the country of the Hindus or Sindus. Compare the modern Sinde, in the north-west of India, which contains the lower course of the Indus. In Hebrew India was called Hodu, which is a contraction of Hondu, another form of Hindu. See Esther i. 1; viii. 9. Krüger changed ωδοποιειτο into ωδοποιει

|611| This city was probably on the site of Jelalabad.

|612| επει τε. This is the only place where Arrian uses this Ionic form for the simple επει.

|613| The Indians worship a god Homa, the personification of the intoxicating soma juice. This deity corresponds to the Greek Dionysus or Bacchus.

|614| The slopes of this mountain were covered with vines. See Ovid (Fasti, ii. 313; Metamorphoses, xi. 86); Vergil (Georgics, ii. 98); Pliny, xiv. 9.

|615| φανειη. Arrian does not comply with the Attic rule, that the subjunctive should follow the principal tenses in the leading sentence. Cf. V. 6, 6; 7, 5; vii. 7, 5; 15, 2.

|616| Cf. Pliny (Nat. Hist., vi. 23; viii. 60; xvi. 62). The ordinary reading is αλση παντοια και ιδειν συσκιον. For this Krüger has proposed αλση παντοια υλη συσκια.

|617| The other names of Dionysus were: Bacchus, Bromius, Evius, Iacchus, Lenaeus, Lyacus. The Romans called him Liber.

|618| Curtius (viii. 36) says that the Macedonians celebrated Bacchanalia for the space of ten days on this mountain.

|619| The 1st aor. pass. εσχεθην is found only in Arrian and Plutarch. Cf. vii. 22, 2 infra.

|620| The celebrated Geographer and Mathematician, who was born B.C. 276 and died about B.C. 196. His principal work was one on geography, which was of great use to Strabo. None of his works are extant. He was made president of the Alexandrian library, B.C. 236.

|621| Cf. Arrian (Indica, v. 11).

|622| The earliest mention of India which has descended to our times is in Aeschylus (Suplices, 284).

|623| Arrian frequently uses the Ionic and old Attic word, σμικρος.

|624| About £480,000.

|625| Alexander probably crossed the Indus near Attock. The exact site of Taxila cannot be fixed.

|626| The Hydaspes is now called Jelum, one of the five great tributaries of the Indus.

|627| Herodotus considered the Danube the largest river in the world as known to him, and the Dnieper the largest of all rivers except the Danube and the Nile. See Herodotus, iv. 48-53.

|628| "Amnis Danubius sexaginta navigabiles paene recipiens fluvios, Beptem ostiis erumpit in mare. Quorum primum est Peuce insula supra dicta, ut interpretata sunt vocabula Graeco sermone, secundum Naracustoma, tertium Calonstoma, quartum Pseudostoma: nam Boreonstoma ac deinde Sthenostoma longe minora sunt caeteris: septimun ingens te palustri specie nigrum."—Ammianus (xxii. 8, 44). Pliny (iv. 24) says that the Danube has six mouths, the names of which he gives.

|629| The Indus does not rise in the Parapamisus, but in the Himalayas. It has two principal mouths, but there are a number of smaller ones. Ptolemy said there were seven. The Delta is between 70 and 80 miles broad. "Delta, a triquetrae litterae forma hoc vocabulo signatius adpellata."—Ammianus, xxii. 15.

|630| The territory included by the Indus and its four affluents is now called Punjab, a Persian word meaning five rivers.

|631| Ctesias was the Greek physician of Artaxerxes Mnemon. He wrote a history of

Persia and a book on India. His works are only preserved in meagre abridgement by Photius. Aristotle says that he was false and untrustworthy {Hist. of Animals, vii. 27; De Generatione Animalium, ii. 2). Subsequent research has proved Ctesias to be wrong and Herodotus generally right in the many statements in which they are at variance.

[632] The fact is, that the Indus is nowhere more than 20 stades, or 2.5 miles broad.

[633] See Strabo, xv. 1; xvi. 4; Herod., iii. 102, with Dean Blakesley's note.

[634] ουδαμων is the Ionic form for ουδενων.

[635] The Greek name Αιθιοψ means sun-burnt. The Hebrew name for Aethiopia is Gush (black). In ancient Egyptian inscriptions it is called Keesh. It is the country now called Abyssinia. Aethiopas vicini sideris vapore torreri, adustisque similes gigni, barba et capUlo vibrato, non est dubium. (Pliny, ii. 80).

[636] Cf. Xenophon (Cyclopaedia, vii. 5, 67).

[637] Called the Indica, a valuable little work in the Ionic dialect, still existing.

[638] Nearchus left an account of his voyage, which is not now extant. Arrian made use of it in writing the Indica. See that work, chapters xvii. to lxiii.

[639] Megasthenes was sent with the Plataean Deimachus, by Seleuous Nicator, the king of Syria and one of Alexander's generals, as ambassador to Saudraootus, king of the country near the Ganges. He wrote a very valuable account of India in four books.

[640] Taurus is from the old root tor meaning high, another form of which is dor. Hence Dorians=highlanders.

[641] The ancient geographers thought that the Jaxartes bifurcated, part of it forming the Tanais, or Don, and flowing into the lake Maeotis, or Sea of Azov; and the other part falling into the Hyrcanian, or Caspian Sea. The Jaxartes and Oxua flow into the Sea of Aral, but the ancients thought that they fell into the Caspian, as there is indeed evidence to prove that they once did. Hyrcania is the Greek form of the old Persian Virkâna, that is Wolf's Land. It is now called Gurgân.

[642] Herodotus (i. 203) states decidedly that the Caspian is an inland sea. Strabo (xi. 1), following Eratosthenes, says that it is a gulf of the Northern Ocean.

[643] The Euphrates, after its junction with the Tigres, flows through the marshes of Lamlum, where its current moves less than a mile an hour.

[644] Cf. Arrian, vi. 27 infra.

[645] Probably the Chaudragupta of the Sanscrit writers. He conquered from the Macedonians the Punjab and the country as far as the Hindu-Koosh. He reigned about 310 B.C.

[646] Mount Dindymus, now called Murad Dagh, was sacred to Cybele, the mother of the gods, who was hence called Dindymene.

[647] Hecataeus of Miletus died about B.C. 476. He wrote a work upon Geography, and another on History. His works were well known to Herodotus but only fragments survive.

[648] See Herodotus, ii. 5.

[649] See Herodotus, ii. 10-34.

[650] See Homer's Odyssey, iv. 477, 581. In Hebrew the name for Egypt is Mitsraim (dark-red). In form the word is dual, evidently in reference to the division of the country by the Nile. The native name was Chem, meaning black, probably on account of the blackness of the alluvial soil

[651] αλλοι is Abicht's reading instead of πολλοί.

[652] Arrian, in his Indica, chap. 4, gives the names of these rivers.

[653] See Herodotus, vii. 33-36; iv. 83, 97, 138-141. Bosporus = Oxford. The name was applied to the Straits of Constantinople, and also to those of Yenikale, the former being called the Thracian and the latter the Cimmerian Bosporus. Cf. Aeschylus {Prom., 734). Ad Bosporos duos, vel bubuB meabili transitu; unde nomen ambobus (Pliny, vi. 1).

[654] Diodorus (xvii. 86) says that Alexander crossed on a bridge of boats. Cf. Strabo, p. 698; Curtius, viii. 34.

[655] There was another river called Rhenus, a tributary of the Po, now called the Reno.

It was called Rhenus Bononiensis, being near Bononia or Bologna.

[656] αι πρύμναν κρουόμεναι. For this nautical term compare Thucydides, i. 51; Herodotus, viii. 84; Diodorus, xi. 18; Aristophanes, Wasps, 399. κατα ρουν is Krüger's reading for the usual κατα πόρον.

[657] The explanation of this passage given in Liddell and Scott's Lexicon, sub voce κλιμαξ is evidently incorrect, as there is nothing about a chariot in the original.

[658] Compare the description of Caesar's bridge over the Rhine (Gallic War, iv. 17).

[659] The place where Alexander crossed the Indus was probably at its junction with the Copheu or Cabul river, near Attock. Before he crossed he gave his army a rest of thirty days, as we learn from Diodorus, xvii. 86. From the same passage we learn that a certain king named Aphrices with an army of 20,000 men and 15 elephants, was killed by his own men and his army joined Alexander.

[660] The kingdom of Porus lay between the Hydaspes and Accesines, the district now called Bari-doab with Lahore as capital. It was conquered by Lords Hardinge and Gongh in 1849.

[661] Diodorus (xvii. 87) says that Porus had more than 50,000 infantry, about 3,000 cavalry, more than 1,000 chariots, and 130 elephants. Curtius (viii. 44) says he had about 30,000 infantry, BOO chariots, and 85 elephants.

[662] επιστεψας is Krüger's reading instead of επιτάξας

[663] About the month of May. See chap. 12 infra; also Curtius, viii. 45, 46. Strabo (xv. 1) quotes from Aristobulus describing the rainy season at the time of Alexander's battle with Porus at the Hydaspes.

[664] Cf. Arrian, i. 14 supra.

[665] αλλα κενόν is Krüger's reading, instead of αλλ' εκεινον.

[666] αλσει is Abicht's reading for ειδει.

[667] About 17 miles.

[668] This use of πρίν with infinitive alter negative clauses, is contrary to Attic usage.

[669] The perf. pass. πέπηγμαι is used by Arrian and Dionysius, but by Homer and the Attic writers the form used is πέπηγα. Doric, πέπαγα.

[670] Seleucus Nicator, the most powerful of Alexander's successors, became king of Syria and founder of the dynasty of the Σελευcidae, which came to an end in B.C. 79.

[671] For this use of όσον, cf. Homer (Iliad, ix. 354); Herodotus, iv. 45; Plato (Gorgias, 485Α; Euthydemus, 273Α).

[672] Compare the passage of the Rhone by Hannibal., (See Livy, xxi. 26-28; Polybius, iii. 45, 46.)

[673] 100 Greek and 101 English feet.

[674] See Donaldson's New Gratylus, sec. 178.

[675] πριν κατιδωσιν. In Attic, πριν αν is the regular form with the subjunctive; but in Homer and the Tragic writers αν is often omitted.

[676] Cf. Arrian's Tactics, chap. 29.

[677] Diodorus (xvii. 89) says that more than 12,000 Indians were killed in this battle, over 9,000 being captured, besides 80 elephants.

[678] According to Diodorus there fell of the Macedonians 280 cavalry and more than 700 infantry. Plutarch (Alex. 60) says that the battle lasted eight hours.

[679] Curtius (viii. 50, 51) represents Porus sinking half dead, and being protected to the last by his faithful elephant. Diodorus (xvii. 88) agrees with him.

[680] Cf. Curtius, viii. 44; Justin, xii. 8.

[681] Cf. Arrian, ii. 10 supra. δεουλωμένος τη γνωμη. The Scholiast on Thucydides iv. 34, explains this by τεταπεινωμένος φοβω.

[682] Cf. Plutarch (Alex., 60); Curtius, viii. 51.

[683] Diodorus (xvii. 87) says that the battle was fought in the archonship of Chremes at Athens.

|684| Nicaea is supposed to be Mong and Buoephala may be Jelalpur. See Strabo, xv. 1.

|685| Cf. Plutarch (Alex., 61). Schmieder says that Alexander could not have broken in the horse before he was sixteen years old. But since at this time he was in his twenty-ninth year he would have had him thirteen years. Consequently the horse must have been at least seventeen years old when he acquired him. Can any one believe this? Yet Plutarch also states that the horse was thirty years old at his death.

|686| Curtius (vl. 17) says this occurred in the land of the Mardians; whereas Plutarch (Alex., 44) says it happened in Hyrcania.

|687| Diodorus (xvii. 89), says Alexander made a halt of 30 days after this battle.

|688| Cf. Arrian, v. 8 supra, where an earlier embassy from Abisares is mentioned.

|689| Strabo (xv. 1) says that this Porus was a cousin of the Porus captured by Alexander.

|690| This is the Chenab. See Arrian (Indica, iii.), who says that where it joins the Indus it is 30 stades broad.

|691| Diodorus (xvii. 95) says that Alexander received a reinforcement from Greece at this river of more than 30,000 infantry and nearly 6,000 cavalry; also suits of armour for 25,000 infantry, and 100 talents of medical drugs.

|692| Μέλλειν is usually connected with the future infinitive; but Arrian frequently uses it with the present.

|693| Now called the Ravi.

|694| Sangala is supposed to be Lahore; but probably it lay some distance from that city, on the bank of the Chenab.

|695| Compare Csesar (Bell. Gall., i. 26): pro vallo carros objecerant et e loco superiore in nostros venientes tela conjiciebant, et nonnulli inter carros rotasque mataras ac tragulas subjiciebant nostrosque vulnerabant.

|696| εγκυρειν is an epic and Ionic word rarely used in Attic; but found frequently in Herodotus, Homer, Hesiod, and Pindar.

|697| The Greeks had only three watches; but Arrian is speaking as a Roman.

|698| Eumenes, of Cardia in Thrace, was private secretary to Philip and Alexander. After the death of the latter, he obtained the rule of Cappadocia, Paphlagonia, and Pontus. He displayed great ability both as a general and statesman; but was put to death by Antigonus in B.C. 316, when he was 45 years of age. Being a Greek, he was disliked by the Macedonian generals, from whom he experienced very unjust treatment. It is evident from the biographies of him written by Plutarch and Cornelius Nepos, that he was one of the most eminent men of his era.

|699| Now called the Beas, or Bibasa. Strabo calls it Hypanis, and Pliny calls it Hypasis.

|700| In the Hebrew Bible Javan denotes the Ionian race of Greeks, and then the Greeks in general (Gen. x. 2, 4; Isa. lxvi. 19; Ezek. xxvii. 13; Joel iii. 6; Zech. ix. 13). In Dan. viii. 21, x. 20, xi. 2, Javan stands for the kingdom of Alexander the Great, comprising Macedonia as well as Greece. The form of the name Javan is closely connected with the Greek Ion, which originally had a digamma, Ivon. Pott says that it means the young, in opposition to the Graikci, the old. According to Aristotle (Meteorologica, i. 14) the Hellenes were originally called Graikoi. Cf. Sanscrit, jewan; Zend, jawan; Latin, juvenis; English, young.

|701| Coele-Syria, or the Hollow Syria, was the country between the ranges of Libanus and Antilibanus. Syria between the rivers is usually called by its Greek name of Mesopotamia. It is the Padan Aram of the Bible. Cappadocia embraced the whole northeastern part of the peninsula of Asia Minor. Slaves were procured from this region. See Horace (Epistles, i. 6, 39); Persius, vi. 77. The name Pamphylia is from παν and φυλὴ, because of the mixed origin of the inhabitants.

|702| Cf. Arrian (Anabasis, vii. 1; Indica, 43). Herodotus (iv. 42) says that Pharaoh Neco sent a Phoenician expedition from the Bed Sea, which circumnavigated Africa and returned by the Straits of Gibraltar, or the Pillars of Hercules. The Carthaginian Hanno is said to have sailed from Cadiz to the extremity of Arabia. See Pliny (Historia Naturalis, ii. 67; v. 1).

Herodotus (iv. 43) says that the Carthaginians asserted they had sailed round Africa. There is a Greek translation of Hanno's Periplus still extant. As to the Pillars of Hercules, see Aelian (Varia Historia, v. 3). They are first mentioned by Pindar (Olym. iii. 79; Nem. iii. 36).

[703] Arrian, like many other ancient writers, includes Africa, or Libya, as a part of Asia. The boundaries were the Eastern Sea and the Atlas Mountains. Cf. Arrian, iii. 30; vii. 1 and 30. The name Asia first occurs in Homer (Iliad, ii. 461), in reference to the marsh about the Cayster, and was thence gradually extended over the whole continent.

[704] The interior of Africa, from the Straits of Gibraltar to Egypt, and from the Mediterranean to the then unexplored South.

[705] Heracles, from whom the Macedonian kings claimed to be descended.

[706] Hence Hercules is called Tirynthius. (Virgil, Aeneid. 662; viii. 228).

[707] See chap. 1 of this book.

[708] Cf. Xenophon (Anab., i. 7, 4).

[709] Cf. Curtius, ix. 12.

[710] Arrian (iii. 19) says that the Thessalians were sent back from Eubatana.

[711] Pontus Euxinus antea ab inhospitali feritate Axenos appellatus (Pliny, vi. 1).

[712] The Latin name Carthago and the Greek Carchedon were corruptions of the Phoenician Carth-Hadeshoth, the "new city."

[713] Pliny (vi. 21), says that Alexander erected the altars on the farther bank of the Hyphasis, whereas Arrian, Diodorus, and Plutarch say they were on this side of the river. Curtius (ix. 13) does not specify the side of the river.

[714] Herodotus (iv. 44) says that the Indus is the only river besides the Nile which produces crocodiles. He does not seem to have known the Ganges.

[715] This was the Nelumbium speciosum, the Egyptian bean of Pythagoras the Lotus of the Hindus, held sacred by them. It is cultivated and highly valued in China, where it is eaten. The seeds are the shape and size of acorns.

[716] I.e. the Mediterranean.

[717] See Arrian, v. 6 supra. The native name of Egypt was Chem (black). Compare Vergil (Georgic. iv. 291):— Viridem Aegyptum nigrâ, fecundat arenâ. Usque ooloratis amnis devexus ab Indis.

[718] This use of αμφί with the dative is instead of the Attic περί with the genitive or accusative.

[719] Plutarch (Alex. 66) informs ua that Alexander's army numbered 120,000 infantry and 15,000 cavalry. Cf. Arrian (Indica, 19).

[720] Arrian, in the Indica (chap. 19), says that Alexander embarked with 8,000 men.

[721] Strabo (xv. 1) says that the realm of Sopeithes was called Cathaia.

[722] As Alexander was at this time east of the Indus, the expression, "beyond the Indus," means west of it.

[723] Cf. Arrian, v. 2 supra.

[724] Only fragments of this narrative are preserved. Strabo (xv. 1) says that the statements of Onesicritus are not to be relied upon.

[725] Curtius (ix. 13) and Diodorus (xvii. 95) say that there were 1,000 vessels. Arrian (Indica, 19) says there were 800. Krüger reads χιλίων in this passage instead of the common reading δισχιλίων.

[726] From Arrian (Indica, 18) we learn that ηe sacrificed to his country gods, and to Poseidon, Amphitrite, the Nereids, the Ocean, as well as to the three rivers. Cf. i. 11, supra.

[727] Cf. iii. 3 supra.

[728] Cf. Arrian (Indica, 7).

[729] Cf. Curtius;; (ix. 15); Diodorus (xvii. 97). The latter says that Alexander offered sacrifice to the gods for having escaped the greatest danger, and having contested with a river like Achilles.

[730] According to Diodorus (xvii. 96) and Curtius (ix. 14) Alexander here made an

The Diary of Alexander the Great

expedition against the Sibi; defeated an army of 40,000 Indians, and captured the city of Agallassa.

[731] The chief city of the Mallians is the modern Mooltan.

[732] Μήπω. In later writers μή is often used where the Attic writers would use ου.

[733] Strabo and Curtius call this river Hyarotis.

[734] The Brachmans, or Brahmins, were a religious caste of Indians. The name was sometimes used for the people whose religion was Brahminism. Cf. Arrian (Indica, 11); Strabo, xv. 1; p. 713 ed. Casaubon.

[735] Cf. Arrian i. 11 supra.

[736] The Romans called these men duplicarii. See Livy, ii. 59; vii. 37.

[737] τοις εποιτα πυθέσθαι. Cf. Homer (Iliad, xxii. 305; ii. 119).

[738] Curtius (ix. 22) calls the physician Critobulus. Near the oity of Cos stood the Asclepieum, or temple of Asclepius, to whom the island was sacred, and from whom the chief family, the Asclepiadae, claimed descent. Curtius says:— Igitur patefaoto latius vulnere, et spiculo evolso, ingens vis sanguinis manare coepit, linquique animo rex, et caligine oculis offusa, veluti moribundus extendi.

[739] Cf. Plutarch (Alex. 63); Diodorus (xvii. 98, 99); Curtius (ix. 18-23); Justin (xii. 9).

[740] As to Fame, or Rumour, see Homer (Iliad, ii. 93; Odyss. xxiv. 412); Hesiod (Works and Days, 758-762); Vergil (Aeneid, iv. 173-190); Ovid (Met. xii. 39-63); Statius (Theb. ii. 426).

[741] Curtius (ix. 18) says it was the town of the Oxydracians.

[742] Nearly 70 miles.

[743] Isthmus is from the same root as ιέναι, to go, and thus means a passage. Pindar (Isthmia, iv. 34) calls it the "bridge of the sea."

[744] We learn from Curtius (ix. 21) that the authors who stated that Ptolemy was present in this battle were Clitarchus and Timagenes. From the history of the former, who was a contemporary of Alexander, Curtius mainly drew the materials for his history of Alexander.

[745] Ptolemy received this appellation from the Rhodians whom he relieved from the assaults of Demetrius. The grateful Rhodians paid him divine honours as their preserver, and he was henceforward known as Ptolemy Soter. B.C. 304. See Pausanias, i. 8, 6.

[746] The word αταλαιπωρος is used in a similar way by Thucydides, i. 20, 4.

[747] Curtius (ix. 24) says that Craterus was deputed by the officers to make this representation to the king, and that he was backed up by Ptolemy and the rest.

[748] This line is a fragment from one of the lost tragedies of Aeschylus: δράσαντι γάρ τι και παιθειν οφειλεται

[749] Curtius (ix. 23) says that he was cured of his wound in seven days. Diodorus (xvii. 99) says that it took many days.

[750] Arrian does not mention the Sutledj, which is the fifth of the rivers of the Punjab. Pliny (vi. 21) calls it Hesidrus; Ptolemy (vii. 1) calls it Zaradrus.

[751] About 12 miles. Ita se findente Nilo ut triquestram terrae figuram effioiat. Ideo multi Graeoae literae vocabiilo Delta appellavere Aegyptum (Pliny, v. 9).

[752] This tribe dwelt between the Acesines and the Indus. Diodorus (xvii. 102) calls them Sambastians; while Curtius (ix. 30) calls them Sabarcians. The Xathrians and Ossadians dwelt on the left bank of the Indus.

[753] We find from Curtius (ix. 31) and Diodorus (xvii. 102) that the name of this was Alexandria. It is probably the present Mittun.

[754] Curtius (ix. 31) calls this satrap Terioltes, and says he was put to death. His appointment as viceroy is mentioned by Arrian (iv. 22 supra).

[755] This king is called Porticanus by Curtius (ix. 31), Diodorus (xvii. 102), and Strabo (xv. 1).

[756] An expression imitated from Thucydides (iv. 34). Cf. Arrian, ii. 10; v. 19; where the

393

same words are used of Darius and Porus.

[757] Diodorus (xvii. 102) says that Sambas escaped beyond the Indus with thirty elephants.

[758] See note, page 327 supra.

[759] The Indica, a valuable work still existing. See chapters x. and xi. of that book.

[760] These people inhabited the Delta of the Indus, which is now called Lower Scinde. Their capital, Patala, is the modern Tatta.

[761] Cf. Arrian (Indica, ii.).

[762] Aristobulus, as quoted by Strabo (xv. 1), said that the voyage down the Indus occupied ten months, the fleet arriving at Patala about the time of the rising of Sirius, or July, 325 B.C.

[763] Curtius (ix. 34) calls this king Moeris.

[764] The right arm of the Indus is now called the Buggaur, and the left Sata.

[765] I.e. caused a heavy swell of waters. Cf. Apollonius Rhodius, ii. 595; Polybius, i. 60, 6. This wind was the south-west monsoon.

[766] Cf. Curtius (ix. 35, 36); Caesar (Bell. Gall. iv. 29). τα σκάφη εμετεωρίζοντο. Arrian does not comply with the Attic rule, that the plural neuter should take a verb in the singular. Compare ii. 20, 8; v. 17, 6 and 7; etc.

[767] Plutarch (Alex. 66) says that Alexander called the island Scillustis; but others called it Psiltucis. He also says that the voyage down the rivers to the sea took seven months.

[768] In regard to this expedition, see Arrian, vii. 20 infra.

[769] About 200 miles. Arrian here follows the statement of Nearchus. Aristobulus said that the distance was 1,000 stades. See Strabo, xv. 1.

[770] See Curtius, ix. 38. This lake has disappeared.

[771] These periodical winds are the southerly monsoon of the Indian Ocean. Cf. Arrian (Indica, 21).

[772] This occurs at the beginning of November. The Romans called the Pleiads Vergiliae. Cf. Pliny (ii. 47, 125): Vergiliarum occasus hiemem inchoat, quod tempus in III. Idus Novembres incidere consuevit. Also Livy (xxi. 35, 6): Nivis etiam casus, occidente jam sidere Vergiliarum, ingentem terrorem adjecit.

[773] This river, which is now called the Purally, is about 120 miles west of the mouth of the Indus. It is called Arabia by Arrian (Indica, 21); and Arbis by Strabo (xv. 2).

[774] These were a people of Gadrosia, inhabiting a coast district nearly 200 milles long in the present Beloochistan. Cf. Arrian {Indica, 22 and 25); Pliny, vi. 23.

[775] The Arabitians dwelt between the Indus and the Arabius; the Oritians were west of the latter river.

[776] Rhambaoia was probably at or near Haur.

[777] According to Diodorus (xvii. 104) the city was called Alexandria.

[778] Ora was the name of the district inhabited by the Oritians.

[779] Cf. Pliny (Nat. Hist. xii. 33-35).

[780] Cf. Strabo (xv. 2); Pliny (Nat. Hist. xii. 26).

[781] Probably the snow-flake.

[782] This is the well-known catechu, obtained chiefly from the Acacia Catechu. The liquid gum is called kuth or cutch in India.

[783] These people were called Ichthyophagi, or Fish-eaters. They are described by Arrian (Indica, 29); Curtius, ix. 40; Diodorus, xvii. 105; Pliny (Nat. Hist. vi. 25, 26); Plutarch (Alex. 66); Strabo, xv. 2. They occupied the sea-ooast of Gadrosia, or Beloochistan. Cf. Alciphron (Epistolae, i. 1, 2).

[784] A man of Callatis, a town on the Black Sea in Thrace, originally colonized by the Milesians.

[785] Cf. Herodotus, i. 193.

[786] Pura was near the borders of Carmania, probably at Bampur. The name means town.

[787] Cf. Strabo, xv. 2; Diodorus, ii. 19, 20. According to Megasthenes, Semiramis died before she could carry out her intended invasion of India. See Arrian (Indica, 5). Neither Herodotus nor Ctesias mentions an invasion of India by Cyrus; and according to Arrian (Indica, 9), the Indians expressly denied that Cyrus attacked them.

[788] Strabo says that some of these marolies extended 200, 400, and even 600 stades; most of the marching being done in the night. Kruger substitutes ξυμμέτρους for ξύμμερτος ουσα.

[789] Cf. Thucydides, ii. 49, 3.

[790] Cf. Xenophon (Anab. vii. 5, 13); Homer (Odyss. vii. 283).

[791] Curtius (vii. 20) mentions a similar act of magnanimity as having Occurred on the march in pursuit of Bessus through the desert to the river Oxus. Plutarch (Alex. 42) says it was when Alexander was pursuing Darius; Frontinus (Strategematica, i. 7, 7) says it was in the desert of Africa; Polyaemus (iv. 3, 25) relates the anecdote without specifying where the event occurred, μετεξέτεροι is an Ionic form very frequently used by Herodotus.

[792] Compare note on page 146.<this is the page number in the original book, or note 356 in this book>

[793] This man had been placed over the Oritians. See page 351 supra. < in original text or Chapter 166: Campaign against the Oritians in this text>

[794] Curtius (ix. 41) says that Craterus sent a messenger to the king, to say that he was holding in chains two Persian nobles, Ozines and Zeriaspes, who had been trying to effect a revolt.

[795] The Areians were famed for their skill as professional mourners. See Aeschylus (Choëphorae, 423). For the origin of the name see Donaldson (New Cratylus, sect. 81.)

[796] εξηλέχθη is substituted by Sintenis for the common reading εξηγγέλθη.

[797] According to Curtius (x. 1), Cleander and his colleagues were not slain, but put into prison; whereas 600 of the soldiers who had been the agents of their cruelty were put to death. Curtius says Oleander was spared for having killed Parmenio with his own hand. Cf. iii. 26 supra.

[798] The thriambus was a hymn to Bacchus, sung in festal processions in his honour. It was also used as a name of that deity, as we learn from Diodorus, iv. 5. It was afterwards used as synonymous with the Roman triumphus, by Polybius, Dionysius, and Plutarch.

[799] The Bacchanalian procession through Carmania is described by Curtius (ix. 42); Plutarch (Alex. 67); and Diodorus (xvii. 106).

[800] Diodorus (xvii. 106) says that the port into which Nearchus put was called Salmus.

[801] ἐκπεριπλεύσοντα. The Attic future of πλέω is πλεύσομαι. πλεύσω is only found in Polybius and the later writers.

[802] See Arrian (Indica, 18-43).

[803] The name for Persia and the Persians in the Hebrew Bible, is Paras. Cyrus is called Koresh (the sun) in Hebrew; in the cuneiform inscriptions the name is Khurush. Cambyses is called Ahasuerus in Ezra iv. 6; and Smerdis the Magian is the Artaxerxes who was induced by the Samaritans to forbid the further building of the temple (Ezra iv. 7-24). The Ahasuerus of the Book of Esther is probably Xerxes. Artaxerxes the Long-handed was the patron of Ezra and Nehemiah (Ezra vii. 11-28; Neh. ii. 1-9, etc). " Darius the Persian," mentioned in Neh. xii. 22, was probably Darius Oodomannus, who was conquered by Alexander. The province of Susiana, previously called Elymais, appears in the Hebrew under the name of Eilam or Elam. Persis is still called Fars.

[804] B.C. 325.

[805] Aria. See chap. 27 supra.

[806] Curtius (x. 4) says Orxines was descended from Cyrus.

[807] See iii. 25 supra.

[808] Cf. Strabo, xv. 3, where a description of this tomb is given, derived from Onesioritus, the pilot of Alexander. See Dean Blakesley's note on Herodiotus i. 214.

[809] Just a few lines above, Arrian says that the couch was by the side of the coffin.

[810] Cf. Ammianus, xxiii. 6, 32, 33. The Magi were the priests of the religion of Zoroaster, which was professed by the Medes and Persians. Their Bible was the Avesta, originally consisting of twenty-one books, only one of which, the twentieth (Vendidad), is still extant.

[811] See iii. 18 supra.

[812] According to Curtius (x. 4, 5) Orxines was not only innocent, but was very devoted and attached to Alexander. The favourite eunuch, Bagoas, poisoned the king's mind against him, and suborned other accusers against him. He was condemned unheard.

[813] Purpura et nitor corporis, ornatusque Persicus multo auro multisque gemmis. — Cicero (de Senectute, 17).

[814] Pasargadae was the ancient capital of Cyrus, but Persepolis was that of the later kings of Persia. The tomb of Cyrus has been discovered at Murghab; consequently Parsagadae was on the banks of the river Cyrus, N.E. of Persepolis. The latter city was at the junction of the Araxes and Medus. Its extensive ruins are called Chel-Minar, "the forty columns."

[815] The Tigris rises in Armenia, and joins the Euphrates ninety miles from the sea, the united stream being then called Shat-el-Arab. In ancient times the two rivers had distinct outlets. In the Hebrew the Tigris is called Chiddekel, i.e. arrow. The Greek name Tigres is derived from the Zend Tighra, which comes from the Sanscrit Tig, to sharpen. Its present name is Dijleh. The respective lengths of the Euphrates and Tigris are 1,780 and 1,146 miles.

[816] Among these were Curtius (x. 3); Diodorus (xviii. 4); and Plutarch (Alex., 68).

[817] Gadeira or Gades was a Phoenician colony. The name is from the Hebrew 'li, a fence. Cf. Pliny (iv. 36); appellant Poeni Gadir ita Punica lingua septum significante. Also Avienus (Ora Maritima, 268): Punicorum lingua conseptum locum Gaddir vocabat. According to Pliny (v. 1), Suetonius Paulinus was the first Eoman general who crossed the Atlas Mountains.

[818] See note 3, page 309.

[819] Now called Capo di Leuoa, the south-eastern point of Italy.

[820] Cf. Arrian (Indica, 11).

[821] Cf. Alciphron (Epistolae, i. 30, 1), with Bergler and Wagner's notes.

[822] This must have occurred B.C. 336. See Plutarch (Alex. 14); Cicero (Tusculanae Disputationes, v. 32). Alexander said: " If I were not Alexander, I should like to be Diogenes." Cf. Arrian, i. 1; Plutarch (de Fortit. Alex., p. 331).

[823] Cf. Strabo, xv. 1.

[824] Strabo calls this sage Mandanis.

[825] Strabo says, Alexander's messengers summoned Mandanis to the son of Zeus.

[826] Plutarch (Alex., 65) says this philosopher's name was Sphines; but the Greeks called him Calanus, because when he met them, instead of using the word χαῖρε in greeting them, he said καλέ The same author says that he was persuaded to come to Alexander by Taxiles. See also Strabo (xv. 1).

[827] Strabo (xv. 1) says that the voluntary death of Calanus occurred at Pasargadae; Aelian (Varia Historia, v. 6) says it was at Babylon; but Diodorus (xvii. 107) says it happened at Susa, which statement is confirmed by the fact of Nearchus being seemingly present.

[828] Cf, Arrian (Indica, 10).

[829] Cf. Arrian, vii, 13 infra; and Herodotus, vii. 40.

[830] Cf. Cicero (Tusc. Disput. v. 27).

[831] Media. See vi. 29 supra.

[832] Oxathres wag killed by Alexander himself with a sarissa, or long Macedonian pike. See Plutarch (Alex. 68), who calls him Oxyartes.

[833] For this use of φθείρομαι, cf. Aristophanes (Plutus, 610); Alciphron, i. 13, 3; with Bergler's note.

[834] Cf. Curtius, x. 5.

[835] She was also called Statira. See Diodorus, xvii. 107; Plutarch (Alex., 70). She is called Arsiuoe by Photius.

[836] "By these two marriages, Alexander thus engrafted himself upon the two lines of antecedent Persian kings. Oohus was of the Achaemenid family, but Darius Codomannus, father of Statira, was not of that family; he began a new lineage. About the overweening regal state of Alexander, outdoing even the previous Persian kings, see Pylarchus apud Athenaeum, xii. p. 539."—Grote.

[837] See p. 242.

[838] Cf. Aelian (Varia Historia, viii. 7). A copious account of this celebrated marriage feast is given in Athenaeus, xii. p. 538.

[839] Cf. Curtius, X. 8.

[840] About £4,600,000. Justin, xii. 11, agrees with Arrian; but Diodorus (xvii. 109); Plutarch (Alex., 70); Curtius (x. 8) say 10,000 talents.

[841] Cf. Curtius (ix. 41); Arrian (vi. 22) supra.

[842] The Epigoni, or Afterborn, were the sons of the seven chiefs who fell in the first war against Thebes. See Herodotus, Pindar, Sophocles, etc.

[843] For this mesanculon see Gellius (Noctes Atticae, x. 25); Polybius, xxiii., 1, 9; Euripides (Phoenissae, 1141; Andromache, 1138); Alciphron, iii. 36.

[844] It was at this time that Harpalus, viceroy of Babylon, having squandered a great deal of the treasure committed to his charge, became frightened at the return of Alexander, and fled to Greece with 50,000 talents and 6,000 mercenary troops. See Diodorus, xvii. 108.

[845] The Eulaeus is now called Kara Su. After joining the Ooprates it was called Pasitigris. It formerly discharged itself into the Persian Gulf, but now into the Shat-el-Arab, as the united stream of the Euphrates and Tigris is now called. In Dan. viii. 2, 16, it is called Ulai. Cf. Pliny, vi. 26, 31; xxxi. 21.

[846] The Greeks and Romans sometimes speak of Mesopotamia as a part of Syria, and at other times they call it a part of Assyria. The Hebrew and native name of this country was Aram Naharaim, or "Syria of the two rivers."

[847] The Tigris now falls into the Euphrates.

[848] Cf. Arrian, iii. 7, supra; Curtius, iv. 37.

[849] Cf. Strabo, xvi. 1; Herodotus, i, 193; Ammianus, xxiv. 3, 14.

[850] Probably this city stood at the junction of the Tigris with the Physcus, or Odoneh. See Xenophon (Anab. ii. 4, 26); Herodotus, i. 189; Strabo, (xvi. 1) says that Alexander made the Tigris navigable up to Opis.

[851] Cf. Justin (xii. 11); Diodorus (xvii. 109); Curtius (x. 10, 11). These authors put the punishment of the ringleaders after the speech instead of before.

[852] Thracians mean mountaineers; Hellenes, warriors; Dorians, high-landers; Ionians, coast-men; and Aeolians, mixed men. See Donaldson (New Cratylus, sect. 92).

[853] The gold and silver mines at Mount Pangaeon near Philippi brought Philip a yearly revenue of more than 1,000 talents (Diodorus, xvi. 8). Herodotus (v. 17) says that the silver mines at Mount Dysorum brought a talent every day to Alexander, father of Amyntas.

[854] This is a Demosthenic expression. See De Falsa Legatione, 92; and I. Philippic, 45.

[855] B.C. 346.

[856] He here refers to his own part in the victory of Chaeronea, B.C. 336. See Diodorus, xvi. 86; Plutarch (Alex. 9).

[857] This fact is attested by Demosthenes (De Haloneso, 12).

[858] The Thebans under Pelopidas settled the affairs of Macedonia, and took young Philip to Thebes as a hostage, B.C. 368.

[859] About £122,000. Cf. Plutarch (Alex. 15); Curtius, x. 10.

[860] "Iων is the Hebrew Javan without the vowel points. In the Persian name for the Greeks Ἰάονες, one of these vowels appear. See Aeschylus Fersae, 178, 562).

[861] Larger Phrygia formed the western part of the great central table-land f Asia Minor. Smaller Phrygia was also called Hellespontine Phrygia, because it lay near the

Hellespont. See Strdbo, xii. 8.

|862| A blue band worked with white, which went round the tiara of the Persian kings.

|863| Cf. Ammianus, xxv. 4, 15: " (Julianus) id aliquoties praedioans, lexandrum Magnum, ubi haberet thesauros interrogatum, apui amicos enevole respondisse."

|864| Cf. Arrian, i. 16 supra.

|865| It is supposed that the Saxones, i.e. Sacasuna, sons of the Sacae, originated from this nation.

|866| At the Persian court, kinsman was a title bestowed by the king as a mark of honour. Curtius says they were 15,000 in number. Cf. Diodorus, xvi. 50; Xenophon (Cyropaedia, i. 4, 27; ii. 2, 31).

|867| As to this Persian custom, see Xenophon (Agesilaus, v. 4; Cyropaedia i. 4, 27).

|868| Cf. Justin, xii. 7; Plutarch (Eumenes, 16); Curtius, viii. 17; Livy xxxvii. 40; Polybius, v. 79, 4:

|869| ἔμενον λιπαροῦντες. The more usual construction would be ἐλιπάρουν μένοντες. Cf. Herodotus, ix. 45 (λιπαρέετε μένοντες); iii. 51 (ἐλιπάρεε ἱστορέων).

|870| The paean was sung, not only before and after battle, but also after a banquet, as we see from this passage and from Xenophon (Symposium, ii. 1).

|871| About £240.

|872| Literally "with his own head," an Homeric expression. We learn from Plutarch (Eumenes, 6), that Craterus was a great favourite with the Macedonians because he opposed Alexander's Asiatic innovations. See also Plutarch (Alexander, 47); Diodorus, xvii. 114:— Κράτερον μὲν γὰρ εἶναι φιλοβασιλέα, Ἡφαιστίωνα δὲ φιλαλέχανδρον.

|873| The use of κελεύειν with the dative, is in imitation of Homer. Cf. i. 26, 3 supra.

|874| We learn from Diodorus (xviii. 4) that when Alexander died, Craterus had got no farther than Cilicia on his return journey. He had with him a paper of written instructions, among which were projects for building an immense fleet in Phoenicia and the adjacent countries for conveying an expedition against the Carthaginians and the other western nations as far as the pillars of Hercules; for the erection of magnificent temples, and for the transportation of people from Europe into Asia and from Asia into Europe. Alexander's generals put these projects aside, as too vast for any one but Alexander himself.

|875| Cf. Curtius, x. 31.

|876| The Greeks reckoned according to the lunar months, and therefore they talked of ten months instead of nine as the period of gestation. Cf. Herodotus, vi. 63; Aristophanes (Thesmoph. 742); Menander (Plocion, fragment 3); Plautus (Cistell, i. 3, 15); Terence (Adelphi, iii. 4, 29).

|877| For this expression, cf. Dion Cassius, xlii. 57; Homer (Iliad, 23, 538); Pausanias, vii. 10, 2; Herodotus, viii. 104.

|878| Here there is a gap in the manuscripts of Arrian, which probably contained an account of the flight of Harpalus, the viceroy of Babylon, with the treasures committed to his care, and also a description of the dispute between Hephaestion and Eumenes. See Photius (codex 92).

|879| Cf. Plutarch (Eumenes, 2).

|880| The march was from Opis to Media, as we see from the next chapter.

|881| Cf. Herodotus (iii. 106; 7ii. 40); Strabo, xi. 7 and 14; Diodor. xvii. 110; Ammianus, xxiii. 6. Sir Henry Eawlinson sajs: " With Herodotus, who was most imperfectly acquainted with the geography of Media, origiaated the error of transferring to that province the Nisea (Nesd) of Khorassan, and all later writers either copied or confounded his statement. Strabo alone has escaped from the general confusion. In his description we recognise the great grazing plains of Khawah, Alishtar, Huru, Silakhur, Burburud, Japalak, and Feridun, which thus stretch in a continuous line from one point to another along the southern frontiers of Media." Alexander probably visited the westernmost of these pastures which stretch from Behistun to Ispahan along the mountain range. The form διαρπαγῆναι is used only by the

later writers for διαρπασθῆναι.

[882] Cf. Strabo, xi. 5; Diodorus, xvii. 77; Curtius, vi. 19; Justin, xii. 3; Arrian, iv. 15; Homer (Iliad, iii. 189); Aeschylus (Eumenides, 655); Hippocrates (De Aere, Aquis, et Locis, p. 553).

[883] The queen is called Thalestris by Diodorus and Curtius.

[884] This is a mistake, for Xenophon does mention the Amazons in the Anabasis (iv. 4, 16). For Trapezus and the Phasians see his Anabasis (iv. 8, 22; v. 6, 36.)

[885] See Diodorus, iv. 16. This was one of the twelve labours of Hercules.

[886] See Plutarch (Theseus, 26).

[887] "The Battle of the Amazons" was a celebrated painting in the Stoa Poecile at Athens, executed by Mioon, sou of Phaniohus, a contemporary of Polygnotus about B.C. 460. Cf. Aristophanes (Lysistrata, 678): "Look at the Amazons whom Micon painted on horseback fighting with the men." See also Pausanias (i. 15; viii. 11).

[888] Cf. Herodotus, iv. 110-117; ix. 27.

[889] See Isocrates (Panegyricus, 19); Lysias (Oratio Funebris, near the beginning).

[890] Strabo (xi. 5) declined to believe in the existence of the Amazons altogether. However, even Julius Caesar spoke of them as having once ruled over a large part of Asia. See Suetonius (Life of Julius Caesar, 22). Eustathius, on Dionysius Periegetes, p. 110, derives the name Amazones from ἀ, not, and μᾶζα, barley-bread:—διὸ καὶ Ἀμαζόνες ἐκαλοῦντο οἷα μὴ μάζαις ἀλλὰ κρέασι θηρίων ἐπιστρεφόμεναι. This is not the usual derivation of the word.

[891] Cf. Plutarch (Alex. 72); Diodorus (xvii. 110).

[892] Plutarch makes this statement.

[893] See Homer (Iliad, xxiii. 141, 162); Arrian (i. 12).

[894] See Herodotus (vii. 35). Xerxes means the venerable king. Cf. Herod., vi. 98. See Donaldson's New Cratylus, sections 161, 479.

[895] Epidaurus in Argolis was celebrated as the chief seat of the worship of Aesculapius.

[896] This is an Homeric expression, meaning myself.

[897] Equal to £2,300,000. Plutarch (Alex. 72) agrees with Arrian. Diodorus (xvii. 115) and Justin (xii. 12) say 12,000 talents.

[898] Cf. Aelian (Varia Historia, Tu. 8); Diodorus (xvii. 114, 115); Plutarch(Alex. 72, 75; Eumenes, 2; Pelopidas, 34).

[899] See p. 392, note 3.

[900] Cossaea was a district on the north-east of Susiana, which the Persian kings never subdued, but purchased the quiet of the inhabitants by paying them tribute. It is supposed to be the Cush of the Old Testament. Diodorus (xvii. Ill) says that Alexander completed his conquest of the Cossaeans in forty days. Plutarch (Alex. 72} says he called the massacre of the Cossaeans his offering to the manes of Hephaestion.

[901] Cf. Livy, Tii. 37, 38; Pliny, xxii. 4; Justin, xii. 13.

[902] The Romans called these people Etruscans.

[903] Justin (xxi. 6) says that the Carthaginians sent Hamiloar to learn Alexander's real designs against them, under the pretence of being an exile oficring his services.

[904] Cf. Diodorus, xvii. 113.

[905] Aristus was a man of Salamis in Cyprus. Neither his work nor that of Asclepiades is extant. Aristus is mentioned by Athenaeus (x. 10) and Strabo (lib. xv.).

[906] Livy (ix. 18) says he does not think the contemporary Bomans even knew Alexander by report.

[907] These are what Hirtius (Bell. Alex. 11) calls " naves apertas et constratas."

[908] See p. 155, note 6.

[909] See p. 199, note 1. Strabo (xi.7) says that Aristobulus declared the Oxus to be the largest river which he had seen except those in India.

[910] See p. 198, note 3. The Oxus and Jaxartes really flow into the Sea of Aral, or the

Palus Oxiana, which was first noticed by Ammianus Marcellinus (xxiii. 6, 59) in the 4th century a.d. Ptolemy, however, mentions it as a small lake, and not as the recipient of these rivers. Cf. Pliny, vi. 18.

[911] The Araxes, or Aras, joins the Cyrus, or Kour, and falls into the Caspian Sea. It is now called Kizil-Ozan, or Yellow River. Its Hebrew name is Chabor (2 Kings xvii. 6). Pontem indignatus Araxes (Vergil, Aeneid, viii. 728). See Aeschylus (Prometheus, 736), Dr. Paley's note.

[912] As to the Chaldaeans, see Cicero (De Div., i. 1) and Diod. (ii. 29-31).

[913] This is a verse from one of the lost tragedies of Euripides. It is also quoted by Cicero (De Divin., ii. 5): Est quidam Graecus vulgaris in hanc sententiam versus; bene qui oonjiciet, vatem huno perhibebo optimum."

[914] See Herodotus (i. 32); Plutarch (Solon, 27).

[915] See p. 171, note 3. Herodotus (i. 181) gives a description of this temple, which he says existed in his time. Strabo (xvi. 1) agrees with Arrian that it was said to have been destroyed by Xerxes. He also says that Alexander employed 10,000 men in clearing away the rubbish of the ruins. Professor Sayoe and others adduce this passage of Arrian to prove that Herodotus is not to be trusted even when he says he had seen the places and things which he describes. The words of Herodotus are ἐς ἐμὲ τοῦτο ἔτι ἐόν, meaning, not that he had himself seen the temple, but that it existed till his time. In chap. 183 he expressly states that he did not see other things which he is describing, but that he derived his information from the Chaldaeans. He was about twenty years of age when Xerxes was assassinated. It must not be forgotten that Strabo and Arrian lived five or six hundred years after Xerxes. The veracity of Strabo is never doubted; yet in his description of Babylon this author speaks of the walls and hanging gardens as if they were still in existence, though not expressly saying so.

[916] Cf. Arrian, iii. 16 supra.

[917] See Arrian, iii. 16 supra.

[918] Cf. Philostratus (Life of Apollonius, viii. 7, 5).

[919] Perdiccas was killed by his own troops at Memphis, B.C. 321. See Diodorus, xviii. 36.

[920] The battle of Ipsus was fought B.C. 301. See Plutarch (Demetrius, 29).

[921] Diodorus (xvii. 113) says that embassies came from the Carthaginians, Liby-Phoenicians, Greeks, Macedonians, Illyrians, Thracians, and Gauls.

[922] Cf. Arrian, iii. 16 supra.

[923] The name Athens is said to have been derived from the worship of Athena. See Euripides (Ion, 8): Πόλις τῆς χρυσολόγχου Παλλάδος κεκλημένη. Attica is ἀττική or ἀκτικὴ γῆ, the "promontory land."

[924] Clazomenae was an Ionian city on the Gulf of Smyrna, celebrated as the birthplace of Anaxagoras. It is now called Kelisman.

[925] About £1,200,000.

[926] The Hebrew name for Arabia is Arab (wilderness). In Gen. xxv. 6 it is called the "East country," and in Gen. xxix. 1 the "Land of the Sons of the East."

[927] Cf. Arrian, v. 26; vii. 1 and 15 supra.

[928] Cf. Herodotus, iii. 8.

[929] Cf. Herodotus, ii. 40, 86; iii. 110-112; Strabo, xvi. 4; Pliny (Nat. Hist. xii.).

[930] About 17 miles.

[931] One of the Sporades, west of Samos, now called Nitaria. Cf. Horace (Carm., iv. 2, 2) and Ovid (Fasti, iv. 28).

[932] Called Tyrus by Strabo (xvi. 3). It is now called Bahrein, and is celebrated for pearl fisheries.

[933] A fragment of the work of Androsthenes descriptive of his voyage is preserved by Athenaeus (iii. p. 936).

[934] Probably Ramses. Its ruins are at Abu-Kesheb.

The Diary of Alexander the Great

|935| Probably the projection now called Ras-al-Had.

|936| Cf. Arrian (Indica, 82).

|937| About 90 miles. This canal fell into the Persian Gulf at Teredon. No trace of it now remains.

|938| The Hebrew name for Armenia is Ararat (2 Kings xix. 37; Isa. xxxYii. 38; Jer. li. 27).

|939| The country called Assyria by the Greeks is called Asshur (level) in Hebrew. In Gen. x. 11 the foundation of the Assyrian kingdom is ascribed to Nimrod; for the verse ought to be translated: "He went forth from that land into Asshur." Hence in Micah v. 6, Assyria is called the "land of Nimrod."

|940| The Hebrew name for Babylon is Babel, i.e. Bab-Bel, court of Bel: porta vel aula, civitas Beli (Winer). In Jer. xxv. 26; li. 41, it is called Sbeshach, which Jewish commentators, followed by Jerome, explain by the Canon Atbash, i.e. after the alphabet put in an inverted order. According to this rule the word Babel, which is the Hebrew name of Babylon, would be written Sheshach. Sir Henry Rawlinson, however, says it was the name of a god after whom the city was named; and the word has been found among the Assyrian inscriptions representing a deity.

|941| The perfect passive δεδόμημαι is equivalent to the Epic and Ionic form δέδμημαι.

|942| σχεθῆναι. See p. 268, note 4.

|943| τῶν τὶς ναυτῶν. This position of τίς is an imitation of the usage in Ionic prose. Cf. Herod, i. 85; τῶν τὶς. See Liddell and Scott, sub voce τίς. Cf. Arrian, ii. 26, 4; vi. 9, 3; vii. 3, 4; 22, 5; 24, 2.

|944| Cf. Arrian v. 13 supra.

|945| Cf. Arrian, iii. 6; iv. 18.

|946| The Macedonian stater was worth about £13s. 6d.

|947| f. Arrian (Tactics, 12, 11).

|948| Cf. Arrian, p. 379, note 1.

|949| We read in the speech of Demosthenes against Dionysiodorus (1285), that Cleomenes and his partisans enriched themselves by monopolizing the exportation of com from Egypt. Cf. Arrian, iii. 5 supra.

|950| This island is mentioned by Homer (Odyssey, iv. 355). Alexander constructed a mole seven stades long from the coast to the island, thus forming the two harbours of Alexandria. See Strabo, xvii. 1. The island is chiefly famous for the lofty tower built upon it by Ptolemy Philadelphus, for a lighthouse. Cf. Caesar (De Bella Civili, iii. 112); Ammianus, xxii. 16,

|951| Consult Lucian (Calumniae non temere credendum, 17).

|952| After Alexander's death Cleomenes was executed by Ptolemy, who received Egypt as his share of the great king's dominions.

|953| I.e. the Mediterranean.

|954| Diodorus (xvii. 116) and Plutarch (Alex., 73) say that he was a bound prisoner. The latter says his name was Dionysius, and that he was a Messenian.

|955| Plutarch (Alex., 75) and Justin (xii. 13) say that he gave a banquet to Nearchus the admiral, and that, as he was leaving it, he was invited to the revel by Medius the Thessalian. Cf. Diodorus, xvii. 117.

|956| We learn from Athenaeus (x. p. 434 B) that this Court Journal was kept by the royal secretary, Eumenes, afterwards so famous, and by the historian, Diodotus of Erythrae. As to the last days of Alexander, cf. Plutarch (Alex., 76, 77).

|957| Cf. Curtius, ix. 23: Mos erat principibus amicorum et oustodibus corporis exoubare ante praetorium, quotiens adversa regi valetudo incidisset.

|958| Serapis, or more correctly Sarapis, was an Egyptian deity, whose worship was introduced into Greece in the time of the Ptolemies. His worship was introduced into Borne, with that of Isis, in the time of Sulla. Strabo (xvii. 1) gives an account of his cultus in the

401

celebrated temple at Canobus. The Serapeum at Alexandria, which contained the famous library, is described by Ammianus, xxii 16.

|959| I.e. the most valiant.

|960| To decide who was to succeed to his power. Cf. Curtius, x. 14; Diodorus, xvii. 117; Justin, xii. 15.

|961| Cf. Curtius, X. 31; Diodorus, xvii. 117, 118; Justin, xii. 13. Plutarch (Alex., 77) asserts that nothing was said about Alexander's being poisoned, until six years after, when Olympias, the enemy of Antipater, set the charge afloat.

|962| See Arrian, iv. 10 supra.

|963| Cassander was afterwards king of Macedonia and Greece. He put Olympias, Roxana, and her son Alexander Aegus to death, and bribed Polysperchon to put Barsine and her son Hercules to death. He died of dropsy, B.C. 297.

|964| Cf. Pausanias, xviii. 4; Curtius, x. 31; Plutarch (Alex., 77). The ancients called the poison, "the water of Styx"; it was obtained from Nonacris in the north of Arcadia, near which the river Styx took its origin. Justin (xii. 14) says: Cujus veneni tanta vis fuit, ut non aere, Hon ferro, non testa contineretur, neo aliter ferri nisi in ungula potuerit. Pliny (Hist. Nat., xxx. 53) says: Ungulas tantum mularum repertas, neque aliam ullam materiam quae nou perroderetur a veneno Stygis aquae, cum id dandum Alexandre magno Antipater mitteret, dignum memoria est, magna Aristotelis infamia excogitatum.

|965| Diodorus (xvii. 117) states that after drinking freely, Alexander swallowed the contents of a large goblet, called the cup of Heracles, and was immediately seized with violent pain. This statement, however, is contradicted by Plutarch. It seems from the last injunction of Calanus, the Indian philosopher, that it was considered the right thing to drink to intoxication at the funeral of a friend. See Plutarch (Alex., 69).

|966| June, 323 B.C.

|967| Ptolemy took the embalmed booty of Alexander to Egypt, and placed it in Memphis, but removed it a few years after to Alexandria. See Curtius, X. 31. Cf. Aelian (Varia Historia, xii. 64; xiii. 29).

|968| Cf. Diodorus, xvii. 4; ἡ ὀξύτης τοῦ νεανίσκου.

|969| Cf. Curtius, x. 18: Gloriae laudisque, ut justo major cupido, ita ut javeni et in tautis admittenda rebus.

|970| Plutarch (Alex., 28) attributes the same motive to Alexander in representing himself to be the son of Zeus. Livy (ix. 18) says: Referre in tanto rege piget superbam mutationem vestis et desideratas humijacentium adulationes, etiam viotis Macedonibus graves, nedum victoribus; et foeda supplioia, et inter Tinum et epula, caedes amicorum at vanitatem ementiendae stirpis. Consult the whole of the interesting passage in Livy, ix. 17-19. See also Aelian (Varia Historia, n. 19; v. 12; ix. 37).

|971| Cf. Herodotus, vii. 41; Arrian, iii. 11 supra.

|972| Xenophon (Cyropaedia, vii. 5, 85) says that the Persian Equals-in-Honour, or Peers, spent their time about the Court.

|973| Cf. Arrian, iv. 14 supra; Justin, ix. 8; Athenaeus, x. p. 431 B; Aelian (Varia Historia, iii. 23; ix. 3; xii. 26).

|974| Europe and Asia. Arrian reckoned Libya, or Africa, as a part of Asia. See iii. 30; v. 26; vii. 1.

|975| Dr. Leonhard Sohmitz says:—"Arrian is in this work one of the most excellent writers of his time, above which he is raised by his simplicity and his unbiassed judgment. Great as his merits thus are as an historian, they are yet surpassed by his excellence as an historical critic. His Anabasis is based upon the most trustworthy historians among the contemporaries of Alexander, such as Ptolemy, Aristobulus, which two he chiefly followed, Diodotus of Erythrae, Eumenes of Cardia, Nearchus of Crete, and Megasthenes; and his sound judgment as to who deserved credit, justly led him to reject such authors as Onesicritus, Callisthenes, and others. No one at all acquainted with this work of Arrians can refuse his assent to the opinion of Photius (p. 73; comp. Lucian, Alex., 2), that Arrian was

the best among the numerous historians of Alexander. One of the great merits of the work, independent of those already mentioned, is the clearness and distinctness with which he describes all military movements and operations, the drawing up of the armies for battle, and the conduct of battles and sieges.' In all these respects the Anabasis is a masterly production, and Arrian shows that he himself possessed a thorough practical knowledge of military affairs. He seldom introduces speeches, but wherever he does he shows a profound knowledge of man; and the speech of Alexander to his rebellious soldiers, and the reply of Coenus, as well as some other speeches, are masterly specimens of oratory. Everything, moreover, which is not necessary to make his narrative clear is carefully avoided." See Smith's Dictionary of Greek and Roman Biography.

ABOUT THE AUTHOR

Dr Hutan Ashrafian, BSc Hons, MBBS, MRCS, MBA, PhD is a scientist, surgeon, philosopher and historian.

He is currently lecturer in surgery at Imperial College London and senior surgeon registrar at Chelsea and Westminster Hospital in London. Awarded the Arris and Gale Lectureship by the Royal College of Surgeons of England and the Hunterian Prize, he leads a team focusing on the development of innovative technological, pharmaceutical and economic strategies to resolve the global healthcare burden of obesity, metabolic syndrome and cancer.

His historical and paleopathological work spans the classical era exploring preeminent leadership styles notable in Alexander the Great, Xenophon, Hannibal Barca and Julius Caesar. His investigations into ancient innovation include the earliest world literature from the Ancient Near East and the integration of science with art in the renaissance focusing on the work of Leonardo da Vinci, Raphael and Michelangelo. As an Egyptologist, he has offered the first pathological analysis of the Great Sphinx and his analysis of the death of Tutankhamun and 18th Dynasty Pharaohs received world-wide attention through documentaries on the BBC, National Geographic and the Smithsonian Channel. He is founder and executive chair of the Institute of Civilisation.

Printed in Great Britain
by Amazon

19998986R00241